Queering Law and Order

Queering Law and Order

LGBTQ Communities and the Criminal Justice System

Kevin Leo Yabut Nadal

LEXINGTON BOOKS
Lanham • Boulder • New York • London

Published by Lexington Books
An imprint of The Rowman & Littlefield Publishing Group, Inc.
4501 Forbes Boulevard, Suite 200, Lanham, Maryland 20706
www.rowman.com

6 Tinworth Street, London SE11 5AL, United Kingdom

Copyright © 2020 by The Rowman & Littlefield Publishing Group, Inc.

All rights reserved. No part of this book may be reproduced in any form or by any electronic or mechanical means, including information storage and retrieval systems, without written permission from the publisher, except by a reviewer who may quote passages in a review.

British Library Cataloguing in Publication Information Available

Library of Congress Control Number: 2020932605

ISBN 978-1-7936-0106-3 (cloth : alk. paper)
ISBN 978-1-7936-0108-7 (pbk : alk. paper)
ISBN 978-1-7936-0107-0 (electronic)

∞™ The paper used in this publication meets the minimum requirements of American National Standard for Information Sciences Permanence of Paper for Printed Library Materials, ANSI/NISO Z39.48-1992.

For my son—who I hope grows up in a world
where he will be able to live as his greatest and most authentic self.

Contents

Preface		ix
Acknowledgments		xiii
Introduction		1
1	A History of LGBTQ People and the Law	17
2	Finding Our Pulse: LGBTQ Experiences with Hate and Historical Trauma	37
3	Neither Protected, Nor Served: LGBTQ People and Law Enforcement	53
4	Gender and Sexuality on Trial: LGBTQ People and the Courts	71
5	Locked Up in a Binary: LGBTQ People and Incarceration	93
6	The Workplace Closet: LGBTQ People and Employment Law	115
7	Queer and TransParent: LGBTQ People, Family Court, and the Child Welfare System	135
8	Over the Rainbow and Across the Border: LGBTQ People and Immigration	151
9	The Queer Criminal Mind: LGBTQ People and Forensic Psychology	177
Conclusion		207
References		215
Index		243
About the Author		251

Preface

As a queer person of color who grew up in the United States, I often tell people that I am surprised that I am alive today. LGBTQ young people are three times as likely than heterosexual, cisgender youth to die by suicide (Bostwick et al., 2014); are seven times as likely to be homeless (Quintana, Rosenthal, & Krehely, 2010); and are three times as likely to use illicit drugs (Marshal et al., 2008). Gay and bisexual men are the most vulnerable to HIV/AIDS and account for two-thirds of all new HIV diagnoses (Centers for Disease Control [CDC], 2016). Factoring in my racial identity, the odds were grimmer: LGBTQ youth of color are five times as likely than heterosexual and cisgender youth to die by suicide (Bostwick et al., 2014) and are five times as likely to have lower GPAs or miss school due to bullying (Diaz & Kosciw, 2009). And for a brief era, gay Asian American and Pacific Islanders had the greatest annual percentage increases in HIV/AIDS diagnoses of all major racial groups (Chin, Leung, Sheth, & Rodriguez, 2007).

As a gay man of color who engaged in a lot of risky behaviors during the height of the AIDS epidemic, I somehow steered clear of the virus—one that I witnessed kill some of my friends and many others who were just like me. Growing up in a time when I also saw some of my peers of color die by gang violence or become incarcerated, or when anti-LGBTQ hate crimes were on the rise, I somehow managed to stay relatively safe and even succeed. I've never viewed this as a sign of resilience or perseverance; instead, I have just considered myself a lucky one. Perhaps understanding my upbringing and intersectional identities would help further illustrate why I have always felt this way, while also explaining why I do the work that I do.

I knew I was different since I was six years old. I didn't really know what "gay" was, but I knew it was bad and that I didn't to be it. I also knew *bakla* (the Tagalog word for gay, feminine, or transgender) meant something negative, and that it hurt my feelings when my older brothers or cousins called me it. As I grew older, I would learn that being gay or *bakla* meant that my family would have a hard time accepting me. It meant that I would be terrified that people would discover who I really was. It would mean that I would live in constant fear that I would die early—either by contracting the virus or getting killed by hate violence. This belief was one I would later learn many of my queer peers feared too.

As a child of color (and a child of immigrants), I learned about racism pretty early on. My Philippines-born father taught me about discrimination when I was in elementary school; he stressed that education was the only way to combat the ignorance or prejudice I would face. My first experiences with racial or ethnic bias were when I was six years old and non-Filipino classmates made fun of the foods I brought for lunch, or how I pronounced certain words—a result of having parents who learned English as a second language. My first experiences with racism and the law occurred when I first started driving, and I found myself frequently getting pulled over by police officers (who did not ever provide any valid reasons for detaining me). I'd been stopped, padded down, or had my car searched three times before my eighteenth birthday. I'd have police officers accuse me of being in a gang or look at me suspiciously while I was doing the most mundane of things. I would later learn that this was a common practice called police profiling and it occurred most often when people were driving (or walking or breathing) while Black or Brown. Yet, knowing this was a common encounter did not make these experiences feel any less stressful, annoying, or sometimes terrifying.

As a teenager, when I began to internally acknowledge and accept that I was gay and more fluid in my gender expression, I tried to externally deny it for as long as I could. Not only did I fear my parents, family, and friends would reject me or disown me (which some did), but part of me felt like I could not be gay, because it would just add even more discrimination and emotional distress in my life. Coming out would mean having to work even harder because now I had multiple marginalized identities—each that came with their own sets of obstacles and consequences. So now, not only would I have to combat racial and ethnic discrimination, I also would have to fight against heterosexism, toxic masculinity, and gender binaries too (as well as the myriad ways all of those things would intersect).

During my childhood and adolescence, I picked up on many subtle and overt messages about what it meant to be smart or successful—from my peers in elementary school who taught me that if I got good grades that I was "acting White" to the experience of being one of the few Filipinos in my Honors Classes (despite half of my high school student population being Filipino). Those messages lingered throughout adulthood; as I became more successful, I saw fewer people who looked like me. In fact, studies show that only a small percentage of people of color attain a PhD and even fewer enter academia. For Filipino Americans specifically, my colleague Dr. Dina Maramba and I (2013) surveyed that there were only eighteen Filipino American full professors in the US and that the majority were not American born. So, now that I have a doctorate, am a tenured full professor, and make more money than my entire family in the Philippines would ever see in their lives, it makes me realize how fortunate I really am.

If it was not for the mentors who guided me at every stage of my life, or my parents who loved me unconditionally despite a few challenges along the way, I easily could have become a statistic. When I was teased and bullied persistently in high school, I often felt suicidal, which could have resulted in me being an LGBTQ youth who died by suicide. When my parents initially dismissed or rejected my sexual orientation identity, I could have become homeless. If I coped with that rejection by using illicit substances, I could have failed academically or dropped out of school.

Writing this book has made me realize even more how fortunate I am. Although I thought I knew a lot about the justice system from my work as a professor at a leading college of criminal justice; a former trainer of the largest police department in the US; and an expert witness in several court cases, I learned so much in conducting the research for this book. I have realized that if I was born in a different period of time, or if I had been in the wrong place at the wrong time, I easily could have had a different experience with the law and the justice system. For example, when I was a young adult, if I lived in a different state, I could have been arrested for sodomy. If I was born twenty years earlier, I would have been diagnosed with mental illness and perhaps subjected to conversion therapy. If I was born thirty years ago, and my parents never immigrated into the US, I could have been prevented from entering the country myself, as LGBTQ people were not legally allowed to migrate into the US until 1990.

I wrote this book because I want to make sure that people know about the history of LGBTQ people and the law. I want LGBTQ people to understand what our ancestors and trailblazers had gone through and fought for, so that we could have what we do today. I want people to know the government has not historically been kind to historically marginalized groups, and that if we do not speak out against injustice, they have the power to do that again. So, whether you identify as LGBTQ or as an ally or as someone who just wants to learn more, I hope that whatever new knowledge or critical view you take away or develop, that you always use your voice to fight for justice. In doing so, I sincerely hope that we can all eventually live in a world where people don't feel like "lucky ones" and instead feel able to live their greatest and most authentic selves, in a world where love is love is love and justice prevails.

Acknowledgments

This book has been guided and supported by a community of people who have surrounded me with unconditional love and strength. Thank you to my parents, Leo and Charity Nadal, for giving me life and my voice. Thank you to my mentors for teaching me how to find my power and use my voice. Thank you to the numerous friends and chosen family for constantly stimulating my brain and my heart. Thank you to my students and mentees for keeping me grounded and reminding me why I do this work. Finally, thank you to my husband and my son for being my safe space and my home.

Introduction

THE CASE OF CECE MCDONALD

On June 5, 2011, CeCe McDonald, a twenty-three-year-old Black transwoman, was walking down the street with four friends in Minneapolis, Minnesota, when a crowd of White bar patrons began to yell racial and homophobic slurs at them, calling them "niggers" and "faggots." McDonald and her friends (who are all Black) began to walk away, but the group continued to harass them. One of the White men, Dean Schmitz, began screaming transphobic comments at McDonald, saying, "Look at that boy dressed like a girl, tucking her dick in" (Pasulka, 2012). One of the White women, Molly Flaherty, then approached McDonald and struck her with a cocktail glass, slicing McDonald's cheek open and initiating a physical altercation between the two groups. As McDonald began to walk away, the group continued to verbally harass her—with Schmitz being most vocal. She preemptively grabbed a pair of scissors out of her bag for protection and turned around to face her harasser (who she did not know was now directly behind her). As a result, Schmitz was fatally stabbed in the chest. After police arrived at the scene, McDonald was arrested. After hours of interrogation, McDonald contested that she was merely acting in self-defense; yet, she was charged with second-degree intentional murder.

While awaiting her trial, McDonald was housed in two different men's prisons, as the state of Minnesota did not allow transgender women to be housed in women's facilities. She reported she even spent some time in solitary confinement, which some prisons view as a compromise for not housing transgender women in men's facilities (Arkles, 2009). Feeling hopeless after being incarcerated for almost a year, McDonald accepted a plea deal of second-degree manslaughter—a crime that would result in a 41-month prison sentence. She was told that if she went to trial, the jury would have enough evidence to convict her; she was also informed the sentence from the plea bargain would be much shorter than what would be expected if she was convicted of murder. Yet, in accepting the plea, she would have to forfeit her defense that Schmitz's death was an act of self-defense.

Throughout the case, local media did not paint McDonald in a positive light and most even used her male-assigned birth name instead of her chosen female name. Meanwhile, a social media campaign, led by transgender activist groups, used the hashtag #Free_CeCe to publicize the injustices related to McDonald's case (Fischer, 2016). Journalists picked up on the story in May 2012 (see Hill, 2012; Pasulka, 2012), and actress LaVerne Cox of *Orange is the New Black* became involved. After a total of 19 months in prison, and months of community organizers actively lobbying and protesting, McDonald was released from the men's prison. She served the remainder of her 41-month sentence on parole (Gares & Cox, 2016).

LGBTQ PEOPLE AND THE LAW

Throughout history, governments and legal systems have pathologized and criminalized lesbian, gay, bisexual, transgender, and queer (LGBTQ) people on the basis of their sexual orientations and gender identities. In the first two centuries of the United States, lynching, burning, or jailing of people who engaged in same-sex sexual acts were common and legal (Bronski, 2011). Fifty years ago, LGBTQ people were arrested for dressing in ways that were deemed inappropriate for their gender, or for gathering in public spaces with other LGBTQ people (Eskridge, 2009). Fifty years ago, homosexuality was diagnosed as a psychiatric disorder, with treatments including electroshock therapies, lobotomies, and castrations (Herek, 2010; Nadal, 2013). Twenty years ago, it was still illegal for people to engage in consensual same-sex sexual activity, even in the privacy of their own homes (Kane, 2007). Today, LGBTQ people have continued to be targets of hate violence (Herek, 2017), discrimination (Nadal, 2013), and police harassment and brutality (Grant et al., 2011)—potentially increasing their contact with the criminal justice system, should they choose to seek legal remedies.

Despite this wrought relationship with the law, academic scholarship on LGBTQ people within the criminal justice system has been relatively minimal. While there has been an increase in literature in understanding the relationship between race, racism, and the justice system (see Alexander, 2012), research on LGBTQ people within the criminal justice remains in its nascent stages (Buist & Stone, 2014; Nadal, Quintanilla, Goswick, & Sriken, 2015; Woods, 2017). Some community advocacy organizations have written about LGBTQ concerns within the prison industrial complex (Hunt & Moodie-Mills, 2012; Lydon, Carrington, Low, Miller, & Yazdy, 2015), LGBTQ experiences within court systems (Majd, Marksamer, & Reyes, 2009), and negative police interactions (Amnesty International, 2005; Lambda Legal, 2015; Waters, 2017). Some empirical research has examined LGBTQ experiences with hate crimes (Herek, 2017), LGBTQ perceptions of police (Satuluri & Nadal, 2018; Serpe & Nadal, 2017), and LGBTQ prisoners' incarceration experiences (Meyer et al., 2017; Sexton, Jenness, & Sumner, 2010). Some government agencies have released reports on their LGBTQ data, including the U.S. Department of Justice (DOJ)'s report on incarcerated LGBTQ people (Beck, 2014) or the annual Federal Bureau of Investigation (FBI, 2018) report on anti-LGBTQ hate crimes. Moreover, there is a growing body of literature in other legal specialties, like employment law (Resnick & Galupo, 2019), family law (Knauer, 2012), criminal law (Woods, 2014; 2017), and immigration law as it relates to undocumented LGBTQ immigrants (Cisneros, 2018) and LGBTQ asylees (Shuman & Hesford, 2014).

I began this book with the case of CeCe McDonald, as her story exemplifies multiple ways the criminal justice system has been oppressive to LGBTQ people—particularly Black transgender women and other LGBTQ people with multiple oppressed identities. In reviewing the case, there are four recurring themes that will be prevalent throughout this text: 1) LGBTQ people are both victimized and criminalized; 2) Intersectional identities matter; 3) Gender binaries are harmful and dangerous; and 4) Advocacy creates change.

LGBTQ People are Both Victimized and Criminalized

When CeCe McDonald was walking down the street with her friends on that summer day in 2011, she had no idea her life would change drastically. She was only placed in this predicament because of the White bar patrons who chose to harass her and her friends. It is also clear that Molly Flaherty's assault on McDonald was motivated by bias alone (i.e., she did not have any personal reason to attack McDonald), hence fitting the criteria for a hate crime. However, when police were notified of the incident, they immediately searched for, and arrested, McDonald, but they did not arrest Flaherty. In doing so, they disregarded that McDonald and her friends were targeted first, or that McDonald was actually a survivor of a hate crime.

Further, the police officers invalidated McDonald's claim of self-defense. When she walked away and tried to escape after the biased incident had escalated, Schmitz continued to provoke her. She had already been slashed in the face for no reason; she did not know what else the mob would be capable of. At that moment, McDonald made a split-second decision, knowing it would be a lose-lose situation either way. If she reached into her purse and armed herself, she would have a better chance of staying alive, but could potentially be criminalized and blamed for the incident. If she did not arm herself, her perpetrators may have injured her more, or worse, may have even killed her. In choosing to fight to survive, she instinctually found something that could be used as a weapon in her purse, ended up killing her harasser, and was arrested for it.

Intersectional Identities Matter

CeCe McDonald's case also demonstrates that when people hold multiple marginalized identities, they may face increased obstacles—particularly when they are Black, trans, or both. When Schmitz and his friends, who were all White, began to antagonize McDonald and her friends, they did so not only because of her transgender identity or their perceived sexual orientations, but also because of their race. While it is unknown if Schmitz and his friends would have harassed the group if they only had one marginalized identity (i.e., if McDonald and her friends were White, or if they were Black but appeared to be heterosexual and cisgender), it is known they did use racial, homophobic, and transphobic epithets from the start. Sadly, this dynamic of harassing LGBTQ people of color is not unique in any way, as evidenced by research which has found LGBTQ people of color, particularly Black transgender women, are more likely to experience more verbal harassment and hate violence than their White LGBTQ counterparts (Waters, 2017).

Moreover, racial bias imparted by the police was evident early on in the case, when they arrested and questioned the Black trans woman, but not the White woman who initiated the whole altercation. In doing so, the police officers immediately drew the conclusion of the Black group being the perpetrators and the White group being the victims. This presumed criminality or deviance of Blacks and favoritism or innocence of Whites is an implicit bias that is quite common for police officers and is one that can even result in the disproportionate amount of police killings of Black civilians (Nadal, Davidoff, Allicock, Serpe, & Erazo, 2017).

Police bias is one of the primary reasons why the criminal justice system is disproportionately overrepresented with Black prisoners, in comparison to other racial groups. In 2014, 35 percent of state prisoners were White, 38 percent were Black, and 21 percent were Hispanic (Carson, 2015), which is significantly disproportionate to the racial breakdown of the general American population, in which 60.4 percent are non-Hispanic White, 13.4 percent are Black, and 18.3 percent are Hispanic (U.S. Census, 2019). When police officers engage in racial profiling of Black Americans, the number of arrests and incarceration of Black Americans increases (Alexander, 2012). Other factors that may contribute to the disproportionate number of Black prisoners include the implicit biases of jurors, judges, and attorneys in the courtroom, which then negatively influence verdicts and sentencing. Other extraneous factors associated with race—such as socioeconomic status, educational status, and access to resources—also result in an increased likeliness of unfair trials, resulting in more incarceration (see Burch, 2015 for a review). Because of these factors, Michelle Alexander (2012) describes the criminal justice system as a reincarnation of slavery and Jim Crow laws—citing how the system is fueled by racism and classism and how it is designed to legally disenfranchise Black Americans and other poor communities of color.

Furthermore, the intersectional identities of being Black and transgender also increases the likeliness that a person would be incarcerated. The National Transgender Discrimination Survey of 2008–2009 revealed almost half (47 percent) of the Black transgender sample had been incarcerated at some point in their lives (Grant et al., 2011) and that Black transgender women were 3 times more likely as White trans women to have ever been incarcerated (Reisner, Bailey, & Sevelius, 2014). When police officers hold implicit or explicit biases about Black transgender women and other queer people of color, they set a tone for how the rest of the investigation and case will go. If they immediately do not believe a Black transgender woman like Ms. McDonald was a survivor of a hate crime, and instead paint her as a perpetrator, their biases influence the evidence they collect, the district attorney's decision to prosecute, and the ways the jurors deliberate on verdicts and sentences. Perhaps if the Minneapolis police officers were more knowledgeable or aware of the general experiences of Black transgender women, they would have been more sensitive in working with McDonald and the case would have been handled very differently.

Gender Binaries Are Harmful and Dangerous

CeCe McDonald's time in prison demonstrates some of the systemic issues that transgender people experience in correctional facilities. Because transgender people are not housed in the prisons that match their gender identities and instead are placed in prisons that match their sexes assigned at birth, they are more likely to experience physical and sexual violence, especially if they are transgender women or transwomen of color. For example, one study in California found transwomen placed in in men's prisons are 13 times more likely to be sexually assaulted than the general prison population (Jenness, Maxson, Matsuda, & Sumner, 2007), while another study found transwomen of color were more likely to be sexually assaulted in correctional facilities than White transwomen (Reisner et al., 2014). Further, when transgender prisoners are housed in solitary confinement—not for their behavior, but for their gender identities—they may experience an array of harmful and damaging psychological effects, like hallucinations, delusions, and self-harm (Arkles, 2009; Haney, 2018). So, by being transgender alone, they are treated with the most extreme forms of punishment. In fact, Ms. McDonald accepted the plea because she felt psychologically defeated and saw it as a way for her time in prison to be shorter. Perhaps had she not spent so much time in isolation, she would have been in a clearer frame of mind when making such a major decision.

Furthermore, through Ms. McDonald's case, it also becomes evident that because the criminal justice system was created in ways that presume rigid gender binaries, people who live and exist outside of those gender binaries are at a disadvantage when they come in contact with the system (Buist & Stone, 2014; Spade, 2015). For instance, as more people—especially young people—identify as transgender or gender nonconforming (TGNC)—particularly as genderqueer or gender nonbiary—prisons must figure out ways to house them, protect them from unnecessary violence, and protect them from unnecessary psychological trauma. While some states have become more affirming in allowing TGNC prisoners to be housed in correctional facilities matching their gender identities (or in facilities with other TGNC prisoners), other states have continued to house TGNC people in facilities that match their sex assigned at birth (Routh, Abess, Makin, Stohr, Hemmens, & Yoo, 2017). In doing so, correctional facilities create dangerous and harmful spaces for TGNC people—resulting in punishments that exceed what is actually appropriate for their crimes.

Advocacy Creates Change

A final major lesson that we learn from Ms. McDonald's story is about the power of advocacy and community organizing (Fischer, 2016). Because systems and institutions have historically been discriminatory toward people of color, LGBTQ people, LGBTQ people of color, and other historically marginalized groups, it is crucial for people to actively advocate for social justice, particularly when those historically marginalized groups are unable to. Without community activism, McDonald would have served more time behind bars—possibly in a men's prison or in solitary confinement—where she may not feel safe or sane. It took community organizing of transgender rights groups to share McDonald's story to the media and celebrities, who then used their power to broadcast the injustice to the masses. It took journalists and filmmakers to document her story as a way of educating people about the injustices bestowed upon transgender people, especially Black trans women, in the criminal justice system. It took tweeting and letter writing and lobbying and picketing for prison staff to agree that McDonald could be released on parole.

In this way, CeCe McDonald's story is a call to action. It is a reminder that in order for systemic change to occur, and for justice to prevail, people have to first identify the problems that exist. Then, they have to collectively work together to address the wrongdoings that have occurred, while creating solutions and assessing alternatives for the future. While it is a daunting task to challenge the status quo, we have learned from history how it takes the masses to speak out against injustice in order for major change to occur.

Introduction

WHAT THIS BOOK COVERS AND WHO IT IS FOR

Queering Law and Order will provide an overview of LGBTQ experiences with the justice system—reviewing current theoretical and empirical literature, while applying past and present legal cases. Chapter 1 will review the history of anti-LGBTQ legislation which has created a culture of heterosexism and transphobia in American society. Chapter 2 will examine hate violence and historical trauma, using a critical lens of the Pulse nightclub shooting in Orlando, Florida, in 2016. Chapters 3 through 5 will cover LGBTQ experiences with law enforcement, the courts, and the prison industrial complex—integrating the stories of Brandon Teena, Michael L. Johnson, and Lindsay Saunders-Velez, as a way of understanding how anti-LGBTQ biases can result in wrongful sentencing, violence, and even death. Chapters 6 through 8 will focus on employment law, family law, and immigration law—highlighting legal aspects that are often not included in criminal justice scholarship. In chapter 9, the case of Andrew Cunanan will be analyzed as a way of conceptualizing how sexual orientation, gender identity, and other cultural factors influence criminal behaviors of LGBTQ offenders. Finally, the conclusion will provide recommendations for best addressing heterosexism and transphobia in the justice system, highlighting best practices for serving LGBTQ communities.

This book is intended for a few audiences. First, it can serve as a resource text for individuals of all sectors—including academics, clinicians, attorneys, law enforcement officers, government personnel, and students. Practitioners in the helping professions (such as psychologists, physicians, counselors, social workers, and attorneys) may use the book to gain an understanding of the current issues facing their LGBTQ clients. Leaders of government institutions, non-profit organizations, prisons, schools, and hospitals may use some of the information presented to improve their policies and procedures for working with and serving their LGBTQ constituents. Finally, general readers who are committed to social justice and who want to learn more about improving the human condition may gain knowledge about people whom they may have limited knowledge about, due to the lack of integration of LGBTQ issues into our educational systems or mainstream media.

REFLEXIVITY AND THEORETICAL FOUNDATIONS

It is critical for me to identify the lenses and underpinnings from which I formulate my thoughts and approaches to this work. First, I acknowledge my worldview as a queer person of color from an immigrant family, who has gained access and privilege through education. As a gay person who is considered an Xennial (i.e., the generation between Generation X and millennials), I am old enough to remember how terrifying it was to come out of the closet, but young enough to have experienced acceptance in many of my familial and social circles when I was an adult. As a non-Black person of color with medium brown skin, I am hypervigilant of the ways that my race has affected various aspects of my life—including my membership and participation within LGBTQ communities. I recognize my identities as a cisgender person who fluctuates in gender conformity; a child of immigrants; a Filipino American who is perceived in racially diverse ways; a spiritual, recovering Catholic; a California-bred New Yorker; a husband; and a father—knowing each have individually and collectively shaped how I understand, absorb, filter, connect to, and disseminate all of this information.

Second, I acknowledge my theoretical orientations in which this text is grounded: (a) Queer Theory, (b) Intersectionality Theory, and (c) Womanism. Queer Theorists acknowledge that historical definitions, conceptualizations, and ideologies of gender, sex, and sexuality are socially constructed and rely on binary systems (Ghaziani & Brim, 2019). Through this type of gendered and sexual socialization, one group is considered normal (and thereby privileged) and other groups are considered abnormal or deficient (and thereby less privileged). Queer theorists challenge cissexist and heterosexist conceptualizations of gender and sexuality—while normalizing the experiences of LGBTQ individuals and communities. In this way, I aim to "queer" the field of criminal justice and forensic psychology by disrupting what has been considered standard or truth in American and Western societies.

This text is also grounded in Intersectionality Theory, which Kimberlé Crenshaw (1989) first proposed, as a way of recognizing how Black women have been oppressed by both racism and sexism. Through Intersectionality Theory, I will examine the ways race, ethnicity, gender, socioeconomic status, age, immigration, religion, and other identities may affect LGBTQ people's experiences in various sectors of the justice system, particularly considering the ways that systemic power and privilege negatively impact individuals with multiple marginalized identities (e.g., Black people, transgender women, undocumented queer immigrants, etc.).

Aligned with this, I borrow concepts from Womanism, which was originally coined by Alice Walker (2004). Womanism breaks away from traditional White feminism (which minimizes the influence of race and racism) and centers Black women's experiences, perspectives, and narratives with historical and contemporary context. In doing so, I make an intentional effort to normalize the voices of Black women and other groups who have been the most marginalized in society. Centering Black women is crucial in this text, as they have been overlooked, ignored, or even silenced. From the dismissal of Sojourner Truth in the earliest formations of the (White) Feminist Movement to the silencing of Black and Brown transwomen like Marsha P. Johnson and Sylvia Rivera in both historical and contemporary LGBTQ advocacy efforts, it is critically necessary for LGBTQ people to acknowledge how the "LGBTQ Movement" has focused predominantly and consistently on White, cisgender, gay, male experiences. And while many of the issues that White gay cisgender people have addressed, or advocated for, affect LGBTQ people of color too (e.g., same-sex marriage bans, military bans, hate crime reform, etc.), it is crucial to recognize how LGBTQ people of color are significantly challenged by other issues that do not affect LGBTQ White people. In this way, there is no umbrella LGBTQ experience, nor is there one LGBTQ community; rather, there are spectrums of LGBTQ experiences, subgroups, and communities.

IDENTIFYING TERMINOLOGY

Throughout this text, there are several terms that may need defining for some readers. Understanding such terminology is necessary not just for absorbing the content to be presented but is also important for recognizing the fluidity and progression of LGBTQ-related language and identities over time.

Sexual Orientation

Sexual orientation refers to the identity involving three parts: (a) the gender one is sexually or romantically attracted to, (b) the behaviors, relationships, and lived experiences that develop from those attractions, and (c) the identity that results from all of those experiences. In other words, people's sexual orientations are not just based on who they are sexually or romantically attracted to, but also how they relate to others, how they live their lives, and how they identify. For example, a heterosexual person might be sexually or romantically attracted to someone of the opposite binary gender (e.g., a heterosexual man is attracted to women); however, their heterosexuality still exists whether or not they engage in any sexual activity (e.g., whether or not they are celibate or impotent). Further, their sexual orientation influences their everyday behaviors (e.g., sex, extracurricular activities, social networks), as well as long-term goals (e.g., who to date, whether to marry or have children, etc.). Finally, whether conscious or not, they form an identity (e.g., if someone asks about their sexual orientation, they likely label themselves as heterosexual or straight).

Within LGBTQ communities, there is a spectrum of sexual orientation identifiers. Gay is usually used by people who are sexually and romantically attracted to their same gender (e.g., a man who is attracted to other men). Some women may also identify as gay, but many gay women prefer the term "lesbian"—or a woman who is attracted to other women.

In this text, lesbian will be used as a term for women who only have same-sex attractions, while gay men will be used for men who only have same-sex attractions. Furthermore, lesbian, gay, and heterosexual identities are all considered monosexual identities, or sexual orientations which involve individuals who are sexually or romantically attracted to one gender.

Bisexual refers to people who are sexually and romantically attracted to more than one gender (e.g., a woman who is sexually attracted to men and women, a man who is attracted to men and genderqueer people). One common misconception about bisexuality is that bisexuality utilizes gender binaries (i.e., bisexuals are attracted to men and women). Another misconception is that bisexuality is defined by having an equal amount of attraction to different genders. For example, bisexuals are often presumed or expected to alternate between male and female sexual or romantic partners or are told they are not really bisexual if they have maintained a long-term monogamous relationship with a person of any gender.

Pansexual refers to people who are sexually and romantically attracted to people of any gender, usually based on personality, energy, or spiritual connection. Demisexual refers to people who are only sexually attracted to people to whom they have a strong emotional connection. Fluid refers to someone who is flexible or adaptable with their sexual orientation, particularly regarding relationships, attractions, and behaviors. Polyamory refers to the consensual practice or desire of having more than one intimate or sexual partner; it can take several forms (e.g., open relationships, threeways, etc.) and can be common for many LGBTQ people.

Asexual is a term used to identify an individual who has an enduring lack of sexual attraction to people of any gender. It is estimated 1 percent of the population is asexual, and that there is a spectrum of asexual identities and behaviors (e.g., some asexual people repulse sex, while other asexual people engage in sex, but do not experience sexual attraction to other people; Deutsch, 2017). Relatedly, aromantic is used to identify an individual who has an enduring lack of romantic attraction to people of any gender. Some people identify as both asexual and aromantic, while others identify with one, but not the other. Asexuals sometimes identify as part of the LGBTQ umbrella, as they share a historically marginalized sexual identity; however, many asexuals do not, due to their unique experiences or exclusion by LGBTQ people.

Finally, queer is an umbrella term that generally refers to someone who is not heterosexual. Many people use the term "queer" when they do not feel that other terms properly describe their authentic identities or experiences. Other people identify with queer in addition to another sexual orientation (e.g., a man describes himself as gay or queer, depending on contexts or situations). Queer is also a politically charged identifier, particularly for individuals who wish to reclaim a word that was solely a pejorative and was used in violent ways.

Sex and Gender

Sex is determined by many biological or physiological traits, including chromosomes, gonads, reproductive organs, and hormones. Many people tend to assume that sex is binary—in that there are only males and females; however, approximately 1 out of every 2,000 people of the American population (or 0.5 percent) is intersex, or people who were born with biological or physiological traits countering typical or rigid definitions of female or male (Hill & McCaughan, 2017). For instance, an intersex person may have external male genitalia but internal female reproductive organs. Relatedly, the term "sex assigned at birth" is used instead of "sex," "biological sex," or "birth sex" to recognize how intersex people are given a sex label immediately after birth, in order to fit into gender binaries that permeate throughout society. However, such decisions, especially those requiring medical surgeries or genital mutilations, can cause severe physical, sexual, or psychological damage in the future (Hill & McCaughan, 2017).

Unlike sex, gender is a socially constructed identity involving how people are socialized, perceived, or emotionally connected to their sex assigned at birth, as well as their desire or ability to perform masculinity, femininity, both, either, or neither. Accordingly, gender identity refers to one's self-identification regarding their sex assigned at birth, as well as their connection to masculinity, femininity, both, either, or neither. The majority of people are cisgender, which means they identify as male or female, matching their sex assigned at birth. However, about 1 percent of the population identifies as transgender or trans—umbrella terms for anyone who does not identify with their sex assigned at birth.

Many transgender people transition, which means they undergo gender-affirming treatments or gender-confirmation procedures (e.g., hormones, surgery), so that their bodies can match (or align more with) their authentic gender identities. Some transgender people transition along a binary, which means they transition from their sex assigned at birth to the gender identity of the opposite side of the binary (e.g., a transman was assigned female at birth but transitioned through hormonal treatments or medical procedures). Sometimes transgender people include their transition in their identities (e.g., someone identifies as a "male-to-female transgender woman" or an "MTF transwoman"). Some transgender people identify simply as the gender they transitioned into (e.g., a transwoman may identify solely as a woman). Under the trans umbrella are other gender identities such as genderqueer, gender nonconforming (GNC), or gender non-binary—all describing individuals who do not identify as male or female, or identify with a gender beyond a binary.

Some transgender and gender nonconforming (TGNC) people do not transition via hormones or medical procedures at all, while some may engage in only the partial gender-confirmation procedures. As an example, a transwoman may have "top surgery" (i.e., breast implants), but she may not engage in "bottom surgery" (i.e., genitalia reconstruction). TGNC people can identify with a variety of pronouns; some use gender neutral pronouns like they/them/theirs, while others may interchange between male (he/him/his), female (she/her/hers), and gender-neutral pronouns. Some nonbinary people may create other pronouns like ze, zis, or zers. TGNC people who have transitioned use (as well as request and expect others to use) the pronouns that match their gender identity (e.g., a transman who was assigned female at birth would use he/him/his, while a transwoman who was assigned male at birth would use she/her/hers). When cisgender people do not respect transgender people's pronouns or continue to refer to them as their sex assigned at birth, they are engaging in the act of misgendering. When they call transgender people by their names assigned at birth, they are engaging in the act of deadnaming.

Gender Presentation

Gender presentation involves the ways people perform gender through their clothing, hairstyle, mannerisms, speech, and behaviors. Many cisgender heterosexuals perform traditional gender roles and presentations on unconscious or subconscious levels, as a result of gender socialization from a very early age. Some cisgender lesbians, gay men, and bisexuals may hold more traditional gender presentations (e.g., queer women who are feminine or queer men who masculine); sometimes these individuals are viewed as "passing," which means that others may presume they are heterosexual, which may result in more privilege and less discrimination (Davis, 2017a). Similarly, many trans people can "pass" as cisgender, particularly after completing gender-confirming medical treatments. They are sometimes referred to being "in stealth" or "in stealth mode"—similar terms for passing, used for transgender people.

Other cisgender lesbians and gay men may present in ways that counter traditional gender role norms (e.g., masculine lesbians are often referred to as "butch," while feminine gay men are often referred to as "femme"). People across various LGBTQ identities, particularly genderqueer, gender nonbinary, or GNC people, may present as androgynous, which means they dress in gender neutral ways—sometimes resulting in passersby incorrectly identifying their gender identities, sexes, or both. Other GNC people may fluctuate in their gender presentation—with some wearing more traditionally male clothing sometimes, traditionally female clothing other times, or some combination other times. Some cisgender people experiment with gender presentation through cross-dressing or performing drag, yet still present and identify as cisgender in their daily lives. Meanwhile, some people come to terms with their gender identities through the art of drag, resulting in self-identifying as trans or GNC. As an example, Peppermint, a contestant of *RuPaul's Drag Race*, came out as a transwoman while on the show (Reynolds, 2017). Finally, it is important to note that gender nonconformity demonstrates incongruent presentation to one's gender identity. Thus, when a gender nonbinary person presents in gender neutral ways, they may assert that they are actually conforming to their self-identified gender.

Intersectionality and Other Identity-Related Terminology

Intersectionalities are crucial in understanding how many people identify, in that some groups intentionally include their racial identities when describing their sexual orientations or gender identities (e.g., "queer people of color," "trans women of color," "Black transwomen," "trans Latinas"). Some people identify with their gender presentation and sexual orientations (e.g., "butch lesbian," "queer femme"). Others use language and terminology from their respective cultural or heritage groups (e.g., Native Americans use "two-spirit" or "two-spirited" to capture gender variance or sexual fluidity; many queer Black men identify as "same gender loving"; and Native Hawaiians use *mahu* to describe gay men and *mahu wahine* to describe transwomen). It is necessary to acknowledge how identity terms have changed over time—with some terms emerging or growing in popularity and other terms becoming more outdated. In fact, depending on when readers come in contact with this book, terms used may be outdated too. For instance, many younger people today identify with the term "queer" more than they do with more traditional labels like gay, lesbian, or bisexual (Davis, 2017b). However, because "queer" had historically been a derogatory term, used when inciting homophobic and transphobic violence, many older people find the word "queer" to be problematic, due to its association with their own personal and historical experiences with trauma. Relatedly, while "homosexual" had been used as a clinical or medical term to identify people who are attracted to, or have sexual relations with, people of the same sex, it is now viewed as an outdated term and is hardly used as a self-identification. Similarly, while transsexual was more commonly used in the past, transgender has been used more in contemporary times, to signify the emphasis is on gender and not on sex. Finally, in describing LGBTQ history, some contemporary terms will be used that may not have existed back then. As an example, while many of the women involved in the Stonewall Uprising of 1969 would have then self-identified as drag queens or transvestites, I will refer to them as transgender women, or more specifically transgender women of color.

Anti-LGBTQ Discrimination

There are many terms related to discrimination used throughout the text. First, some people opt out of using the term "homophobia" to describe anti-gay prejudice, as phobias involve intense or irrational fears of people, animals, objects, or ideas (e.g., persons who suffer from arachnophobia would scream in terror upon seeing a spider). Given that many people do not have intense or irrational fears about gay people, homophobia may not accurately describe anti-gay sentiment. Thus, I primarily use the term "heterosexism" to describe anti-gay sentiment. Conversely, while many people may not have intense or irrational fears about transgender people, many cisgender people are still vocal and overt in their biases against TGNC people. Transgender people—especially TGNC people of color and TGNC people who do not pass—are subjected to copious amounts of hate violence, as well as harassment, ridicule, or microaggressions. Additionally, while other terms have emerged to describe anti-trans bias (e.g., genderism, cissexism), neither term is currently used as widely within general American society, nor specifically within transgender communities. Therefore, transphobia will be the term used to describe anti-trans sentiment.

Finally, I will refer to how discrimination manifests in a variety of ways. Systemic discrimination involves the ways that societal structures or institutions enact bias, discrimination, stigmatization, or exclusion of certain identity groups; thus, systemic heterosexism and systemic transphobia refer to structures that specifically target LGBQ or TGNC people respectively. Hate violence can include hate crimes which involve physical or sexual assaults or abuse but also refers to hate speech or other behaviors that promote anti-LGBTQ sentiment. Overt discrimination involves the verbal and behavioral manifestations of prejudice that is malicious, deliberate, or spiteful. Microaggressions are the subtle forms of discrimination encountered by people of historically marginalized groups, that are often unintentional or ambiguous, but result in an array of short-term and long-term psychological and behavioral consequences (Nadal, 2018). Microaggressions are said to derive from individuals' stereotypes (i.e., learned presumptions about people, places, or things, based on socialization and lived experiences) or implicit biases (i.e., socialized beliefs about people and groups that may not be readily available in one's consciousness; Jost et al., 2009). Implicit bias differs from the concept of "stereotypes" because individuals may consciously or vocally deny stereotypes, or they attempt to cognitively work through such stereotypes they had previously been conditioned with. However, even if individuals attempt to alter the stereotypes they may have learned, they are still likely to have implicit biases. Thus, if people have an implicit bias, and engage in a microaggression based on that bias, they may not recognize how their implicit bias influenced the behavior.

BEGINNING OUR JOURNEY

Now that you understand more about (a) where I am coming from; (b) why this book is important to me; and (c) what I will be covering, I convey my appreciation that you will embarking on this journey toward justice. I hope you will find that this book is a call to action—for both me (as the author) and you (as the reader). Together, we are identifying a problem—that the criminal justice system has been rooted in heterosexism and transphobia (intersected with racism, classism, sexism, and other types of oppression). We are recognizing that, embedded in the system, there are issues related to bias, unfairness, or inequity. As the author, I will provide examples of how these injustices have manifested in all aspects of the system—from law enforcement to courts to legislation—covering historical and contemporary contexts. As a reader, I hope you will reflect on how these issues have personally touched your life—as a result of your historically privileged or historically marginalized identities, as well as the communities and networks you have surrounded yourself with. Finally, I will describe the collective work that has historically been used to advocate for justice, while providing grassroots and alternative recommendations for improving or uprooting the system. In doing so, I hope you will reflect on the ways you can assist in decreasing oppressive policies and practices, or how you individually or collectively can improve the lives of LGBTQ people.

While all of this is indeed a daunting task, let's reconsider a quote by the great Audre Lorde—renowned Black American lesbian writer and activist, who writes:

> I have come to believe over and over again that what is most important to me must be spoken, made verbal and shared, even at the risk of having it bruised or misunderstood. That the speaking profits me, beyond any other effect . . . I was going to die, sooner or later, whether or not I had even spoken myself. My silences had not protected me. Your silences will not protect you. (Lorde, 2007, p. 41)

Breaking the silences that have suppressed the generations before me, and verbally addressing these problems in our justice system, are important for me for two primary reasons. First, speaking my truth and sharing the truths about people who are like me is, selfishly, for my own healing. As a queer person of color with a platform, I often fluctuate between guilt and passion and fatigue. I often transform my guilt into passion, which often leads to fatigue and then cycles back to guilt. But as my dear friend Dr. Allyson Tintiangco-Cubales has taught me: "Pain + Love = Growth."

Thus, I use my pain to transform into growth. Second, giving voice to people who have been disenfranchised now feels like a responsibility. I can no longer be silent as people in power attempt to push us down. I can no longer allow myself to be complicit to the spreading of lies and propaganda. Our LGBTQ pioneers—especially the queer and transgender people of color—did not sacrifice their lives for us to be complicit. We must unite. We must fight. And we must all do our parts to bring justice back into the justice system.

ONE
A History of LGBTQ People and the Law

THE STONEWALL UPRISING

In the 1960s, it was illegal for people who were attracted to others of the same gender (now commonly known as lesbian, gay, bisexual, or queer people) or people who dressed in ways traditionally aligned with their birth sex (now commonly known as transgender or gender nonconforming people) to gather in bars and other public spaces. While societal stigma prevented LGBTQ people from being able to live as their true and authentic selves, cities and states also maintained explicit homophobic and transphobic laws which were upheld by law enforcement. For example, sodomy laws existed in most states prior to the 1960s—making it illegal for anyone to engage in oral and anal sex, regardless of consent or whether they were in the privacy of their own homes (Kane, 2007). Because of these sodomy laws, police officers often raided establishments where they knew lesbians, gays, and transgender people frequented. Patrons often paid off the police officers, to avoid being arrested and publicly "outed" or having sodomy listed on their criminal record (Bronski, 2011).

By June of 1969, police raids of bars where LGBTQ people gathered (and where bar owners did not have proper liquor licenses) were quite frequent (Carter, 2004; Duberman, 2019). Some police officers were undercover—posing as gay customers, so they could get past the bouncer at the door. Other times, police officers would force their entry into the establishments—arresting customers, seizing alcohol, or bribing bar owners or managers in order to keep the bar open for the night. People who were arrested most often were those who were not dressed in gender conforming ways—namely drag queens and butch lesbians (Bausum,

2015), especially if they were people of color (Gan, 2007). In fact, at the time, patrons were aware that there was a "three-article" rule—in which individuals had to be wearing a minimum of three articles of clothing that matched their assigned birth sex (Ryan, 2019). Because the majority of the cisgender men donned male-presenting clothes, cisgender gay men were less likely to be arrested, despite being most predominant in lesbian and gay bars (Bausum, 2015).

On Saturday, June 28, 1969, the Stonewall Inn in New York was packed with at least 200 patrons inside—in spite of a police raid that occurred a few days prior. Shortly after midnight, a group of 6 undercover police officers (4 men and 2 women) raided the bar again and began to arrest patrons who were inside. While the officers started their regular process of confiscating alcohol, checking IDs, and making arrests, some patrons were able escape the premises and began to tell others outside of the raid happening on the inside—either by calling their friends from payphones or spreading the news to passersby on the street. Crowds of about 500 to 600 gathered outside of the bar and in the Christopher Street Park—located directly across the street from the Stonewall Inn and where many homeless LGBTQ youth lived. While it is unclear of the chronological order of incidents that followed, what is known is that the events of that night began what would later be known as the Stonewall Uprising. It was the first time the crowds fought back physically against the police, resulting in several days of anti-police riots and protests. It was documented as the first major uprising that led to LGBTQ community organizing and advocacy for civil rights (Bausum, 2015; Carter, 2004; Duberman, 2019).

Historians cite the first visible act of resistance was from a transgender woman who hit a police officer with her purse, as she was being thrown into a police van. When the officer hit her with his baton, the crowd began to jeer and rock the van, colloquially known as a paddy wagon (Carter, 2004). Some witnesses say the uprising began when a butch lesbian complained her handcuffs were too tight and resisted arrest; when a police officer hit her on the head with a baton and she began bleeding, she yelled to the crowd to do something (Bausum, 2015; Carter, 2004). While it is uncertain who that butch lesbian was, some have identified the woman as Stormé Delarverie—a butch Black drag king lesbian (Santos, 2018). Other witnesses say the first ones to act were homeless street youth (Carter, 2004), while others claim Black transgender activist Marsha P. Johnson threw a shot glass at a mirror inside the bar, before being arrested, yelling: "I got my civil rights" (Santos, 2018, p. 70). Others say that Marsha P. Johnson and Sylvia Rivera (a transgender Latina activist) both joined the crowds outside Stonewall and were among those leading the riots (Duberman, 2019; Gan, 2007). Sylvia Rivera later recalled: "I remember when someone threw a Molotov cocktail, I thought, 'My god, the revolution is here! The revolution is finally here!'" (Feinberg, 2006).

Some witnesses describe those who fought the longest and the hardest were the most marginalized of the community—the homeless street youth and the gender deviant (Carter, 2004), many who were people of color (Gan, 2007).

Regardless of what initiated the revolt, the crowd began to act quickly, collectively, and in myriad ways. Because they had felt they had tolerated enough police violence and harassment, they began to throw various objects at police officers—ranging from coins to oranges to garbage cans. When the police barricaded themselves in the bar for their own safety, the crowd threw Molotov cocktails through the bar's windows and doors. Some individuals attempted to physically fight with police by pushing them to the ground, resulting in some foot chases and wrestling. Michael Fader, a Stonewall veteran, shared:

> We all had a collective feeling like we'd had enough of this kind of shit. It wasn't anything tangible anybody said to anyone else, it was just kind of like everything over the years had come to a head on that one particular night in the one particular place, and it was not an organized demonstration. It was spontaneous. That was the part that was wonderful. (Carter, 2004, p. 160)

So, whether it was a brick or a stone or a high-heeled that was first thrown at the police, the Stonewall Uprising is a representation of the contentious relationship between LGBTQ people, the police, and the criminal justice system in general.

Pre-Stonewall Uprisings

In spite of this momentous event, Stonewall was not the first LGBTQ revolt against law enforcement, nor was it the last. At Cooper's Doughnuts, in downtown Los Angeles, police would regularly harass and arrest queer and transgender patrons. One night in May 1959, as police officers were arresting a group of gay men and transgender women, patrons began throwing doughnuts and other objects at them, resulting in a riot and several arrests (Faderman & Timmons, 2009). Similarly, Compton's Cafeteria in the Tenderloin District in San Francisco was one of the few locations that transgender and gender nonconforming people could frequent after hours; however, the restaurant's owners often called the police who would then harass or arrest the patrons. One night in August 1966, after being jostled by a police officer, a transgender woman threw a cup of coffee at the officer, resulting in a riot, in which many of the transwomen fought back with their heavy bags and high heel shoes (Stryker, 2008). Despite both events occurring years prior to Stonewall, both riots did not become known as the start of the LGBTQ Civil Rights movement for a few reasons. For example, the media never reported on either event, and police reports were never filed (or were deleted). Thus, relying only on the oral histories from people who were present, the exact dates are not even known. Second, both riots were smaller in size, which reduced the impact the event could have had on media and policy, as well as the number of people who could even share the happenings of the night. For the Compton's Cafeteria riot, specifically, being led primarily by transgender women may have prevented cisgender gay men in San Francisco (and beyond) from connecting to the event. In this way, cisgender gay men may have contributed to the erasure of the event from LGBTQ history too. Either way, the uprisings in Los Angeles, San Francisco, and New York inspired LGBTQ people and communities all over the world to fight back against the systems that oppressed them. No longer would LGBTQ people allow police officers to harass them or raid their spaces. They now knew they were not alone, and they had the power to advocate for their freedoms, equities, and justice.

A HISTORY OF LGBTQ PEOPLE AND CRIMINAL JUSTICE

Fifty years after the Stonewall Uprising, there have been several major wins for LGBTQ rights. For instance, while many states had put an end to sodomy laws as early as 1961, the Supreme Court of the United States (SCOTUS) ruled in *Lawrence v. Texas* (2003) that sodomy laws were unconstitutional—thus decriminalizing sodomy on a federal level (Kane, 2007). In 2009, President Barack Obama put an end to "Don't Ask, Don't Tell" policies in the US military—allowing LGBTQ people to serve openly in the armed forces; President Obama also signed the Matthew Shepard and James Byrd, Jr. Hate Crime Act—adding sexual orientation and gender identity as protected classes under federal hate crime law (Nadal, 2018). Relatedly, through the Violence Against Women Reauthorization Act of 2013, LGBTQ people who were victimized through intimate partner violence (IPV) became protected through federal law—as the prior version of the act included heteronormative definitions of family as involving marriage or having a biological child in common (Stapel, 2008). Furthermore, while states began to permit same-sex marriage as early as 2004, SCOTUS ruled, in *Obergefell v. Hodges* (2015), that state marriage bans were unconstitutional—resulting in the legalization of marriage equality across the US.

Despite these encouraging signs of acceptance for LGBTQ people, there are still many types of legal obstacles LGBTQ people face. While President Obama had advocated for many LGBTQ rights and protections, Donald Trump's presidential administration reversed many of those protections—including the right for transgender people to serve in the military or considering sexual orientation and gender identity as protected classes in federal employment (Byne, 2018). Many states prohibit discrimination on the basis of sexual orientation (and some states also prohibit discrimination on the basis of gender identity), yet there is no federal law that ensures that people cannot be discriminated against in education or employment based on one's sexual orientation or gender identity (Resnick & Galupo, 2019). Many states have introduced "religious freedom" bills that permit people and institutions to legally discriminate against LGBTQ people, if their biased behaviors align with their religious beliefs (Bindewald, Rosenblith, & Green, 2017). Finally, LGBTQ people are still unfairly targeted by law enforcement in numerous ways; as an example, LGBTQ people, particularly transwomen, are stopped, questioned, frisked, and subsequently arrested for prostitution when they have condoms on their person (Wurth, Schleifer, McLemore, Todrys, & Amon, 2013). With these few examples, it is evident that LGBTQ rights are still threatened by government and the law and why, even 50 years after Stonewall, we still need to advocate for systemic change for LGBTQ people.

Before delving into these various chapters, let's first review the history of heterosexism and transphobia in the legal system, as a way of contextualizing how LGBTQ people have interacted with the justice system throughout history. First, we will review historical legislation that has directly and indirectly targeted LGBTQ people. We will also review major events and important time periods for LGBTQ people, which resulted in assorted interactions with law enforcement and government. While it is often painful to revisit the past, we must understand how history influences current and modern-day situations. In order for people to really advocate for social justice, equity, and change, they must understand how systems and institutions have unfairly privileged certain groups and marginalized others (and how they continue to today).

As renowned Black American gay writer and activist James Baldwin once said: "I want to suggest that history is not the past. It is the present. We carry our history with us. We are our history. If we pretend otherwise, to put it very brutally, we are literally criminals" (Baldwin, 1981, p. 53). We remember that history must not be forgotten. History is part of who we are, and whether we are conscious of it or not, it is part of who we will become.

Sodomy Laws

In recognizing the history of LGBTQ people and the law, one must understand sodomy laws, or legislation targeting LGBTQ people by criminalizing sexual acts considered to be deviant and immoral (Kane, 2007). While same-sex acts and gender nonconformity were found to be accepted or neutral in various civilizations like Ancient Egypt, Ancient Greece, Ancient Rome, pre-colonized Thailand, pre-colonized Philippines, and pre-colonized North America (Nadal, 2013), the criminalization of sodomy was believed to originate in European countries influenced by Christianity (Eskridge, 2009). Some sodomy laws explicitly described forbidden sexual acts; as an example, the Buggery Act of 1533 was enforced in England for over three centuries and made "buggery" (i.e., sex between two men or a man and a beast) punishable by hanging (Nadal, 2013).

When the English settlers first arrived in what is now the United States in the 1600s (and stole lands from the indigenous people of North America), sodomy laws came too. Disregarding Native American practices of honoring a continuum of human sexuality and gender expression, as well as the existence of two-spirit people (Pope, 2017), British sodomy laws were enforced in the early America. So, although the Pilgrims escaped moral and religious persecution from the British monarchy, they ended up applying their own system of moral codes and persecuting those who did not abide. For the first two centuries, the punishment for sodomy in the US was death; however, as time progressed, punishments for sodomy, across most states, usually included fines and jail time (Crompton, 1976), with some offenders serving up to a year in jail (Chauncey, 1995). By the 1900s, sodomy was considered a major felony or a "crime against nature" (Eskridge, 2009, p. 109), even if both parties consented to the sexual acts in their own homes. For example, Bérubé (2003) notes that in California in the early 1900s, "landlords, housekeepers, neighbors, policemen, and YMCA janitors drilled tiny holes in walls, peeped through keyholes, transoms, and windows or broke down doors to discover men having sex with each other. Because *all* sex acts between men were considered public and illegal, gay men were forced to become sexual outlaws" (p. 33). In New York, NYPD began raiding bathhouses as early as 1903 and arresting patrons on sodomy charges; by 1910, they moved on to other methods, including following two men suspected of being gay into hotels, spying on them through a transom in a neighboring hotel room, and arresting them after watching them have sex (Chauncey, 1995).

Sodomy laws were typically used as a rationale for police entrapment of gay men (Bausum, 2015; Chauncey, 1995). Because of societal stigma, many queer men—some who were closeted and some who had no other way to meet romantic or sexual partners—would cruise for sex in public spaces. Cruising is defined as "the purposeful search for a socio-sexual partner, in some cases for a limited relationship (one-night stand) and in others for an indeterminate period" (Bullock, 2004, p. 4). In the early 1900s, the NYPD targeted men in rumored cruising areas (e.g., parks, beaches, public bathrooms, etc.)—arresting men on charges of degeneracy, indecent exposure, loitering, or prostitution, often without catching the men in any overt sexual act (Chauncey, 1995). In the 1950s, NYPD police officers in plain clothes went to gay bars or cruising spots, convincing patrons they wanted to have sex, and then luring them to hotel rooms. Once arrested, the hotel would become makeshift holding cells, as police officers continued to deceive other men; the detainees were transferred to police precincts for processing together at the end of the night (Bausum, 2015). Similar stings occurred across the country; in Mansfield, Ohio, in 1962, police set up surveillance cameras at a public restroom and arrested 38 men, after watching them engage in a variety of sexual acts. Thirty-one of those men were convicted on sodomy charges, which resulted in a mandatory minimum sentence of one-year imprisonment in a state penitentiary (Biber & Dalton, 2009).

Finally, sodomy laws were used to target and punish businesses that served or attracted LGBTQ clientele. For instance, from 1954 to 1965, the San Francisco Police Department, the SF District Attorney's office, and local media worked together to lobby for the state legislature to pass a law that revoked liquor licenses of bars with a reputation for serving LGBTQ clients. In their campaigns, these agencies even referred to lesbian and gay bars as "resorts for sexual perverts" (Bérubé, 2003, p. 47). So, even if businesses were not allowing customers to engage in actual acts of sodomy in these spaces, being affiliated with LGBTQ people made them susceptible to being targeted by the government.

Illinois became the first state, in 1961, to remove sodomy laws from its criminal code; however, most states still recognized sodomy laws for decades—with varying levels of enforcement of those laws (Nadal, 2013). In spite of the 2003 SCOTUS ruling which deemed sodomy laws unconstitutional, as of 2019, sixteen states have not officially removed sodomy laws from their criminal codes. While sodomy could not legally be used as the official reason for arrests, some states have still tried to criminalize LGBTQ people based on this now outdated and unconstitutional statute (Dart, 2019), or they use any number of other vague general laws like "loitering with the intent of soliciting" as a reason to arrest innocent LGBTQ people (Make the Road, 2012).

Masquerade Laws

In the 1800s, several state and local jurisdictions began to criminalize cross-dressing or gender-bending through various "masquerade laws." For example, in 1850, Chicago adopted an ordinance in which cross-dressing was considered a criminal offense. Arrests could be made

> if anyone shall appear in a public space in a state of nudity, or in a dress not belonging to his or her sex, or in an indecent or lewd dress, or shall make indecent exposure of his or her person or be guilty of an indecent act of lewd act of behavior. (Eskridge, 2009, p. 27)

While over 50 cities adopted similar ordinances, two states passed such laws. In 1845, New York criminalized being "disguised" in public places, while California, in 1874, prohibited people from "masquerading" in another person's attire for criminal purposes. Many masquerade laws did not overtly refer to cross-dressing or gender-bending (and were initially intended to prevent people from using disguises to commit crimes); however, many law enforcement departments began to interpret such laws to criminalize transgender and gender nonconforming people (Eskridge, 2009; Ryan, 2019). For instance, in 1913, in Brooklyn, an individual named Elizabeth Trondle was sentenced to three years in a correctional facility for masquerading in men's clothing. The judge stated: "I sent her to the Bedford Reformatory because I believe she is a moral pervert. No girl would dress in men's clothing unless she is twisted in her moral viewpoint" (*Brooklyn Daily Eagle*, 1913, p. 16).

The aforementioned three-article rule, which was used to arrest transgender and gender nonconforming people (which includes cisgender lesbian and gay people whose gender presentation was nonconforming or nonbinary) during the era of the Stonewall Uprising, is one example of how masquerade laws were applied and enforced. One lesbian named Rusty Brown, who was born in the 1920s, described her experiences with the three-article rule:

> I had been arrested in New York more times than I have fingers and toes, for wearing pants and a shirt. . . . You had to have three pieces of female attire. Now, let's put it this way. At the time I was young, I had nothing on top, so what the hell was I going to put in a brassiere? I'm not exactly the type for lace panties. And if I'm wearing pants I sure as hell didn't need a pretty coat. So, there goes your three pieces of female attire. (Ryan, 2019, pp. 241–242)

While many LGBTQ people were being targeted by this rule, there was no actual documentation of the "three-article rule" as an actual police policy (Ryan, 2019). Therefore, it was a mere scare tactic that was used to arrest LGBTQ people without actually having any legal standing in courts.

After the Stonewall Uprising of 1969, it appears that masquerade laws or the three-article rule were no longer enforced in New York City, nor were they used as the legal reason to arrest a transgender or gender nonconforming person. However, masquerade laws were never formally removed from the local laws, as evidenced by the law being used to arrest Occupy Wall Street protestors in 2011 (Gardiner & Firger, 2011). Further, police officers still utilize other obscure laws to arrest transgender people, including a 2018 incident in which NYPD officers arrested a trans Latina woman on the grounds of "false personation"—a crime in which someone knowingly misrepresents themselves with intent to prevent police from knowing their identity (Stafford, 2019). Even if masquerade laws are not used explicitly to arrest transgender people, trans people are still being arrested for numerous unjustifiable reasons. For instance, in the 2015 U.S. Transgender Survey, out of the participants who were arrested or detained in the past year, nearly one-fourth believed it was because of their gender identity alone (James et al., 2016).

Sexual Psychopath Laws

Beginning in the 1930s, several states enacted sexual psychopath laws, usually implemented in response to a series of serious sex crimes committed in quick succession in a given area. The laws allowed for certain people to be arrested on suspicion they could possibly commit a sex-related crime (and not because of actually committing a crime; Lave, 2008). While there were broad definitions of sexual psychopaths across state laws, many jurisdictions criminalized queer men on the basis they would commit violent sexual crimes, due to their sexual orientation identities (Sutherland, 1949). For example, in 1954, after the murder of two children in Sioux City, Iowa, twenty gay men were arrested and sentenced to a mental institution to be cured of their homosexuality (Miller, 2002). Further, while lesbianism was indeed stigmatized and pathologized, it was evident that these sexual psychopath laws (and sodomy laws in general) primarily targeted men. Prior to 1952, Kinsey, Pomeroy, Martin, and Gebhart (1953) reported there were no known cases of a woman being convicted of any homosexual activity.

These laws emerged during a time when homosexuality was pathologized and labeled as an abnormal, deviant, and even violent disorder. The American Psychiatric Association (1952) first introduced the concept of homosexuality as a sociopathic personality disturbance in the *Diagnostic and Statistical Manual of Psychiatric Disorders*; in doing so, homosexual thoughts and behaviors were deemed pathologies that needed to be cured or medically treated through heinous means like electroshock therapy, lobotomies, or castration (Drescher, 2015). Moreover, national media continued to paint LGBTQ people as dangerous sexual deviants; as an illustration of this, a 1950 article in *Coronet* described how homosexuals recruited younger people to their homosexual lifestyle and how homosexuals sexually abused children (Major, 1950).

While many law scholars at the time did indeed believe homosexual acts were "perversions" (Sutherland, 1949, p. 546), others argued how homosexuality, in itself, should not be classified in the same category as violent sex crimes. As an example, Ploscowe (1962) writes: "These individuals are nuisances for the most part. They create scandal and annoyance, but they are not a serious danger to the women and children of a community" (p. 8). Bowman and Engle (1956) were more sympathetic to homosexuals, citing treatment was costly and ineffective and only caused psychological distress; they further argued if consensual heterosexual sexual acts done in private were not criminalized, consensual same-sex sexual acts in private should not be criminalized either. Eventually, many sexual psychopath laws were removed from criminal codes, primarily for the reason that predictions of behavior were not reliable and therefore not justifiable in accusing one of criminal behavior (Bowman & Engle, 1956). Among the repealed laws was the Iowa sexual psychopath law that was used to convict 20 homosexuals in 1954; that conviction was repealed in 1978 (Miller, 2002).

While sexual psychopath laws do not exist in explicit form today, there are myriad ways that similar sentiments may emerge in more covert ways. For instance, some LGBTQ offenders, especially youth offenders, have reported experiencing sentences in which they are presumed to be sex offenders for crimes that have nothing to do with sexual misconduct (Majd et al., 2009). In more subtle ways, LGBTQ people in general may experience microaggressions in which they are presumed to be sexually deviant (e.g., someone presumed that LGBTQ people are sexual predators, child molesters, or hyper promiscuous; Nadal, 2013).

The Lavender Scare and Other Anti-LGBTQ Witch Hunts

In the 1940s and 1950s, alongside McCarthyism and the fear that communists were infiltrating the US government, many Americans began to learn about, and subsequently, ostracize "homosexuals"—a group which included gay men and lesbians, but likely referred to anyone who would identify today as LGBTQ. For example, prior to World War II, if service members were found to be homosexual in the military, they would be dishonorably discharged, court-martialed, and imprisoned for sodomy. By 1946, 9,000 homosexuals were previously discharged from the military—with 5,000 discharges from the army and 4,000 from the navy. Yet, by the end of World War II, the mere confession by an individual to a psychiatrist of homosexual tendencies did not itself result in a discharge, but instead required hospitalization (Bérubé, 2003).

Similar types of pathologizing for LGBTQ people occurred in different parts of the country and resulted in varying levels of disciplinary actions for people who were suspected of being LGBTQ, caught engaging in sodomy, or both. First, in the 1920s, male students had been expelled from two elite universities, Harvard and Dartmouth. Although the official reason may not have been listed as such for engaging in homosexual activity, their suspected sexual orientations were believed to be the primary reasons for the expulsions (Syrett, 2007; Wright, 2005). In the 1940s, similar purges occurred in three major public universities—University of Texas, University of Missouri, and University of Wisconsin. This time, however, such instances included both students and faculty who had been expelled or terminated on the suspicion of being homosexual (Nash & Silverman, 2015).

Perhaps the greatest overt and intentional targeting of LGBTQ people by a single entity was when an executive order forbade LGBTQ people from working in the federal government. Later labeled by Johnson (2009) as the "Lavender Scare," this time period was an era where homosexuals were viewed as communist sympathizers, traitors to the government, or both. Homophobic fears gained momentum during a congressional hearing in 1950 when Undersecretary of State for Administration John Peurifoy testified that most of the federal employees dismissed for "moral turpitude" were homosexuals (D'Emilio, 2012, p. 41).

In 1950, a subcommittee of the U.S. Senate's Committee on Expenditures in the Executive Departments released a report that stated: "In the opinion of this subcommittee, homosexuals and other sex perverts are not proper persons to be employed in Government for two reasons; first, they are generally unsuitable, and second, they constitute security risks" (p. 3). Immediately following, U.S. Senator Charles Hoey determined the department heads of five federal agencies (e.g., U.S. Army, U.S. Navy, Washington, DC Police, U.S. State Department, and U.S. Parks) kept records of over 16,500 names of individuals who were considered or suspected of being homosexual or sexual deviants (Johnson, 2009). In the latter half of 1951, the number of homosexuals who were dismissed from federal positions averaged 60 per month—12 times the number of dismissals from a few years prior (D'Emilio, 2012). By 1953, the Truman administration fired 425 federal employees on suspicion of homosexuality (Brown, 1958).

Shortly after being inaugurated, President Dwight Eisenhower signed an executive order in which "sexual perversion" could be used as a reason to terminate employment from federal employment, including both civilian and military positions (D'Emilio, 2012, p. 44). Without explicitly referring to homosexuality, the order states: "Employees could be a security risk and still not be disloyal or have any traitorous thought, but if their personal habits are such they might be subject to blackmail by people who seek to destroy the safety of our country" (Johnson, 2009, p. 123). Some scholars interpreted the executive order as being "based on a consensus of various intelligence agencies who presume that because most homosexuals lack emotional stability and have weak moral fibre, they are an unnecessary risk to government service" (Bowman & Engel, 1956, p. 579). In other words, because LGBTQ people could keep secrets (i.e., their sexual orientations) and were presumed to be emotionally and psychologically weak, they would be security threats for blackmail.

Accordingly, an era of anti-LGBTQ "witch hunts" ensued—in which individuals who were suspected of being gay were interrogated, spied on, publicly outed, and subsequently humiliated and ostracized. It is estimated more than 5,000 federal civil servants lost their jobs, as a result of their sexual orientations (actual or alleged), with thousands of LGBTQ applicants who were denied federal employment (D'Emilio, 2012; Johnson, 2009). The federal employment ban based on sexual orientation ended when the Circuit Court of Appeals in San Francisco found homosexuality itself did not negatively affect job performance and ordered the

Civil Service Commission to cease the excluding and discharging of employees on the basis of their sexual orientations (Johnson, 2009).

Although President Eisenhower's executive order in 1953 specifically targeted federal employees, anti-LGBTQ witch hunts transpired in many other public, private, and corporate sectors. Private investigation businesses began to emerge, offering assistance to employers in uncovering current and prospective LGBTQ employees (Johnson, 2009). Anti-LGBTQ witch hunts did not only affect people who were formerly employed by the federal government. They occurred when rumors amassed about LGBTQ people in particular communities. As an example, in 1955, *Time* magazine published an article which cited the existence of a secret society of homosexuals in Boise, Idaho, which resulted in investigators uncovering and "outing" these individuals—many who were teachers who lost their families and jobs and were sentenced to psychiatric treatment centers (Blount, 2006).

Anti-LGBTQ witch hunts (and subsequent termination from employment) occurred in educational systems too. In Florida, from 1956 to 1965, lesbian and gay schoolteachers were outed and fired because of the fear that "homosexuality was spreading throughout state educational systems" (Graves, 2009, p. xii). In California, legislation was passed in which an educator's teaching credentials would be immediately suspended if they were convicted of any statute related to sex or morality (Bronski, 2011). In Washington, an openly gay high school teacher named James Gaylord was terminated because of his "immoral sexual orientation" after a student reported his sexual orientation to school administration (Blount, 2006, p. 118). All of these early teachers who appealed or sought retribution lost their legal battles—mostly due to loopholes or clauses in existing local and state laws.

Taken together, these are just a few examples of the ways that LGBTQ people had been outed and subsequently targeted, due to their sexual identities. While many state laws now protect LGBTQ people from discrimination based on their sexual orientations or gender identities, there are still no federal laws to do so. And although Title VII of the Civil Rights Act of 1964 was created to prohibit workplace discrimination based on sex, race, color, religion, and national origin, sexual orientation or gender identity were not included as protected classes. Thus, a repeat of the Lavender Scare is entirely possible in several states.

HIV/AIDS Stigma and Legislation

In the early 1980s, when gay and bisexual men began getting severely sick in metropolitan areas, they were initially diagnosed with Gay Related Immune Deficiency (GRID). As a result, gay people began to be blamed for the disease, which would later be known as HIV/AIDS. Media outlets continued to propagate homophobic connections to HIV/AIDS leading to the start of LGBTQ people being criminalized, pathologized, or blamed for their illness (Nadal, 2018). For example, *National Review* (1985) published:

> Many homosexuals, in the Seventies and early Eighties, had a conviction, amounting to a political dogma, that "freedom" could only be asserted through compulsive sexual license. That attitude is bitterly condemned by some homosexuals now, as the death tolls mount. But the phenomenon of promiscuity was more than the result of a conscious philosophy. Abnormal sex is, simply, normless. (p. 18)

As people living with HIV/AIDS (most who were queer and trans) got sick and subsequently died, the American government did not take any action for over five years—despite the rapid number of deaths that occurred. In 1987, President Ronald Reagan first spoke publicly about AIDS, and he issued an executive order to create the President's Commission on the AIDS Epidemic; however, by that time, a total of 20,849 people had already died, which equates to a rate of 9.5 people per day over a six-year span (Nadal, 2018).

Thirty years since the first cases of AIDS were discovered in 1981, over 700,000 people have died; today, over 1.1 million people are currently living with HIV/AIDS (CDC, 2018). Because HIV/AIDS has been highly prevalent among LGBTQ communities—particularly for men who have sex with men and transgender women—it has continued to be a primary issue for LGBTQ people. Additionally, because of the ongoing stigma toward LGBTQ people, HIV/AIDS has continued to be considered a gay disease, resulting in several controversial issues regarding HIV/AIDS and government. Legislation involving HIV/AIDS centers around three major themes: (a) systemic policies involving people living with HIV/AIDS, (b) laws in which people living with HIV/AIDS are criminalized, and (c) laws which protect people living with HIV/AIDS when they are discriminated against because of their serostatuses.

Systemically, there are numerous policies concerning HIV/AIDS that have negatively impacted LGBTQ communities. First, in 1983, the Food and Drug Administration (FDA) instituted a ban on blood donations from men who had ever had sex with men. For three decades, this policy was in place, regardless of its empirical logic or common sense (i.e., all blood was screened for disease anyway, sexually active heterosexual people could transmit HIV, celibate queer men could not donate, etc.). In 2015, the FDA lifted its lifetime ban on blood donations from gay and bisexual men, and instead instituted that men who refrained from any sexual activity in the past year could donate blood (Printz, 2018). Though reduced in severity, the policy still discriminates against men who have sex with men, while not discriminating against others who may be at greater risk of contracting the virus. For instance, a monogamous gay male couple who were sexually active could not donate blood, while a sexually promiscuous heterosexual man could.

Immigration policies have included many controversial issues related to HIV/AIDS. As an example, in 1987, under President Ronald Reagan, the US mandated all new immigrants to be tested for HIV/AIDS and subsequently deemed anyone living with HIV/AIDS be inadmissible to the US. This policy had remained virtually unchanged for decades, until the Department of Health and Human Services, under the direction of President Obama, voted to remove HIV from the list of inadmissible infections (Winston & Beckwith, 2011). Accordingly, refugees living with HIV/AIDS could seek political asylum in the US, if they could prove they would be persecuted in their home country because of their serostatus.

Regarding criminalization, 26 states maintain specific HIV-related laws criminalizing exposure, with 19 states in the US requiring people living with HIV to disclose their serostatuses to anyone they may expose to the virus—including sexual partners or people with whom they share hypodermic needles (CDC, 2019). Scholars have argued how the criminalization of HIV/AIDS is problematic, in stigmatizing and pathologizing HIV; discourages HIV testing and treatment; and erodes the norms of mutual responsibility for prevention and sexual health (Mykhalovskiy, 2015). Furthermore, as the virus has historically and disproportionately affected LGBTQ communities—including gay and bisexual men, transgender women, and queer people of color from lower socioeconomic statuses, criminalizing HIV/AIDS further puts marginalized groups in contact with the justice system and hinders their ability to thrive.

Conversely, people living with HIV/AIDS are also subject to discrimination as a result of their diagnosis. Within the first decade of the epidemic, the National Gay and Lesbian Task Force reported more than 1,200 incidents in which harassment or victimization was both anti-gay and anti-HIV/AIDS (Berrill, 1990). Eventually, HIV/AIDS would be protected under the American Disabilities Act of 1990, as it would become classified as a type of disability. Employers would know they were not allowed to ask people about their HIV status, nor were they allowed to terminate, demote, or make any job-related decision based on one's knowledge of their HIV status (Elliott, Utyasheva, & Zack, 2009). Finally, while discrimination toward people living with HIV/AIDS may be illegal, it is still common for people to encounter an array of microaggressions regarding their serostatuses—ranging from stigmatizing language to endorsement of stereotypes (Vitiello & Nadal, 2019).

Anti-LGBTQ Discrimination and Freedom of Speech

In the 1980s and 1990s, there were a series of federal and state supreme court cases, in which several entities were accused of sexual orientation discrimination. While many of the cases were not favorable for

LGBTQ people, their arguments and verdicts opened the doors to subsequent SCOTUS cases which were successful. In 1982, Michael Hardwick was arrested in Georgia, in his own bedroom, for engaging in consensual adult same-sex sexual activity and charged with sodomy. While the district attorney decided not to prosecute them, Hardwick filed a federal civil rights challenge to the Georgia statute, which classified that same-sex sexual activity was considered illegal sodomy. In *Bowers v. Hardwick* (1986), SCOTUS upheld the state statute because there was no constitutionally protected right to engage in homosexual sex because sodomy was indeed "a crime against nature" (Goldstein, 1988, p. 1084).

In 1992, the Irish American Gay, Lesbian and Bisexual Group of Boston, Inc. (GLIB) was denied participation in the St. Patrick's Day Parade by the South Boston Allied War Veterans Council (who were the sponsors of the parade). Through *Hurley v. Irish-American Gay, Lesbian, and Bisexual Group of Boston* (1995), SCOTUS upheld a Massachusetts statute prohibiting discrimination based on sexual orientation could not be applied, as it would violate the First Amendment rights of the parade organizers. The majority ruled requiring GLIB's participation would force a particular message which countered the organizers' message, violating the Council's First Amendment right to choose the content of its expression (Brower, 2001).

In 1992, Colorado voted in support of Amendment 2, which prevented protected status to lesbians, gays, and bisexuals in the Colorado constitution. In other words, LGB people would not be considered a protected minority group and could be legally discriminated against. Richard G. Evans, a gay municipal employee, filed suit to enjoin the amendment. In *Romer v. Evans* (1996), SCOTUS struck down the amendment because there was no rationale for it being a legitimate state interest, stating the amendment was created merely based on "animus toward the class that it affects" (Koppelman, 1997, p. 90).

In 1990, James Dale, an openly gay man, was terminated from his role as an assistant scoutmaster of the Boy Scouts of America, Inc. in New Jersey, after the organization learned of his gay identity. The New Jersey Supreme Court ruled the organization violated the state's public accommodation anti-discrimination statute. *Boy Scouts of America, Inc. and Monmouth Council, et al., Petitioners v. James Dale* (2000) reversed that decision—citing it would unconstitutionally burden the organization's First Amendment freedoms of expressive association. One of the determining factors was that because Dale was open about his sexual identity, he was deemed as flaunting it, communicating that LGBTQ should just be quiet about their identities and go back into the closet to avoid discrimination (Brower, 2001).

Hate Violence Legislation

Hate crimes are criminal acts in which an individual (or survivor) was targeted because of the actual or perceived race, color, religion, national origin, ethnicity, disability, or sexual orientation, or gender identity; examples may include physical assaults, hate mail, threatening phone calls, vandalism, fires, and bombings (Herek, 2017). Prior to Stonewall, violence toward LGBTQ people was viewed as natural crimes toward a group of people who were deserving of it (Herek, 2017; Nadal, 2013). Further, hate crimes based on sexual orientation or transgender identity are typically underreported; not only do survivors experience emotions like shame, guilt, and fear, but police officers and others often do not label incidents as hate crimes (Herek, 2017).

Hate crimes toward LGBTQ people became more popularized in both media and law when a young gay White man named Matthew Shepard was violently killed in Laramie, Wyoming, due to his sexual orientation (Nadal, 2013). Shepard's murder eventually led to changes in hate crime legislation on local, state, and eventually federal levels, most notably with the Matthew Shepard and James Byrd, Jr. Hate Crimes Prevention Act—which added sexual orientation and gender identity as protected classes in federal hate crime law (Nadal, 2018). Until then, it was not required for hate crimes based on sexual orientation or gender identity to be tracked; the actual number of hate crimes against LGBTQ people had not been known prior. Moreover, with the emergence of social media, hate crimes toward other groups have become more documented, particularly toward transgender and gender nonconforming (TGNC) people. The first International Transgender Day of Remembrance (ITDOR) was held on November 20, 2009 and has been held annually to recognize the thousands of TGNC people who had been murdered within that past year and throughout history (Chang & Skolnik, 2017).

While the FBI (2018) reported that out of 5,803 hate crime incidents, 15.8 percent were targeted because of their sexual orientation, community organizations have created their own systems to accurately track violence and cite different numbers. In 2017, the National Coalition of Anti-Violence Programs reported 71 percent of anti-LGBTQ hate crime homicides involved people of color; that 52 percent involved transgender or gender nonconforming victims; and that 40 percent involved transgender women of color (Waters, 2017). Moreover, in 2018, 29 anti-transgender murders occurred in the US, with an overwhelming majority of these victims being Black transgender women (Human Rights Campaign [HRC], 2019b).

Military Policies on Sexual Orientation and Gender Identity

While the Lavender Scare in the 1950s resulted in thousands of federal employees, including military personnel, being terminated from their jobs, LGBTQ people in the military have continued to struggle in their ability to serve in the military. Beginning in 1982, the U.S. Department of Defense implemented a policy that stated: "Homosexuality is incompatible with military service. The presence in the military environment of persons who engage in homosexual conduct or who, by their statements, demonstrate a propensity to engage in homosexual conduct, seriously impairs the accomplishment of the military mission" (Herek, 1993, p. 539).

In the early 1990s, "Don't Ask, Don't Tell" (DADT) policies were first enacted as a compromise between more conservative people who did not think that lesbian and gay people could serve effectively in the military and more liberal people who thought they could. Opponents of lesbians and gays in the military often cited the notion of living and working in close quarters as a reason why they would be ineffective. Thus, DADT was created as a way of allowing military personnel to continue to serve, as long as they did not publicly divulge their sexual orientations (Burks, 2011). While initially viewed as a compromise, DADT was actually discriminatory and therefore unconstitutional, in allowing a group of people to be treated differently as a result of their sexual orientation identities. In fact, while DADT was meant to allow military service people to keep their jobs, it had opposite effects, such as increasing sexual stigma, heterosexist prejudice, anti-LGBTQ aggression, victimization, and violence (Burks, 2011). Moreover, concealing one's identity under DADT was quite psychologically distressing for its LGBTQ service personnel, with many reporting increased hypervigilance, isolation, and other mental health symptoms (Van Gilder, 2017).

In 2011, President Obama signed a federal bill which put an end to DADT—allowing LGBTQ individuals to openly serve in the military (Nadal, 2018). Yet, it is necessary to understand the individuals affected from the 1982 ban and the DADT policy. From 1980 to 1993 (prior to DADT), it is estimated over 19,000 service members were discharged, with another 13,000 who were discharged during DADT, from 1993 to 2009 (Burks, 2011). While spanning three decades, the number far surpasses the 9,000 military officers who were discharged during the Lavender Scare (see Bérubé, 2003).

Finally, DADT policies did not explicitly address transgender military personnel at all. However, in 2017, the presidential administration threatened to discharge all transgender people from the military (Byne, 2018). While several court cases are still pending as of the time of this writing, it is unclear if 15,000 current trans servicepeople (and future trans service members) will be allowed to serve in the military.

Marriage Equality and LGBTQ Family Law

While historians have documented that many same-sex couples had found ways to legally wed over the past two centuries (Cleves, 2015), federal laws regarding same-sex marriage first became challenged in Colorado in 1971, when an Australian man, Tony Sullivan, tried to apply for American citizenship, after being issued a marriage license with his husband, Richard Adams (a Filipino American naturalized citizen). The Immigration and Naturalization Service replied with: "You have failed to establish that a bona fide marital relationship can exist between two faggots" (Cathcart & Gabel-Brett, 2016, p. 7). Because their appeal was rejected, they self-exiled out of the country, so they could continue living together. State bans on same-sex marriage began to emerge in the 1970s, after Christian groups and former beauty queen Anita Bryant led crusades to demonize LGBTQ people and take away their civil rights (Blount, 2006; Bronski, 2011). In 1990, a group of three couples applied for marriage licenses in Hawai'i; a judge held that preventing them from doing so was unconstitutional and a violation of their civil rights. In 1995, Congress passed the Defense of Marriage Act (DOMA) which stated marriage was between a man and a woman (Haldeman, 2017).

The act of marrying was important for many LGBTQ people because it afforded them the same types of rights as heterosexual couples. Prior to the SCOTUS decisions, it was legal for same-sex couples to be rejected from seeing their life partners in hospital rooms because they were not considered immediate family. It was also financially burdensome. When Edie Windsor lost her wife, Thea Spyer, whom she had been married to for 2 years, but partnered with for over 40 years, she was taxed $363,000 by the Internal Revenue Service (IRS), simply because their marriage was not recognized by federal law (Cathcart & Gabel-Brett, 2016).

In 2004, Massachusetts became the first state to recognize same-sex marriage, after a Massachusetts Supreme Judicial Court ruled the state ban on same-sex marriage was unconstitutional. For the decade following, many states voted on same-sex marriage bans (e.g., Proposition 8 in California in 2008), while many state legislatures voted on ending bans on same-sex marriage (e.g., Marriage Equality Act in New York in 2011; Nadal, 2013). Two major SCOTUS decisions in 2013 opened the door for federal law and marriage equality: (a) *Hollingsworth v. Brown* found the bans on same-sex marriage in California were unconstitutional, legalizing same-sex marriage again in the state; and (b) *US v. Windsor* which invalidated the DOMA's clause that defined marriage as the union between a man and a woman, allowing married same-sex couples to access federal benefits of marriage, such as Social Security survival benefits and sponsoring a spouse for immigration. The latter decision would have made it legal for Tony Sullivan and Richard Adams' marriage to be recognized by INS in 1975 and for Edie Windsor's marriage to Thea Spyer to be recognized by the IRS after Spyer passed in 2009. Finally, in 2015, in *Obergefell v. Hodges*, SCOTUS deemed state bans on same-sex marriage to be unconstitutional—thus requiring all states to issue marriage licenses to same-sex couples, and for same-sex marriages to be recognized as legal (Haldeman, 2017).

Regarding laws toward LGBTQ families, the legality of adoption by LGBTQ people, prior to 2017, had been determined through state laws—most with unique language or clauses. For example, Mississippi had banned same-sex couples from adopting or fostering children, while Alabama had banned single LGBTQ people from adopting or fostering children. Further, Florida first enacted a ban on lesbians and gays from adopting and fostering of children in 1977; that law lasted for three decades before it was deemed unconstitutional (Averett, Nalavany, & Ryan, 2009). In 2016, a Federal District Court deemed Mississippi's law prohibiting adoption by same-sex couples as unconstitutional (Villaseñor, 2019). Despite these wins, there are still attempts to challenge the current laws—with some legislatures proposing bills to allow organizations to discriminate against adoptions by LGBTQ people if it aligns with their religious beliefs.

QUEERING LEGISLATION

Queering legislation means examining all laws which are deemed conventional and acceptable by contemporary community standards, as well as determining if they are actually oppressive to LGBTQ people and other historically marginalized groups. For instance, in 2019, New York lawmakers introduced a bill that would decriminalize sex work in the state—making it the first of its kind in the nation (McKinley, 2019). One reason for this push is because transwomen of color are often profiled, arrested, and charged with prostitution, when such acts may be their only option due to job discrimination or the lack of employment opportunities for transwomen. As transgender activist Cecilia Gentili stated: "For people like me, sex work is not 'one' job option. It's the *only* option" (Garsd, 2019). Further, when transgender women (many who are transwomen of color) are victimized by their clients, they are unable to seek help due to fears of being arrested—further marginalizing the group (Campero & Nanclares, 2019). Therefore, advocating for sex work as consensual sex between two adults involving money exchange would reduce police profiling of trans women of color, while providing measures to ensure their safety.

Everyday advocates can queer legislation by educating themselves on local, state, and federal laws and the impacts of these policies on LGBTQ people. Such education can come from watching documentaries like *Free CeCe!* or television programs like *Pose*, which tell stories of queer and trans people from their own voices and perspectives. People can encourage their peers and families to read works of queer and transgender writers like Raquel Willis, Darnell Moore, or Janet Mock, or to become familiar with the research of queer and trans scholars like Cathy Cohen, Barbara Smith, Sara Ahmed, Andrea Richie, Anneliese Singh, Beverly Green, Martin Manalansan, Jose Esteban Muñoz, Susan Stryker, Dean Spade, Sarah Schulman, Gregory Herek, Martin Duberman, and others. People can also learn about criminal justice issues affecting LGBTQ communities by following the social media pages of New York City's Anti-Violence Project, the Audre Lorde Project, the Sylvia Rivera Law Project, Gay Men of African Descent, and other LGBTQ non-profit organizations. With this education, people can lobby for legislators to advocate for changes to laws and policies that are inequitable or unjust. They can participate in the political process when propositions need to be voted on and for change to occur, and they can encourage others to become educated and politically involved too.

Finally, queer legislation means an acknowledgment of the many ways history appears to be repeating itself and a commitment to stopping historical cycles of oppression. Law enforcement had previously arrested LGBTQ people for wearing gender-conforming clothes, and now they are arresting LGBTQ people for carrying condoms. Lesbians and gay men were banned from working in the federal government in the 1950s (solely for their sexual orientations) and were later banned from joining the military in the 1980s (solely for their sexual orientations), and now transgender people are being banned from joining the military (solely for their gender identities). In this way, it appears the Lavender Scare is happening again, but this time, with a new subgroup of LGBTQ people in 2020; and we need to organize to stop it from continuing.

TWO
Finding Our Pulse

LGBTQ Experiences with Hate and Historical Trauma

THE PULSE MASSACRE

On the morning of June 12, 2016, I woke up as I would on most summer Sundays—without an alarm clock and without anything stressful planned for the day. As I slowly arose and casually checked my email and social media accounts, I was shocked to read a link to an LGBTQ news site indicating there was a mass shooting at a gay club in Orlando. I quickly turned on the television to see in fact the shooting took place at Pulse nightclub—a club I remember visiting many years before—and that officials feared that dozens of people were killed. Glued to the television, I awaited a couple of hours for these cable news reporters to mention that Pulse was a gay club; that detail never came. Republican presidential candidates began to tweet messages about ending terrorism against American citizens; they, too, failed to identify the venue as a gay establishment, or how the victims and survivors were likely to identify as LGBTQ.

By the end of that day, journalists eventually acknowledged that Pulse was indeed one that catered to LGBTQ patrons. News outlets also began to report it was "Latin Night" on Saturdays at Pulse—and that the majority of the 49 victims were Latinx (or people of Latin or Hispanic American origins). Later reports indicated that 90 percent of the victims were Latinx, with almost half being Puerto Rican and some being Afro-Latino (Brydum, 2016; Hancock & Haldeman, 2017; Ramirez, Gonzalez, & Galupo, 2018). Photos and stories of the victims began to pour in. The oldest victim was Brenda Lee Marquez-McCool, 49, a mother of 11 children who went to Pulse with her son Isaiah. Shortly before the shooting, she had posted a Facebook video of same-sex couples dancing to Latin music. As the shooting began, Isaiah witnessed his mother get struck by the gunfire. Fortunately, he survived—unfortunately, without the mother who he reported having accepted his sexual identity from when he first came out. The youngest victim was Akya Murray, 18, who had just graduated from high school and earned a full ride to attend college in the fall. She was traveling with her family on vacation, and her parents dropped her off at the club, presuming that she would have a good time.

The victims included couples like Christopher Andrew Leinonen and Juan Guerrero (ages 32 and 22); Jean Carlos Mendez Perez and Luis Daniel Wilson-Leon (ages 35 and 37); and Juan P. Rivera Velazquez and Luis Conde (ages 37 and 39). There were best friends like Amanda Alvear and Mercedez Flores (ages 25 and 26), as well as Pulse employees like Deonka Deidra Drayton and Kimberly Morris (ages 32 and 37). Enrique L. Rios, 35, flew in from New York to celebrate his friend's 21st birthday. Cory James Connell, 21, went to Pulse with his girlfriend, Paula Andrea Blanco; she was one of the 53 people who were wounded but who survived.

The Pulse massacre was the deadliest mass murder of LGBTQ people in modern history; at the time, it was also the deadliest mass shooting of any group of people in one setting in modern American history (Ben-Ezra, Hamama-Raz, Mahat-Shamir, Pitcho-Prelorentzos, & Kaniasty, 2017). It was a reminder of the centuries of oppression that LGBTQ people have experienced in the US and around the world. Though the U.S. Supreme Court granted same-sex couples the legal right to get married in the US almost exactly one year prior, and though LGBTQ rights were gradually increasing under President Obama's administration, the tragedy demonstrated the reality that some Americans still held hateful biases against LGBTQ people and the fear that LGBTQ people still had reason to feel unsafe in this country (Nadal, 2018).

Pulse and Terrorism

In the morning hours of June 12, media outlets first identified the shooter as Omar Mateen. Journalists then attributed radical Islamic terrorism as Mateen's main motive (Hancock & Haldeman, 2017), despite that Mateen was an American-born child of Afghan immigrants, that he grew up in New York, and there was no evidence that Mateen had any actual ties to Al-Qaeda or any other terrorist organization. Yet, questions about terrorism and national security became a focus in the mainstream media. The Republican politicians who led these charges (many who were running for president at the time) were the same politicians who had previously vocalized an array of anti-LGBTQ sentiments (Haider, 2016). In fact, many had even voted against LGBTQ civil rights (e.g., they voted against adding sexual orientation and gender identity as protected classes in workplace discrimination or hate crime legislation). So, although these elected officials had not previously advocated for LGBTQ rights, they had politicized the Pulse shooting for their own anti-terrorist agendas or political campaigns.

Turning to terrorism as the main factor of this tragedy was problematic for other reasons too. First, the "terrorist" narrative furthered a culture of fear that distracted the general public on the roles of gun accessibility or sensible gun control laws. Given the previous research which found gun law reforms have resulted in fewer deaths, firearm suicides, and mass shootings in other countries (Gius, 2015), it is plausible there would be fewer victims of Pulse if Mateen was unable to obtain, or had more difficulties in obtaining, a semi-automatic weapon. Yet, because politicians wanted to appease their conservative pro-gun voters (who also potentially espoused homophobic views), they focused the attention on terrorism.

Similarly, in labeling the massacre as an act of terrorism, the media failed to recognize the tragedy was a hate crime toward LGBTQ people (Hancock & Haldeman, 2017). According to the Federal Bureau of Investigation (FBI) (2019a), a hate crime is a "criminal offense against a person or property motivated in whole or in part by an offender's bias against a race, religion, disability, sexual orientation, ethnicity, gender, or gender identity." While hate crimes have been part of American vernacular since the 1980s, research on hate crimes toward LGBTQ people are often not labeled as such or are underreported (Herek, 2017). While the Pulse shooting may have fit the definition of a hate crime (i.e., Mateen committed a criminal act toward a targeted group), the FBI investigation failed to identify the event as a hate crime, due to a lack of evidence supporting Mateen had overt homophobic biases (Nadal, 2018).

Yet, regardless of whether it was officially deemed as a hate crime, LGBTQ people, particularly LGBTQ Latinx people and other LGBTQ people of color, reacted to the tragedy like they would to any hate crime. Hate crimes can be especially daunting because of the negative impact they have on the victims or survivors, as well as on the surrounding community members with shared identities. Herek (2017) shares:

> Hate crimes are different from other crimes in that they not only attack the victim physically, they also attack a core aspect of the victim's personal identity and community membership, components of the self that are particularly important to many sexual and gender minority individuals because of the stress they experience as a consequence of societal stigma. (p. 144)

Haider (2016) describes how some initial media reports struggled to identify whether the shooting was an act of terrorism or if it was a hate crime, with some even labeling the event as "homophobic terrorism" (p. 555). Yet, such terminology does not fully address the difficulty in labeling a mass shooting as one crime over another.

Finally, a final problem with labeling the Pulse shooting as a terrorist attack is because of the quickness in labeling the tragedy as an act of terrorism, while other mass shootings are immediately labeled as "senseless act of violence." For instance, when Dylann Roof used assault rifles to kill 9 Black churchgoers at Mother Emmanuel Church in Charleston, South Carolina in 2015, or when Nikolas Cruz killed 17 students and teachers at Marjory Stoneman Douglas High School in Parkland, Florida in 2018, news reports labeled these young men as "troubled," "a lone wolf," or as someone who suffered from mental health issues. However, when an American who is non-White, like Mateen, engages in a similar act, it is labeled as an act of terrorism.

In order to decipher between senseless acts of violence and terrorism, it is helpful to understand current FBI definitions of terrorism—which are broken down into international and domestic terrorism. Domestic terrorism includes acts that "espouse extremist ideologies of a political, religious, social, racial, or environmental nature (FBI, 2019b). Both Roof and Cruz describe their prejudiced political views before their violent acts, particularly their anger and disgust toward historically marginalized groups (e.g., Black people, immigrants, etc.). Both Roof and Cruz appear to not have had any personal motives for killing any of the specific victims (e.g., they shot at random and did not aim for specific targets they knew) and rather they just wanted a whole group of people to suffer. So, if Mateen is labeled as a terrorist, then Roof, Cruz, and others should be labeled as such, too.

Pulse and Queer Sanctuaries

For many queer and transgender people, the Pulse shootings were particularly shocking because they occurred at a gay bar—which traditionally had been a "safe space" or a queer sanctuary for LGBTQ people (Croff, Hubach, Curin, & Frederick, 2017). Unlike the churches or other religious sanctuaries that demonized queer and trans people, the gay or lesbian bar is (or had been) where queer or trans people take the first steps to explore their sexual orientations or gender identities. For some LGBTQ people who may not be able to fully express themselves in their families, communities, or workplaces, the gay bar is an escape. While the heteronormative world can be a place where they feel stifled, restricted, or unsafe, the gay bar was a place where people were free to be themselves. They could dress, talk, move, and laugh in manners which led to bullying and punishment. They could flirt with, dance with, and kiss strangers; they could also have intimate moments with the loves of their lives. In some parts of the country, some people travel for dozens of miles to find this escape. And while varying group dynamics may transpire at each location (e.g., many gay bars are known to have histories of racial or transphobic biases), patrons might take some comfort in knowing they may find at least one other person who they can connect with on their shared sexual identities.

Post-Pulse, this sense of safety was challenged. While many LGBTQ people may have mastered how to navigate heterosexism and transphobia in their everyday lives—through smaller decisions like whether they can hold their partners' hands in public, to bigger decisions like whether or not to disclose their identities to their loved ones or colleagues—they would now have to be hypervigilant of their surroundings in what they once deemed to be their sanctuaries. In fact, with the Pulse massacre, studies reported LGBTQ people experienced a greater lack of safety, increased psychological distress, and more traumatic stress symptoms (Ben-Ezra et al., 2017; Jackson, 2017), particularly for transgender and genderqueer people (Stoltz et al., 2017).

Adding to this threat to queer safe spaces was how these innocent lives were taken in June—a month traditionally reserved for LGBTQ people to proclaim pride in their sexual orientations and gender identities. While Pride Month was usually a time when queer and trans people could reflect on how progressive and accepting the US has become, June 2016 was a month in which many LGBTQ people may have believed the opposite.

Pulse and Intersectional Identities

Complicating the tragedy were the many ways that gender, race, ethnicity, religion, immigration status, and other multiple identities played a role in the aftermath of the shootings (Ramirez, Gonzalez, & Galupo, 2018). First, race and ethnicity were very salient in the tragedy, but they were rarely discussed in both mainstream media and within White-dominated LGBTQ communities. While mainstream media and political candidates tried to erase sexual orientation from the original narrative, LGBTQ media outlets attempted to whitewash race and ethnicity from the narrative too (Ramirez et al., 2018). Though it was clear that all of the victims were non-White, that most were Latinx, and that almost half were Puerto Rican, it was a fact that was not thoroughly discussed by White LGBTQ people, media sources, or both.

The erasure of race and ethnicity (and the false notion of colorblindness) is not new. For decades, LGBTQ people of color (LGBTQPOC) have described how experiences of racism within mainstream LGBTQ communities are often dismissed or invalidated and how racial hierarchies within White-dominant LGBTQ communities are pervasive, but unspoken about (Nadal, 2013; 2018). For some LGBTQPOC, experiences of racism by people with shared sexual orientations and gender identities feels more disturbing, hurtful, and disappointing. While LGBTQPOC may expect heterosexual and cisgender White people to hold oppressive and prejudicial biases, they are triggered when they experience such microaggressions and other forms of discrimination from LGBTQ White people. For instance, Ramirez and colleagues (2017) conducted an online analysis of LGBTQPOC responses to Pulse, finding "participants voiced their frustrations with the lack of an intersectional focus across race/ethnicity, gender, and sexuality" (p. 590). Relatedly, Meyer (2019a) described instances documented by journalists in which queer Latinx people were viewed as dividing or harming White cisgender spaces when they brought up issues of race and ethnicity.

In spite of this, the massacre led to conversations about homophobia and transphobia among Latinx communities. In July 2016, Puerto Rico installed its first LGBTQ monument to memorialize the victims, particularly recognizing the 23 victims who were Puerto Rican (Brydum, 2016). Among the inscription (translated from Spanish), it reads: "This tribute to life strengthens our commitment to fight hate—the product of homophobia—with love and respect. Our slogan resounds in all our hearts: Love is love, is love, is love" (Brydum, 2016).

Moreover, it was reported Omar Mateen was the shooter, that he was an American-born child of Afghan immigrants, and that he grew up in New York. Investigators discovered that Mateen traveled over a hundred miles to target Pulse, and he identified himself to emergency services as someone who has "pledged allegiance to the Islamic State" (Meyer, 2019, p. 7). As a result, the shooting (like many other terrorist acts) resulted in an increase in Islamophobia, or biases toward Muslim people in general American society and within LGBTQ communities specifically. When terrorist acts become publicized, Muslim people (or people who are mistaken as Muslim) often become alert to the various ways they are treated or targeted by others. For instance, LGBTQ media may have contributed to the misinformation that Mateen was a foreigner with racial Islamic beliefs, while erasing any narratives related to xenophobia or Islamophobia (Meyer, 2019). Though most major religious groups may generally maintain anti-LGBTQ teachings, White LGBTQ people are often quick to stereotype LGBTQ communities of color (and the religions they belong to) as being more homophobic or transphobic, as being less open-minded in general, or both. In doing so, they fail to recognize how many White cultural and religious groups (e.g., evangelical Christians, Mormons, etc.) and countries (e.g., Russia, Bosnia) demonstrate as much (and sometimes more) homophobic or transphobic biases than communities of color. In buying into these types of dynamics, people of historically marginalized groups are pitted against each other, instead of being encouraged to work together toward social justice.

Such dynamics are especially damaging because they fail to recognize people with relevant intersectional identities (i.e., LGBTQ Muslim Americans or LGBTQ people who are perceived to be Muslim). Like other Muslim people, LGBTQ Muslim Americans may have learned to prepare for everyday Islamophobic microaggressions they may encounter in general society. Like other LGBTQ people, LGBTQ Muslim Americans in a post-Pulse era may be more cognizant about their safety in queer spaces. And also, in a post-Pulse era, LGBTQ Muslim Americans might be mindful of how they are treated within LGBTQ spaces too. Omar Sarwar (2016) describes the conflict that arose from his intersectional identities:

> As a gay American Muslim, I feel especially vulnerable in a society infected both by homophobia and a highly racialized Islamophobia, constantly trying to encourage the gay community to be more accepting of Muslims. . . . But there is one question that many on the left are too afraid to explore: To what extent has the mainstream American Muslim community enabled the kind of homophobic bigotry which corrupted Mateen's heart?

In this way, it is clear that when any individual from a historically marginalized group commits a crime, the group suffers tremendously.

Finally, rumors surfaced that Mateen may have been struggling with his own sexual orientation identity (Hancock & Haldeman, 2017). Former Pulse patrons revealed Mateen was known to frequent Pulse before the shooting. Witnesses describe him as being defensive, conflicted, or "on edge"—with some identifying him as drinking heavily and becoming belligerent. Mateen's ex-wife even described him as possibly being gay—or at least being very defensive when one presumed him to be gay. Perhaps Mateen struggled with his own internalized oppression and the negative messages he learned about sexuality prevented him from developing a healthy sexual orientation identity. Gender role socialization may have led to Mateen's development of a hegemonic masculinity, which is defined as the ways that patriarchy and heteronormativity may impede men's ways of being loving, vulnerable, and empathetic (Connell & Messerschmidt, 2005). Such learning may often lead to more violent, misogynistic, or competitive attitudes or behaviors, otherwise known as toxic masculinity (Haider, 2016). Instead of learning to cope with his emotions or turning to others for help, Mateen may have turned to aggression. Instead of potentially exploring sexual curiosities or healthily challenging gender role norms, Mateen chose violence instead.

Investigators would later dismiss assertions about Mateen's sexual orientation as mere rumors—due to a lack of sufficient supporting evidence. However, given that many LGBTQ people learn to master the art of concealing their identities, one might wonder if any sufficient evidence would ever be found. In fact, if Mateen chose Pulse as a random place to enact terror, one may wonder why he decided to drive 125 miles south of where he lived, instead of targeting a local shopping mall or school. Despite this, Hancock and Haldeman (2017) warn that this narrative may actually contribute to the pathologizing of "closeted" LGBTQ people.

Regardless, because we will never know for sure, it is part of the narrative that must be considered.

Though most LGBTQ people were nowhere near Pulse nightclub on June 12, 2016, many LGBTQ people may have felt historical trauma. They may have felt the centuries of pain and suffering that LGBTQ people have encountered across the world. They may have felt the fear that what happened at Pulse could have happened at any venue or any night that was reserved for queer and trans people. For LGBTQ Latinx people (and other LGBTQ people of color), they may have been hit with guilt that they had survived all the times they had gone to a "Latin Night" or a "Hip Hop Night" or an anxiety they may no longer have a place where they would be able to feel fully safe.

THE CONTEXT OF HISTORICAL TRAUMA

This chapter will focus on historical trauma, or the "complex and collective psychological distress that is experienced over time and across generations of a group of people who share an identity, affiliation, or circumstance" (Mohatt, Thompson, Thai, & Tebes, 2014, p. 128). Previous scholars have written about historical trauma as it has been experienced by many groups—including, but not limited to—Black Americans and the trauma of slavery and racism; Jewish people and the trauma of the Holocaust; Native Americans and the trauma of genocide (Nadal, 2018). While the term "survivors of trauma" often refers to people who experience palpable, first-hand trauma (e.g., surviving a hate crime assault), historical trauma refers to the collective pain that a community of people may experience over time.

Within LGBTQ communities, historical trauma may result in a number of emotional reactions and psychological outcomes. For example, when LGBTQ people are victims of hate crime homicides, LGBTQ people who learn about these experiences may feel some of the symptoms of trauma—such as difficulty in concentrating; difficulty sleeping; avoidance of people, places, or stimuli; intense guilt or shame; or anger, irritability, mood swings (Nadal, 2018). While they may not know the victim or survivor personally, they recognize it easily could have been them who was harmed—muddying their own senses of safety or justice. Noelle (2002) referred to this process as the "ripple effect"—in that LGBTQ people may feel triggered by anti-LGBTQ trauma or violence they hear or read about. When the secondary trauma is experienced by a helping professional, McCann and Pearlman (1990) refer to this process as vicarious trauma, or the process by which an individual indirectly encounters trauma and develops similar symptoms that are usually felt intensely by a direct survivor of trauma.

As Black transgender author and activist Janet Mock once wrote: "I believe that telling our stories, first to ourselves and then to one another and the world, is a revolutionary act. It is an act that can be met with hostility, exclusion, and violence. It can also lead to love, understanding, transcendence, and community" (Mock, 2014, p. xviii). With this, we understand that trauma can be painful and daunting. However, by sharing our stories of violence and agony, people may also be able to find healing, connection, and understanding with others who may have overcome similar struggles and obstacles.

Hate Crimes

Prior to Pulse, there were two hate crime homicides that have been considered national tragedies in the US, by both general society and by mainstream LGBTQ communities. First, in November of 1978, San Francisco Mayor George Moscone and City Supervisor Harvey Milk were assassinated. While Moscone was much more well-known at the time, Milk was one of the first openly gay people to hold any public office in the US, as well as one of the most vocal opponents of anti-gay legislation in the state and in the country (Eyerman, 2012). So, when former City Supervisor Dan White walked into San Francisco City Hall and killed both of them, many gay people in San Francisco and across the country were devastated. Allegedly, White shot both men point-blank, several times each, with a service revolver that he obtained as a police officer; he specifically shot Milk in the head to ensure he was dead (Eyerman, 2012).

Years after his death, Milk's legacy has resulted in a new approach to anti-gay hate crimes (Berrill, 1990), integration of LGBTQ history into California's public school curriculum (Donahue, 2014), and even a high school in New York in his name that was created to provide a safe environment for LGBTQ-identified adolescents (Bethard, 2004). A biopic about his life, *Milk*, won many awards, including an Oscar for actor Sean Penn, who played the title role.

Twenty years later, in October of 1998, Matthew Shepard, a gay White man, was killed in Laramie, Wyoming, by two men who targeted him because of his sexual orientation. He was brutally beaten and tied to a cow fence, where he was left to die (Dunn, 2010; Noelle, 2002). While Shepard's death was not the first anti-LGBTQ hate crime murder, it was the first to gain so much media attention (first by LGBTQ media and later by mainstream media), with one of the reasons being the heinous acts of hate violence inflicted toward him. His assailants were found guilty of robbing him, verbally abusing him, and torturing him; they left him cold, unconscious, and bleeding, with his hands tied behind his back. A biker found Shepard the next morning, unconscious; he was brought to the hospital and he died five days later, without ever regaining consciousness (Dunn, 2010). The court trial was one of the first of its kind in

American history—with the general public taking an interest in the outcomes of an anti-LGBTQ hate crime (Dunn, 2010; Kaufman, Fondakowski, Pierotti, & Paris, 2014). It was also historic in being one of the few times at that point in history in which the gay panic defense (i.e., the rationale that someone murdered or assaulted a gay person out of fear of being sexually assaulted themselves) had been rejected and the assailant was found guilty of murder (Dunn, 2010).

While Shepard's murder was clearly horrendous and traumatizing for both his loved ones and others who felt collective trauma, there were a number of positive outcomes for LGBTQ communities in the US. First, in 2009, the Matthew Shepard and James Byrd, Jr. Hate Crimes Act was enacted by President Barack Obama; the executive order added sexual orientation and gender identity as protected classes in federal hate crime law (Nadal, 2018). Moreover, Judy Shepard (Matthew's mother) founded the Matthew Shepard Foundation in 1999, with the original goals being to "replace hate with understanding, compassion, and acceptance" (Shepard, 2009). Finally, several media projects told the story of Matthew Shepard, including the Laramie Project—a play that documents the aftermath in the town where Matthew was killed and has been used as an educational tool in high schools and communities across the US (Kaufman et al., 2014).

In spite of the positive outcomes of both Milk's and Shepard's murders, one of the critiques to how both cases have been adopted and integrated into LGBTQ mainstream narratives and Queer Studies is how they centered the tragedies of two White cisgender educated gay men—painting Harvey Milk as "the gay movement's martyr" (Krutzch, 2019, p. 19), while labeling Matthew Shepard as a "secular saint" (Dunn, 2010, p. 78) and a "common man" (Dunn, 2010, p. 86). Perhaps such tactics were used to convince mainstream heterosexual audiences to empathize with, or better relate with the victims. However, these media strategies are ones that are only available to White cisgender men. When innocent Black men are killed by police or vigilantes, the media often paints them in the most negative of ways—often using photos that portray them as violent, criminal, and in some cases, older (Jackson, 2016). Thus, even in death, there is a privilege that comes with being White, cisgender, and male—even if one is gay or queer.

It is also problematic to only recognize the deaths of Milk and Shepard as a typical type of hate crime, because LGBTQ people of color are consistently more likely to be targeted for anti-LGBTQ hate crimes. In 2018, it was reported 71 percent of hate crime victims were people of color; 52 percent were transgender or gender nonconforming people, and 40 percent were transgender women of color—prevalence rates that have been consisted over the past decade (Tillery, Ray, Cruz, & Waters, 2018). However, their stories do not tend to be told—especially in mainstream media. Here are some examples of hate crime homicides of LGBTQ people of color in the past two decades:

- In 2003, Sakia Gunn, a 15-year-old Black lesbian (who people described as a butch-aggressive) was killed in Newark, New Jersey; her assailant's motive was that she rejected his sexual proposition and told him she was a lesbian (Townsend, 2012).
- In 2009, Jorge Steven López Mercado, a 19-year-old Latino gay man, who often performed in drag, was burned, dismembered, and decapitated in Puerto Rico (La Fountain-Stokes, 2018).
- In 2013, Mark Carson, a Black gay man, was walking down the street with another Black gay man in the Greenwich Village neighborhood of New York City. Another man followed them for blocks, screaming homophobic slurs; he then shot Carson in the face within point-blank range (Nadal, 2018).
- In 2013, Islan Nettles, a Black transgender woman, was murdered outside of a police precinct in the Harlem neighborhood of New York City; allegedly, she rejected a sexual advance and disclosed her gender identity. Nettles was one of thirteen Black transgender women to be killed in the US that year (Nadal, 2018).
- In 2019, Muhlaysia Booker and Chynal Lindsey were two Black transgender women who were killed in Dallas, Texas, within a one-month period. Months prior in Dallas, another Black transgender woman named Brittany White was killed, and another unnamed Black transgender woman was stabbed multiple times, but survived (Gold, 2019).

While there are clearly many other hate crime victims and survivors, race and gender identity both influence whose stories get told, whose stories are presumed to be relatable, and whose stories may not neatly fit in the LGBTQ narrative.

Finally, while naysayers may assert the primary reason why Milk's story was covered most was because of his fame and activism, Shepard's story is quite similar to Gunn's, Mercado's, Carson's, Nettles', Booker's, Lindsey's, and White's. They were all young LGBTQ people trying to live their authentic lives before a hateful person tragically took that away from them. Thus, we must question why Shepard's story get told the most and the others are erased.

Anti-LGBTQ Bullying

When LGBTQ people learn about the many LGBTQ teens who die by suicide as a result of being bullied or victimized, they may experience historical trauma. This became evident in the fall of 2010, when journalists across the US reported stories of at least six young people living in different parts of the country who, within a 1- to 2-month span, died by suicide. In September 2010, Billy Lucas, a multiracial 15-year-old boy from Indiana, was found dead, hanging in a barn at his grandmother's home. His mother filed a wrongful death lawsuit against the school, citing that administrators knew about the bullying and did nothing; the case was settled out of court. That same month in September 2010, Seth Walsh, a White 13-year-old boy in Kern County, California, died by suicide after months of homophobic bullying. Days later, Tyler Clementi, a White 18-year-old student in New Jersey, who was cyberbullied by his roommate and another classmate who posted an Internet video of him having sex with another man. In October 2010, Raymond Chase, an openly gay Black student in Rhode Island was found dead by hanging in his dorm room. The commonality between them was they were LGBTQ-identified or had been victimized by pervasive teen bullying due to their actual or perceived sexual orientation (Eliason, 2010).

Similar cases were found in the years prior, including Carl Joseph Walker-Hoover, a Black 11-year-old boy from Springfield, Massachusetts, who died by hanging in April 2009, after school bullies repeatedly called him "gay" (García & Slesaransky-Poe, 2010). Stories of trans teens began to emerge too: in 2014, Leelah Alcorn, a White 17-year-old trans girl, died by suicide, after posting a blog about her struggles in being trans (Jennings, 2015). In 2015, Blake Brockington, a Black 18-year-old trans man who was the first trans man to be homecoming king at his high school, died by suicide (Kellaway, 2015). Among these all, there were many similar story lines: the young people were LGBTQ (either openly or presumed to be); they were bullied in person or cyberbullied at home; when the youth tried to seek help from authority figures, they were unsuccessful; they lost all hope and viewed suicide as the only resort.

Shortly following the death of Billy Lucas, author Dan Savage and Terry Miller started the "It Gets Better" media campaign, as a way of encouraging LGBTQ youth to be hopeful for the future. The initial video inspired many others—celebrities and everyday LGBTQ people—to make their own videos to offer their own messages of hope (Gil, Shifman, & Kampf, 2016). By January 2014, over 60,000 people made videos with personal testimonials of how it gets better, and the videos were cumulatively watched over 50 million times (Ciszek, 2014). Some of the most popular videos were by Ke$ha, President Obama, Adam Lambert, Chris Colfer, Tim Gunn, and Lady Gaga (Ciszek, 2014). The number of older LGBTQ adults who felt compelled to share their stories of heterosexist bullying and suicidal ideations from their adolescent years demonstrated a collective trauma that many LGBTQ people can relate to, while the number of views symbolized the collective trauma felt by current LGBTQ youth.

In spite of these well-intentioned efforts, there were several critiques of the campaign. Goltz (2013) described how many critical LGBTQ community members viewed it as "passive, impractical, homogenizing, and exclusionary" (p. 135), and "deceptive, condescending, homonormative, lazy, self-congratulatory" (p 136). Similarly, Majkowski (2011) offered: "This temporal rhetoric of 'wait it out' and 'what doesn't kill you will make you stronger' is not the best we can do . . . [instead, we need] an active, passionate commitment and plan on the part of our politicians and policymakers to protect and foster our queer youth into queer adults" (p. 164). In both of these critiques, there is an underlying question of how the campaign actually helps LGBTQ youth to get through bullying, particularly if they don't have support, resources, or privileges of those adults who tell them to wait.

One of the other critical aspects of the campaign was how little it focused on intersectional identities. Goltz (2013) said the campaign was "inextricably tied to racial, gendered, and economic privilege" (p. 136), while Majkowski (2011) argued the campaign communicated "all queer youth end up wealthy, white and famous to boot" (p. 164). Perhaps this lack of intersectionality was due to the colorblindness that was instituted from the project's inception. For instance, Billy Lucas, the teen whose death sparked Savage to start the campaign, was bullied not just for his perceived sexual orientation, but also for his ethnicity and disability status. In the lawsuit filed by his mother, she listed how her son was bullied for all the ways that he was different, which included his mixed ethnicity and learning disability (Brown, 2010).

Similarly, the erasure of stories of people of color, trans people, or trans people of color from the start of the campaign is indicative of who gets to represent LGBTQ teen suicide. Again, White cisgender faces are displayed (and their stories are told), while Black, Brown, and trans faces and stories are not. For instance, when Aubrey Mariko Shine, a 22-year-old transgender woman of color died by suicide, after jumping off the Golden Gate Bridge, community members commented there was not even a ripple in LGBTQ media—unlike the quantity and quality of coverage of gay White cisgender teens (Busey, 2015). Further, like many transgender people who die, her family erased her transgender identity at her funeral, calling her by her name-assigned-at-birth, using incorrect pronouns, and not displaying any recent photos of her (Martela, 2015). When trans people who die are "deadnamed"—or referred to by the gendered name they do not identify with, the act promotes violence, while also retraumatizing other trans people who witness this act of trans erasure (Tillery et al., 2018). In this way, experiencing other trans people's identities being erased or invalidated is also a form of collective trauma.

HIV/AIDS Epidemic

Specific to LGBTQ people is also the historical trauma of the HIV/AIDS epidemic. As stated in chapter 1, when the AIDS virus was first discovered in New York, Los Angeles, and San Francisco, it was initially labeled in 1981 as a "rare cancer seen in 41 homosexuals" and "Gay Related Immune Disorder," because it was found mostly in gay men (Bronski, 2011, p. 224). While there was little known about the causes and symptoms of the disease, the national conversation focused on criminalizing and pathologizing gay men. In the first six years of its discovery, approximately 20,000 people had died of the virus; by 1990, the death toll increased to 31,000 (Nadal, 2018). Because the majority of the victims were gay and bisexual men, many LGBTQ people lost so many friends and loved ones they may have experienced some of the symptoms of survival guilt (Boykin, 1991). Scholars also examined how LGBTQ people in metropolitan areas like New York City and San Francisco suffered from bereavement overload—or the loss of multiple friends and lovers in such a short amount of time. One qualitative study revealed some LGBTQ people knew up to 50 people who died of the virus; many people lost numerous people from their most intimate social support group; and there were very short intervals between deaths (Biller & Rice, 1990). Because many LGBTQ people coped with this excessive amount of loss, while overcoming the discrimination and stigma of the virus, the HIV/AIDS epidemic is one that still triggers painful feelings and memories; hence, it should be considered a historical or collective trauma among LGBTQ people, especially for LGBTQ people who witnessed or survived it all.

QUEERING TRAUMA

Some studies have found queer and trans people report higher frequencies of exposure to traumatic life experiences, as well as greater prevalence of trauma symptoms, than their heterosexual or cisgender counterparts (Nadal, 2018). Research studies have revealed a large majority of transwomen have experienced at least one diagnosable trauma in their lifetime and that most have experienced multiple traumatic events in their lives (Shipherd, Maguen, Skidmore, & Abramovitz, 2011). Researchers have discussed how oppression itself is a predictor of post-traumatic stress disorder (PTSD) symptoms, suggesting traumatic events like violence or physical injury are not the only types of predictors of trauma (Bryant-Davis, 2019). Accordingly, the trauma of experiencing so much discrimination and bias, that has persisted over time, has also been referred to as microaggressive trauma (Nadal, 2018).

Perhaps the most important way to "queer" trauma is to ensure that trauma is conceptualized through queer lenses—meaning that people are not limited to simple or rigid definitions of trauma. Nadal (2018) describes how psychology, psychiatry, and other helping professions have been inflexible and strict in what is considered trauma, resulting in misdiagnoses or ineffective treatment plans. If historical trauma or microaggressive trauma does not fit formal classifications of trauma (e.g., witnessing death or violence, surviving physical or sexual violence, etc.), people who suffer from these traumas not be considered for any PTSD treatments, even though their symptoms are similar. Similarly, if people of color suffer from racial trauma, or the experiences of trauma resulting from a lifetime of navigating systemic racism and racial discrimination (Bryant-Davis, 2019), but are not classified by clinicians as having a trauma, their abilities to heal and thrive from those traumas are often limited.

Moreover, with historical trauma also comes opportunities for healing. Some studies find connections to community are most important for people who experience trauma (Schultz et al., 2016). One study highlighted how LGBTQ graduate students turned to an online forum immediately after the Pulse shooting to provide emotional support and a sense of validation from others (Jackson, 2017). Therefore, we must acknowledge the historical traumas of LGBTQ communities, in order to provide individuals with the care and connections they need.

Finally, aligning with the notion that only advocacy creates change, it would be crucial for psychologists, psychiatrists, and other practitioners to advocate for historical trauma, microaggressive trauma, and other related forms of trauma to be included as legitimate types of trauma in the *Diagnostic and Statistical Manual of Psychiatric Disorders* (DSM). If these types of traumas continue to be ignored, then individuals who suffer with these trauma symptoms will continue to be underserved. In the same way that activists lobbied to have homosexuality removed from the DSM, or to have Gender Identity Disorder changed to Gender Dysphoria, activists can also lobby for trauma to be inclusive of all types of trauma.

THREE
Neither Protected, Nor Served

LGBTQ People and Law Enforcement

THE MURDER OF BRANDON TEENA

On Christmas Day 1993, Brandon Teena, a White transgender man living in Nebraska who had just turned 21 years old, was kidnapped and raped by John Lotter and Marvin Thomas Nissen (Hale, 1998; Muska & Olafsdottir, 1998). The two assailants were Mr. Teena's acquaintances who had recently learned about Mr. Teena's gender identity, after he was detained in the local women's jail. Mr. Teena was apprehended for forging checks, and the arrest was publicized in the local newspaper. Upon learning this, the assailants abducted Mr. Teena and took him to a remote area in the country. After the rape, Mr. Teena's girlfriend took him to the hospital, where a rape kit was administered. A police report was then filed with Charles Laux, the local sheriff.

While Mr. Teena described the assault, Sheriff Laux made a number of sexually inappropriate and transphobic comments. These include:

- "After he pulled your pants down and seen you was a girl, what did he do? Did he fondle you any?"
- "You were all half-ass drunk. I can't believe that if he pulled your pants down and you are a female that he didn't stick his hand in you or his finger in you."
- "Why do you run around with girls instead of guys being you're a girl yourself?" (Fairyington, 2013).

Later, Sheriff Laux questioned Lotter and Nissen about the assault, but he chose not to arrest them—in spite of having sufficient medical evidence to do so. He even informed them of the police report, not considering the impact on Mr. Teena's safety. On New Year's Eve in 2003, Lotter and Nissen found Mr. Teena at a friend's home—where they shot and killed him at point-blank range. They also killed two of Mr. Teena's housemates, Lisa Lambert and Phillip DeVine, in an attempt to silence any witnesses and cover up their crimes.

Later, Laux said he did not believe Mr. Teena's rape accusation because he perceived Mr. Teena as lying about his gender. Laux's transphobic bias and lack of sensitivity was evident, as demonstrated by a quote he later made to a journalist: "You can call it an *it* as far as I'm concerned" (Hale, 1998, p. 312). Other colleagues reveal that he views himself as "blameless" for the incident, while recognizing it might be a defense mechanism (Fairyington, 2013). While his actions (and inactions) reflect how common anti-LGBTQ sentiment was among police officers at the time (see Berrill, 1990), it is also clear that he is partially responsible for the murders of Mr. Teena and his two friends. If he had arrested the two rapists or had filed some sort of order of protection for Mr. Teena, it is highly possible the murders would have been circumvented.

Twenty years later, Brandon Teena's story has become nationally and internationally known—with a documentary, *The Brandon Teena Story*, and the award-winning movie *Boys Don't Cry*, for which actress Hilary Swank would win an Oscar for portraying Mr. Teena. In 2001, a lawsuit against Richardson County and Sherriff Laux for their negligent treatment (filed by Mr. Teena's mother, Joanna Brandon) resulted in an award of nearly $100,000. While Mr. Lotter and Mr. Thomas are both serving life in prison, Sheriff Laux was never formally reprimanded (Fairyington, 2013).

INTRODUCTION

In the early 1900s, when the New York Police Department (NYPD) first started raiding LGBTQ bathhouses and bars and also began to entrap and arrest people who were suspected of being LGBTQ, they could legally do so because of state sodomy laws (see chapter 1 for a review). Thus, the relationship between police and LGBTQ communities was already one of distrust and contention. As described in chapter 1, the Stonewall Uprising signified the beginning of a revolution—in which LGBTQ people demanded for the police to treat them with respect and in which the power of demonstration led to actual change in policy.

However, even as state sodomy laws began to be repealed or no longer enforced, and eventually deemed unconstitutional by the Supreme Court of the US in 2003, being LGBTQ, itself, was no longer considered a crime in any capacity. So, in theory, there should not be any legal reason for police officers to target, mistreat, or discriminate against LGBTQ people any further. Yet, many police officers still maintain anti-LGBTQ biases, resulting in continued criminalization of LGBTQ people and a tense relationship between LGBTQ people and the criminal justice system, particularly with the police.

The purpose of this chapter is to examine the current state of law enforcement and LGBTQ communities. We will focus on several related concepts, beginning with LGBTQ people and their perceptions of police officers. We will also describe research on the various types of interactions that police have had with LGBTQ communities—including police violence and brutality; police anti-LGBTQ profiling; and anti-LGBTQ microaggressions. Additionally, we will examine perspectives of police departments, highlighting the current state of LGBTQ competency training for officers across the country, as well as experiences of LGBTQ people within the police department.

LGBTQ Perceptions of Police

Procedural justice is the notion that all aspects of the legal process are fair and unbiased (Tyler, 2007; 2008). Procedural justice examines whether individuals perceive various parts of the criminal justice system to be fair; these include people's attitudes about laws, law enforcement departments, judges, courts, and every other aspect of the system. Because law enforcement officers are often the first or only contact that people have with the justice system, they are highly influential as to how people will perceive the entire justice system.

According to the procedural justice model of policing, police are able to build better relationships with their constituents when they act in fair and just ways (Tyler, 2008). Further, people view police more positively when they are confident of police officers' abilities, when they believe that police officers treat others fairly, and when they know that police avoid using excessive force (Callanan & Rosenberger, 2011). When police officers enact behaviors that are viewed as negative or unfair, communities become more distrustful or skeptical of police officers' abilities to serve and protect their communities.

The general public's perceptions of the police vary—with some studies finding police are typically viewed positively, while other studies find people hold more negative attitudes about the police (see Nadal et al., 2017 for a review). Previous literature has found historically marginalized groups tend to view police more negatively than historically privileged groups. For example, studies have found people of color tend to trust the police significantly less than White people, mostly due to the knowledge of police brutality and racial profiling toward the communities, and found that regular, negative contact with police increases individuals' mistrust of police and increase mental health symptoms (Nadal et al., 2017).

While there is still a dearth of literature that examines LGBTQ people and perceptions of police, there are some studies that do provide initial support. In one study, LGBTQ participants describe how variables like feminine and masculine gender presentations and intersectional identities influenced how police treat them, as well as how these encounters shaped their views of the police (Nadal et al., 2015). Another study found LGBTQ people's attitudes toward police became more positive when they viewed police as being helpful when they reported a crime (Gillespie, 2008). Moreover, to examine the potential differences in attitudes toward police between LGBTQ people and heterosexual, cisgender people, two studies utilized Nadal and Davidoff's (2015) Perceptions of Police Scale (POPS), which measures general perceptions of the police and perceptions about police bias and discrimination. One study found LGBTQ participants held less favorable perceptions of the police than heterosexual participants, and that LGBTQ participants also viewed police as being more discriminatory than heterosexuals (Satuluri & Nadal, 2018). Another study reported transgender and gender nonconforming (TGNC) participants held less favorable perceptions of the police than cisgender participants, and they also viewed the police as being more biased. Additionally, in comparison to both cisgender women and cisgender men, TGNC participants reported being less comfortable in seeking police for help than their cisgender counterparts (Serpe & Nadal, 2017). Wolff and Cokely (2007) describe how LGBTQ civilians' negative experiences with police officers involve rudeness, disrespect, and retraumatization, while positive experiences involve being taken seriously, feeling respected, and feeling assisted. Finally, one study found LGBTQ participants were significantly less likely than heterosexual, cisgender participants to perceive police officers as being fair, and that transgender participants scored police officers' fairness significantly lower than lesbian, gay, and bisexual participants (Owen, Burke, Few-Demo, & Natwick, 2018).

One aspect of procedural justice is whether or not people trust the police enough to seek help when they need it. Previous research has found when LGBTQ people are afraid and distrustful of police, they avoid police altogether and even avoid reporting hate crimes—out of fears of being further mistreated by the police, beliefs that reporting would be futile, or the rationale that the hate crime was not serious enough to be reported (Herek, 2017). For example, a recent study found only 12 percent of queer and transgender youth would feel comfortable turning to police (Stoudt, Fine, & Fox, 2012). Yet, earlier studies on LGBTQ people and hate crime reporting reveal that not much may have changed in the past twenty years, in that they found LGBTQ survivors did not report crimes for fear that police officers would blame them for the incident; would invalidate or dismiss anti-LGBTQ crimes as mere pranks; or would fail to protect survivors from further violence from their assailants (Berrill, 1990; Comstock, 1991). All of these trends appeared to be present when Brandon Teena reported his rape.

TGNC people may hold a greater amount of mistrust toward law enforcement, resulting in not reporting crimes, or not cooperating with law enforcement (Stotzer, 2009). Reasons for TGNC people not seeking help include the belief that police officers are not trustworthy or that police are indifferent or ineffective (Wolff & Cokely, 2007). Further, some TGNC people choose not to report hate crimes or any sort of violence toward them because they believe they would be retraumatized after reporting their incidents (Fiani et al., 2017; Stotzer, 2009).

Many LGBTQ people are hesitant in reporting incidents of intimate partner violence (IPV) for similar reasons. Previous research has found police respond differently to intimate partner violence calls, minimizing the violence between same-sex couples or transgender survivors, notably more than they would with heterosexual, cisgender couples (Calton, Cattaneo, & Gebhard, 2016). Previous studies reveal police officers are more likely to arrest lesbians than gay men (Pattavina, Hirschel, Buzawa, Faggiani, & Bentley, 2007). Some potential reasons for arresting women more than men include police homophobia and toxic masculinity; because police officers presume two men should be able to protect themselves from other men, or because they would rather not get involved in cases with gay men, they may avoid arrest. For instance, one gay man of color shared how police did not take his report of violence seriously: "I think if I was a 90-pound woman and I said, 'No, he held me against my will for 45 minutes. My wrist is bleeding. I want to press charges,' I don't think they would've questioned it. I think they would've immediately have taken him away" (Nadal et al., 2015, p. 469). Regardless of the reason, if LGBTQ survivors do not feel that police would protect them from their aggressors, or if they fear they would have to face homophobia or transphobia when they sought help, they may avoid seeking assistance from law enforcement.

Race plays a salient factor in whether LGBTQ people would seek help from police, in that LGBTQ White people are more trusting of police than LGBTQ people of color, particularly in places they presume to be more liberal. As a poignant example, when asked about whether she would seek police for help, a Black queer woman revealed: "I just don't really want to go and get help from the police unless I have to. I just don't want to, like, disturb them. They might be having like a bad day and then for whatever might boomerang back onto me" (Nadal et al., 2015, p. 474). Meanwhile, one gay White man said: "I would definitely be more comfortable here approaching a, even just walking up and approaching a police officer on the street, of my own volition, and saying, 'Hey. I was either a victim or I saw something happen. I need your help.'" (Nadal et al., 2015, p. 476). Through these disparate reactions, we are reminded of the diversity of LGBTQ communities, and how intersectional identities may influence one's experiences with the justice system. Perhaps, the White gay male feels more trusting of police, due to his privileged racial and gender identities, while the Black queer woman is less trusting because of her marginalized racial and gender identities.

Police Profiling of LGBTQ Communities

While sodomy laws are illegal and no longer used to persecute LGBTQ people, there are many ways that police officers may target LGBTQ using other laws as a reason for arrest. For instance, while the act of engaging in consensual sex in private locations is not illegal, engaging in sex in public areas or indecently exposing oneself are both misdemeanors. Some scholars have found police departments still set up "sting operations" in which undercover police officers arrest gay men after consenting to have sex with them in public locations (Woods, 2009). While these men can no longer be arrested on sodomy charges, they can be charged with indecent exposure or lewd conduct—both are misdemeanor crimes. In general, these sting operations are legal; yet, scholars argue if they are unconstitutional, in that they set up people to engage in acts they may not have, if the police officer did not instigate it, and they intentionally target gay or bisexual men (Strader & Hay, 2019). Because sting operations are not set up to entrap heterosexual men and women, who also potentially have sex in public spaces, sting operations that set up gay and bisexual men should be considered discriminatory.

Unjust or random police searches, often known as Stop, Question, and Frisk (SQF) policies, have been used to target historically marginalized groups. SQF policies were set in place as a way of reducing crime, in that police officers could randomly stop people who they viewed as being likely to commit a crime, question them, and search them if they felt they had a reason to do so. In New York City, SQF policies had been found to disproportionately target Black or Latinx people more than Whites and to be only marginally effective in reducing crime, and in 2013, a U.S. District Court judge ruled SQF was unconstitutional (Nadal et al., 2017).

While sexual orientation and gender identity were not measured in official NYPD SQF datasets (as both categories are not legally mandated to be collected across most jurisdictions), some community studies describe the types of experiences that LGBTQ people have with police profiling and SQF practices. Make the Road New York [MRNY] (2012) reported in Queens, New York, that 54 percent of their LGBTQ participants reported they had been stopped by police, as compared to 28 percent of their non-LGBTQ sample; 59 percent of transgender participants had reported being stopped. Out of those who had been stopped, 51 percent of LGBTQ participants said they encountered verbal or physical harassment by police, and 61 percent of transgender participants reported verbal or physical harassment by police. Additionally, 38 percent of the total

LGBTQ sample reported physical abuse by police and 46 percent of transgender participants reported physical abuse by police. Similarly, lesbian, gay, bisexual, and queer (LGBQ) youth in New York City were more likely to report any police contact than their heterosexual counterparts in the past 6 months (Stoudt et al., 2012). Compared to heterosexual youth, LGBQ youth were also more likely to report negative police experiences, including verbal contact, physical contact, and sexual contact.

Previous reports have also described many first-hand accounts of LGBTQ people being profiled and targeted by police officers for their sexual orientation or gender identity, often intersected with their race and other identities (Amnesty International [AI], 2005; Center for Constitutional Rights [CCR], 2012). Some studies have found butch women, or cisgender women who may appear to be more masculine, tend to be stopped frequently by police (CCR, 2012; Dwyer, 2011). For example, one butch-identified pansexual female shared:

> Well I'm a pretty butch girl so I've never had any really good relationships with police. I was locked up when I was younger . . . and I didn't really get treated that well [because] they were like "Ah you should stand up for yourself you're butch" and it was just like "Yeah I'm a 14-year-old kid with shaved head like that's just me." I think the way you look is the way you get judged when it comes to the police. (Dwyer, 2011, p. 210)

Butch women (especially Black butch women and other butch women of color) are often racially profiled in similar ways as Black men and other men of color. Previous research has found the intersection of gender presentation and race impact how people are treated by police officers, with masculine or butch Black women often stereotyped as being aggressive (Nadal et al., 2015).

There have also been many reports of how the NYPD has disproportionately arrested transgender women—particularly transgender women of color—for prostitution and other sex-related crimes (Daum, 2015). In New York City, police often arrest trans women on the charge of "loitering with intent to solicit" (MRNY, 2012)—a charge that is so vague it can be used at essentially any time. In this way, transgender women have adopted the term "walking while trans" to depict how they can be criminalized for simply living their lives (Scharron-del Rio, 2017). To illustrate this, a Latina transgender woman describes an arrest, in which she was presumed to be a sex worker (and her boyfriend was suspected to be a client):

> One night I was with my boyfriend at a club in Jackson Heights, Queens. At around 4AM we left the club together and walked home. We were walking next to each other. At one point an undercover police van stopped next to us. Eight undercover cops got out from the van and some of them threw me against the wall. While they were hand-

> cuffing me, my boyfriend was also thrown to the wall and they frisked him. They told me I was being arrested for sex work. I told them that I was not doing anything like that. After they frisked my boyfriend, they frisked me and found 3 condoms, after seeing the condoms they asked if I was sure that I was not working. I told them that I was with my boyfriend and they said that he was not my boyfriend. . . . My boyfriend came to the 110th Precinct where I was held and spoke to the captain; he tried to explain that I was his girlfriend and that I was with him. But the captain said that he couldn't do anything. I was taken to court and was accused of sex work. (Daum, 2015, p. 566)

While most reports on profiling LGBTQ people as sex workers focus on the experiences of transgender women, some scholars describe how young gay men of color are also presumed to be sex workers. Amnesty International (2005) describes a case in Chicago, in which three gay men of color (two Black and a Latino) were stopped by officers who allegedly told them: "You fucking faggots, put your hands on the car," "You're out here selling your ass, but no one is going to buy it," and "I'll find a reason to arrest you" (p. 25).

When queer and trans people are searched by police officers, condoms are often used as evidence in arresting them for sex work; in fact, in many major metropolitan areas, possessing condoms is enough to be arrested for prostitution (McLemore, 2012; Wurth et al., 2013). So, now not only were police officers able to randomly search trans and queer people because they looked suspicious, they now had "evidence" for arresting them. One transgender Latina shared: "If I took a lot of condoms, they would arrest me. If I took a few or only one, I would run out and not be able to protect myself. How many times have I had unprotected sex because I was afraid of carrying condoms? Many times" (McLemore, 2012, p. 1).

In one case, finding condoms on a person resulted in a suicide. In Schuylkill County, Pennsylvania, in 1997, Marcus Wayman, an 18-year-old and his 17-year-old friend were found drinking in a car in an empty lot (Dale, 2001). When the arresting officer Scott Willinsky found two condoms on the 17-year-old, he called them "queers" (which would have been considered a derogatory term at the time) and charged them on underage drinking. He allegedly lectured them on what the Bible says about homosexuality and threatened to "out" them to their families. After returning home, Wayman died by a suicidal gunshot wound to the head. Wayman's family sued and received a settlement of $100,000; the case set a precedent for people's constitutional right to privacy regarding their sexual orientation or gender identity (Weinstein, 2004).

Public health scholars have argued that using condoms as evidence is problematic because it discourages people from carrying condoms, which then increases their chances of engaging in unprotected sex (Wurth et al., 2013). Furthermore, using condoms as evidence is counterintuitive in cities where condoms are distributed to promote safer sex practices. One transgender woman stated: "Why is the city giving me condoms when I can't carry them without going to jail?" (McLemore, 2012, p. 3). In this way, the contradiction between city departments (e.g., health departments versus police departments) may unintentionally result in entrapment or criminalization for LGBTQ people and others.

Police Misconduct and Brutality

Over the past twenty years, there has been an increase in literature focusing on the experiences of police misconduct, brutality, and violence toward LGBTQ people (Mallory, Hasenbush, & Sears, 2013; Stotzer, 2009; Wolff & Cokely, 2007). Berrill (1990) found that from 1985 to 1987, there were a total of 550 incidents of police harassment reported to the National Gay Task Force, and that out of all of the anti-LGBTQ-related incidents participants experienced, 20 percent were from police; many occurred after police officers were responding to a previous anti-LGBTQ incident. Additionally, Berrill (1990) found across four different samples that police harassment and anti-LGBTQ victimization ranged from 23 to 31 percent of the gay male samples and 8 to 16 percent for the lesbian samples.

Decades later, similar dynamics still occur, with some slight changes. For instance, in a national study on survivors of hate violence, Waters (2017) discovered that out of all reported anti-LGBTQ hate violence incidents in 2016, 10 percent were perpetrated by police officers (an increase from 3 percent in 2015). The analysis also found a little less than half of the sample (40 percent) of LGBTQ survivors of violence interacted with police; out of that group, about one-third of the sample (35 percent) reported the police officers were indifferent, and another one-third of the sample reported the police to be hostile (Waters, 2017). Several survivors even indicated police officers ended up using excessive force as a result of their interaction, with Black survivors being significantly more likely to encounter excessive force than all others. Lambda Legal (2015) found 14 percent of their sample had experienced verbal assault by police in the past five years, 3 percent reported sexual harassment, and 2 percent reported physical assault. Percentages increased significantly for people of color: 4 percent had been physically assaulted by police, 5 percent had been sexually harassed, and 25 percent had been verbally assaulted. Similarly, LGBTQ people from low-income backgrounds also reported higher frequencies—including 5 percent reporting physical assault, 7 percent reporting sexual assault, and 25 percent reporting verbal assault.

A national report found in 2017 there were a total of 52 hate violence homicides toward LGBTQ people and people living with HIV/AIDS; out of those incidents, it was reported three of those homicides were by police responding to incidents (Tillery et al., 2018). Additionally, the report revealed 55 percent of hate violence survivors who interacted with police reported law enforcement was indifferent and 20 percent were hostile; meanwhile, 47 percent of IPV survivors who interacted with police reported they were indifferent, and 11 percent reported they were hostile. Finally, 13 percent of hate violence survivors reported police misconduct (with 44 percent reporting excessive force), while 5 percent of IPV survivors reported police misconduct (with 20 percent reporting excessive force).

In searching through media articles, one can easily find how common these types of anti-LGBTQ police brutality can be. Below are some examples:

- In 2008, in Memphis, videos emerged of police verbally and physically assaulting Duanna Johnson, a Black transgender woman, at the Shelby County Jail. Ms. Johnson filed charges and the officers were fired; she was found shot dead several months later; no suspects were arrested (Brown, 2008).
- In 2009, outside of a bar in Brooklyn, New York, Jeanette Grey and Tiffany Jimenez, two lesbians of color, were beaten by police with nightsticks while allegedly using homophobic slurs, including "We are having some dyke pussy in here tonight" (Smith, 2009).
- In 2013, in Brooklyn, New York, police raided the home of Jabbar Campbell, a gay Black man, during a party. Upon entering the building, police officers turned a security camera off, so it could not capture the event; Campbell sustained multiple injuries and required several surgeries. A judged ruled the NYPD was liable for false arrest, battery, and malicious prosecution (Riley, 2017).

TGNC individuals are generally more likely to experience violence from the police; as an example, the National Transgender Discrimination Survey found 29 percent of their sample experienced police harassment and that 46 percent of respondents were uncomfortable in seeking police assistance (Grant et al., 2011). In that same study, 7 percent of the transgender participants reported being arrested or jailed strictly due to police officer bias toward their gender identity—with rates being higher for Black transgender participants (41 percent) and Latinx transgender participants (21 percent). Another study reported police officers often used excessive force when searching gender nonconforming individuals—often in an attempt to determine their sex assigned at birth (CCR, 2012). For TGNC people of color, encounters with police tend to worsen; as an example, one study reported transgender people of color were likely to report twice as much police violence than the remainder of the LGBTQ population (Waters, 2017). Similarly, studies have revealed how transgender women, especially transgender women of color, reported sexual abuse or unnecessary sexual contact by police officers, like being touched or frisked inappropriately or being strip-searched in front of cisgender men (Nadal, Davidoff, & Fujii-Doe, 2014; Stotz, 2009). One Latina transgender woman described a very humiliating experience of being arrested and spending time in the jail, recalling:

> I remember the first comment: "Ohh, look at this one! This is a gorgeous one. We haven't had one like you in a long time," starting with the commanding officers. Then the [inmates start] yelling "Put it in our cell. C'mon, we'll have some fun tearing up that asshole." You all get into a line and you're going to get strip searched, you're gonna take a shower, and you know, they put your clothes through the metal detectors, and you take your clothes [back after]. (Nadal, Skolnik, & Wong, 2012, p. 73)

These types of humiliating incidents appear to be common experiences, that may even result in lawsuits. For instance, in 2010, in Boston, Massachusetts, Brenda Wernikoff, a transgender woman, was arrested by police for refusing to leave a woman's bathroom in a homeless shelter; when they arrested her, they allegedly forced her to expose her breasts and jump up and down. The case was settled for $20,000 (Cramer, 2013).

For many other TGNC people, arrests often turn to violence. One Black transgender woman shared what she encountered regularly when she was arrested:

> A lot of times the officer would come up to you, pat you down, you know if you were dressed as a female, then find out I have this birth defect between my legs, he'd freak out . . . I've been hit with a billy club, I've gotten both of my legs broke, I've gotten my ankles broke, my hips broke. I'm almost blind in one eye [because] he hit me upside the head so hard. I've gone to the hospital with a shattered skull. (Nadal, Vargas, et al., 2012, p. 131)

Even though these types of experiences are quite known among LGBTQ communities, they are often not discussed elsewhere because police officers do not report them or they do not gain media attention. Thus, their stories are deemed false and their experiences are invalidated.

Microaggressions and Police Officers

Microaggressions or the subtle, often unintentional forms of discrimination, which convey bias about particular individuals and groups (Nadal, 2018), are the more covert ways biases manifest among police officers. For example, a gay Latino man said: "I think that it has become really frowned upon to be antigay, even though it's totally common. But police are less explicit about it. There's still a lot of it. So. It's, like, shifting slowly, but it's not at all" (Nadal et al., 2015, p. 474). People cope with microaggressions in different ways; in one study, gay men say they cope with microaggressions from police officers by reminding themselves they "need to act straight" (Nadal et al., 2015, p. 467). Across multiple studies, there are several types of microaggressions that occur for LGBTQ people in the criminal system—particularly from police.

Use of Derogatory Language and Misgendering

While several examples of anti-LGBTQ language have been described throughout the chapter, language and terminology can be used in more innocuous, but hurtful ways. Calling someone a homophobic or transphobic slur while attacking them is considered both a verbal and physical assault; however, saying things that are meant to be humorous, or in which a person can deny any malicious intent would be considered more of a microaggression. Within police departments, LGBTQ police officers describe how embedded homophobic language and jokes are in police culture (Miller, Forest, & Jurik, 2003). Amnesty International (2005) found across multiple cities and jurisdictions, LGBTQ people reported hearing police officers use language like "faggot," "dyke," "freak," and "he/she" (p. 56). When a Black transgender woman was brought into a county jail, she recalled: "The two arresting officers asked, 'Where do we put this one?' to which a deputy responded, 'It has tits and ass, so let's put it in the queer tank'" (AI, 2005, p. 93). While there may not be violence involved when making these comments, hearing such remarks can be extremely humiliating and dehumanizing.

Homophobic language has been embedded into formal or informal policies or codes; for example, Detroit state troopers referred to sting operations as "bag a fag" (AI, 2005, p. 33), while bribing closeted gay men after being caught for sodomy was referred to by Washington, DC's Metropolitan Police Department as "fairy shaking" (Fillichio, 2006, p. 57). Thus, before even arresting anyone, police enter situations with homophobic bias that influences how they were treat all LGBTQ people they will interact with.

Misgendering is a common microaggression committed by police officers toward transgender people. Sometimes the misgendering is accompanied by violence, but sometimes it is used in subtle or less threatening ways. For instance, a transgender woman described an incident at a police station in trying to report a crime: "The detectives were passing by and they [sang] 'Transformers . . . men up in disguise' . . . Just like that" (Nadal et al., 2013, p. 73). Other times, misgendering involved calling a TGNC person by their name assigned at birth, instead of their chosen name; one transgender woman disclosed: "When I told them my real name, Rachel, they refused to recognize that and continued to call me by my male name" (AI, 2005, p. 73).

Assumptions of Criminality, Pathology, or Abnormality

As discussed throughout this chapter and previous chapters, LGBTQ people are often stereotyped to be sexually deviant criminals. As aforementioned, some transgender women are automatically presumed to be sex workers, or gay men are presumed to be engaging in lewd conduct, when police officers see them. While police officers often profile, entrap, or arrest them as a result of these biases, sometimes they engage in microaggressions. As an example, one transgender woman shared an experience of reporting a crime in which she was victimized: "The detectives in the victim's unit asked if we were prostitutes. So, I said, 'I'm not a prostitute, why are you saying that?' He said, 'Because all you transsexuals are all prostitutes'" (Nadal, Skolnik, & Wong, 2012, p. 65). A transgender person shared a similar sentiment: "I've had experiences where I've had to call to the police to diffuse situations, and it felt like they were always turning it, somehow, against me as being the aggressor" (Fiani et al., 2019, p. 9). Sometimes even when an individual does engage in a crime, they perceive their treatment being extra biased because of their sexual orientation or gender identity.

Sexualization/Exoticization/ Dehumanization

Because many people are unfamiliar with LGBTQ people, they may hold many stereotypes or curiosities about their bodies or their behaviors—resulting in sexualization, exoticization, or dehumanization. For instance, gay men are often sexualized by police officers—in ways that are meant to be derogatory and demeaning, or to mock or provoke LGBTQ citizens. Stoudt and colleagues (2012) found several LGBTQ youths of color in New York City experienced several instances of sexualization. One gay Black male disclosed: "A group of police walked by and it just so happen [my friend] and I were sucking on dollar ice pops, so they were long, and the police said, 'I like the way y'all sucking on them icy. Y'all should come in the park and suck on us'" (Stoudt et al., 2012, p. 1344).

Transgender people particularly are often harassed or violated because of their physical bodies—with police officers touching them in inappropriate ways. One trans woman shared:

> "I've been stopped and frisked, and some dude like definitely scurried his way across my waistline . . . but like took like 5 seconds too long . . . borderlining on non-consensual touching" (Fiani et al., 2019, p. 10). Another transgender woman recalled how when waiting at a precinct, some police officers referred to another transgender woman with "many derogatory remarks such as 'Did you see the size of the tits on that freak?' until we informed them that we too were transsexuals. At that they held their tongues." (AI, 2005, p. 84)

LGBTQ POLICE OFFICERS

In January 1978, New York City Mayor Ed Koch signed an executive order that banned discrimination against homosexuals in all city agencies. Many high-ranking police officers were upset by this decision, including Samuel DeMilia, who was then the president of the Police Benevolent Association. In an op-ed in the *New York Times*, DeMilia wrote that a ban on discrimination can "do more harm than good. . . . The idea is unworkable in the Police Department because of the paramilitary nature of the job. Policemen form closer working and personal relationships than people in other fields. . . . This sociability, vital to building a cohesive, effective force, can never develop with homosexuals for obvious reasons" (DeMilia, 1978, p. 28). Years later, in 1981, when the New York City Council considered passing legislation to ban discrimination on gays in employment, housing, and public accommodation, Sergeant Charles Cochrane, Jr. outed himself as a gay man at a packed City Council meeting. When he did so, he had become the first publicly open gay NYPD officer—the first since the department was founded in 1845. He later helped to find the Gay Officers Action League to support LGBTQ members of law enforcement (Quindlen, 1981).

In other major cities, police officers were also publicly disclosing their sexual identities—mostly through major local newspapers. The earliest documented openly transgender police officer was Bonnie Davenport of Washington, DC, who transitioned, in 1979, after serving on the job for nine years. When she returned to work, she was assigned a new partner—a rookie officer named Bobby Almstead who was the first openly gay officer of the Metropolitan Police Department (Wheeler, 1983). In 1981, Woody Tennant became the first openly gay officer of the San Francisco Police Department; he was later interviewed on CBS' *60 Minutes*, where he described the amount of hate mail and phone calls he received, including one in which an anonymous caller even threatened: "It's pretty hard to be number one if you're a dead faggot" (Wallace, 1992).

In 1989, the International Association of Chiefs of Police, the leading professional organization of police administrators at the time, rescinded its decades-old policy of opposing the hiring of lesbian and gay police officers (Serrano, 1990). As a result, many police departments across the country lifted official or unofficial bans on LGBTQ officers, and at least ten departments in major metropolitan areas began to recruit lesbian and gay police officers in the 1990s. Some departments specifically cited a need for lesbian and gay officers, in response to a growing increase of anti-gay hate crimes and a need to gain trust in the community.

Lesbian officers first came out in some cities, with Dorothy Knudson and Mary Boyle starting the Lesbian and Gay Police Association in Chicago (Griffin, 1993). One of its earliest members was Ron Bogan, the first openly gay police officer in the Chicago Police Department (Schmich, 1992), and likely the first known openly gay Black police officer in the US. Meanwhile, other police departments continued to disallow lesbian and gay officers, mainly because their sodomy laws were still in place; they could not hire a person to enforce the law if they were known to be breaking the law.

Given the anti-LGBTQ stigma existing for centuries, particularly in the military (see chapter 1 for a review), it may not be surprising that many police officers did not publicly disclose their sexual orientations. Because the field of policing is an occupation that is highly gendered and sexualized, many LGBTQ people may not choose a career in policing, while existing police officers navigate norms related to heterosexuality and masculinity (Colvin, 2012; Miller et al., 2003). Some scholars have described the ways heterosexism and transphobia are pervasive throughout police culture, while also manifesting through interactions with peers and colleagues (Colvin, 2009, 2012; Nolan, 2009). From 2000 to 2013, the Williams Institute reported a total of 57 court cases and administrative complaints involving anti-LGBTQ discrimination within police departments across the US (Mallory et al., 2013). In 2019, *USA Today* reported 11 lawsuits were filed against law enforcement departments since 2016 (Lam, 2019).

In this way, police culture is a demonstration of hegemonic masculinity, which is defined as "the creation and maintenance of a gendered hierarchical structure within a given sociopolitical context" (Smith, 2017, p. 830). Hegemonic masculinity may explain why many out lesbian and gay officers are viewed as "outsiders" even within police departments—leading to unique barriers to equal employment opportunities in ways that are similar for women and people of color (Colvin, 2009). The culture has developed steadily over time, as illustrated best by former PBA President Samuel DeMilia (1978) who said: "The predominant attitudes of this latter group toward homosexuality, which are characterized by a refusal to develop any close personal relationships with homosexuals, were formed and hardened over many years. They are part of a morality whose origins date back to pre-biblical times" (p. 28). Further, police cultures across the country and in many other parts of the world often maintain a "blue wall of silence," which is defined as "a phenomenon that suggests that the police engage in a pervasive pattern of deception and withholding of the truth in ritual cover-up for their brethren" (Nolan, 2009, p. 250), which then prevents LGBTQ officers from being able to speak out against any discrimination they may face. In fact, when they do file complaints, they are often silenced, stigmatized, or ostracized by their peers, or ignored by internal affairs (Mallory et al., 2013). Despite these obstacles, one positive aspect of having more LGBTQ police officers is how they support more humane and less violent approaches to policing, making them more capable and competent in working with LGBTQ communities and other historically marginalized groups (Miller et al., 2003). So, although they work for an entity that has historically discriminated against LGBTQ people, they themselves have learned to be resilient in overcoming bias within the system.

QUEERING LAW ENFORCEMENT

While one obvious way to queer law enforcement is to increase the number of LGBTQ officers in police departments, we must acknowledge how such a practice would be meaningless if law enforcement systems remained heterosexist or transphobic. In other words, if a large number of LGBTQ police officers emerged, but those individuals assimilated into current hegemonic police cultures (e.g., they engaged in acts of toxic masculinity, they promoted gender binaries, etc.), then heterosexist and transphobic biases would continue to persist.

Thus, queering police departments must come through changes in systems and the ways that police officers are trained to engage in police practice and to enforce the law. For instance, while policing has traditionally been viewed as people who enforce the law through physical strength and prowess, perhaps policing needs to be transformed so that police officers are viewed as community liaisons who promote safety and use their emotional prowess. Such practices have been referred to by some as community policing, which has been defined as "new organization strategies that seek to redefine the mission, the principal operating methods, and the key administrative arrangements of police departments" (Moore, 1992, p. 103). Weisheit, Falcone, and Wells (1999) further the definition by referring to community policing as having three parts:

> The first has to do with the police being accountable to the community as well as to the formal police hierarchy. The second is that police will become more connected with and integrated into their communities, which means that police will interact with citizens on a personal level, will be familiar with community sentiments and concerns, and will work with the community to address those concerns. A third and final theme requires that police will be oriented to solving general problems. (p. 115)

Kingshott (2013) describes how "the police department should reflect the society being policed where the police accept that their role has a duty of care and is not solely about crime fighting" (p. 377)—suggesting community policing includes representation from historically marginalized groups, while also shifting attitudes from solely fighting crime to building community. DOJ (2014) defines community policing as "a philosophy that promotes organizational strategies that support the systematic use of partnerships and problem-solving techniques to proactively address the immediate conditions that give rise to public safety issues such as crime, social disorder, and fear of crime" (p. 3).

Specific to LGBTQ communities, one study found LGBTQ people viewed community policing positively, particularly if LGBTQ participants were being assisted with something (Gillespie, 2008). In spite of this, the authors mention a caveat that the data was collected at an Atlanta Pride event in 2004, and that such views may not have held true the following year when Atlanta police arrested six gay men and used homophobic slurs. Therefore, we acknowledge how the tenets of community policing need to be practiced at all times and integrated into all aspects of police culture. Relatedly, Colvin (2014) found lesbian and gay police officers believed in the philosophy behind community policing (especially the creation or utilization of LGBTQ community liaisons), but how it often meant they were given extra responsibilities to serve as liaisons to LGBTQ communities. If community policing insists that all police officers are able to integrate into the communities they serve, then LGBTQ police officers should not be the only ones who are effective and trusted by LGBTQ people.

Moreover, queering law enforcement means that police profiling must end, as it promotes the criminalization of historically marginalized groups, but because it also perpetuates systems of violence. Specific to LGBTQ communities, criminal justice reform may include ensuring police officers' accountability and transparency regarding discriminatory practices (National Center for Transgender Equality, 2018). In order to gain LGBTQ community members' trust, civilians must know police officers face consequences when they engage in biased behaviors.

One effective way to queer law enforcement is to ensure all police officers are trained properly in working with LGBTQ communities—particularly being mindful of intersectional identities within the LGBTQ umbrella. Training cannot simply involve a one-time, one-day model, as such trainings have little effect on reducing biases or transforming systems of prejudiced policing (Israel, Harkness, Delucio, Ledbetter, & Avellar, 2014). Trainings must be interactive and can be most effective when they involve police officers brainstorming their own solutions and approaches, while integrating new LGBTQ-related information (Israel et al., 2016). Moreover, while police trainings on reducing implicit racial biases are still nascent (Smith, 2015), understanding implicit bias must be a factor to be explored before becoming a police officer. Implicit bias training toward LGBTQ people and other marginalized groups must be integrated into all aspects of training—from tactics to firearm training to mental health training. In order for LGBTQ-affirming trainings to be most effective, they must be integrated as values of police culture; as a result, leadership in police departments must model the type of behavior that should be adopted by police officers across all levels. In doing so, perhaps LGBTQ people and others of historically marginalized groups would have more confidence and faith in police officers, increasing their abilities to feel protected and served.

In order to advocate for change, communities must utilize their collective voices when they believe their local or state law enforcement engages in any unjust or biased behaviors. Individuals can do so through protests, petitions, rallies, or education. While it is necessary for people to be vocal regarding unjust behaviors toward LGBTQ people, they must speak up against all injustices—including police brutality and violence toward people of color, women, people with mental illness, or people with many marginalized identities—even if it does not directly affect them. In this way, LGBTQ people of all racial groups should be just as outraged when an innocent, unarmed trans woman is brutalized by police officers, as when an innocent, unarmed gay man is beaten by police officers, or as when an innocent, unarmed Black man is killed by police officers. History demonstrates that activism is also more effective when people from different groups form larger coalitions to advocate for diverse marginalized communities. For example, when the Filipino farmworkers began their strike against their employers, they knew they would be more effective with the support of Mexican farmworkers; together, they built the United Farmworkers and led one of the greatest labor movements in history (Mabalon, 2013). Thus LGBTQ community leaders must work alongside other community organizers (e.g., Black Lives Matter or #MeToo activists), in order to successfully create change.

Finally, it is crucial to note how people with multiple marginalized identities, particularly Black women, are often at the frontlines of activism—fighting against systemic oppression, as well as discrimination within their identity groups. Two of the early leaders of the LGBTQ rights movement in New York, Sylvia Rivera and Marsha P. Johnson, were two women of color. Two of the three founders of the #BlackLivesMatter movement, Alicia Garza and Patrisse Khan-Cullors, are queer Black women. While people with multiple marginalized identities are the most vocal because they have historically felt intersectional oppression, it is critical for people with privilege to step up to become the allies and accomplices needed to advance justice. In doing so, perhaps others in positions of power will have an easier time hearing the message, which can assist in systemic change too.

FOUR
Gender and Sexuality on Trial
LGBTQ People and the Courts

THE CASE OF MICHAEL L. JOHNSON

On October 10, 2013, Michael L. Johnson, a 23-year-old Black gay male college wrestler at Lindenwood University in St. Charles, Missouri, was pulled out of his class and taken away by police officers in handcuffs (Lawless, 2017; Thrasher, 2014). Unbeknownst to him, Johnson was being arrested for failing to disclose to his sexual partners that he was HIV positive and for allegedly spreading the virus to them. Later, his official charges would be 1 count of recklessly infecting another with HIV and 4 counts of attempting to recklessly infect another with HIV—all classified as felonies in the state of Missouri. While awaiting trial, he would spend 18 months in the local county jail, primarily in solitary confinement.

As a student, Johnson was an out gay man on the conservative Catholic campus—where he became popular for his good looks and athletic physique. As one of the few Black students on campus, he stood out even more, and many of his gay White classmates admitted to hooking up with him—mentioning how they had not been with any (or many) Black men sexually besides him. He met many of his sexual partners through the dating app Grindr—using the alias Tiger Mandingo, a name that he picked up when he walked in the ballroom scene. He regularly engaged in consensual, condomless anal sex—mostly with gay White men as the anal recipients. Journalist Steven Thrasher—who received accolades for his investigative reporting of Johnson's story—quoted someone as saying: "Everyone wanted a piece of him, until he had HIV" (Thrasher, 2014).

It appears that Mr. Johnson had been diagnosed with HIV in January 2013 and had signed a form (sanctioned by the state of Missouri) acknowledging his diagnosis. Johnson, who was dyslexic, signed the form without any counsel and admitted later to not fully understanding what the document was about. In spite of this, signing this form meant that anytime he had sex with someone without disclosing his HIV status, he would commit a felony in the state of Missouri.

Reports suggest Johnson was initially acquainted with the first plaintiff in January 2013—a week after he learned of his HIV status. That plaintiff waited several months before he first approached police about his HIV status and his presumption of contracting the virus from Johnson—again, through consensual condomless sex—at the end of May 2013. Police then waited for four months before talking to and arresting Johnson. If police would later classify Johnson's HIV status as a dangerous weapon, it is unclear why they would wait for so long to prevent him from "assaulting" other men. Nonetheless, five other plaintiffs eventually came forward, with four of them identified as White. Each of the plaintiffs claimed they contracted HIV from Johnson—though there would be no scientific evidence to actually prove that. All of the plaintiffs admitted to engaging in consensual unprotected sex, but they all claimed Johnson lied about his HIV status to them prior to the intercourse.

Herein lies the problem and the major controversy of the case. When two parties choose to engage in unprotected (or "bareback") sex, knowing all of the risks involved, who should be held responsible? There is the possibility Johnson did not know of his HIV status when he had sex with any of the plaintiffs, as well as a possibility any of these men contracted the virus from a different sexual partner. There is also a possibility they potentially passed the virus on to Mr. Johnson. Without testing the strains of HIV of each of the parties (at the time each was diagnosed), there would inevitably be many reasonable doubts and multiple possibilities. Yet, Mr. Johnson, the Black man, was the only one held accountable.

Mr. Johnson was vilified on campus and in the surrounding community—both which were predominantly White. The university sent an announcement urging anyone who had sex with Johnson to get tested for HIV; the same university is one that did not allow for the word "gay" to be in the name of a student organization and is one that did not provide condoms or promote safe sex on campus (Thrasher, 2014). In May 2015, Johnson was convicted on multiple felony counts, including recklessly infecting another with HIV, which carries a 10-year minimum sentence. The jury sought the maximum penalty of 60.5 years—despite the lack of genetic evidence that linked Mr. Johnson to any of his partners. In July 2015, the judge ultimately sentenced him to 30 years in prison.

While laws involving HIV criminalization vary by state, Missouri is one of 19 states where exposing another person to HIV without disclosure is considered a crime (Centers for Disease Control and Prevention

[CDC], 2019). Many states, including Missouri, view nondisclosure as a felony; other states, not including Missouri, require people who are convicted of HIV-related crimes to register as sex offenders (CDC, 2019). Laws about HIV/AIDS are limited because they were written in the 1980s and 1990s—a time when there was little scientific knowledge about the virus and how it was transmitted. Back then, contracting HIV was considered a "death sentence"—which is why some state laws may treat it similarly to a murder or manslaughter conviction. However, today, HIV is a manageable, chronic disease, which can even be undetectable and non-transmittable (Cortopassi, Driver, Eaton, & Kalichman, 2019)—making extreme punishments seem cruel, unnecessary, and even unconstitutional.

Race became a prevalent factor in how the case proceeded—with Johnson being criminalized as a Black man, and the plaintiffs (the majority were White) being painted as innocent victims. While the criminalizing of Black men in general is pervasive in numerous ways (e.g., Black men being viewed as dangerous, physically violent, or involved in gangs), the criminalizing of Black men as sexual predators dates back to slavery, when Black men were falsely stereotyped as raping White women (Alexander, 2012). The trope of Black men being deemed predators while White women were deemed victims was evident in the case of Emmett Till—a 14-year-old Black boy who was brutally murdered in Mississippi because he allegedly whistled at or spewed insults at a White woman (Onwuachi-Willig, 2016).

Michael Johnson was criminalized as a sexual predator in numerous ways. First, when the media picked up on the story, he was repeatedly referred to as Tiger Mandingo, his social media alias, and not by his actual legal name. While "Mandingo" may refer to an ethnic group in Western Africa, the term became popularized in the US through a 1975 film called *Mandingo*—which depicted a slave who killed other slaves and impregnated his master's female slaves. In allowing for this narrative to persist in the media, Johnson was intentionally or unintentionally depicted as a dangerous and oversexualized criminal. Further, during the actual trial, jurors were shown photos of Johnson's naked torso and even his penis—furthering the narrative of Johnson as a sexual predator (Thrasher, 2019). The all-White jury found Johnson to be guilty on all counts, despite a lack of evidence—aligned with previous literature which asserts that Black Americans were more likely to be convicted of criminal HIV exposure related to a sexual interaction than White Americans (Galletly & Lazzarini, 2013). When the jury recommended the maximum sentence and the judge ordered a sentence that was longer than the state average for second-degree murder (Thrasher, 2019), it aligned with previous literature that noted Black offenders who were convicted of HIV-related crimes received significantly longer sentences than those who were White (Galletly & Lazzarini, 2013).

In December 2016, the Missouri Court of Appeals for the Eastern District overturned his conviction because prosecutors had waited until the last moment to disclose evidence, which was condemned as being "fundamentally unfair." Mr. Johnson avoided another trial by accepting a no-contest Alford plea deal, in which he still did not admit fault, but acknowledged that prosecution had enough evidence to convict him. In July 2019, Mr. Johnson was released on parole—serving only 5 years of his 30-year sentence (Thrasher, 2019). Despite this, his case is one that has stirred many conversations about HIV-criminalization and how, or if, HIV-related cases should be treated in a court of law.

INTRODUCTION

As evidenced in chapter 1, heterosexist and cissexist legislation had historically infiltrated all parts of the criminal justice system—from the earliest sodomy laws of the US to contemporary LGBTQ issues like being able to adopt children or serve in the military. In reviewing that history, one may notice how quickly LGBTQ rights have progressed in the past two decades. In the 1990s and early 2000s, it seemed that LGBTQ people's lives were constantly at the forefront of political debates and the law, with many debating whether LGBTQ rights should be regulated or removed altogether (Knauer, 2012). Yet, by 2010, across all branches of government, there were many successful attempts in advocating for LGBTQ rights—from the SCOTUS decisions on marriage equality to the executive orders to include sexual orientation and gender identity as protected classes in federal hate crime legislation (Nadal, 2018).

Despite these victories, there have been many anti-LGBTQ biases that have permeated the courts—affecting everything from trials to sentences. Prior to *Lawrence v. Texas* (2003), which outlawed sodomy on a federal level, most legal scholarship on LGBTQ people focused on the pathology of "homosexuals" and did not examine the ways judicial bias may have been unfair or discriminatory toward LGBTQ people. In the 1990s and early 2000s, a noticeable amount of LGBTQ-affirming legal scholarship began to emerge for the first time—focusing on bias and discrimination within the legal profession and discrimination within the courts. This chapter will cover the scholarship on LGBTQ experiences in courts and sentencing, citing the ways that biases have oppressed, and continue to oppress, LGBTQ people. Because the Supreme Court has not always been favorable toward LGBTQ rights, it makes sense why LGBTQ people would hold negative perceptions of the court system.

HISTORICAL BIASES IN THE JUDICIAL SYSTEM

One of the first comprehensive explorations regarding anti-LGBTQ sentiment in the courts was Durkin's (1998) analysis of eleven studies that focused on sexual orientation bias in the legal profession from 1991 to 1996. Each study surveyed lesbian and gay attorneys and was conducted by different bar associations across different regions and jurisdictions (i.e., city, county, state bar associations). Major themes include the need for anti-discrimination policies and more lesbian and gay attorneys. Some studies examined perceptions of homophobia in courts (e.g., in Massachusetts, 23 percent of participants heard anti-LGBTQ remarks while at work, and 14 percent heard homophobic comments by judges or mediators). Rubenstein (1998) described the same aforementioned eleven studies—applauding the bar associations for their efforts, while citing their limitations. First, the studies focused primarily on experiences of attorneys; thus, results may not necessarily reflect other lesbian and gay court constituents (e.g., plaintiffs, defendants, judges, court employees). Second, because judges and attorneys exhibit homophobic bias openly in courtroom and without any repercussions, Rubenstein argued how research should examine judicial bias in legal rulings, as well as discriminatory motives or intent by court officials (attorneys, paralegals, courthouse employees, jurors, litigants, etc.) against court users (attorneys, witnesses, litigants, etc.). Further, with nearly half of the lesbian and gay sample reporting they are closeted at work, as well as nearly all of the participants being White and mostly gay men, Rubenstein critiqued how the studies were not generalizable to lesbians, gay people of color, bisexuals, or transgender people.

Shortnacy (2001) describes two major studies conducted by states to assess sexual orientation bias in their court systems: (a) the Judicial Council of California lesbian and gay court users and court employees of any sexual orientation in 2001; and (b) the State Bar of Arizona Board of Governors surveyed Arizona judges, attorneys, law students, and members of the gay and lesbian community in 1999. In both studies, a notable percentage witnessed anti-gay comments or actions: 56 percent of court users in California; 20 percent of court employees in California; 77 percent of judges and attorneys in Arizona; and 29 percent of lesbian and gay court employees in Arizona. Many of these comments occurred in open court and were made frequently by judges, lawyers, or court employees. In California, 30 percent of lesbian and gay court users believed those who knew their sexual orientation did not treat them with respect, while 39 percent believed their sexual orientation was used to invalidate their credibility. In Arizona, 60 percent of judges had little to no knowledge about statutes protecting lesbian and gay people, while only 17 percent of law students ever had classes that addressed issues involving lesbian and gay people. Twenty-nine percent of the court employee participants in California reported it was unsafe for employees to be open about their sexual orientation.

Forbes (2014) examined how an individual's level of gender conformity or gender nonconformity influenced one's perceived treatment by the courts. Results indicated people who reported higher scores of gender nonconformity were more likely to report negative court experiences. Further, while sexual orientation was a significant predictor of gender nonconformity (i.e., LGBTQ people were more likely than heterosexual/cisgender people to report higher levels of gender nonconformity), sexual orientation, alone, did not significantly predict how one would be treated by courts. Thus, the findings suggest gender presentation predicts how people will be treated in court more than sexuality alone. Perhaps when an LGBTQ person is able to "pass" or conceal a marginalized identity (Davis, 2017a), they are able to avoid stigmatization and discrimination, leading to more favorable experiences in courts.

Regarding juvenile justice, studies have found LGBTQ youth perceive the court system to be biased. In a study of LGBTQ youth in New York City who had come into contact with the criminal justice system, 44 percent reported negative experiences with the courts, with many reporting being misgendered through incorrect pronouns or experiencing heterosexist and transphobic language and discrimination (Dank et al., 2015). LGBTQ youth also described how adults make decisions that they do not deem to be safe or fair; for instance, when asked about her experiences in family court, a Black lesbian young woman shared: "Of course they are going to listen to the adult more as a solution. Because, at the end of the day, that person is older and everything. But they're not listening. They did not listen to the young person who is actually going through the situation" (Dank et al., 2015, p. 115).

Finally, qualitative studies on LGBTQ perceptions of procedural justice provide insight on issues related to the courts. First, Nadal and colleagues (2015) recruited a randomized sample of lesbian, gay, bisexual, and queer (LGBQ) participants to discuss their experiences with the criminal justice system; participants mainly discussed experiences with police, without any describing first-hand experiences with courts or incarceration. Meanwhile, Nadal, Erazo, Fiani, Murrillo Parilla, and Han (2018) utilized a similar method to recruit transgender and gender nonconforming (TGNC) participants and found many of the sample could describe experiences related to the courts and correctional facilities. For instance, one Black trans person shared: "The court system . . . I believe is just as biased as the police officers. And you—I know I keep referring to my ethnic background—you know me being African American, it doesn't even matter what judge it is that you get; I cannot afford an attorney and based on that I am often railroaded by the judicial system" (Nadal et al., 2018, p. 67). Many TGNC participants described being held in custody (e.g., in a holding cell or jail), sharing anxiety about being surrounded by other detainees of their sex assigned at birth.

In general, TGNC participants describe the normalcy of being mistreated in the criminal justice system—a view that is typically learned through direct experiences of discrimination or maltreatment. For example, James and colleagues (2016) reported 22 percent of the TGNC participants in their sample who interacted with judges felt only sometimes treated with respect, while 2 percent felt like they were never treated with respect. Meanwhile, Grant and colleagues (2011) reported 12 percent of their TGNC sample had been denied equal treatment or felt harassed by judges or court officials. To demonstrate this sentiment, one trans participant shared: "I'm treated like an individual who has to take what is in fact being given to them . . . because I don't have anyone to fight for me"; meanwhile, another participant shared: "I assume, um, and then accept, a certain level of disrespect, sadly, more than I think a straight person would" (Fiani et al., 2017, pp. 9–10). In this way, TGNC people have learned, through first-hand experience, how the criminal justice system is not meant for them; accordingly, they may resign to the reality that they will continually encounter obstacles in the justice system due to their gender identities.

The next sections will focus on the ways that specific aspects of the judicial system may exhibit bias and in turn discriminate against LGBTQ people. I will review four main areas of literature: (a) judicial bias, (b) attorney bias, (c) jury bias, and (d) bias in sentencing.

Judicial Biases

Procedural justice is highly influenced by whether or not individuals trust judges, or believe that judges act in fair and impartial manners (Tyler, 2007). Ethically, one would expect that judges would withhold biases. For instance, according to the American Bar Association's (2011) Model Code of Judicial Conduct, it reads:

> (A) A judge shall perform the duties of judicial office, including administrative duties, without bias or prejudice.
> (B) A judge shall not, in the performance of judicial duties, by words or conduct manifest bias or prejudice, or engage in harassment, including but not limited to bias, prejudice, or harassment based upon race, sex, gender, religion, national origin, ethnicity, disability, age, sexual orientation, marital status, socioeconomic status, or political affiliation, and shall not permit court staff, court officials, or others subject to the judge's direction and control to do so. (p. 18)

Despite this, previous research has found judges are often unable to avoid engaging in their homophobic biases—as evidenced by homophobic language used by judges in courts (Brower, 2001; Shortnacy, 2001) or allowing attorneys to exhibit discriminatory animus and bias in influencing jurors (Brower, 2001; Brown, 2000; Clemens, 2005). Perhaps these behaviors are why 50 percent of lesbian and gay participants in an aforementioned study in California believed the courts did not provide fair and unbiased treatment (Shortnacy, 20010). LGBTQ youth themselves have expressed their perceptions that judges are not fair, or even biased against LGBTQ people. For instance, one LGBTQ youth said: "The judges aren't welcoming if they know you're gay. No one seemed interested in working with me" (Laver & Khoury, 2008, p. 23).

Given the research that demonstrates that human beings all develop implicit biases, or the attitudes, beliefs, and assumptions about groups and individuals that are unknown or unconscious, typically learned through socialization (Jost et al., 2009), it would be illogical to believe that judges would somehow be immune from bias. In fact, multiple studies have supported that judges and other court personnel have a number of biases that can influence their various decisions (Brower, 2001; 2006). In analyzing court decisions, scholars have found judges who are more likely to rule in favor of gay rights include: (a) judges appointed by Democrats, (b) Black judges, and (c) Jewish judges (Pinello, 2003). Some scholars have cited that judges are often motivated by anti-LGBTQ prejudice and seek to punish people who clash with their own morals (Ritenhouse, 2001). Other scholars argued how judicial biases could be assessed by looking at judges' past rulings, as well as their behavior beyond the courtroom including presentations made to civic, bar, press, community, and religious organizations (Stern, Oehme, & Stern, 2016).

In the juvenile judicial system, judges make custody decisions for children across many cases—determining whether minors will be placed with relatives, or in foster care, group homes, or detention facilities. Previous scholars describe how custody decisions for minors have detrimental effects for queer and trans youth who are often placed in unsafe homes or facilities (Laver & Khoury, 2008; Marskamer, 2008; Valentine, 2010). For example, in *R.G. v. Koller* (2006), a juvenile detention center in Hawai'i was found to violate the constitutional rights of LGBTQ youth who endured verbal, physical, and sexual abuse, and were often put into solitary confinement—allegedly for their own safety. Further, judges' biases can also lead to inappropriate custody decisions for LGBTQ offenders. As an example, a court employee described an instance in which a transgender client who committed no sexual offenses (and displayed no signs of physical or sexual aggression) was sent by a judge to a "center where we send deviant youth who are likely to commit sexual offenses against children" (Majd et al., 2009, p. 63). Some judges have reportedly even hospitalized LGBTQ youth in an attempt to stop their same-sex attractions; for example, a probation officer recalled a judge placed a lesbian youth in a private hospital for 14 days, so she could be "treated and diagnosed for this behavior" (Majd et al., 2009, p. 64).

In parental custody battles, judges often rule for children to be placed with their heterosexual parents or family members, rather than with an LGBTQ parent or relative. In fact, in the past, several states had adopted and enforced the "per se rule" in which a judge deemed an LGBTQ parent to be viewed as "unfit"—preventing an LGBTQ parent from being awarded custody of their children and sometimes from having contact with their children (Cohen, 2017).

Some states have made efforts to avoid anti-LGBTQ judicial bias, adding clauses to their ethical codes. For instance, the California Supreme Court (2018) added an amendment to their judicial codes, stating: "A judge shall not hold membership in any organization that practices invidious discrimination on the basis of race, sex, gender, gender identity, gender expression, religion, national origin, ethnicity, or sexual orientation" (p. 12). The clause is informally known as the "Boy Scout exception"—in response to the previous cases involving the Boy Scouts of America, Inc., an organization which has historically banned LGBTQ people who are open about their sexuality from joining their membership. Some legal scholars have argued the exception is a violation of their First Amendment rights; however, others argue judges who maintain membership in biased organizations demonstrate bias against certain groups (Mondel, 2016).

Perhaps there would be less judicial bias if there were more LGBTQ-identified judges, as judges from diverse backgrounds are more likely to represent the best interests of their constituents (Pinello, 2003). Thus, it may be important to know the number of federal judges who identify as LGBTQ. Twenty years ago, Rubenstein (1998) estimated only one in every 1,000 state court judges identified as gay and identified that there was only one Article III judge in the entire US who identified as openly gay—Justice Deborah Batts, who was appointed by President Bill Clinton. For 25 years, Justice Batts remained the only openly gay federal judge in the US; she retired in 2012. Prior to 2009, it was reported there were fewer than 100 openly gay judges (out of roughly 30,000 local, state, and federal judges in the US, or 0.003 percent) who mostly held local-level judicial appointments in New York, California, and Chicago (Fradella, Owen, & Burke, 2009). When President Obama was inaugurated in 2009, he appointed 10 openly gay federal court judges—multiplying the number of federal judges tenfold (Tobias, 2018). While it is not guaranteed that LGBTQ judges will always rule in favor of LGBTQ cases, the lack of LGBTQ judges does suggest the many systemic or institutional barriers for LGBTQ people to become judges (especially federal judges). And if those systemic issues exist in the appointment of judges, it is possible that those biases would seep into every aspect of the law.

Attorney Bias

While attorneys are typically assumed to be individuals who fight for their clients' rights and abide by their clients' wishes, many attorneys (especially state or state-appointed attorneys) may hold an array of biases which may interfere with their ability to advocate for their clients' best interests (Valentine, 2010). These biases can include (a) presuming LGBTQ people have mental health disorders; (b) LGBTQ people deserve punishment; or (c) anti-LGBTQ discrimination or anti-LGBTQ violence does not really exist.

LGBTQ people have described multiple ways in which they have perceived their attorneys to be biased. Some have described how attorneys may victim blame LGTBQ survivors of violence. For example, one court user noted how attorneys, witness, and court audience implied a gay man "asked for it" by being out (Brower, 2001, p. 618). Previous authors have described how prosecutors often disclose defendants' sexual orientation during trials and sentencing, when it is not relevant to the case, and how prosecutors use disrespectful or biased language as a tactical way of influencing jurors who may also have homophobic views (Brown, 2000; Brower, 2001). For instance, one LGBTQ court user said: "[A lawyer] questioned potential jurors about whether they would accept unbiased testimony from gay witnesses. The manner of question implied gays were unreliable witnesses, thus placing a bias in the minds of potential jurors" (Brower, 2001, p. 621). One transgender participant said a prosecutor intentionally used the wrong honorific (i.e., "Mr." instead of "Ms.") as a way to prey on jury bias (Fiani et al., 2017). Similarly, an LGBTQ court user said: "Defendant's lawyer . . . used my relationship and my partner a subject of focus to denigrate my loss and income claim and create smoke and mirrors. That would not have been used in a nongay situation" (Brower, 2001, p. 608). In this section, I will describe three aspects of attorney bias: (a) Overt Attorney Bias, (b) Covert Attorney Bias, and (c) Attorney Bias and Sentencing.

Overt Attorney Bias

Sometimes attorney bias is so overt that it dominates their legal strategies—particularly against LGBTQ defendants. In one case in which a lesbian teen assaulted her homophobic family members, one judge described how "the whole case was about sensationalizing lesbians . . . and that the [the prosecuting attorney] played it like she was a deranged lesbian lunatic" (Majd et al., 2009, p. 52). Sometimes attorney anti-LGBTQ biases are so engrained that many attorneys do not advocate for their clients or recognize how anti-LGBTQ bias may affect their cases. As an example, in a Florida case, after a man was sentenced to death, it was discovered that his trial attorney failed to block a juror who said: "If I felt the person was a homosexual, I personally believe that person is morally depraved enough that he might lie, might steal, might kill" (Saunders, 2018). The Florida Supreme Court ordered a new sentencing hearing.

A specific case of using lesbians' sexual orientation as a way of influencing biased jurors is the case of Elizabeth Ramirez, Kristie Mayhugh, Cassandra Rivera, and Anna Vasquez, later informally known as "The San Antonio Four." In 1994, the four women were convicted of gang-raping Ramirez's 7- and 9-year-old nieces. The girls alleged how, while on vacation at Ramirez's home for a week, the four women (all in their 20s) pinned them down and sexually assaulted them on two occasions. However, the girls' accounts varied from their initial police reports to their testimonies on the stand. Inconsistent details included how many women were present; if other children were in the home; who was holding the gun to their heads; and more. A medical examiner testified how both girls had vaginal injuries which could only come from "painful trauma" from a foreign object. All four women maintained their innocence—refusing plea bargains, testifying in court, and sharing corroborating accounts of the week in question. In spite of these reasonable doubts, all four women were found guilty; Ramirez was sentenced to 37.5 years in prison, while the remaining women were sentenced to 25 years. Three of the women had young children who were removed from their mothers immediately and raised by other family members.

One of the major factors in the case was how the women's sexuality became a factor in court. At the time of questioning, police officers asked many irrelevant questions involving the women's sexuality. Prosecuting attorneys also asked many questions that alluded to the women being hypersexual and promiscuous. For example, from Ramirez's trial, an exchange included:

Attorney: Did you have a gay relationship with Anna?

Ramirez: No.

Attorney: Did you have a gay relationship with Cassie?

Ramirez: No.

Attorney: Well, you were gay, and they were gay—

Ramirez: That doesn't mean you have to be together. (Chammah, 2014, p. 18)

Further, the medical examiner wrote in her notes, "This could be satanic"—a sentiment that was not supported by any physical evidence, but rather on her stereotypes or biases of lesbians as witches or demonic. One of the jury members was a minister who said that he believed homosexuality was a sin; however, he asserted it would not affect his judgment. At the trial's conclusion, he stated he believed the women should have gotten life in prison (Chammah, 2014).

In 2012, the younger of the girls recanted her testimony, saying that she was coached by her father and grandmother to say the women had raped her. Her father's motive appeared to be to gain full custody of the girls (as their mother is the sister of Ms. Ramirez), as well as to retaliate against Ms. Ramirez who had rejected his romantic advances and subsequently came out as a lesbian. Later, the medical examiner also recanted her testimony, saying that she would not have come to the same conclusions if she used new and updated scientific standards that were available nearly twenty years later. In 2016, the women were fully exonerated of their crimes and their records were expunged in 2018. Each woman was then eligible to collect $80,000 in restitution for every year they were wrongfully imprisoned (Fitzsimmons, 2018).

Another example of overt attorney bias is the use of gay and trans panic defenses in the courts. Gay panic, also sometimes referred to legally as the Nonviolent Homosexual Advance Defense, is the defense used in criminal court cases in which a plaintiff claims they only committed the violent crime because the gay or bisexual person was sexually assaulting or harassing them in some way (Tomei & Cramer, 2016). Similar to gay panic, trans panic is the defense used when a defendant claims their crime was influenced by learning of the gender identity of a transgender person, most commonly a transgender woman (Lee & Kwan, 2014; Steinberg, 2005). In these cases, defendants attempt to convince jurors their motives were clouded by bad judgement and they were victimized in some way by their gay or trans targets. For example, in *Michigan v. Schmitz* (1998), often colloquially known as the "Jenny Jones Murder." In 1995, Scott Amedure was a guest on *The Jenny Jones Show* (a popular 1990s television talk show) and disclosed to his best friend Jonathan Schmitz how he had a crush on him. Three days later, Schmitz killed Amedure, telling police he was distressed from the show. Schmitz was sentenced to prison for 25 to 50 years; he was released in 2017 (Swanson, 2017).

Covert Attorney Bias

Sometimes, attorney bias is less malicious and results from a lack of knowledge or exposure to LGBTQ issues. For example, one youth offender divulged: "When [my attorney] saw the letter from my doctor about being transgender, [he] panicked, and the probation officer didn't understand. The probation officer didn't even know what it was to be transgender!" (Majd et al., 2009, p. 46). Sometimes, attorneys (especially state-appointed attorneys) are apathetic or unaware of issues affecting LGBTQ youth, which then impacts their ability to advocate for their clients. One youth offender revealed: "Defenders are ignorant. Because you are

LGBT, they don't work as hard because they don't know what to do. They don't try to defend you as much" (Majd et al., 2009, p. 129). Regardless of the reason, when defense attorneys do not advocate for their clients or abide by their wishes, they are violating their ethical codes as attorneys.

Under the umbrella of attorney bias are instances in which public defenders may not advocate for LGBTQ clients effectively (and other inmates in general), especially when they are overworked and under-resourced. For instance, one Latina trans woman shared:

> They just want you out in and out; very, very, very rarely do you find someone who is genuinely passionate to help you and really hear your story and want to argue and get you out genuinely. But at the end of the day, you know, they're public defenders or you know, appointed attorneys. Usually they just don't want to deal with this type of work, it's like, oh it's either easy for them or it's not a priority or important. So, it's like, you know, you are not important. (Dank et al., 2015, p. 50)

A specific example that demonstrates covert bias is the case of Ky Peterson, a Black 20-year-old trans man in Georgia who was serving time for killing a man who raped him. Living in a trailer and not having financial resources for his own attorney, Mr. Peterson was appointed a public defender, David Grindle, whom Mr. Peterson did not meet for a whole year, while he was detained in county jail—demonstrating how little time his attorney would have for his case. When Mr. Grindle finally met his client for the first time, he said that he may have believed Mr. Peterson's story, but he felt it would be hard to convince the jury and win the case due to Mr. Peterson's multiple marginalized identities, so he suggested Mr. Peterson agree to a plea. Meanwhile, Mr. Peterson asserts that Mr. Grindle did not advocate hard enough for him, later saying, "I really don't like how [my attorney] defended me, because I feel like he could have done more. He could have at least come more [often] and tried to talk to me. I feel like he really didn't do a good job at representing me" (Brydum & Kellaway, 2015). While it is typical that public defenders are overworked and inundated with excessive caseloads (Benner, 2011), it would be even harder to advocate for LGBTQ clients, especially trans people of color, when they have very little drive, energy, or resources to do so—setting up the criminal justice system to fail.

Attorney Bias and Sentencing

Attorney bias can also affect sentencing and custody for LGBTQ offenders—with some punishments not reflecting the actual crimes. As an example, a gay male young person said that a prosecutor in his case argued in court that he should be placed in a more restrictive setting for high-risk youth "so [he] won't become a pedophile" (Majd et al., 2009, p.

63). A young gay Black male described: "My lawyer doesn't know me, but he knows I'm gay. He knows I want to leave this place, but he told the court: 'Don't let him leave there.' I don't think that's fair" (Majd et al., 2009, p. 120). Some attorneys appear to be aware of the ways their colleagues' anti-LGBTQ biases affect sentencing for LGBTQ people. As an example, in response to two minors engaging in oral sex in a school, one attorney shared: "The prosecutor wouldn't give the kid a deal because it was a 'gay' crime in a school . . . I think [heterosexual youth] would have gotten a better deal" (Majd et al., 2009, p. 63).

In another case, a 15-year-old transgender girl was sentenced to a high-security juvenile detention center, where she experienced sexual and physical violence (Marksamer, 2008). When she asked her state-appointed attorney to remove her from the facility, the attorney refused to advocate for her. In court, he told a judge: "I think this young man has a lot of things—and I use the word *man*—to think about, so I would just ask the court to be cautious in any decision that it makes" (Marksamer, 2008, p. 77). While this example clearly demonstrates how an attorney's transphobic biases resulted in a transgender client's continued exposure to violence, it is also a demonstration of how juvenile defense attorneys often make decisions on behalf of minors based on their presumption of the minor's "best interests."

A final example of attorney bias that can influence both verdicts and sentencing can be found in the case of Michael Johnson—the aforementioned gay Black man who was criminalized for his HIV status in Missouri. It was noted that Timothy Lohmar, the prosecuting attorney whose office had tried Johnson, asked the jury for a life sentence—which would surpass the maximum sentence for the felony of HIV transmission and was often reserved for murder charges (Thrasher, 2019). While Mr. Lohmar vehemently denied that any racial or homophobic bias influenced his approach to the case (Thrasher, 2014), it is likely that his implicit bias influenced his passion or motivation for criminalizing Mr. Johnson.

Jury Bias

While there has been a growing amount of literature on jury bias and race (see Hunt, 2015), there has been a limited amount of research that has examined jury bias and LGBTQ communities. In general, studies support that politically conservative jurors are more likely to hold anti-LGBTQ beliefs (Salerno et al., 2015), which may then influence their decisions in hate crime penalty enhancement laws (Cramer et al., 2017), as well as sentences involving execution (Clemens, 2005). In response to new federal laws on hate crimes, some scholars have examined individuals' beliefs about hate-crime legislation, offenders, and victims. One study found liberal people were more likely to be in favor of hate crime legislation and that conservative people were more likely to victim blame

LGBTQ survivors of hate crimes (Cabeldue, Cramer, Kehn, Crosby, & Anastasi, 2018). Qualitative data suggests court users themselves are able to identify bias in juries, with one court user proclaiming: "Jury member suggested that witness was gay and therefore his testimony could not be trusted" (Brower, 2007, p. 237).

Studies with mock jurors provide some insight for understanding anti-LGBTQ jury bias. For instance, in one study, a researcher investigated surveys from over 7,800 mock jurors from 2002 to 2008, revealing:

- Approximately 45 percent of people think that homosexuality is not an acceptable lifestyle.
- Approximately 40 percent of people believe that gays and lesbians could change their sexual orientation and become heterosexuals if they really wanted to.
- Approximately 33 percent of people think that sexual orientation should not be a civil right that is protected by the government. (Overland, 2009, p. 2)

One of the ways in which juror bias may influence verdicts and sentencing is through the aforementioned gay or trans panic defenses. While the defense was first used in 1965 (and was then unsuccessful), scholars estimate that, prior to 2013, it had been used anywhere from 45 to 189 times in court and it has only lessened sentences a small percentage of the time (Tomei & Cramer, 2016). Experimental studies report conservative jurors are more likely than liberal jurors to empathize more with defendants who utilized gay panic defenses (Salerno et al., 2015). Because the defense is believed to not bear any merit (and is merely used as a legal strategy that relies solely on jurors' anti-LGBTQ bias), many states have passed legislative bans that prevent the defense from being used in court.

Anti-LGBTQ Bias in Sentencing

Depending on the courts and the jurisdiction, sentencing is determined by either judges or juries. While there is a dearth of literature on actual sentencing disparities for LGBTQ offenders, there are some studies that offer some preliminary insight. Meyer and colleagues (2017) revealed some disparities between LGBTQ prisoners and cisgender heterosexual prisoners: (a) self-identified lesbian and bisexual women were significantly more likely to have longer sentences than heterosexual women; (b) self-identified gay and bisexual men were more likely than were heterosexual men to have sentences longer than 10 years in prison; and (c) self-identified lesbian and bisexual women were more likely to have a sentence of longer than 20 years in prison. These findings align with what many LGBTQ court users and court employees already believe to be true. For instance, one participant shared: "[Courts] don't take crimes against homosexuals/lesbian people as seriously. It appears that the perpetrators of crimes against gays are given lighter sentences."' (Brower, 2007, p. 174). A clinical social worker revealed "sentencing patterns are clearly stricter [gay offenders] than [for] heterosexual sex offenders" (Brower, 2007, p. 174). While more studies are needed to further support these perceptions, Meyers and colleagues demonstrate some initial support.

Sometimes, blatant heterosexist laws negatively affect sentencing for LGBTQ people. For instance, in most states, when an adult who is under 19 years old commits statutory rape with a child who is no younger than three or four years, they are likely to receive shorter prison terms and more lenient sex offender registration requirements than if general rape statutes apply. However, these exceptions (often referred to as "Romeo and Juliet" laws) are limited to cases if the parties involved were of the opposite sex, resulting in unfair sentencing for parties involved in same-sex cases (Higdon, 2009). One case demonstrating this injustice occurred in Kansas in 2000 when a young man named Matthew Limon who, just a week after his eighteenth birthday, engaged in voluntary oral sex with a fourteen-year-old boy, in a mental health facility where both were residents. Because the "Romeo and Juliet" exception did not apply to him, he was sentenced to 17 years in prison and mandated to register as a sex offender. He served five years in prison before an appeals court reversed the decision—citing the exception violated the Equal Protection Clause of the U.S. Constitution and discriminated on the basis of sexual orientation (Higdon, 2009).

Regarding the death penalty, previous scholars have described how prosecutors often introduce a criminal defendant's sexual orientation in calculated and prejudicial ways, while presenting arguments that blatantly stereotype and degrade LGBTQ people (Brown, 2000; Shortnacy, 2001). For example, prosecutors are likely to portray lesbians and gender nonconforming women as "masculine" as a way of influencing juries to consider the death penalty (Streib, 1995). Further, prosecutors have often introduced lesbian defendants' sexual orientation identities as a way of dehumanizing them and illustrating "the defendant as an animal and the crimes as monstrous" (Streib, 1995, p. 111). In doing so, jurors would be more likely to consider the death penalty for the female offender—an occurrence that is far less frequent for women. Shortnacy (2001) argued that sexual orientation should not be used as a factor in considering the death penalty, in the same ways that race, religion, and other identity groups should not be used as a factor in death penalty sentences either.

One real-life example of how jury bias may influence sentencing of LGBTQ offenders includes the case of Charles Rhines. In 1993, Rhines was found guilty for the brutal murder of 22-year-old Donnivan Schaeffer; the jury in South Dakota sentenced him to death. In 2015, Rhines was assigned new public attorneys who investigated whether jury bias influenced the sentence. In conducting interviews with jurors producing affidavits, jurors recollect that during deliberations there was "disgust" over

Rhines being gay and because he was gay that "he shouldn't be able to spend his life with men in prison" (De Vogue, 2019). However, in April 2019, SCOTUS denied hearing the plaintiff's case, upholding his death penalty.

Another example of how negligence in the court system negatively influenced sentencing is in the aforementioned case of Ky Peterson, the Black trans man who killed his rapist. It appeared that a mere typo may have resulted in a longer sentence for Mr. Peterson. While he signed a plea deal for voluntary manslaughter, which would result in a maximum 10-year sentence in the state of Georgia, his plea was listed as involuntary manslaughter, which instead resulted in a 20-year sentence. The error was likely a typo recorded by a clerk, but it was not reviewed and corrected by either the attorney or the judge before it was signed (Brydum, 2015). This oversight added another 10 years to a young man's sentence; it is also a clear example about how easy it is to be negligent in the system and how people can be unfairly treated.

Microaggressions and the Courts

Within the criminal justice system, there are many types of microaggressions, or subtle, often well-intentioned forms of discrimination, faced by LGBTQ people (Nadal, 2013). Within courtrooms, microaggressions appear to be quite common and innocuous; people may not necessarily express heterosexist or transphobic bias overtly, but instead through their behaviors and subtle comments. For example, one gay young person said: "The judges aren't welcoming if they know you're gay. No one seemed interested in working with me" (Laver & Khoury, 2008, p. 23). Microaggressions result in LGBTQ court users feeling uncomfortable, demoralized, or distressed, perhaps influencing their abilities to believe the justice system is fair and impartial.

Homophobic and Transphobic Language

There are many microaggressions involving homophobic or transphobic language; sometimes, the language is intentionally malicious, while other times, the biased language is so engrained in a person's vernacular. One gay court employee noted, "I've heard derisive references such as 'faggot' from judges, co-workers, and bailiffs" (Brower, 2007, p. 616). In 1991, U.S. District Court Judge Oliver Gasch repeatedly referred to the plaintiff and gay men in general as "homos" (Shortnacy, 2000, p. 318).

For transgender court users, the misuse of gender pronouns is a common type of microaggressions. James and colleagues (2016) found 23 percent of their TGNC sample who had interacted with judges or the court were referred to by the wrong gender pronouns or title (e.g., Mr. or

Ms.) during their interactions. When incorrect pronouns are used, intentionally or unintentionally, they create an environment where a transgender court user may already feel a lack of affirmation for their gender identity.

Disapproval or Discomfort of LGBTQ People

One type of microaggression includes instances in which heterosexual or cisgender people make snide remarks or engage in subtle or obvious body language that conveys disapproval, disgust, or dehumanization of LGBTQ people (Nadal, 2013). For instance, one LGBTQ court user shared: "One defendant was a gay man suing an ex-lover [and you could hear] snickers and comments from jury members" (Brower, 2001, p. 237). One lesbian youth revealed: "Even my [defense attorney] would look at me funny. He wouldn't say anything, but he'd look at me like, 'That's a girl?' He probably thought I didn't notice but I did" (Majd et al., 2016, p. 129). A gay young man reported a judge in open court implied the youth's identity was just "a fad" by saying, "*So you're gay* now?" (Laver & Khoury, 2008, p. 20).

LGBTQ people have described experiencing dehumanization or humiliation in court, due to heterosexism or transphobia. One gay multiracial male discussed a situation where his sexual orientation was made public:

> When I was being arraigned, they were like, "[Name of defendant] had an altercation inside the hotel with his lover" and they say his name and everyone started laughing—the whole courtroom the judge, the bailiff, everybody. They all started laughing. I was so mad. I could only see the people in front of me, so that means that the prosecutors were laughing, the judge was laughing, the bailiff was laughing, the two cops over here were laughing. Everyone was laughing . . . I was embarrassed. I just stood there. They finished laughing and they kept going, and then you know my bail was out and I bounced. (Dank et al., 2015, p. 51)

A Black transgender woman described a time in which she felt unfairly treated by a judge:

> I had a judge that was so disrespectful to me. I mean, I got locked up on a prostitution charge and when I went to her courtroom, I had on heels—some red bottoms and everything you know. I'm so tired, and my make-up was coming off, and she told me, I was doing disorderly conduct. She said, "I don't want her in my courtroom. Bring her to the other one," and everybody in the courtroom started laughing, like it was a joke. So, the officer had to take me and put me in the other courtroom. (Dank et al., 2015, p. 51)

Assumption of Pathology or Criminology

Some microaggressions involve the assumption of stereotypes of sexual pathologies or criminal behavior. In general, LGBTQ people face this when people presume them to be sexually violent or assaultive, hypersexual, immoral, or mentally ill (Nadal, 2013). For LGBTQ people in the criminal justice system, these microaggressions can occur from judges, correctional officers, or anyone within the system. As an example, in a 1997 sentencing, a judge told a lesbian defendant, "I'll tell you ma'am. This is a sick situation. I've seen a lot of sick situations since I've been in this court. I've been in this profession for 27 years and this ranks at the top" (Shortnacy, 2001, p. 318). In one case, *Gay Student Services v. Texas A&M University* (1984), in which an LGBTQ student organization sued for their right to be officially recognized by their university, an expert witness testified that "sexual activity would certainly take place at, or shortly after, group meetings" (Brower, 2007, p. 587). One multiracial young gay male shared even though there was no evidence of any wrongdoing and that his alleged victim did not show up to testify in court, the prosecuting attorney declared in court: "He's a menace to society. He needs to be behind bars" (Dank et al., 2015, p. 50).

An LGBTQ court employee recalled: "When helping lesbians or gays, some of the clerks handle their paperwork touching only the tips or edges of the paper. One stated, 'You never know what they did or touched.'" (Brower, 2007, p. 616). Meanwhile, another gay court user stated: "I was discredited as a witness because they said I was probably 'out at a club or something' before I witnessed the accident" (Brower, 2001, p. 237).

Endorsement of Heteronormativity

Some microaggressions involve messages that heterosexuality and cisgenderism are viewed as normal, while LGBTQ identities are viewed abnormal, wrong, or unnatural (Nadal, 2013). One court employee described how he felt pressured to be closeted, due to the heteronormativity that was presumed in the court culture.

> I have to lead two different lives. Sometimes my co-workers ask me if I have a girlfriend, if I am married, how many children I have, and I have to answer with a lie. All this makes me feel very unhappy. In addition, sometimes the people that I work with make fun of gay people in front of me, and I have to laugh about it and pretend that it does not bother me. (Brower, 2001, pp. 193–194)

One LGBTQ court user described the need to hide their sexual identity as a way to protect themselves: "I felt intimidated—didn't want them [two clerks and a police officer] to talk about me the way they were talking about other gays—kept my mouth shut" (Brower, 2007, p. 610).

Systemic Microaggressions

A final type of microaggression involved behavioral interactions that conveyed bias in policies. As an example, for many transgender people who are not able to change their gender markers on their legal identification cards or other legal documents, microaggressions are likely to occur. One transgender participant recalled: "I recently had to renew my Medicaid . . . I changed my name on the forms, and they called me out and said, 'This isn't you because your social security says something different.'" (Fiani et al., 2017, p. 10). Similarly, another transgender individual disclosed: "I'll show my license to the security guards often times, not always but often um I present more masculine these days depending on the day. Um I'll get like a double take or like a raised eyebrow or is this fake? *What are you?*" (Fiani et al., 2017, p. 9).

QUEERING COURT SYSTEMS

In order to queer the courts, we must identify and amend any laws or policies that then affect how LGBTQ people engage in the criminal justice system. For example, laws criminalizing sex work or HIV/AIDS unnecessarily increase the number of LGBTQ people in the court systems. Within the courts themselves, policies must be examined for the ways they encourage both explicit and implicit bias against LGBTQ people and other historically marginalized groups. Some ways to disrupt these inequities are to mandate conversations about implicit bias at the beginning of every trial, in which judges, juries, attorneys, and other court employees identify how their own experiences influence their positions and approaches to the case; they can also undergo annual mandated LGBTQ microaggression training, so they are vigilant in creating a safe and inclusive environment for their constituents. Scholars have argued that prosecutors who introduce unrelated or prejudicial evidence, such as an LGBTQ offender's sexual orientation, should be considered a reversible error and result in a mistrial (Shortnacy, 2001). Others argue how defenses like gay or trans panic defenses should not be admissible in courts, as they play on jurors' biases (Lee & Kwan, 2014; Tomei & Cramer, 2016). Perhaps jurors must undergo required implicit bias training as a way of being cognizant of how their personal beliefs and identities impact their views of the case. While these recommendations may seem excessive to some, as they challenge the status quo, such actions are necessary to ensure that impartiality is genuinely present for a speedy and fair trial.

One way that LGBTQ community members and allies can advocate for change in court systems is by becoming educated on various laws that are discriminatory toward LGBTQ people and potentially result in the unfair criminalization of LGBTQ people. In the case of Michael Brown, the thorough investigative reporting by Steven Thrasher is what led people from all over the US to become aware of HIV criminalization laws of Missouri and other states. In becoming familiar with such laws, community members can lobby their elected officials to pass more equitable laws, while educating others how to navigate discriminatory legislation.

Another way to advocate for change is to become aware of wrongful convictions of LGBTQ people (and people of other historically marginalized groups). Similar to the release of CeCe McDonald, the exoneration of the "San Antonio Four" would not be possible without the creation of a documentary that told the story from their perspectives; *Southwest of Salem: The Story of the San Antonio Four* was released in 2016 and described how the conviction of the four women was reminiscent of the Salem witch trials. When community members are aware of unfair trials and convictions, they can then pressure district attorneys and courts to revisit certain cases, which may lead to more justice. Perhaps community members can work directly with organizations like the Innocence Project—a nonprofit organization which has successfully assisted in overturning many wrongful convictions—particularly through the use of DNA testing and more advanced ways of analyzing evidence (West & Meterko, 2015). Knowing that there has been some success in overturning cases can encourage community members to know that change is possible, even when it seems like it might be too late.

FIVE
Locked Up in a Binary

LGBTQ People and Incarceration

THE CASE OF LINDSAY SAUNDERS-VELEZ

Lindsay Saunders-Velez is a 20-year-old transgender woman of color in Colorado who began experiencing sexual abuse when she was 8 years old—shortly after she first announced her gender identity as a girl. She first entered the juvenile justice system, as a result of fighting back against her abusers, resulting in being placed in foster care for years. At 15 years old, she began hormone therapy and was living in all aspects of her life as a young woman (Mitchell, 2018).

In 2014, Ms. Saunders-Velez was placed in the Colorado Division of Youth Services—a juvenile justice facility where she was housed with female residents and searched by female guards. However, when she was 18, she was sent to Arkansas Valley Correctional Facility and housed with the male inmates. On the first day she arrived, she was harassed and threatened to be raped. Prison guards misgendered her consistently; refused to call her by her name; and confiscated her feminine undergarments and makeup. In December 2017, she was brutally raped, yet she was not removed from the facility. To avoid being sexually assaulted further, she swallowed razor blades, leaving her hospitalized and temporarily safe from her assailants.

In April 2018, prison guards accused Ms. Saunders-Velez of kissing a male inmate, and her punishment was to spend 30 days in a disciplinary pod. She pled to Chief U.S. District Judge Marcia Krieger to stop this transfer, because four inmates who resided in the pod had previously harassed her and threatened rape. Hours after the judge denied Saunders-Velez's request, an inmate entered her cell and demanded sex.

When she declined, he slammed her head against a metal bunk bed and brutally raped her. She was hospitalized for her injuries, which included rectal tears, and she was transferred to the prison infirmary a day later (Mitchell, 2018). When Justice Krieger learned that she was raped (now a second time), she still refused to place Saunders-Velez into a female prison, and instead offered her choices of other male prisons (including prisons where she had previously experienced abuse and violence).

On May 7, 2018, Colorado representatives passed a resolution in which they requested the Colorado Department of Corrections (CDOC) to create, revise, and continually review a policy to protect transgender inmates; affirm inmates' gender identities; and ensure policies abided by the Prison Rape Elimination Act of 2003 (HR18-1007, 2018). Citing Ms. Saunders-Velez in the document, the resolution was sent to the Colorado governor and the House and Senate Fiduciary Committees. Two months later, Saunders-Velez filed a lawsuit against the Colorado Department of Corrections for (a) allowing sexual violence, assault, and harassment; (b) correctional officers refusing to acknowledge her gender identity, name, or pronouns; and (c) creating a discriminatory and dangerous environment for her. A year later, in July 2019, the two parties reached a $170,000 settlement, with $10,000 set aside specifically for medical expenses.

Sadly, the story of Ms. Saunders-Velez is not unique. Transgender women have reported undergoing sexual violence in prison facilities for years—with over one-third of transgender women being sexually assaulted while incarcerated (Beck, 2015a). Transgender women of color are especially susceptible to sexual violence in prison, with some studies reporting that Black, Native American, and Latina trans women being sexually assaulted significantly more than White trans women (Reisner et al., 2014). Because transgender women who are housed with male inmates are especially prone to sexual victimization, there have been many steps taken across various states to ensure that transgender women are placed in facilities that match their gender identity and not their sex assigned at birth (Routh et al., 2017). Unfortunately, in many states, that decision is left to the discretion of a warden, a facility, or a judge—resulting in recurring violence and lack of protections for these transwomen.

At the same time, the story of Ms. Saunders-Velez is indeed unique. While so many transgender women of color experience violence, few are able to speak their truth in court. Even fewer are able to win court cases or reach large financial settlements. Trans people, especially trans people of color, should not have to experience such blatant and heinous physical and sexual violence in order for political leaders and others to value their humanity. Instead, people in power can demonstrate they value trans lives, by making policy changes to the systems which continue to promote or normalize violence against trans people.

INTRODUCTION

Prior to the 1990s, studies involving sexuality among LGBTQ prisoners focused primarily on gay men—with hardly any literature examining lesbians, bisexuals, or transgender inmates. Aligning with the public opinion of the time, Eigenberg (1992) critiqued how the existing studies utilized four primary essentialist perspectives, which limited understandings of prison sexuality—particularly utilizing contemporary knowledge of gender and sexuality. First, sexuality was rigid and dichotomous: heterosexuality was deemed normal and acceptable, while homosexuality or bisexuality were abnormal or inappropriate. Second, when heterosexual men resorted to same-sex sex in prison, the main determinant was sexual deprivation and not actual sexual identity or sexual orientation. Third, all gay men were deemed to be weak and effeminate; and fourth, distinctions between rape and consensual same-sex sex were blurred.

In an attempt to look beyond these rigid views and binary perspectives, Alarid (2000) used a social constructivist approach with a sample of gay and bisexual offenders; results indicated that 83.7 percent of the total sample felt other inmates treated bisexual and gay men with more disrespect than heterosexual inmates, while 90.7 percent believed deputies and officers treated bisexual and gay men with more disrespect than heterosexuals. Furthermore, sexual orientation differences among the sample led to diverse experiences (e.g., gay men were more likely to be comfortable with their sexual identities than bisexuals; gay men were more likely to always engage in submissive roles in sex and bisexual men who had greater sexual attraction to women over men reported only taking the dominant role in sex). Only 7 percent of the sample reported having more sex in jail than outside of jail. Taken together, the study revealed how there is a spectrum of sexual orientations for people who are incarcerated, which then influence their sexual experiences both inside and outside of prison.

Perhaps the greatest shift in attention toward LGBTQ experiences in correctional facilities occurred when the Prison Rape Elimination Act (PREA) was passed by the U.S. Congress and signed by President George W. Bush in 2003. Though it was not fully enacted until 2012, the PREA forced governments and correctional facilities to become aware of the many atrocities that occurred toward all inmates—particularly LGBTQ inmates who were being sexually and physically abused by other inmates, by correctional officers, and by other staff members. Along with increasing awareness of sexual abuse, researchers began to uncover some of the other common, often horrific and violent, experiences of incarcerated LGBTQ people.

This chapter will focus on the ways that correctional systems are oppressive and violent toward LGBTQ people. When referencing corrections or incarceration, I am referring primarily to prisons, or long-term facilities run by the state or federal government, that typically house felons and inmates who are serving sentences over a year. However, I will also describe jails, which tend to be local city and county facilities, are short term, and house inmates who are awaiting trial, sentencing, or both. I will also highlight immigration detention centers, which house immigrants who await their asylum or deportation hearings.

The chapter will begin by reviewing the current demographics of the incarcerated LGBTQ population; I will then discuss types of violent and discriminatory practices within correctional facilities, including the ways that violence and bias manifests interpersonally and systemically. Throughout the chapter, I will describe the multiple ways incarceration negatively influences an array of mental health issues and quality of life for LGBTQ inmates.

INCARCERATED LGBTQ PEOPLE

Research on LGBTQ people in incarceration is limited, primarily because there are no mandated federal sanctions (and few state requirements) to collect data on sexual orientation and gender identity. However, there are a few major studies which have provided some insight to the experiences of LGBTQ prisoners. First, Black and Pink, a prison abolitionist organization that supports LGBTQ and HIV-positive prisoners, collected data from a national sample of 1,118 LGBTQ prisoners. Recruited from the free newsletter that has been distributed to LGBTQ-identified prisoners across the US since 2010, Lydon et al. (2015) found the following:

- Nearly a fifth of the sample were homeless or transient prior to incarceration.
- 58 percent of first arrests occurred when they were under the age of 18.
- Over a third were unemployed prior to their incarceration.
- 39 percent reported they had traded sex for survival in the past.
- 29 percent of respondents completed high school outside of prison.
- The average time spent in prison on their current sentence was 10 years.
- Nearly three-quarters were held in jail prior to their conviction. Of those held in pretrial detention, more than half were detained for a year or more.

While the study may not be generalizable to the entire LGBTQ incarcerated population, it highlights some of the common themes affecting LGBTQ prisoners—including some of the social determinants related to incarceration (i.e., being homeless, being unemployed, engaging in survival sex, not completing high school). Further, the study demonstrates some of the disparities affecting the population. For instance, the sentence time of their LGBTQ sample was 10 years—almost four times longer than the 2016 average rate of 2.6 years (Kaeble, 2018). Meanwhile, the unemployment rate of the sample was 33 percent, which is almost 7 times more than the national unemployment rate of 4.4 percent in 2016 (Brundage & Cunningham, 2017).

The National Inmate Survey of 2011–2012, which consisted of a sample size of about 80,000 prison and jail inmates, has been examined to reveal different common experiences for LGBTQ people in incarceration. First, Beck, Berzofsky, Caspar, and Krebs (2013) reported 7.9 percent of individuals in state and federal prisons identified as lesbian, gay, or bisexual, as did 7.1 percent of individuals in city and county jails. Examining gender differences, Meyer, Flores, Stemple, Romero, Wilson, and Herman (2017) found the breakdown of LGBTQ people in prison included: 9.3 percent of men in prison, 6.2 percent of men in jail, 42.1 percent of women in prison, and 35.7 percent of women in jail were queer or transgender. Incarcerated LGBQ men and women were more likely than were heterosexual men and women to be incarcerated for violent sexual and nonsexual crimes rather than crimes related to property, drugs, or parole violations (Meyer et al., 2017). Further, the incarceration rate of self-identified lesbian, gay, or bisexual persons was 1,882 per 100,000, more than 3 times that of the US adult population (Meyer et al., 2017).

Race and education may play a significant role in incarceration rates for LGBTQ people of color, with some studies finding Black men who have sex with men (MSM) are arrested more frequently than White MSM (Lim et al., 2011). Furthermore, a study with 1,553 Black MSM found 60 percent of the sample had been incarcerated at least once in their lifetimes (Brewer et al., 2014a), and that Black MSM with lower educational attainment and household income were significantly more likely to have been incarcerated (Brewer et al., 2014b).

Regarding transgender prisoners, data collection and analysis has been difficult, as jurisdictions are not mandated to collect data, do not collect data on gender identity, do not collect data on gender identity correctly, or are divergent where they house transgender prisoners (i.e., according to their gender identity, gender presentation, or their sex assigned at birth). According to the Bureau of Justice Statistics, there were at least 3,209 self-reported transgender inmates across various prisons and jails in 2012 (Beck, 2014). Yet, this is likely an underestimation, as the estimate is based on the number of individuals who self-reported as transgender or those who responded to the survey.

Despite this, there are some community studies that shed some light on the prevalence of incarceration for transgender people. First, in the National Transgender Discrimination Study (NTDS)—which surveyed 6,456 transgender and gender nonconforming participants in the US and three American territories (Grant et al., 2011)—it was reported 1 out of 6 transgender participants (or 16 percent of the sample) had been to jail or prison. Race influences those numbers, with nearly 1 out of 2 Black transgender participants (or 47 percent) and nearly 1 out of 3 Native American transgender participants (or 30 percent) in the sample having gone to jail or prison for any reason at any point in their lives. Further, 21 percent of transgender women participants reported having been sent to jail for any reason, in comparison to 10 percent of transgender male participants. In another study that analyzed the NTDS and examined 3,878 transgender women's experiences, researchers found Black and Native American trans women were more likely to have been incarcerated, and that those who had been incarcerated were likely to have more negative health issues, including being HIV-positive (Reisner et al., 2014)

In their sample of 515 transgender participants, Clements-Nolle, Marx, Guzman, and Katz (2001) found approximately 65 percent of transgender women and 30 percent of transgender men in the United States had ever experienced incarceration in their lifetimes. In the US Transgender Survey (USTS; 2015), which surveyed 27,715 transgender participants, James and colleagues reported about 2 percent of the sample had been held in jail, prison, or a juvenile center in the past year—a rate that is more than twice the national incarceration rate of 0.6 percent (Kaeble & Cowhig, 2018). Yet, we must acknowledge these studies recruited a general sample of transgender participants (and did not recruit transgender inmates specifically); thus, it is very telling that such a high prevalence of incarceration exists for a general sample of transgender people.

Sexton and colleagues' (2010) study of 332 transgender inmates in California may also provide some insight to transgender experiences in general. First, they found transgender inmates are more likely to be middle-aged (with 40 percent being aged 36–45), and that transgender inmates are more likely to be convicted of a property crime than cisgender inmates. Second, they found transgender inmates were more likely to be classified as a sex offender than cisgender inmates yet are less likely to be affiliated with a gang. Further, they are more likely to be classified as Level 3 or Level 4 inmates, which requires more security, more armed coverage, and less open spaces. Transgender inmates were more likely to be in mental health treatment or to be diagnosed with a mental health disorder than the cisgender inmates. Prior to incarceration, only 8 percent of the transgender inmates reported having a college degree, about 30 percent reported being unemployed, over 20 percent reported being homeless, and almost 60 percent reported having a drug or alcohol problem. Finally, anywhere from 60 to 80 percent of transgender inmates in California were living with HIV, which exceeds the average of 1.6 percent of the general prisoner population.

Regarding LGBTQ youth in the juvenile justice system, there are some studies that provide some insight. First, Hunt and Moodie-Mills (2012) estimate that there are approximately 300,000 LGBTQ youth who are arrested or detained annually—representing 13 to 15 percent of those in the juvenile justice system. Of these youth, it is estimated 60 percent are Black or Latinx, supporting a significant racial disparity and overrepresentation of LGBTQ youth of color in the system. Furthermore, in analyzing data from the 1990s, LGBTQ youth (both those who are self-identified and those who may engage in same-sex sexual or romantic behavior) are more likely than heterosexual youth to be stopped by police officers, expelled from their school, or arrested and convicted (Himmelstein & Brückner, 2011). LGBTQ youth were significantly more likely to report arrests and conviction as both juveniles and adults, while non-heterosexual male youth were at a higher risk than are heterosexual males for arrest, conviction, school expulsion, and police stops and harassment (Himmelstein & Bruckner, 2011).

Irvine (2010) surveyed 2,100 youth inmates across six different juvenile detention centers and found 15 percent of youth in detention facilities could be identified as LGBTQ. Irvine and Canfield (2016) surveyed 1,400 youth inmates at seven juvenile detention facilities across the country and found 20 percent of the inmates identified as LGBTQ. Regarding gender breakdown, the percentage was higher for girls—with 40 percent of girl inmates and 14 percent of boy inmates who identified as LGBTQ. Garnette, Irvine, Reyes, and Wilber (2011) reported 23 percent of incarcerated girls are lesbian, bisexual, or queer, a much higher rate than the 13 percent of incarcerated boys who are gay, bisexual, or queer. Such findings align with previous studies which indicate three-fifths of girls in juvenile detention facilities identify as lesbian, bisexual, or not completely straight (Wilson et al., 2017).

Irvine, Wilber, and Canfield (2017) surveyed juvenile detention facilities across California that revealed 19 percent of incarcerated youth identified as LGBTQ or gender non-conforming—with 51 percent of girls who identified as LGBTQ or gender non-conforming, and 12 percent of boys identifying as LGBTQ. Belknap, Holsinger, and Little (2012) examined experiences of 404 boys and girls in juvenile detention centers across the state of Ohio and found 13.4 percent of the juvenile population identified as LGBQ. Of these, 32.5 percent of girls of color identified as LGBQ—a proportion that was much higher than White girls (21 percent), White boys (6.3 percent), and boys of color (4.3 percent). If population experts estimate that 7 to 9 percent of the entire youth population is LGBTQ (Quintana, Rosenthal, & Krehely, 2010) or that 8 percent of girls and 3 percent of boys identify as LGBTQ (Chandra, Mother, Copen, & Sionean, 2011), these studies demonstrate a notable disproportionate amount of incarcerated LGBTQ youth in the juvenile justice system, particularly for girls.

Garnette and colleagues (2011) also argue that LGBTQ youth are disproportionately criminalized for non-violent crimes, in comparison to heterosexuals. For example, their findings indicate a number of disparities: (a) while 12 percent of heterosexual youth were detained for running away, 30 percent of LGBTQ youth were; (b) while 1 percent of heterosexual youth were detained for sex work, 9 percent of LGBTQ youth were; and (c) while 11 percent of heterosexual youth were detained for truancy, 19 percent of LGBTQ youth were detained. It is important to note that within LGBTQ communities, these non-violent crimes are often referred to as survival behaviors—or necessary actions people of marginalized groups must engage in in order to stay alive. For example, homeless LGBTQ youth often turn to survival sex as a means of gaining money, food, or shelter (Walls & Bell, 2011). Given that approximately 40 percent of LGBTQ youth is homeless (Quintana et al., 2010), LGBTQ youth are more likely to engage in these behaviors; by doing so, they are also more likely to come into contact with the justice system.

Race plays a significant factor in LGBTQ youth experiences with incarceration. Irvine (2010) reported the rates of LGBTQ youth were much higher in certain racial and ethnic groups, particularly among Asian Americans (12 percent), Native Americans (24 percent), and multiracial people (18 percent). Irvine and Canfield (2016) reported 85 percent of their sample of incarcerated LGBTQ youth identified as being people of color—with 37.9 percent who identified as Black, 32.6 percent who identified as Latinx, 13.1 percent who identified as White, 11.8 percent multiracial, 2.3 percent who identified as Native American, and 1.7 percent who identified as Asian American. Results indicate similar racial breakdowns for the heterosexual youth population (i.e., 85 percent of heterosexual youth are people of color), suggesting race is a predominant factor in youth incarceration, regardless of sexual orientation or gender identity. In Irvine and colleagues' (2017) study of California incarcerated youth, 90 percent reported being people of color, with 50.4 percent who identified as Latinx, 18.6 percent who identified as Black, 17.1 percent who identified as multiracial, 9.8 percent who identified as White, 1.8 percent who identified as Asian American, and 1.5 percent who identified as Native American. With a higher incarceration rate of Latinx youth, we must examine how geographic and population factors may influence racial disparities in the justice system.

Regarding other salient factors in the juvenile justice system, LGBTQ youth inmates are more likely than heterosexual, cisgender youth inmates to have come from foster care systems backgrounds, with 23 percent of LGBTQ youth having been previously placed in a group or foster home as compared to 3 percent of heterosexual, cisgender youth (Irvine & Canfield, 2016). In comparison to heterosexual, cisgender youth, LGBTQ youth in California were twice more likely to have a history of running away or being homeless, seven times more likely to be incarcerated for sex work, and four times more likely to have been placed in a group or foster home because someone was hurting them (Irvine et al.,

2017). Incarcerated LGBTQ youth in general are also susceptible to more severe punishments (i.e., longer prison and jail terms); sexual victimization; and solitary confinement than their heterosexual counterparts (Wilson et al., 2017). Thus, further research is crucial to understand LGBTQ juvenile offenders' lives.

A final population to consider are LGBTQ people who are housed in immigration detention centers. These individuals are either migrants who recently arrived in the US and are seeking asylum, or individuals who have been living in the US and were apprehended by Immigration Customs Enforcement. Some of these individuals have not committed any crimes at all. They arrived in the US and have been placed in these detention centers as they await trials to determine whether they qualify for asylum. The other individuals are undocumented individuals who were living in the US without legal documents (e.g., green cards or with current visas). Many of these undocumented immigrants were apprehended after committing misdemeanor crimes; others were targeted by Immigration and Customs Enforcement (ICE) through raids and other forced arrests. While there is limited empirical data on this population, we will consider their experiences in the following sections.

VIOLENT AND DISCRIMINATORY PRACTICES IN CORRECTIONS

There are many ways that correctional facilities have maintained violent and discriminatory environments for incarcerated people, particularly those who identify as LGBTQ. In this section, I review six main areas of literature: (a) oppressive systems of gender binaries; (b) sexual victimization; (c) physical and emotional abuse; (d) solitary confinement and other biased punishments; (e) microaggressions; and (f) psychological consequences of incarceration.

Oppressive Systems of Gender Binaries

Perhaps one of the major biases of the correctional system is the dichotomous categorization of prison inmates as either "male" or "female"—based solely on sex assigned at birth or on genitalia—which subsequently results in numerous difficulties for people who identify as transgender, gender-nonconforming, intersex, or as anything else beyond the gender binary (Peek, 2003). This rigid gender binary has historically been used across all aspects of the corrections system—including police holding cells, city or county jails, or state and federal prisons. For years, most correctional facilities have housed transgender, gender nonconforming, or intersex detainees based on their current genitalia, and not on their actual gender identities (Routh et al., 2017). In doing so, transgender and gender nonconforming inmates who were placed in facilities that matched their sex assigned at birth would be subjugated to an array of sexual and physical violence—as evidenced by the case of Lindsay Saunders-Velez.

For intersex people, discrimination and victimization may be even more severe, particularly for people who are not aware of, or are insensitive toward, intersex issues. One attorney described the trauma that intersex people encounter in corrections:

> People with intersex conditions who have not been surgically "normalized" are seen as "freaks" in the prison system, because their bodies defy easy categorization as "male" or "female." [They] have been put into punitive isolation for no other reason than because administrators did not know whether to place them in men's or women's prisons. One client of mine who has an intersex condition was repeatedly strip searched by custody staff for no other reason than to see her genitalia. (Sylvia Rivera Law Project [SRLP], 2007, p. 22)

For a brief period of time, the federal government had taken steps to address the safety of transgender, gender nonconforming, and intersex inmates; under the direction of President Barack Obama, the Federal Bureau of Prisons added a clause to its Transgender Offender Manual, in which an inmate's gender identity would be used to determine appropriate housing in corrections. However, in 2018, the Federal Bureau of Prisons removed that clause, adding that biological sex should be the main consideration for making housing decisions for transgender and intersex inmates (Moreau, 2018). Furthermore, in the memo that was sent to all correctional facilities, the director of the Federal Bureau of Prisons writes: "The designation to a facility of the inmate's identified gender would be appropriate only in rare cases after consideration of all of the above factors and where there has been significant progress toward transition as demonstrated by medical and mental health history" (Inch, 2018, p. 2).

With this new policy, gender identity is rarely considered when deciding where to house a transgender inmate. So, even if an individual has undergone gender-affirming hormonal treatment (e.g., testosterone blockers, testosterone injections, etc.) or cosmetic surgery (e.g., breast augmentation, breast reduction, etc.), their genitalia and sex assigned at birth still take initial precedence in establishing where the individual will be housed. Consider the example of a transgender woman who was assigned male at birth, who had been on hormone therapy for decades and has undergone breast augmentation surgery and other medical procedures to match her gender identity, but who still has male genitalia. Depending on the state where she resides, she might be placed in an all-female facility, in a transgender section or ward of a prison, in an all-male facility, or in solitary confinement. In 2019, Layleen Cubilette-Polanco—a 27-year-old Afro-Latinx trans woman was found dead in her cell at Rikers Island, after being held in solitary confinement. The medical examiner ruled she had epilepsy and died from a seizure; but because she was in solitary confinement, she could not be saved. What is even more tragic is that Ms. Cubilette-Polanco was being held at Rikers Island because she could not pay a $500 bail that was related to misdemeanor sex work and drug possession charges (Dixon, Ray, & Tillery, 2019).

While the federal government rolled back its protections for transgender inmates, some states have taken steps to address the safety needs of transgender and intersex prisoners. Routh and colleagues (2017) assert that 39 states recognized how a diagnosis of Gender Identity Disorder or Gender Dysphoria warranted housing in a facility that matched their gender identity—with some states even adopting a screening process which involves consultation of medical professionals and mental health specialists. Further, 13 states allowed for transgender inmates to obtain gender-affirming hormone treatment while they were incarcerated, and 7 states allow for gender-affirming medical surgeries. In fact, in 2015, two transgender women in California were granted a request for gender reconstruction surgery, in order to enhance their mental health (St. John, 2015). Upon completion, they would be housed in women's facilities.

Despite some progress, solitary confinement is still practiced regularly in immigration detention centers—particularly for trans women—and often for prolonged amounts of times. One trans woman detainee disclosed:

> They told me I couldn't be housed with other people. They never asked me if I wanted to be in segregation [and] they never told me how long I would be there for. A guard told me it was "because I had long hair and breasts." They would only let me out of my cell for 20 or 30 minutes a day. I couldn't talk to anyone or I would be punished. One of the guards told me that he was "tired of seeing faggots." They treated me like an animal. (Frankel, 2016, p. 36)

Many of these trans women in these detention centers are seeking asylum, which suggests they have already experienced copious amounts of trauma; thus, inhumane treatment is particularly cruel for people who are merely seeking assistance and are not being punished for any crimes.

Sexual Victimization

Across multiple studies that focus on LGBTQ people in incarceration, a common theme that emerges is sexual victimization. Earlier research studies on prison rape and sexual coercion in correctional facilities did not collect data on sexual orientation or utilized smaller samples. For instance, researchers found 22 percent of male inmates and 7 percent of female inmates (out of a sample of 1,800) had experienced forced or coerced sex (Struckman-Johnson, Struckman-Johnson, Rucker, Bumby, & Donaldson, 1996); however, data did not disaggregate whether people identified as queer or trans. In a study focusing on gay and bisexual men in a special housing unit in an urban county jail, all of the participants reported they requested special housing to avoid being sexually assaulted in the general population; however, even within protective custody, one-third of the sample described feeling pressured to have sex with other inmates (Alarid, 2000). Further, these gay and bisexual men who were housed in county jails believed sexual assault was more common in state prisons, with 38 percent reporting a fear of being raped if or when they would be transferred into a prison.

In 2003, the U.S. Congress passed the Prison Rape Elimination Act, which aimed to eliminate sexual assault in all prisons and jails. In order to do so, DOJ's Bureau of Justice Statistics (BJS) began collecting data on the sexual victimization of inmates (Wolff, Blitz, Shi, Bachman, & Siegel, 2006). When disaggregating data on sexual orientation, research has revealed LGBTQ inmates are more likely to have been sexually victimized while incarcerated than their heterosexual counterparts (Beck, 2014; 2015b). LGBQ prisoners, in comparison to heterosexual prisoners, were 10 times more likely to be sexually victimized by another inmate and twice as likely to be sexually victimized by prison staff (Beck et al., 2013). In a study of California prisons, 67 percent of LGBQ inmates reported being sexually assaulted, compared to 2 percent of heterosexual inmates (Jenness et al., 2007). Meyer and colleagues (2017) found both LGBQ men and women were more likely to be sexually victimized by other inmates than their heterosexual counterparts; however, they found only LGBQ men were more likely to report being sexually victimized by prison guards and staff. Moreover, results indicated that self-identified gay and bisexual men were most likely to be raped (17.5 percent of the sample), followed by self-identified lesbian and bisexual women (13.1 percent of the sample), men who have sex with men (8.2 percent of the sample), and women who have sex with women (7.7 percent of the sample). Results also revealed prison staff members had allegedly sexually assaulted 6.1 percent of self-identified gay and bisexual men; 4.8 percent of men who have sex with men; and 1.9 percent of heterosexual men.

For transgender prisoners, sexual assault is very prevalent, but is understudied. Thirty-five percent of trans inmates in prisons and 34 percent of trans inmates in jails reported sexual victimization in the past 12 months. Further, 17 percent of trans inmates in prisons and 23 percent of trans inmates in jails reported staff sexual misconduct (Beck, 2015a). In the aforementioned California study, transgender women in men's prisons were 13 times more likely to experience sexual violence than other prisoners—with 59 percent of transgender women inmates reporting sexual assault, a number significantly higher than the 4.4 percent of the general sample at the male prisons (Jenness et al., 2007).

In the National Transgender Discrimination Survey, Grant and colleagues (2011) reported 15 percent of transgender participants who reported being incarcerated at any point of their lives reported being sexually assaulted. In the 2015 US Transgender Survey, out of those who had been incarcerated, 20 percent were sexually assaulted by facility staff or other inmates (James et al., 2016). Eleven percent of transgender participants who were held in jail, prison, or juvenile detention reported being sexually assaulted by facility staff—a rate that is five times higher than the national average for all other prisoners (James et al., 2016). Using the NTDS, researchers found almost half (47 percent) of transgender women who had been incarcerated reported victimization either by other inmates or by correctional staff; further, Black, Latina, and multiracial transgender women were more likely to report experiences of victimization than White transgender women (Reisner et al., 2014). Again, both studies using the NTDS and the USTS targeted a general population of transgender participants (and not incarcerated individuals); hence, the high prevalence of sexual assault in prison demonstrates the severity of the problem among transgender people.

In order to comprehend the prevalence of sexual victimization, it is also important to understand prison culture, in which incarcerated individuals use rape and coercive sex to establish dominance. Often referred to as "prison code," inmates learn they need to "act tough, lift weights, and be willing to fight to settle grudges, or risk being labeled weak and subjected to beatings and rape" (Peek, 2003, p. 1226). Some authors describe how this hierarchy is not just based on a continuum from gay to straight, but rather includes categories such as gays, queens (i.e., femme men or transgender women), and punks (i.e., individuals who had been sexually assaulted in prison and "turned out" into a submissive sexual servant; Sexton et al., 2010). In this way, LGBTQ people who enter correctional facilities become easy targets for sexual victimization, particularly if they are viewed as gender nonconforming, feminine, or weak.

When transgender prisoners are housed in correctional facilities that align with their genitalia or their sex assigned at birth, they are placed at high risk for sexual assault—by other prisoners or by correctional staff. As an example, one transgender woman described the trauma of being raped by her prison guards:

> There [were] four guys, two came on that side and two came on that side and came in there. The first guy sliced his face with the little cutter thing I had, when I woke up, I could feel them in me, one of the guys were in me and they were holding me and choking me, and someone socked me out again. I woke up again, they choked me out, I could feel, eventually I woke up I had to get 15 stitches in my anus, and they kept doing HIV tests, they didn't find nothing. One month after I got out of prison, I got a HIV diagnosis. They told me I could file charges, but it's hard to prove, [because] can you prove they raped you and can you prove they gave you HIV? (Nadal, Vargas, et al., 2012, p. 133)

In this way, sexual victimization may also be a predictor of the high prevalence of HIV infection in prison (Krebs & Simmons, 2002).

Another incarcerated transgender woman reported how reporting of her sexual assault did not help: "I'm raped on a daily basis, I've made complaint after complaint, but no response" (SRLP, 2007, p. 19). Many gay, bisexual, or queer male prisoners (or former prisoners) have also reported being raped by other inmates and by prison guards; however, their sexual orientation had often been used to blame them for being sexually assaulted. For example, one gay man shared that after he was raped, a correctional staff member "told me I was never raped; I just gave it up" (Mariner, 2001, p. 152). In another case, an inmate was told that he "must be gay" for "letting them make you suck dick" (Mariner, 2001, p. 152).

When sexual assaults occur in prisons, particularly if a correctional officer was the perpetrator or a witness, they are hardly ever reported or documented, for a few primary reasons. First, correctional officers often prohibit survivors from seeking medical care, which prevents any documentation. Second, other physical or forensic evidence (e.g., semen on clothing, camera recordings) are often destroyed—resulting in a lack of evidence. Furthermore, given that LGBTQ prisoners, particularly transgender women, are so ostracized and are characterized as being hysterical, hypersexual, or pathological, they are often not believed.

So, although the Prison Rape Elimination Act of 2003 was put into place to eliminate sexual assault in prison, the culture of rape is so pervasive in prisons that it would require an overhaul of the system for sexual assault to truly diminish. Moreover, because of the many psychological and social factors involved, as well as the lack of systemic accountability, reporting sexual assault may not be effective, or even safe, for survivors.

Regarding immigration detention centers, trans women are put at higher risk for sexual assault both by other detainees and by staff members, primarily because it is still acceptable and common to house trans women in men's facilities. One trans woman shared:

> Three men started touching themselves in front of me. They said, "He thinks he's a woman but he's a faggot [. . .] in our country, we kill these people." They made me feel bad and I started to cry. [After they raped me], the guard came to get me and took me to the [housing] pod. She didn't ask me if I was okay or if anything had happened. (Frankel, 2016, p. 20)

In 2013, the U.S. Government Accountability Office found there were three substantiated cases of transgender women who were sexually assaulted in immigration detention, with two of those cases involving male guards assaulting trans women in solitary confinement (Frankel, 2016).

Nonetheless, there has been some potential improvement, at least for cisgender male inmates; while Struckman-Johnson and colleagues (1996) revealed 18 percent of male inmates reporting sexual abuse by correctional staff, nearly 20 years later, Meyer and colleagues (2017) reported a range of 1.9 to 6.1 percent of male inmates being sexually assaulted by correctional officers and other staff. Given the significant improvement in decreasing rapes toward cisgender men, there is some hope that systemic changes can decrease rapes toward transwomen too.

Physical and Emotional Abuse by Correctional Officers and Staff

A common theme for LGBTQ people who are incarcerated involves the ways that LGBTQ people have been physically and emotionally abused by prison guards and other correctional staff members. In general, research has found LGBTQ people across the spectrum encounter violence or abuse in prison, but that gender identity, sexual orientation, and other identities (e.g., race, age, and immigration status) may influence how that violence may manifest. While sexual and physical violence are frequently interchangeable, this section will focus on the violence and abuse that is not sexual in nature (i.e., non-sexual physical and emotional abuse).

Experiences with correctional officers varied by gender and sexual orientation. First, while cisgender LGBQ women might not be as likely to be sexually abused by prison guards and staff (Meyer et al., 2017), they are prone to experiencing physical violence by correctional staff members—particularly if they are gender nonconforming in any way. For instance, one masculine-identified offender shared her experience with prison guards: "'Oh, you want to be like a man? You want to be a man? Eat this. Eat it.' Boom and every time they'd throw me on the floor, I'd eat that" (Mountz, 2016, p. 275). Second, while many gay, bisexual, and queer men report facing violence by prison guards, others describe how correctional officers ignored the assaults; one participant shared: "The correctional officers didn't care about anything. They watched gay people get raped. They would walk the tier and see a gay person being raped or beaten up in his cell and they would keep on walking" (Maschi et al., 2016, p. 1285). Transgender inmates, particularly transwomen, experienced the most violence—as exemplified by one former inmate who shared: "I had my face smashed into a wall by C.O. after asking him politely to 'Please don't touch me' when he was pulling and tugging at my sweater. . . . Why did he put his hands on me? I am a woman" (SRLP, 2007, p. 20). Because of these experiences, LGBTQ inmates may avoid prison-based rehabilitative services for fear of being assaulted.

Another form of abuse by correctional officers was the withholding of healthcare and gender-affirming medical treatment for transgender inmates. Grant and colleagues (2011) revealed 12 percent of trans people who had been in jails or prisons reported denial of routine health care, and that 17 percent of trans people were denied hormones or medical treatment—even when such medication was prescribed by a physician. Similarly, James and colleagues (2016) found more than one-third of respondents who were taking hormones before incarceration were prevented from taking their hormones while incarcerated. One incarcerated transgender person described: "Medical services are poor for the average inmate. They see gender-related services as cosmetic, not essential to transition and to a healthy life" (SRLP, 2007, p. 27). Another transgender woman, who had all of the proper paperwork for her medication, divulged: "Hormones are sporadic. It's a major chore to get refills. They took me off [my meds] for four months. You have no idea the effect of that. I filed a grievance, wrote letters, finally won them back after four months. They treat hormones like they're narcotics or something" (SRLP, 2007, p. 27). Withholding hormones is perfectly legal in most states; 28 states do not allow inmates to obtain any type of gender-affirming treatment once incarcerated, and 20 states' facilities disallow hormonal treatment for inmates who had already been taking hormones (Routh et al., 2017).

Solitary Confinement and Other Biased Punishments

Within incarceration, LGBTQ prisoners recognize they are treated more unfairly than heterosexual, cisgender prisoners. One formerly incarcerated lesbian shared: "Prison is about punishments. And if you are queer, you are punished more" (Johnson, 2017). Similarly, a trans woman stated: "When someone like myself gets in trouble, it gets blown far out of proportion and usually results in the gay or transgendered prisoner getting much harsher punishments than appropriate for the offense or in comparison to other non-gay or non-transgendered prisoners" (SRLP, 2007, p. 22).

Further, "sexual misconduct" is prohibited in prison—meaning people are barred from engaging in any sexual act, even if consensual. For example, Borchert (2017) shares the results of a hearing for a gay man who was caught in two consensual incidents:

> Prisoner Jackson was classified to Administrative Segregation for two major sexual misconducts. The first incidence took place where Jackson and another prisoner were directly observed in a cell together with erect penises. The second incident took place in 2009 where Jackson and the same prisoner were directly observed standing face-to-face in an embrace, kissing each other on the lips. Prisoner Jackson has been classified to Administrative Segregation for a period of 1 year. (p. 197)

Punishments include lengthening time to parole, access to programs, family visitation, forfeiture of good time, loss of privileges, disciplinary transfer, loss of job, restriction to quarters, and solitary confinement (Borchert, 2017; Meyer et al., 2017); inmates may also be outed or shamed to their families, as indicated by a Black bisexual male and former inmate who shared:

> If you get caught by the guards it's a new charge and they send a letter to your house, which might be to your wife or loved one saying that you got caught having sex with a man and these are the charges. . . . It's a charge like you would get if you get caught fuckin' in the street. It's called public lewdness. (Mackenzie, Rubin, & Gómez, 2016, p. 12)

In this way, such charges are reminiscent of sodomy laws and how engaging in consensual sexual acts, even in the privacy of one's own home, was illegal.

The sexual misconduct laws have also been used to punish transgender inmates who are accused of "impersonating" the opposite gender (Borchert, 2017). For instance, one transgender woman reported being punished with a 30-day sentence in solitary confinement for possessing a bra; she states:

> I am currently serving a 30-day keeplock [disciplinary segregation] for possession of brassieres which were not authorized. Unless I develop breast tissue, I will never get authorization for bras. And I will only develop breast tissue after receiving hormonal therapy, which the state has continuously denied me. (SRLP, 2007, p. 31)

Another transgender woman described:

> It was the most devastating day of my life when they made me cut my hair when I was transferred to [facility removed]. It took me so long to grow it. It was like taking an arm. I wish they would not have done that. They don't do that to female inmates. I have to keep my fingernails trimmed, like they are weapons or something. (SRLP, 2007, p. 31)

Previous research has found LGBTQ people in prison were more likely than cisgender heterosexuals in prison to have experienced solitary confinement and other sanctions in both prisons and jails (Meyer et al., 2017). In the Black and Pink Survey, half of the sample shared they had been put in solitary confinement against their will (Lydon et al., 2015). Sometimes, solitary confinement is used to silence an inmate who had been sexually or physically assaulted, particularly if the perpetrator was a correctional officer. One trans woman described:

> When you get beat up [really] bad and they don't want to take you out to get checked out, they put you in the snake pit. They threw me in the snake pit for 6 months after beating me up. Six months! They're animals . . . I got beat up by 12 officers. I'm only 123 lbs. (SRLP, 2007, p. 19–20)

Other times, LGBTQ inmates are placed in solitary confinement as punishment for engaging in consensual sexual activity (Lydon et al., 2015).

Solitary confinement has also been viewed as a solution to gender binary facilities, in that correctional departments believe they are protecting queer and trans inmates who would potentially be targeted if housed with people who match their sex assigned at birth. In fact, some inmates might unknowingly request to go into solitary confinement, as a means to protect themselves from other inmates (Lydon et al., 2015). However, after spending time in isolation, they may realize it was not what they expected. Decades of research indicate that solitary confinement is actually a cruel and unusual punishment—with astounding physical and psychological effects, including anxiety, panic, confusion, memory loss, hallucinations, delusions, psychosis, self-mutilation, appetite loss, hypersensitivity to external stimuli, lethargy, rage, tremors, heart palpitations, and lack of impulse control (Arkles, 2009; Haney, 2018).

In 2015, the United Nations updated their standard minimum rules for the treatment of prisoners, also known as the Nelson Mandela Rules, which prohibits prolonged solitary confinement, or "the confinement of prisoners for 22 hours or more a day without meaningful human contact . . . for a time period in excess of 15 consecutive days" (p. 17). They also prohibit the "placement of a prisoner in a dark or constantly lit cell" (p. 16). It is evident that solitary confinement is a traumatic experience; thus, placing an LGBTQ person in solitary confinement, particularly if they already have trauma histories or PTSD, is an especially cruel punishment which can worsen or hinder any rehabilitation for offenders in the correctional systems.

Transwomen within immigration detention centers are often placed in solitary confinement; one woman expressed:

> I went to shower one day when the gay boys were there because I felt safer [with them]. A guard accused me of having sex in the bathroom and they took me to segregation. She said, "We don't care about your sexuality. You're going to be in there until you leave." I told them I couldn't go because I was claustrophobic. . . . I hadn't eaten for a week because I was so depressed. I cut my wrists [with an ID card] and wanted to kill myself. (Frankel, 2016, p. 37)

Frankel (2016) described how half of the trans women in their study avowed to being placed in solitary confinement, with some of them being held more than 15 days, violating UN rules.

Microaggressions and Incarceration

For LGBTQ people who are incarcerated, the microaggressions are so pervasive and may even manifest in more aggressive ways that do not feel so micro or miniscule. Regardless, the accumulation of these microaggressions may have a negative impact on LGBTQ people in corrections. One trans person shared: "It's the little things, the things that are just a part of life here, but they add up to hundreds of little things all geared toward making life miserable for prisoners like me, but without risking discrimination complaints or other types of complaints against correctional officers or other staff" (SRLP, 2007, p. 21).

Homophobic and Transphobic Language

Homophobic and transphobic language is very common in correctional facilities, as it is among law enforcement and in courts. However, when used in correctional facilities, it often appeared to be more aggressive in nature. In fact, it appears that homophobic and transphobic language is a common experience for LGBTQ prisoners, as supported by the Black and Pink report which indicated that 83 percent of respondents faced verbal harassment by fellow inmates, while 70 percent experienced verbal harassment by prison staff (Lydon et al., 2015). When homophobic and transphobic terminology is used in threatening or violent ways, those would be considered more verbal assaults; however, when they are used as innocuous or everyday vernacular, they could still be classified as microaggressions.

A transgender woman described experiences at booking: "I remember the first comment: 'Oh, look at this one! This is a gorgeous one. We haven't had one like you in a long time,' starting with the commanding officers. Then the [inmates start] yelling 'Put it in our cell!'" (Nadal, Skolnik, & Wong, 2012, p. 73). A transwoman revealed how multiple correctional staff addressed her as "titty man" and made derogatory references about her breasts (Routh et al., 2017, p. 650). Another trans person shared how after being stripped and searched at a jail, a correctional officer said: "What do we do with *it*?" (Fiani et al., 2017, p. 9). Another trans woman shared: "They'd call me lizard, faggot, homo, or to get me really upset, they'd call me by my boy name. Lizard is a derogatory term directed at a lot of the transsexuals or queens in prison" (SRLP, 2007, p. 25).

Dehumanization and Pathology

Many LGBTQ people in corrections describe how they are pathologized because of their sexual orientation or gender identities, or how they are treated as less than human. For instance, one transgender participant shared: "I'm no longer looked at as even a human being. We are not really looked at as people and it should change" (Fiani et al., 2017, p. 9). A Black bisexual male former inmate said: "When you're in that cell you become an animal. You have to be led out to eat, shower or whatever and become an animal. And I know I'm better than that, even though like I said I used to do things that put me there" (Mackenzie et al., 2016, p. 13).

In a focus group with three Black LGBQ female formerly incarcerated youth offenders they recalled their experiences in juvenile detention centers, which included commonly hearing disparaging remarks from both fellow inmates and staff like: "You are going to hell for being gay. God doesn't like you" or "Stay away from [name omitted] because she is not a good person and is trying to turn everyone out" (Holsinger & Hodge, 2016, p. 33). In a different study, a bisexual man described: "In juvenile hall [staff] ask you, 'Have you been molested?' and then they say, 'Oh, that's why you are gay'" (Majd et al., 2016, p. 52). In another study, a trans man disclosed: "While in solitary, a cop asked me about my gender. I told him I was male, and he told me I sounded female. Next thing I knew, I was being taken to the jail doctor to spread my legs and have him confirm my gender. It was humiliating" (James et al., 2016, p. 188). In each of these examples, perpetrators may not even view their actions as being wrong or offensive; rather, they can be written off as part of their jobs.

Misgendering or Misuse of Pronouns

Because of the oppressive gender binaries in the correctional system, a very common type of microaggression for transgender participants is the act of intentionally or unintentionally misgendering someone. For example, a transgender female sex worker described confronting this issue early on in her imprisonment: "When I got to prison, when I first came in, they go, 'What's your name?' And I told them my name, they go, 'No, no, no, what's your male name?'" (Nadal, Vargas, et al., 2012, pp. 136–137). In another example, a transgender women recollected: "They addressed me with male pronouns and titles, forced me to sleep in a room with four men, even though I didn't feel safe, and periodically raided my belongings and confiscated anything they viewed as remotely feminine" (Lambda Legal, 2016, p. 7). Similarly, another transgender male disclosed: "When I was booked, the officers asked very intrusive questions about my genitalia in a very nonprofessional manner and laughed about it. They ended up booking me into an all-female solitary confinement cell, kept calling me 'miss,' and gave me female colors even though I pass full time as male" (James et al., 2016, p. 188).

Psychological Consequences of Incarceration

LGBTQ prisoners are more likely to report more psychological distress than heterosexual, cisgender prisoners (Meyer et al., 2017). Out of LGBTQ-identified inmates with mental health needs, 14.7 percent of jail inmates and 21 percent of prison inmates reported higher rates of inmate-on-inmate sexual victimization (Beck et al., 2013). A gay Black former inmate shared:

> My abuse started in the County Jail where I was raped by four inmates. In prison, a few years later, I was put in a cell with a gang member who made me give him oral sex. . . . It is truly impossible to put into words

what goes through one's mind when becoming a victim of rape. (Mariner, 2001, p. 39)

Similarly, one gay Latino man who served time shared: "In prison, it's hard. But being gay in prison makes it ten times harder. Being gay, you have to be on your toes. I always had to be the strongest person in the area, and that was really taxing" (Johnson, 2017).

QUEERING INCARCERATION

In order to queer incarceration, we must examine if systems that are founded in oppressive or biased underpinnings can ever really be modified to be equitable for historically marginalized communities. Queering incarceration can include individuals reflecting upon whether the system has ever been one of "criminal justice" or if it has rather been one of "criminal punishment," especially for Black people, trans people, and other historically marginalized groups (Spade, 2015, p. 25). Queering incarceration can involve advocating for criminal justice reform, which includes everything from combatting prison expansion and privatization to fighting gender binaries in correctional facilities to repealing laws criminalizing sex work or HIV status (National Center for Transgender Equality, 2018). Queering incarceration may also mean prison abolition altogether and moving toward a full dismantling of the prison industrial complex (Meiners, 2011; Spade, 2015).

Queering incarceration means understanding the prison industrial complex (PIC) goes beyond the prisoners or correctional departments themselves and rather involves the ways that society polices trans and queer people, people of color, and people of historically marginalized groups. Trans activist Miss Major describes it poignantly:

> One of the things that happens or a girl getting involved in the PIC is we already, from the moment we decide to be a transgendered person, are living outside the law. The moment this dick-swinging motherfucker wants to put a dress on and head on down the street to go to the store or something like that, they have broken the law . . . We can be beaten, attacked, and killed, and it's okay. You are already a convict for just how you express yourself and you might start to live a lifestyle of a person that is living outside the law. Because you can't get a legitimate job, you can't get a chance in school, you can't get a chance to function and survive as a part of mainstream society. So, immediately, once you've done this, your part of the PIC (Donahue, 2011, p. 277).

In this way, queering incarceration also means disrupting the normative ways we criminalize trans and queer people (especially trans and queer people of color) for their identities, behaviors, and the ways they live their lives.

In order to advocate for change, activists may consider an array of tactics like lobbying for decriminalization of certain crimes (e.g., sex work laws, marijuana laws) and pressuring elected officials to advocate for amendments to current laws and policies. If queer and trans people are not convicted and sentenced to prison for misdemeanor crimes, then they will not be exposed to violence within jails or prisons. For instance, if Layleen Cubilette-Polanco was not convicted for drug possession and sex work crimes, she would not have been imprisoned at Rikers, placed in solitary confinement, and left to die when she had a seizure.

Other actions may include changing societal stigma of incarceration and altering societal perceptions that prison is the sole way to maintain order. For example, educating others on the realities of LGBTQ people in prison can assist people in learning that there can be alternative ways of working with people who commit non-violent crimes. For instance, instead of placing someone who is convicted of substance abuse charges in a prison, perhaps government officials can advocate for substance rehabilitation centers instead. Instead of housing asylees and undocumented immigrants (many of whom have not committed any crimes) in detention centers that mirror prison facilities, perhaps elected officials can push to provide special government housing instead. Learning more about the injustices faced by LGBTQ inmates and teaching others about those inequities can assist in holding elected officials accountable. Finally, if people are educated on injustices toward incarcerated individuals, perhaps they will be more compassionate toward their humanity. As Black trans actress Laverne Cox once said: "Just because someone is incarcerated does not mean they are no longer a human being. We can't talk about America without talking about this. We incarcerate more people than anybody else in the world" (Spitznagel, 2014). Thus, it is crucial for the system to recognize that everyone—including people who are incarcerated—is a human being and deserves to be treated as such.

SIX

The Workplace Closet

LGBTQ People and Employment Law

THE CASE OF KIMBERLY HIVELY

Kimberly Hively, a White American lesbian in her fifties, was employed as an adjunct instructor of math at Ivy Tech Community College in South Bend, Indiana, from 2000 until 2014. She was first hired to teach remedial math courses, but she eventually advanced to teaching higher-level math courses (Patti, 2017). In 2009, Hively received a phone call from a school administrator who reprimanded her for her nonprofessionalism, after she was reported "sucking face" on campus. Hively was flabbergasted at the accusation, as she recalled merely giving her girlfriend "a quick goodbye kiss" in the parking lot, as most couples would when they leave each other for the day (Simon, 2017). She believed that this was the first time her employers knew of her sexual orientation as a lesbian, even though she had been out for over 20 years; she presumed that homophobia was involved in the accusation.

In spite of this hostile and punitive interaction, Ms. Hively continued to thrive at her job and in her career. She continually received positive reviews and teaching evaluations, and she even won the Adjunct Faculty Award for Excellence in Instruction. She pursued a master's degree from Indiana University at South Bend, which she was told could make her more marketable in attaining a full-time position at Ivy Tech. She earned this degree in 2011 and shortly after began applying for a full-time teaching position in her department.

Yet, Ms. Hively did not have any success in getting hired. She applied at least six different times, and she was rejected each time, without any reasonable explanation. As semesters went by, she observed that many of her colleagues who were adjuncts (many who taught for a much shorter amount of time than she had been on campus) were hired for full-time positions. Further, she also noticed that her hours were reduced, which caused a significant financial strain for an adjunct instructor who relies on maintaining their teaching loads each semester. When her contract as an adjunct instructor was not renewed in 2014, she was certain it was due to homophobia, and she filed a lawsuit against the college.

She originally filed and represented herself without an attorney, because she reports there were no local attorneys who were willing to take on the case. In her complaint, she argued the school violated Title VII of the Civil Rights Act of 1964 and discriminated against her because of her sexual orientation. However, her case was dismissed in a lower court, because Title VII does not list "sexual orientation" as a protected class—although it does list race, ethnicity, sex, religion, and other identities.

In April 2017, in *Hively v. Ivy Tech Community College* (2017), the Seventh Circuit ruled, with an 8–3 majority, that discrimination based on sexual orientation was, indeed, a type of discrimination based on sex; and thus, sexual orientation would be considered a protected class under Title VII (Simon, 2017). The argument included that if an employer discriminates against someone based on the sex of the person they date or are in a relationship with, they are indeed discriminating against that person because of their sex too. In other words, if man who is in a relationship with a woman is not discriminated against, but a woman who is in a relationship with a woman is discriminated against, that woman is being discriminated against because of her sex. As such, this case sets a precedent that could challenge Title VII to be more explicit in including sexual orientation and gender identity as protected classes under federal law.

INTRODUCTION

Previous research has supported that encountering some type of employment discrimination is a very common experience for LGBTQ people across the United States. A literature review found that in the 1980s and 1990s from 16 to 68 percent of their LGBTQ samples had reported any type of workplace discrimination (Badgett, Lau, Sears, & Ho, 2007). Lambda Legal (2007) revealed 39 percent of their respondents reported experiencing some form of antigay discrimination or harassment in the workplace. James and colleagues (2016) discovered 30 percent of a sample of TGNC people have experienced workplace discrimination, while Grant and colleagues (2011) found that 50 percent of TGNC employees experienced harassment at work.

Alongside employment discrimination, another major concern for LGBTQ people is unemployment or underemployment—which often is a result of job discrimination and can lead to poverty and homelessness. Because the U.S. Census does not currently collect information on sexual orientation or gender identity directly (and only collects information on married or cohabitating same-sex couples), it is difficult to identify the exact unemployment rates of the American LGBTQ population. However, some community samples and probability statistics are used to provide a snapshot of rates of unemployment among LGBTQ people. The Williams Institute (2019) estimated 9 percent of the LGBTQ population is unemployed, while Civic Science (2017) estimated 13 percent of the LGBTQ population is unemployed and that 16 percent of TGNC people are unemployed. Grant and colleagues (2011) used the NTDS and discovered that 14 percent of TGNC participants were unemployed, while James and colleagues (2016) used the USTS and reported 15 percent of TGNC participants were unemployed. Using U.S. Decennial Census 2000 Data, one study found gay men were more likely to be unemployed or out of the labor force at higher rates (7.7 percent) than both married heterosexual men (4.5 percent) and unmarried heterosexual men (6.2 percent; Leppel, 2009). Given the unemployment rates among these LGBTQ samples, which ranged between the 7.7 and 16 percent, it is estimated the LGBTQ unemployment rate was two to three times higher than the national rate of unemployment for the general U.S. population, which ranged from 3.6 to 5 percent between January 2015 and May 2019 (U.S. Department of Labor, 2019).

This chapter will focus on LGBTQ concerns with employment law—focusing on the many ways that LGBTQ people are negatively affected by workplace discrimination, as well as the ways that employment-related laws and policies (or lack thereof) may negatively impact LGBTQ experiences. I will first review the history of employment non-discrimination laws on federal, state, and local levels. I will also provide examples of workplace discrimination, as well as a review of correlates of workplace discrimination and unemployment.

FEDERAL, STATE, AND LOCAL LEGISLATION ON EMPLOYMENT DISCRIMINATION

As of 2019, there are no federal protections that prevent LGBTQ people from being hired, fired, or mistreated in their workplace, on the basis of their sexual orientation or gender identity. While the Civil Rights Act of 1964 prohibits discrimination based on race, color, religion, sex, or national origin, it has not been amended to also include sexual orientation or gender identity. Historically, there have been several attempts to advocate for LGBTQ protections under federal law, namely with the Employment Non-Discrimination Act (ENDA)—a federal bill that was first introduced to Congress in 1994 and was reintroduced almost every year for almost 20 years. In this section, I will discuss the history of ENDA and other attempts at federal legislation, while also highlighting federal court cases and state laws involving anti-LGBTQ employment discrimination.

ENDA and Other Congressional Employment Non-Discrimination Bills

Prior to ENDA, there were several acts that were proposed to Congress that aimed to add sexual orientation as a protected class under federal law; however, they were all unsuccessful. First, there was the Equality Act of 1974, a bill that would ban discrimination based upon sexual orientation, marital status, and gender in public accommodation, housing, and employment; next, there was the Civil Rights Amendment of 1975 which would add "sexual or affectional preference" to existing civil rights laws (Gates, 2010, p. 355). Similar anti-discrimination acts were introduced annually over the next several years, but that advocacy stopped in the 1980s—likely a result of the nation's growing homophobia and the AIDS epidemic. When the Employment Non-Discrimination Act of 1994 was introduced, it utilized much of the language from the Equality Act from 20 years prior. Yet, the bill was unsuccessful for over a decade—mainly due to the Republican majority in Congress (Gates, 2010; Currah, 2008).

In the 2000s, transgender community leaders lobbied and advocated for gender identity to be added as a protected class under the newest proposals of ENDA. After years of trans-led advocacy, Congressman Barney Frank, Congresswoman Nancy Pelosi, and other Democratic congressional leaders agreed to add gender identity to the newest version of the ENDA bill when they introduced the bill to the House of Representatives in April 2007. However, months later, without any clear sign of the bill's impending failure, they decided to remove gender identity from the bill (leaving only sexual orientation as a protected class), while introducing a separate bill including both sexual orientation and gender identity. The ENDA with only sexual orientation (or "bad ENDA"; Currah, 2008, p. 334) passed in the House of Representatives (but later was defeated by the Senate), while the other did not succeed at all (Vitulli, 2010).

Nine prominent national LGBTQ organizations—including PFLAG, the Task Force, National Coalition for Transgender Equality, National Center for Lesbian Rights, the National Coalition of Anti-Violence Projects, and others—released a statement denouncing the decision to remove gender identity from the bill. They wrote: "We are shocked and upset that ... influential members of the House of Representatives have apparently made a decision to remove protections for transgender people from the bill. If true, this decision was made without consultation with leaders of the lesbian, gay, bisexual and transgender community" (as cited in Vitulli, 2010, p. 163). Notably missing from the list of organizations was the Human Rights Campaign—an organization that has claimed to be the largest LGBTQ national organization, but who had historically demonstrated multiple instances of trans exclusion.

The decision to exclude transgender protections from ENDA is one that exemplifies the history of LGBTQ community organizing and activism—with many instances of cisgender gay men and lesbian leaders (mostly who are White and wealthy) excluding or undermining transgender and gender nonconforming people (particularly those who are poor or people of color) within "LGBTQ" advocacy efforts. So, in many ways the decision was viewed not just as a political move, but also as a historical reminder that trans people are often viewed as disposable by cisgender leaders of an umbrella LGBTQ community. In spite of this betrayal, many trans activists viewed the exclusionary decision as a pivotal moment for transgender people, in that it empowered trans people to be more vocal about the transphobia within LGBTQ communities and to push for intentional trans inclusion within LGBTQ organizations (Masters, 2017).

Following the failure of both ENDA bills in 2007, gender identity was added in subsequent introductions of ENDA, but the bills continued to fail. In 2013, ENDA passed in the Senate, with a 64–32 majority in favor; however, it failed in the House of Representatives. In 2015, Democratic congressional leaders decided to repackage ENDA and introduced the Equality Act. Similar to ENDA, the Equality Act aimed to prohibit discrimination on the basis of the sex, sexual orientation, gender identity, or pregnancy, childbirth, or a related medical condition of an individual, as well as because of sex-based stereotypes. With a majority Republican House and Senate, the bill continued to fail from 2015 until 2018. However, in May 2019, the Equality Act passed in the House of Representatives, with a 236–173 majority, where, at the time of this writing, it awaits a Senate vote (Killough, 2019).

Federal Courts and Employment Non-Discrimination Laws

While there have been attempts to advocate for changes to federal law via congressional votes, there have been some court cases that have considered whether or not sexual orientation and gender identity were included in the existing language of the Civil Rights Act that prohibits discrimination on the basis of sex. In the aforementioned case of Kimberly Hively, a federal court in Indiana affirmed the plaintiff was indeed discriminated against because of her sex. However, the ruling did not go as far as to say that she was discriminated against because of her sexual orientation explicitly—a sentiment that would be similar in other instances in which LGBTQ plaintiffs were successful in winning their discrimination-related trials. For instance, plaintiffs in other landmark cases could win for being fired for not fitting gender role norms, but not explicitly because of their sexual orientation; in fact, Sousek (2014) argues that "plaintiffs who 'look gay' often find protection under Title VII, while plaintiffs thought to violate gender norms—through known or suspected sexual activity, friendships, hobbies, or choice of partner—almost never win" (p. 715).

In order to understand if sexual orientation and gender identity would or should be covered under the general umbrella of sex, let's revisit definitions of each term that were previously presented. First, while sex is typically categorized by an individual's biological or physiological traits, such as chromosomes, gonads, reproductive organs, and hormones, gender is socialized and involves how people perform masculine and female behaviors, particularly in relation to their sex assigned at birth. Second, sexual orientation involves an identity that is typically derived by who one is attracted to, how one enacts those attractions, and the community of individuals with whom one identifies.

With these definitions, it seems plausible that both sexual orientation and gender identity could be covered under the category of "sex." As in Hively's case, if a person is being discriminated against because of who they are attracted to, they are in part being discriminated against because of their sex—someone holds bias against a gay person because their sexual attraction is different than what their sexual or romantic attraction should be because of their sex. Similarly, if a transgender person is being discriminated against because of their gender identity, they are being discriminated against due to someone's perception of their sex. In other words, if someone discriminates against a transgender woman because they are uncomfortable in knowing that her gender does not match her sex assigned at birth, the bias and subsequent discrimination is at least partially based on reactions to the transgender person's sex.

Despite this logic, there are a few watershed cases, in which courts ruled gender identity was not a protected class under Title VII of the Civil Rights Act (Currah, 2008). For instance, in *Holloway v. Arthur Andersen and Company* (1977), a transgender woman sued her employer after she was terminated due to her gender identity. The court affirmed how "sex" was made a protective class to address "the economic deprivation of women as a class" (p. 662) and determined Ms. Holloway was not discriminated against "because she is male or female, but rather because she is a transsexual who chose to change her sex. This type of claim is not actionable under Title VII" (p. 664). A similar decision was ruled in *Ulane v. Eastern Airlines* (1984). When Karen Ulane sued her employer Eastern Airlines for terminating her employment after gender-affirming surgeries, and initially won her case, the Court of Appeals reversed the decision stating:

> Ulane is entitled to any personal belief about her sexual identity she desires. After the surgery, hormones, appearance changes, and a new Illinois birth certificate, it may be that society . . . considers Ulane to be

female. But even if one believes that a woman can be so easily created from what remains of a man, that does not decide the case. . . . If Eastern [Airlines] did discriminate against Ulane, it was not because she is female, but because Ulane is a transsexual—a biological male who takes female hormones, cross-dresses, and has surgically altered parts of her body to make it appear to be female. (p. 187)

Both cases set the precedent that gender identity would not be a protected class under Title VII of the Civil Rights Act, at least in the way it was currently written.

While Hively was successful in her trial, a plaintiff in a similar case was not. Jameka Evans is a Black lesbian woman, whose gender presentation can be described as more masculine than feminine. Evans was working as a security guard at Georgia Regional Hospital in 2012 and left her job after a year of harassment; she alleged her supervisors made biased comments about her masculine clothes and her short hair, and how they retaliated through isolation, bullying, and unfavorable hours. In *Evans v. Georgia Regional Hospital Department of Behavioral Health and Developmental Disabilities* (2017), the Court of Appeals ruled Title VII was not intended to cover discrimination against lesbian, gay, or bisexual people, and the Supreme Court refused to hear her case (Ok, 2018).

Politics are likely involved in the Evans decision, as it occurred during a time when federal judges were being considered for the Supreme Court, following the death of Justice Antonin Scalia. Further, racial and gender identity were potentially involved in both the Evans and Hively decisions. Kimberly Hively, a White feminine-presenting lesbian, won her case, while Jameka Evans, a masculine-presenting Black woman, did not. Previous research has found there is a racial disparity in plaintiffs who are successful in filing employment discrimination cases, with a major factor that Black, Latinx, and Asian American plaintiffs are more likely to represent themselves in court without a lawyer (Myrick, Nelson, & Nielson, 2012).

State and Local Employment Non-Discrimination Laws

While there is still no official federal protection for LGBTQ employees, some states have adopted employment nondiscrimination policies and consider sexual orientation and gender identity to be protected classes. As of August 2019, the Movement Advancement Project (MAP) (2019a) reported there are only 21 states that explicitly prohibit discrimination based on sexual orientation and gender identity. Washington, DC, Puerto Rico, and Guam all consider both sexual orientation and gender identity to be protected classes regarding employment discrimination. Two states (Pennsylvania and Michigan) interpret sex discrimination to include both sexual orientation and gender identity, without explicitly having it written into law; meanwhile, Wisconsin only explicitly lists sexual orientation (but not gender identity) as a protected class. MAP (2019a) reports that 26 states do not have any explicit laws protecting LGBTQ people from discrimination, though many of those states reside in circuits with a ruling which interprets existing federal prohibition on sex discrimination (under Title VII) to include sexual orientation and gender identity. Based on current population estimates, MAP (2019a) approximates about 44 percent of the entire American LGBTQ population live in states in which they could be fired from their workplace for no other reason than their sexual orientation, gender identity, or both.

There are a few cities and counties that protect LGBTQ people in the workplace and in other public spaces through local ordinances. Oftentimes, these laws are passed in progressive cities, while not applying to the rest of the more conservative state. For example, in 2002, the New York City Council passed the Transgender Rights Bill, which expanded the NYC Human Rights Law to include gender identity as a protected class and to prohibit discrimination against people whose "gender and self-image do not fully accord with the legal sex assigned to them at birth" (de Blasio & Malalis, 2019, p. 2). Meanwhile, in the state of New York, the Gender Equality Non-Discrimination Act, which prohibits discrimination based on gender identity or expression, and adds transgender New Yorkers to those protected by the state's Hate Crimes Law, did not become state law until 2019. While the bill was initially introduced in 2003 (and passed by the New York House of Representatives each year), it continually was defeated by the New York State Senate for 15 years (Segers, 2019).

The Movement Advancement Project (2019b) cites that within the 26 states that do not have non-discrimination laws based on sexual orientation, there are 245 cities and 30 counties with protections based on sexual orientation. In the 27 states that do not have non-discrimination laws based on gender identity, there are 249 cities and 29 counties with protections based on gender identity. As of 2019, three states explicitly ban cities and counties from passing local non-discrimination laws for LGBTQ people—Arkansas, Tennessee, and North Carolina; finally, two states do not have any local ordinances that prohibit discrimination based on sexual orientation and gender identity: North Dakota and South Carolina.

Corporations and Educational Institutions with Non-Discrimination Policies

Many corporate institutions and educational organizations have taken the initiative to include sexual orientation and identity clauses into their company policies. Ninety-three percent of the Fortune 500 include sexual orientation in their nondiscrimination policies and 85 percent include gender identity; further, 193 of those 500 companies achieved a 100 percent rating, which included policies such as (a) ensuring full spousal and partner health care coverage parity, (b) affirming coverage for transition-related care and eliminating all so-called "transgender exclusions" from plans; and (c) ensuring full LGBTQ inclusion in diverse supply chain programs (HRC, 2019a). Research supports that companies who promote social justice and equity result in more job satisfaction and productivity (DeSouza, Wesselmann, & Ispas, 2017; Sears & Mallory, 2014). So, while affirming LGBTQ employees can be considered a moral or ethical responsibility, it also increases productivity and leads to economic growth.

In the 1980s and 1990s, many educational institutions also developed or amended nondiscrimination policies to prohibit any discrimination based on sexual orientation, gender identity, or gender expression. Zemsky and Sanlo (2005) argued having such policies in place was cited as being very important for numerous reasons. First, they allowed for LGBTQ faculty and staff to feel comfortable in disclosing their sexual orientations without fear of losing their jobs. Furthermore, because LGBTQ students on campus had been tasked with advocating for LGBTQ rights and inclusion on campus, it allowed for LGBTQ faculty and staff to alleviate some of the responsibility placed on students, which often took a toll on students' academic success or psychological well-being. Finally, in enacting such policies, LGBTQ employees were now able to enjoy certain rights and benefits that may not have been afforded by the state—including domestic partner benefits or internal settlements regarding LGBTQ discrimination disputes.

TYPES OF WORKPLACE DISCRIMINATION

In order to understand the types of heterosexist and transphobic discrimination LGBTQ people may face, we must review the wide range of experiences that may occur. When assessing workplace discrimination, previous studies have concentrated on terms like "unfairness" or "harassment." For instance, Burns (2007) revealed approximately 5.6 percent of lesbian and gay professionals and managers in the U.S. have left a job due to workplace unfairness, while Sears, Hunter, and Mallory (2009) reported 37 percent of an LGBTQ sample had experienced workplace harassment in the last five years, and that 12 percent had lost a job because of their sexual orientation. Workplace discrimination can also include interpersonal discrimination (i.e., biased interactions between colleagues or from supervisor toward supervisees) and systemic discrimination (i.e., policies that may discriminate against certain groups or lack language that protects certain groups). As an example, transgender employees are often subjugated to interpersonal discrimination, such as misgendering, transphobic jokes or language, or sexual harassment, as well as systemic and institutional discrimination, such as a lack of support for gender-affirming transition processes while maintaining the same job (Fidas & Cooper, 2019). Finally, discrimination may manifest differently across various sectors and fields. For instance, in the field of technology, one report found 20 percent of LGBTQ employees were likely to be bullied and 24 percent were likely to experience public humiliation or embarrassment (Scott, Klein, & Onovakpuri, 2017).

There are other dynamics which may influence how discrimination may affect certain LGBTQ people. For example, some LGBTQ individuals who do not disclose their identities and are presumed to be heterosexual and cisgender still experience workplace discrimination (e.g., hearing heterosexist language from unknowing coworkers), but they may not report or confront the behavior to avoid potential hostility or repercussions (Ragins & Cornwell, 2001). More recent scholarship has focused on how LGBTQ employees encounter less overt discrimination, particularly in the form of microaggressions—or brief and subtle manifestations of bias—and ostracism, or being ignored and excluded, because of one's sexual orientation identity (DeSouza et al., 2017; Resnick & Galupo, 2019). In this next section, I will cover a few aspects of workplace discrimination, including (a) workplace culture and outness, (b) hiring practices, (c) promotions and wage disparities, and (d) microaggressions.

Workplace Culture and Outness

Previous authors have asserted how the values and experiences of dominant groups in society (e.g., White, heterosexual, Christian, and cisgender men) are considered normative and establish the standard against which all people, ideas, and practices are measured—particularly in the workplace (Ward, 2008). Specifically, heteronormativity is the notion that heterosexuality is the only "normal" sexual orientation and that romantic relationships exist only between men and women (Goodrich, Luke, & Kassirer, 2017). In heteronormative environments, there are two processes that occur: (1) all people are presumed to be heterosexual upon first meeting and (2) non-heterosexual people who are open with their sexual orientation identities are "presumed to be abnormal, unnatural, requiring explanation, and deserving of discriminatory treatment and hostility" (Herek, 2007, p. 2).

Heteronormative behaviors in the workplace can manifest in several ways including: cultural norms that prohibit discussions of LGBTQ romantic or family relationships, formal policies privileging heterosexual family structures, and workplace interactions and behaviors that demean LGBTQ people. Heteronormative workplace environments may prevent LGBTQ employees from participating fully in social activities or in engaging in the same pleasantries their heterosexual colleagues do. Furthermore, the workplace culture of heteronormativity and cissexism may result in unique experiences for specific LGBTQ subgroups. Bisexual individuals report a burden of invisibility, in which people presume they are heterosexual or invalidate their bisexuality (Popova, 2018). Meanwhile, transgender employees may have difficulty in navigating name change policies, binary or gender spaces (e.g., restrooms, locker rooms, etc.), and gendered dress codes (Sawyer, Thoroughgood, & Webster, 2016).

Workplace culture can also influence LGBTQ employees' outness, which is defined as the degree to which individuals self-disclose their sexual orientations to others and may vary across time, place, and/or situation (Whitman & Nadal, 2015). Researchers have investigated the concept of outness for at least two decades—citing the contextual reasons for LGBTQ people's ability to self-disclose their identities, while understanding how outness is related to positive mental health and self-esteem. Outness in the workplace can increase encounters with heterosexism, but it is particularly detrimental when working in a less LGBTQ-affirming workplace; being closeted can take a psychological toll, with consequences such as constant fear, cognitive depletion, and psychological strain. Fidas and Cooper (2019) found notable proportions of their sample reported feeling exhausted from spending time and energy concealing their sexual orientation (17 percent) and gender identity (13 percent).

While some studies report only half of LGBTQ employees are fully out in their workplaces (Fidas & Cooper, 2009), we acknowledge that there is no one way to be "out" as an LGBTQ person, especially in the workplace. Some people disclose openly to their colleagues upon meeting them, while others may not verbally disclose their identity to anyone at all. When choosing to disclose their sexual identities in the workplace, LGBTQ people consider a number of factors, including physical and psychological safety, support systems, and potential repercussions (Fidas & Cooper, 2009; Whitman & Nadal, 2015). Some people are out in their everyday personal lives, but may inadvertently "pass" at work, which means that people may assume them to be heterosexual or cisgender (Davis, 2017). Race may influence outness at work, with some studies finding queer people of color be less likely to disclose their sexual orientation at work (Ragins, Cornwell, & Miller, 2003). Furthermore, LGBTQ people hold internalized negative beliefs about their sexual orientations or gender identities, which may affect their outness; Fidas and Cooper found nearly two thirds (59 percent) of non-LGBTQ employees believe it is unprofessional to discuss sexual orientation or gender identity in the workplace.

In some court cases involving anti-LGBTQ discrimination, a major task of a plaintiff is to prove that an employer was aware of the person's sexual orientation, which is difficult to do given that there are few opportunities for any American citizen to declare their sexual orientation on any official document or public record. Unlike job applications, college applications, standardized test forms, or census forms where race and gender/sex are collected, sexual orientation is never collected—making it difficult to ever assess the true population of LGBTQ people in the US (Nadal, 2013). Marriage certificates are one of the only legal documents which may infer one's sexual orientation, and even then, sexual orientation is not explicitly asked for (i.e., applicants merely indicate their genders and they are identified as a same-sex couple). Transgender people may change gender markers on various identifications and forms, which may result in a legal record of their gender identities; however, lesbian, gay, bisexual, and queer people typically would not have any legal record of their sexual orientations.

A case that exemplifies this plight occurred in Iowa, when Chris Godfrey, a gay White man, refused to resign from his government job when new Republican governor Terry Branstad was elected and encouraged him to; as a result, Godfrey's salary was subsequently cut by 30 percent to the lowest possible salary at that level. In trial, Godfrey and his lawyers had to prove former governor Branstad lowered his salary because of his sexual orientation—despite the governor's assertions he did not even know that Godfrey was gay. The jurors decided in favor of the plaintiff, supporting that Godfrey was discriminated against because of his sexual orientation. It was decided that the state of Iowa owed him $1.5 million in damages (Gruber-Miller, 2019).

Biased Hiring Practices

Previous research has indicated it is common for LGBTQ people to experience discrimination in the hiring process (Sears & Mallory, 2014). The Pew Research Center (2013) reported 21 percent of their respondents reported being treated unfairly by an employer in hiring, pay, or promotions because of their sexual orientation or gender identity. The NTDS reported 44 percent of their TGNC participants reported being denied a job (Grant et al., 2011).

Experimental studies have indicated job applicants are significantly less likely to be invited for interviews when their resumes signal their LGBTQ identities (Neumark, 2014). Applicants with multiple marginalized identities are at higher risk of not being hired, as supported by Dispenza, Kumar, Standish, Norris, and Procter's (2018) study that found the interaction of disability and sexual orientation disclosure led to lower employment ratings for LGBTQ people with disablities. LGBTQ people themselves, especially transgender women of color, have described difficulties in gaining employment. A Black transwoman shared: "Even though in the window it says, 'Now Hiring,' they go, 'If we have an opening, we'll call you.' So, they would say that, but they didn't just come out and go 'How dare you, hell no we ain't gonna hire you.'" (Nadal, Davidoff, & Fujii-Doe, 2014, p. 173). While discrimination in hiring practices is commonly known among LGBTQ people, proving bias is difficult—particularly if perpetrators are not verbally explicit in their heterosexist or transphobic biases.

Biases in Promotions and Wages

Lambda Legal (2007) reported 19 percent of their LGBTQ respondents revealed barriers in job promotions, while Grant and colleagues (2011) reported 26 percent of their transgender respondents lost their job because of their gender identity and 23 percent reported being denied a promotion. James and colleagues (2016) reported 51 percent of TGNC participants were fired or forced to resign, denied a promotion, or not hired in the past year because they were transgender

Regarding wage disparities, previous researchers have found sexual orientation (and subsequent discrimination) impacts one's earning potential (Curley, 2018). A spectrum of studies using the General Social Survey (GSS), the United States Census, and the National Health and Nutrition Examination Survey (NHNES III) have revealed gay men earn 10 to 32 percent less than their heterosexual male counterparts with similarly qualified jobs (Black et al., 2003; Carpenter, 2007). Regarding penalties in wages, Blandford (2003) reports nearly a one-third earnings penalty for behaviorally gay men, while Carpenter (2007) notes that his results are strongest (penalties on the order of 30 to 37 percent) for those who are "most likely" to be openly gay. One study found gay men made 15.6 percent less than similarly qualified heterosexual married men and 2.4 percent less than similarly qualified heterosexual unmarried men (Allegretto & Arthur, 2001). Another study finds that while lesbians make more money than heterosexual women, gay men make less money than married heterosexual men (Antecol, Jong, & Steinberger, 2008).

While these studies are helpful in understanding some preliminary information on LGBTQ wage gaps, it is crucial to acknowledge the limitations. First, because most of these studies use census data (which does not explicitly measure sexual orientation), they are only able to disaggregate data on gay men and lesbian women based on participants who identify as living in cohabitating same-sex relationships. As a result, they already may not be generalizable to bisexual, transgender, and queer people—particularly those who are single and not in cohabitating same-sex relationships. Further, while these studies tend to center gay men in general, they also fail to capture experiences of single, unmarried gay, bisexual, or queer (GBQ) men, as well as differences between single GBQ men, married GBQ men, or GBQ men in cohabitating relationships, or any differences based on race, socioeconomic status, geographic region, or any other demographic. Further, as most studies took place before 2015, they do not investigate any potential changes in wage outcomes with the legalization of same-sex marriage and the increasing societal acceptance of LGBTQ people.

Microaggressions in the Workplace

Quantitative research has focused on anti-LGBTQ microaggressions in the workplace, citing three major areas of microaggressions: (a) workplace values, (b) heteronormative assumptions, and (c) cisnormative culture (Resnick & Galupo, 2019). Scholars have described how microaggressions are so subtle they may not be covered by non-discrimination laws, yet may result in various ramifications; for example, an LGBTQ person who confronts an employer on microaggressions can be retaliated against and deemed a troublemaker who is not a team player. Regardless, previous scholars have described how subtler forms of microaggressions are less likely to result in favorable outcomes in workplace discrimination cases, demonstrating the difficulty in seeking recourse or legal action for microaggressions (King et al., 2011).

Use of Homophobic or Transphobic Language

A common microaggression theme experienced by LGBTQ people is the use of heterosexist or transphobic language. For example, when people use terms like "That's so gay" or "No homo" in the workplace, they demonstrate the normalization of heterosexist terminology. For example, one LGBTQ person shared:

> I get upset when someone says, "Oh that's gay" to mean something is stupid or bad. I feel like it is wrong in the same way that saying "It's retarded" is wrong. But people will say it and look at me and instantly say to me, "Oh, I'm really sorry." It is always upsetting because it's not about me, you shouldn't be saying it anyway. Because I'm in the room, they suddenly have to acknowledge me and apologize. (Platt & Lenzen, 2013, pp. 1022–23)

While this participant is distressed by hearing homophobic language, LGBTQ employees who are closeted (or who have not fully disclosed their sexual orientations) also commonly hear derogatory homophobic or transphobic jokes told by co-workers and superiors. Because of presumed cisgender heterosexuality, biased language is used frequently and unhesitatingly, creating work environments that further discourage disclosing their LGBTQ identities.

A common form of transphobic language is through the misgendering of people through pronouns. Grant and colleagues (2011) cited that 45 percent of their TGNC sample had been frequently called by the wrong pronouns on purpose at work. Resnick and Galupo (2019) described language-related microaggressions, such as employees' experiences related to their name ("Having your name assigned at birth and not your own name appear on official office documents such as a nametag, e-mail address, or nameplate") or gendered language ("Having people address you using incorrect pronouns") (p. 1395). Sometimes, heterosexist and transphobic language is well-intentioned or unconscious, such as referring to a heterosexual employee's romantic partner as a "spouse" but referring to a sexual minority employee's partner as a "friend" or "roommate" (DeSouza et al., 2017, p. 126).

Exclusion

Whether intentional or not, the act of exclusion is a common type of microaggression. Previous studies have found in the workplace, women and people of color (Holder, Jackson, & Ponterotto, 2015) are often excluded from formal and informal social gatherings or meetings, which prevents them from advancing in various workplaces. Similar feelings of exclusion may also occur for LGBTQ employees; one study found 26 percent of their sample reported feeling excluded from their work team, interesting work projects, or social events (Lloren & Parini, 2017). Exclusion of LGBTQ employees from social events or informal/formal meetings can be detrimental to their career trajectories because of the disadvantage of not having access to mentoring or opportunities for networking relationships, or receiving important work-related information that occurs at these events. As an example, one Black LGBTQ woman in tech imparted her experience:

> I was treated as an "other," excluded, and undervalued in my office. I was sat in the back of the office, I was ignored, and it was made apparent that I was a "diversity hire." I was told I was "too sensitive." I was told that other black and lesbian folks in the office didn't feel as I did, after mentioning homophobic and racist jokes being spewed in work-only chat channels. I left my employer because I was being treated unfairly as a black woman and human being. (Scott et al., 2017, p. 5)

As evidenced in this quote, intersectional identities, particularly one's race and gender, may influence an LGBTQ person's experience with exclusion and other types of workplace discrimination.

Assumption of Abnormality, Sexual Pathology, and Other Stereotypes

Another common microaggression that occurs toward LGBTQ people is the assumption of abnormality, sexual pathology, or other stereotypes (Nadal, 2013). For example, one LGBTQ person shared: "Once I tell people I'm not straight the common reaction is, 'Oh, so you think I'm attractive?' It feels like the assumption is I'm so gay I'm automatically attracted to everyone of the same sex. I want to say to them, 'Is it the same thing if you're heterosexual? You're not attracted to every girl or guy?'" (Platt & Lenzen, 2013, p. 1023). A gay man described stereotypes he encounters at work:

> They're making it seem like everybody is sexual and smutty-buddy and, you know, every gay man is an interior decorator or sells hair for a

living, you know. Even at my job . . . if you work in stocks, then it's a straight guy, but if you're on the beauty floor and/or you're a cashier, you're gay. (Nadal et al., 2011, p. 246)

While it is evident that LGBTQ people still face an array of microaggressions in their workplaces, it is less clear that heterosexual or cisgender people are aware of how those microaggressions create a hostile or unsafe work environment for their colleagues.

CORRELATES OF WORKPLACE DISCRIMINATION

In this section, I will highlight some of the social and psychological correlates of both workplace affirmation and workplace discrimination and how they may negatively affect LGBTQ people. Specifically, I will cover (a) mental health and substance use, (b) homelessness and poverty, and (c) survival behaviors.

Mental Health and Substance Use

Both quantitative and qualitative research has found anti-LGBTQ discrimination in general negatively influences LGBTQ people's mental health (McCabe, Bostwick, Hughes, West, & Boyd, 2010; Nadal et al., 2016). Specific to the workplace, studies have found LGBTQ people who encounter discrimination at work are more likely to report myriad negative health issues, including depression, psychological distress, and alcohol use (DeSouza et al., 2017; Nawyn, Richman, Rospenda, & Hughes, 2000).

LGBTQ people who are unable to gain formal employment may also develop mental health issues or engage in unhealthy behaviors. For instance, in the National Transgender Discrimination Survey, 70 percent of the sample who suffered from some form of job bias reported drinking alcohol or using drugs as a way to cope with the mistreatment (Grant et al., 2011). Further, homeless LGBTQ youth tend to have a higher prevalence of mental health and substance abuse issues, including suicidal ideation and attempts and riskier sexual behaviors (Cochran, Stewart, Ginzler, & Cauce, 2002). For transgender people of color, unemployment and substance abuse were both significant predictors of HIV/AIDS status (Xavier et al., 2005), suggesting when trans people of color are unemployed and use substances, they are more at risk for HIV/AIDS. Perhaps one of the most alarming connections between workplace discrimination and mental health is Grant and colleagues' (2011) finding 55 percent of their sample who reported suicide attempts did so after losing a job due to bias. Therefore, discrimination in the workplace does not just impact TGNC people's economic status or vocational aspirations; discrimination can threaten TGNC's people's abilities to survive and continue living their lives.

Homelessness and Poverty

Previous research has found homelessness and poverty are significant issues among LGBTQ people, particularly transgender people and LGBTQ youth of color. For example, Durso and Grant (2012) conducted a national survey of 354 homeless youth organizations and shelters and found approximately 40 percent of the sample identified as LGBTQ, while the National Transgender Discrimination Survey uncovered that about one-fifth of a national sample of TGNC participants had ever been homeless in their lifetimes (Grant et al., 2011).

Unemployment and poverty are typically significantly correlated, with unemployed people more likely to live in poverty and people living in poverty likely to be unemployed. As aforementioned, the unemployment rate for TGNC people is estimated to be 14 to 15 percent, which is anywhere from two to three times the national unemployment rate (Grant et al., 2011; James et al., 2016). However, race may influence unemployment significantly; for example, Grant and colleagues (2011) found unemployment rates were much higher for TGNC participants who are Black (28 percent), Native American (24 percent), Latinx (18 percent), and multiracial (18 percent).

Further, some studies have found poverty is common for lesbian, gay, bisexual, and queer people too. Albelda, Badgett, Schneebaum, and Gates (2009) reported unemployed same-sex couples were more likely to live in poverty than heterosexual couples, with 25 percent of same-sex female couples living in poverty and 13 percent of same-sex male couples living in poverty. Badgett, Durso, and Schneebaum (2013) revealed same-sex female couples were more likely to live in poverty in comparison to married heterosexual couples (7.6 percent versus 5.3 percent) and that single LGBTQ people were more likely to live in poverty in comparison to single heterosexual people (21.5 percent of LGBTQ women and 20.1 percent of LGBTQ men versus 19.1 percent of heterosexual women and 13.4 percent of heterosexual men). Finally, Badgett and colleagues (2013) found bisexual women and men were most likely to live in poverty (29.4 percent of bisexual women and 25.9 percent of bisexual men) versus 22.7 percent of lesbians and 20.5 percent of gay men.

When people are living in poverty, it is common for them to experience homelessness. Grant and colleagues (2011) reported one-fifth of their TGNC sample had experienced homelessness at some point in their lives, and TGNC participants who had lost a job due to bias were four times more likely to have experienced homelessness due to bias (40 percent) than those who did not lose a job due to bias (10 percent). To demonstrate this connection, one transgender participant shared: "I was fired for being transgender. I was on the brink of homelessness and starvation until a friend (who is also transgender) invited me to stay with her in a different state, over 15 hours away" (Grant et al., 2011, p. 66).

In addition to job discrimination, LGBTQ youth often become homeless after being evicted by their families or running away from home, because their families reject their sexual orientations or gender identities (Rosario, Schrimshaw, & Hunter, 2012). When LGBTQ youth become homeless, it becomes difficult for them to ever finish school or obtain formal education, resulting in a lifetime of poverty and potential contact with the criminal justice system.

Survival Behaviors

When people live in poverty, are homeless, or are unemployed, they are often forced to engage in survival behaviors, or nonconventional, often illegal, methods used to obtain their basic needs like money, food, housing, or clothing. Survival behaviors may include sex work or survival sex, dealing drugs, pimping, pornography, adult entertainment, panhandling, theft, selling stolen goods, selling blood or plasma, or conning others (Ferguson, Bender, Thompson, Xie, & Pollio, 2011). Previous research has found homeless LGBTQ youth are significantly more likely than heterosexual youth to engage in survival sex (Walls & Bell, 2011). Previous research has also found LGBTQ youth are more likely to experience physical or sexual victimization and to be assaulted by a greater number of perpetrators (Cochran et al., 2002). For LGBTQ homeless youth and transgender women of color, survival sex is often seen as a last resort—when they have run out of options and are unable to obtain formal employment due to systemic discrimination (Cochran et al., 2002; Nadal et al., 2014).

QUEERING EMPLOYMENT LAW

In order to queer employment law, it is evident that there is a need for sexual orientation and gender identity to be recognized as protected classes when it comes to employment nondiscrimination laws on federal, state, and local levels. Further, it is critical to acknowledge the ways that systems allow for discrimination to perpetuate, which maintains a status quo for LGBTQ people, particularly LGBTQ people from historically marginalized groups. For instance, if LGBTQ youth who are evicted from their homes are criminalized (instead of supported), they potentially endure lifelong suffering and an array of personal obstacles. Therefore, queering employment laws means to look at how employment discrimination is simply one branch of a greater system of oppression.

For people who are committed to advocating against discrimination in the workplace, there are several possible steps that they can take to ensure safer environments for LGBTQ people. First, employees may research whether or not their employer or institution has policies that protect LGBTQ people from discrimination, or if they have policies and benefits that are LGBTQ-affirming (e.g., do their insurance policies cover gender-affirming procedures, are there benefits for non-married same-sex couples or non-gestational same-sex parents?). Second, employers may initiate programs, trainings, or policies to be more inclusive of LGBTQ people and other historically marginalized groups. For example, do departments have policies or trainings on the importance of using correct gender pronouns or addressing microaggressions? Third, people should become aware of, or provide recommendations for revising, reporting procedures involving discrimination, microaggressions, or sexual harassment. When people do experience workplace discrimination, is there a fair and just process for people to report and to control against retaliation, and for a fair and smooth investigation to occur? While it may be difficult to sometimes be the lone voice advocating for change, it is often a necessary act in order for justice to occur.

Aligned with this sentiment, Margaret Cho (queer Asian American comedian, actress, and activist) once said: "All our truth needs to come out. Everything about queerness and survival. As a queer woman of color, it's vital for me to continue to be seen and heard as an active and vocal member of my community" (Jones, 2019). In this way, it is important for queer and trans people to be vocal and to fight for justice—especially when they have the resources or the support to do so. So, whether it is fighting against violence, or speaking for LGBTQ-affirmative policy changes in our workplaces, we must continue speaking our truths, so that our communities can survive and thrive.

SEVEN

Queer and TransParent

LGBTQ People, Family Court, and the Child Welfare System

THE CASE OF LUIS AND JOSEPH DESERRANO

Luis and Joseph DeSerrano first met in 2009 in Bozeman, Montana, when Luis was a doctoral student of microbiology at Montana State University. Joseph had moved to Bozeman, where his parents lived, in 2008 after he found a job. Joseph was raised in New Hampshire, served in Washington State with the Army Reserve, and earned his bachelor's degree in architecture from the University of Washington in 2001. Meanwhile, Luis grew up in Puerto Rico and received his bachelor's degree from the University of Puerto Rico at Mayaguez, before moving to Montana. The two were friends for a year before they officially began dating. Four years later, in August 2014, they were married in Seattle, Washington; they had a marriage blessing ceremony at their Episcopal church in Montana that September. Same-sex marriage was not legalized in Montana until later that year in November (Leitsinger, 2014).

Like many other couples, the DeSerranos were interested in raising children. They decided to turn to the foster system, in hopes they could provide a home to a child who may have been neglected or abused. When they started the process, they started to perceive they were being treated differently because they were gay. They asserted one social worker told them they would always be "on the bottom of her list" for placement; they would never get an infant; and other social workers would not want to work with her because they were a gay male couple (Schontzler, 2016).

Despite this, a 5-week-old boy was placed with the couple in March 2016. They were told the boy's birth father was in jail; the birth mother was living out of a car; and how the infant at birth tested positive for marijuana and methamphetamine. When the boy was placed with them, they were told the state would be looking for longer-term foster placement and they were moving to terminate parental rights. For three months, the DeSerranos took care of the infant: they fed him in the middle of the night; took him to pediatrician appointments; and helped the baby to gain weight. After three months, the baby was happy, healthy, and giggly. They could not help but "fall in love with him," viewing him as their "little angel" (Schontzler, 2016).

It appeared all was going well for the first two months, as they had not heard anything about attempts to reunite the child with his birth parents. However, they began to worry when a family outreach specialist told them they had "a really hard case." The last Friday of May, they were informed the baby would be removed from their care five days later. The agency had found a distant relative—a single woman who was "a stepdaughter to a stepbrother of the birth father." And because family reunification is always the primary goal of foster care, the distant relative had more legal rights than the couple who had taken care of the baby for three months and was deemed to be more appropriate for the baby.

Infuriated and betrayed, the DeSerranos filed a complaint with the Montana Human Rights Bureau alleging anti-LGBTQ discrimination by the Department of Public Health and Human Services. Their complaint alleged the agency delayed and sabotaged their application; didn't check their references or conduct a home study in a timely way; covered up and back-dated documents; retaliated by refusing to answer their phone calls; and fast-tracked moving the baby out of their home (Schontzler, 2016). They claimed it seemed the agency was working really hard to find someone else instead of allowing the baby to stay with them. The agency said they were simply doing their job. The couple realizes they have no legal right to the baby, but they continue with the complaint against the state agency to ensure such discrimination does not happen with anyone else.

The case of the DeSerranos is a story which is sadly common among many people (regardless of sexual orientation or gender identity) who choose to start their family via the foster system. Their intentions are good and commendable—they simply want to provide a child with a loving and secure home, especially for children who may come from a history of trauma, abuse, or neglect. For many LGBTQ couples, they choose the foster system as their method of starting a family because it is the most plausible for them. As two men, having a child through biomedical technology would be costly; it would require finding a surrogate mother who may or may not be willing to donate her egg, as well as the cost of intrauterine or intracervical insemination. Some couples may pay surrogates, which can cost up $60,000 plus medical expenses. In some states, paying a surrogate is illegal, so some couples have to travel across state lines to find a viable surrogate they can pay (resulting in more travel fees).

Given all of these obstacles, some LGBTQ people may research adoption options, particularly if they feel like they would rather spend money on a child who is already born or will be born (rather than birthing a child through scientific means). However, the various other types of adoption may also come with additional fees and stressors. For instance, going through a private adoption agency, an LGBTQ couple may find a pregnant woman who is willing to surrender her parental rights and allow them to adopt her child; however, this process may result in legal fees which match those of surrogacy. Moreover, there is always a slight chance of the birth mother, after giving birth, changing her mind and opting to keep the baby; across different states, there would be differing laws regarding how much time a birth mom has before she can decide to surrender her parental rights.

Finally, a same-sex couple might be interested in international adoption; however, because of global heterosexism, homophobia, and transphobia, there are so few countries who permit adoption by LGBTQ parents, particularly parents outside of their home country (Mertus, 2011). If they are able to find a country without restrictions against LGBTQ parents, other costs may arise, including travel, attorney fees, and other application costs.

So, while the foster care route may seem the most cost-effective route toward building a family, there are major potential risks involved, as demonstrated by the case of the DeSerranos. First, for most children in foster care, "the primary permanency plan is reunification with their parents" and according to federal law, states must make "reasonable efforts to provide birth parents with the services and supports needed to care for their children" (Bass, Shields, & Behrman, 2004, p. 6). Further, in many states, the preferred placement option for foster kids is kinship care (or "safe living arrangements with relatives or individuals known to the child before searching for alternatives"; Bell & Romano, 2017, p. 268). While some studies have found more positive outcomes with kinship care placements, results are marginal and inclusive, suggesting there may not be significant reasons for kinship care to be viewed as being more effective than foster care (Bell & Romano, 2017).

With this in mind, the DeSerranos' case calls into question the notion of who is considered kin. If the newborn baby has never met the kin in question, are they really being placed in a home where the child knows the person and where the child is going to thrive? How is being the stepdaughter of a stepbrother any better than being raised by strangers without any relation? Further, if the birth parents are in contact with the kin, especially due to substance use or severe mental health issues, would the kin expose the child to the birth parents, whom the state has terminated the rights of? Finally, should there be a time limit before a family member can be introduced to take the child away from a foster family? If the child was 6 months old, would it be in the child's best interests to remove from the only parents the child has known? If the child was 9 months or 12 months, would it be wise, safe, or ethical to remove a child from parents who they may have formed a healthy attachment with? And finally, if foster care is the most financially viable way for many LGBTQ couples to start their families, is it moral or ethical to allow parents to feel the psychological distress of knowing the children they raise can be taken away at any moment because the laws believe that blood lineage or legal kinship trumps emotional bonds? These are all important questions to unpack as we consider how people become families, the obstacles people have in choosing their families, and how others may struggle in ever finding a family to call their own.

INTRODUCTION

When gay Puerto Rican singer Ricky Martin first became a father to twins, he shared: "Two toddlers can get hectic, but I wouldn't change it for anything. Every day they teach me different things. The love is there. When you have a two-year-old saying every other hour, 'Papi, te amo. Papi, I love you,' it can't get better" (Hill, 2011). His sentiment reminds us how becoming a parent can be a very rewarding and life-changing experience for many people, and how the experience may feel especially rewarding for LGBTQ people, due to the many obstacles they may have in starting families or legally raising children. According to the Williams Institute, in 2016, there were 700,000 cohabiting same-sex couples in the US (346,000 male same-sex couples and 359,000 female same-sex couples); out of these couples, an estimated 114,000 couples (or 86,000 female couples and 28,000 male couples) were raising children (Goldberg & Conron, 2018). Of these couples raising children, 68 percent of them were raising biological children (i.e., there was at least one birth parent), 21.4 percent were raising adopted children, and 2.9 percent were raising foster children. These numbers are significantly different than heterosexual or different-sex couples in which 96.6 percent raised biological children, 3 percent adopted, and 0.4 percent fostered children.

Meanwhile, in 2017, there were approximately 442,995 children who were in the foster care system; of these, more than half (or 269,690) had entered the system within the past year and about one-fourth (123,437) were waiting to be adopted (Children's Bureau, 2018). While exact data of LGBTQ youth in the child welfare system is not known (due to lack of data collection on sexual orientation or gender identity), previous research has estimated anywhere from 15 to 19 percent identify as LGBTQ

(Dettlaff & Washburn, 2018; Wilson, Cooper, Kastanis, & Nezhad, 2014). Furthermore, previous scholars have revealed LGBTQ youth are more likely than heterosexual and cisgender youth to age out of the system, meaning they do not find adoptive families or other permanent homes (McCormick, Schmidt, & Terrazas, 2017).

This chapter will focus on LGBTQ people's experiences with family law and foster care (also known as the child welfare system). Though same-sex marriage became legal on the federal level in 2015, there are still many obstacles for LGBTQ families or same-sex couples who wish to become parents. Further, as more young people come out as LGBTQ at early ages, when they are in the child welfare system, decisions are made about where (and with whom) they should be housed. Historically, family law has not been inclusive of LGBTQ people, because definitions of "families" had only been conceptualized using heteronormative or cisgender lenses. In recent years, family law has become one of the most rapidly changing aspects of the legal system for LGBTQ people. Thus, this chapter will describe the history of heterosexism and transphobia in family law and child custody, the current state of affairs for LGBTQ families, and LGBTQ youth in foster care.

LGBTQ PARENTING AND FAMILY LAW

As introduced in chapter 1, there were numerous state laws prohibiting LGBTQ people from becoming parents, each with different clauses and regulations. For example, some states prohibited LGBTQ people from fostering or adopting altogether, while some laws banned only LGBTQ same-sex couples from fostering and adopting because they did not allow unmarried couples to foster or adopt. Therefore, for some LGBTQ couples, it was necessary for same-sex marriage to be recognized on a federal level, so that their states would allow them to foster or adopt children. When *Obergefell v. Hodges* deemed state bans of same-sex marriage were illegal, the ruling opened the door to same-sex adoption too. A year later, in 2016, a federal judge in a District Court in Mississippi ruled the state's law that prohibited same-sex couples from adoption was unconstitutional, thus setting a precedent that any bans on adoption by same-sex couples would be unconstitutional and thereby illegal (Villaseñor, 2019). While this ruling was definitely a victory for LGBTQ couples, there are thirteen states with explicit laws prohibiting LGBTQ people from fostering children (Warbelow, Oakley, & Kutney, 2018). Given LGBTQ couples are 7.25 times more likely to start their families through the foster system than heterosexual, different-gender couples (Goldberg & Conron, 2018), such laws significantly hinder LGBTQ people's ability to raise children.

Before we begin, we note how, in general, laws regarding adoption, child welfare, or other instances related to family law are governed at the state level, resulting in an array of different outcomes for similar cases across different states (Shapiro, 2013). Relatedly, by acknowledging family state laws were written hundreds of years ago, and thereby used outdated, rigid, and prejudiced heteronormative or cissexist language, cases involving LGBTQ people typically resulted in unfavorable outcomes (Chambers & Polikoff, 1999). Further, regarding adoption and custody cases of children, states will utilize the "best interest" standard in making their determinations, which essentially means guaranteeing children's well-being by placing them with adults who are best able to care for them (Ritenhouse, 2011). Furthermore, while most states now prohibit judges from using a parent's sexual orientation as an explicit factor in determining custody, judges have historically used numerous anti-LGBTQ rationales for their custody decisions, including fears children will suffer from gender role confusion, will become gay, lesbian, or bisexual themselves, or will suffer unnecessary stigmatization and discrimination (Ritenhouse, 2011). Thus, unless there are explicit laws prohibiting anti-LGBTQ discrimination, judicial bias may always be a factor.

Historical Context of LGBTQ People and Family Law

In the late twentieth century, most of the cases involving LGBTQ people and family courts involved custody battles during or after divorce hearings—typically concerning instances in which one of the parents had come out as LGBTQ (Flaks, 1994; Rivera, 1991). In many of these cases, judges often explicitly imposed their own moral views in their decisions, with some rulings using terms like "unnatural" and "alternative lifestyle" (Arnup, 1999, pp. 10–11). For instance, in 1987, a Missouri appellate judge affirmed a previous decision involving a woman who had come out as a lesbian, after having four children with her ex-husband, asserting:

> We are not presuming that Wife is an uncaring mother. The environment, however, that she would choose to rear her children in is unhealthy for their growth. She has chosen not to make her sexual preference private but invites acknowledgment and imposes her preference upon her children and her community. The purpose of restricting visitation is to prevent extreme exposure of the situation to the minor children. We are not forbidding Wife from being a homosexual, from having a lesbian relationship, or from attending gay activist or overt homosexual outings. We are restricting her from exposing these elements of her "alternative lifestyle" to her minor children. (*S.E.G. v. R.A.G.*, 1987, p. 167)

In a similar example, in 1993, in Virginia, a judge removed two-year-old Tyler Doustou from his biological mother, Sharon Bottoms, and instead gave him to his grandmother Kay Bottoms, because Sharon was living in a romantic relationship with a woman named April Wade

(Chambers & Polikoff, 1999). Although her ex-husband had supported that their biological child should be able to live with his birth mother and her girlfriend, the judge said that "a two-parent home environment where their homosexual relationship is openly practiced and presented to the child as the social and moral equivalent of a heterosexual marriage" would be exposing the child "to a lifestyle that is neither legal in this state, nor moral in the eyes of most of its citizens (Chambers & Polikoff, 1999, p. 542). His ruling was based on knowing Bottoms and Wade had privately engaged in oral sex—an act that would be considered sodomy and thereby was illegal at the time.

In the years following, many cases would follow suit. In 1995, a judge granted custody of an 11-year-old girl to a father who had murdered his first wife, instead of to her lesbian mother whom she had been living with solely for 8 years. The judge declared it was important to give the girl a chance to live "in a non-lesbian world" (Arnup, 1999, p. 3). In 1989, a judge ruled against a father who was unwilling to forgo his romantic relationship with another man, stating, "Surely it cannot be argued that the exposure of a child to unnatural relationships is in the best interests of that child of tender years" (Arnup, 1999, p. 10). Relatedly, there were some cases in which judgments were favorable for LGBTQ parents, as long as they were more discreet or closeted about their sexual orientations. For example, in one case, a judge ruled, "[Parent] is not a missionary about to convert heterosexuals to her present way of life," while another judge stated that "they make no effort to recruit others to their way of living. They make no special effort to associate with others who pursue that lifestyle" (Arnup, 1999, p. 8). Thus, some earlier judges did rule in favor of LGBTQ parents, so long as they did not actively live as LGBTQ people.

In some jurisdictions, there were some judges who began to rule in favor of LGBTQ parents, citing that sexual orientation should not be a factor in ruling against a parent for custody. For instance, in 1987, the *New York Times* published an article about a gay man getting custody of his son. In his opening testimony, he avowed, "Yes, I'm a homosexual. Now let's get on with the case" (Gutt, 1987, p. C-1). Later, the judge's decision stated, "The court finds no evidence of any present or potential harm upon which to make the father's homosexuality a consideration in this custody dispute" and asserted that the boy's "needs can best be met by his father" (Gutt, 1987, p. C-1).

In addition to custody cases regarding divorce or separation, judges in the 1980s and 1990s heard and ruled on an array of cases involving issues related to the prospect of becoming parents—ranging from the right to adopt children, to become foster parents, or to determine parental rights when reproductive technology is used (Flaks, 1994). For example, in 1989, a court in Broward County, Florida, was presented with a case involving deciding the custody of a child, 10-year-old Kristen Pearlman. Pearlman's biological mother, Joanie Pearlman, who became pregnant through a sperm donor, died when she was five years old. At the time of her death, the judge awarded custody to Joanie's parents, instead of Janine Ratcliffe, who was Joanie's partner and had served as Kristen's co-parent since birth. Kristen even pleaded with the judge to live with Janine, who she viewed as her mother. Four years later, a judge determined it would be detrimental to keep Kristen from Janine, whom she still considered her primary parent figure. Additionally, the judge ruled there was no evidence Janine's sexual orientation would have any negative impact on Kristen (Chambers & Polikoff, 1999).

Further, in the 1980s and 1990s, more same-sex couples cohabitated, entered monogamous relationships, or both. As a result, legal issues arose when one person died or if the couple decided to separate (Flaks, 1994; Rivera, 1991). Given the couples were not legally married, family court cases ranged from separation and alimony disputes between long-term couples to the division of estates without wills, particularly when biological families fought against the LGBTQ widowed partner of their deceased relative (Rivera, 1991). Further, because some same-sex couples did not have the legal benefits of marriage, some cases emerged in which one adult in a same-sex relationship adopted their romantic partner, as a way of ensuring they were legally connected (Chamber & Polikoff, 1999; Rivera, 1991).

Concurrent to all of these instances were policies that were created to prevent LGBTQ people from becoming foster parents. One of the first known cases involved Don Babets and David Jean, a gay White male couple, who first went through the process of becoming foster parents in 1984 in Massachusetts (George, 2016; Ricketts & Achtenberg, 1989). Their first placement, which took place a whole year later, was two brothers—one who was three years old and another who was 18 months old. The kids had been removed from their mother, who was aware of and approved of the gay couple as foster parents. However, when the *Boston Globe* ran a story about the first gay foster parents, backlash ensued; social workers came to take the kids later that afternoon. In May 1985, Massachusetts legislators voted (with an overwhelming majority) to ban gay foster parenting on the basis of sexual orientation alone. Governor Michael Dukakis enacted a policy that stated a hierarchy for foster placement: (1) family members, (2) heterosexual married couples with experience raising children, (3) unmarried couples and single people, and 4) gays and lesbians. In the policy, all non–family members would be asked about their sexual orientation, despite any actual evidence supporting any constitutional reason to do so. The couple filed a complaint in *Babets v. Johnston* in 1986; the case was argued for five years before it was eventually settled, and sexual orientation was no longer asked about in foster parent applications in Massachusetts. While Babets and Jean were never reunited with their first two foster children, they eventually ended up adopting four brothers. Scholars affirm the case set precedent for many other landmark LGBTQ rights cases, by shaping the image of LGBTQ people as socially conscious adults who could potentially help children in need.

Current Issues with LGBTQ People and Family Law

Prior to the 2015 SCOTUS decision, there were several studies that focused on same-sex couples' perceptions of the law and adoption. For instance, Patterson and Riskind (2010) revealed how same-sex couples who did want to pursue parenthood did so based on which legal obstacles were less restrictive for them, while Riskind, Patterson, and Nosek (2013) revealed LGBTQ people who lived in less LGBTQ-affirming areas were less likely to believe becoming a parent was possible. Park, Kazyak, and Slauson-Blevins (2015) interviewed same-sex couples with children and examined three aspects of LGBTQ parenting—the methods used to become parents, decisions about where to live, and experiences of family recognition. Findings indicate differences in states with more LGBTQ-affirmative and less LGBTQ-affirmative areas, including parents in more restrictive areas feeling the need to "work within the system" while those living in a more affirmative area feeling they live in "a bubble" (p. 1).

One of the main arguments used by individuals who opposed adoption by LGBTQ parents was that children of LGBTQ parents would be at greater risk of lower-quality parenting or potential psychological effects of being raised by two parents of the same sex or by an LGBTQ parent. However, studies have consistently demonstrated that there are no significant differences in psychological adjustment between children of LGBTQ parents and children of heterosexual parents and that in some areas, children with same-sex parents actually perform better than those with different-sex parents (Patterson, 2009).

While same-sex marriage is now recognized on the federal level, and state laws prohibiting adoption by LGBTQ people are unconstitutional, there are still many obstacles that LGBTQ people face in trying to become parents. First, some states still explicitly prohibit LGBTQ people from becoming foster parents. As of 2018, there were 13 states that have laws which explicitly permit discrimination against LGBTQ people from becoming foster parents; these include Alabama, Arizona, Kansas, Kentucky, Michigan, Mississippi, Montana, North Dakota, Oklahoma, South Carolina, South Dakota, Texas, and Virginia (Warbelow et al., 2018). Under the guise of aforementioned religious freedom laws, many foster care agencies may assert that they will not allow LGBTQ people to become foster parents because it conflicts with their religious values or beliefs. Meanwhile, there are only 16 states that have explicit non-discrimination policies that prohibit discriminating against LGBTQ people from fostering children, with a remaining 21 out of 50 states that do not have any explicit policies that protect against anti-LGBTQ discrimination of foster parents (Warbelow et al., 2018). In the aforementioned case of the DeSerrano's, it is crucial to note they live in Montana—one of the states that permits anti-LGBTQ discrimination in adoption and foster placement, and one without any overt policies against prohibiting anti-LGBTQ discrimination in foster care (Warbelow et al., 2018).

Race influences LGBTQ families in a number of ways. First, Gates (2013a) estimated 39 percent of LGBTQ people in same-sex couples who are raising minor children are people of color, which is similar to 36 percent of those in different-sex couples who are non-White. However, in comparison to same-sex White couples, it was revealed 41 percent of non-White women in same-sex relationships and 20 percent of non-White men in same-sex relationships are raising children under 18, that only 23 percent of White women in same-sex couples and 7 percent of White men in same-sex couples are raising children under 18. Further, one-third of people of color in same-sex couples are raising a biological, step, or adopted child, which is much higher than the 18 percent of their White counterparts. The difference between men is even greater, with 16 percent of men of color in same-sex couples raising a biological, step, or adopted child, as compared to 5 percent of White men. Regarding children and race, Gates (2013) reports that Black children who are raised by two parents are more likely to be raised by same-sex parents (16 percent) versus different-sex parents (8 percent). One explanation for this finding is that Black children in the foster system are being raised or are adopted by same-sex couples.

Gates (2013) also reports some socioeconomic disadvantages: single LGBTQ adults raising children are three times more likely than heterosexual, cisgender single adults raising children to be living at or near the poverty threshold. Similarly, LGBTQ families with two parents and children are twice as likely than different-sex couples with children to be living at or near the poverty threshold. Further, the median house income of same-sex couples with minor children is significantly lower than different-sex couples ($63,900 versus $74,000 respectively).

Currently, there are still many issues involving LGBTQ parents and custody of children. While many judges are more reasonable regarding custody cases in which a parent has come out as LGBTQ after the dissolving of a heterosexual marriage, many family court cases now involve the legality of second-parent adoptions, or adoptions in which a second parent is able to adopt a child they did not give birth to (Maxwell & Kelsey, 2014). In the context of same-sex couples, this typically involves same-sex women couples in which one woman is the gestational mother and the other is her partner who has co-parented the child since birth. However, these instances can also involve a parent who has a biological child and becomes involved with a romantic partner who helps in raising that child.

Regardless, second-parent adoptions are important, because they offer parents who are not biologically related to a child an opportunity to be legally connected to the child (Shapiro, 2013). For example, a major fear that same-sex women couples have in utilizing a donor father is that a non-gestational parent will lose custody of their child because the one who does not bear the child has no implicit, legal right to custody. Further, when couples split, second-parent adoptions are helpful in ensuring that non-gestational parents are not treated like strangers to the children they helped to raise, which can be especially hurtful and humiliating. Moreover, second-parent adoptions increase the likeliness that couples would share custody if the non-gestational parent adopted the child (Gartrell, Bos, Peyser, Deck, & Rodas, 2011), ensuring less psychological distress for children involved.

It is believed the first successful trial court decisions regarding second-parent adoptions involved a lesbian couple in 1991 in Washington, DC; the first case of a successful second-parent adoption to be publicized in the media was the case of a lesbian couple in the *New York Times* in 1992 (Chambers & Polikoff, 1999). Presently, there are only 15 states that have state laws or have court decisions which allow for a second parent of the same sex to petition to adopt their partner's children, regardless of whether they are in a legally recognized relationship (Warbelow et al., 2018). For states that do not have such law or court precedents, judges can determine whether or not second parents have any legal rights. So, depending on the values or biases of judges, LGBTQ people who raise children they are not legally bound to may either gain or not gain any parental rights.

In 2012, there was a landmark case in New York, in which parental rights were granted to a secondary parent instead of a biological or birth parent. Allison Scollar and Brook Altman were never married, but they agreed to have a child together after being in a romantic relationship for several years (Mangan, 2012). They utilized a sperm donor, Robert Frame, then a friend of Scollar's, who later believed he should have parental rights, even though that was not part of the original agreement. When Altman took their daughter out of state without Scollar's consent, a judge granted her temporary custody and an order for the child to return home. In the final custody decision, the judge ruled Altman, a television producer, acted "more as a friend or older sister than a responsible parent"; the judge added: "This does not give her an automatic priority over the adoptive parent. This is analogous to a father getting custody of his own child, where only the best interests of the child are paramount" (Mangan, 2012).

LGBTQ YOUTH IN THE CHILD WELFARE SYSTEM

Throughout this text, we have covered issues related to LGBTQ juvenile offenders and their experiences with law enforcement (see chapter 3 for a review); in courts (see chapter 4 for a review); and in incarceration (see chapter 5 for a review). However, this section will describe the non-criminalized experiences of LGBTQ young people with the law—namely focusing on LGBTQ youth in the child welfare system. As aforementioned, there are close to half a million children and youth in foster care in the US; about one-fourth who await adoption or other permanent opportunities age out of the system (Children's Bureau, 2018) and anywhere from 15 to 19 percent identify as LGBTQ (Dettlaff & Washburn, 2018; Wilson et al., 2014). Given that LGBTQ youth only comprise about 7–10 percent of the general youth population (but represent 15–19 percent of youth in foster care), these numbers suggest LGBTQ youth are twice as likely than heterosexual, cisgender youth to be in the child welfare system.

Race and gender identity may both play a factor in this LGBTQ over-representation in foster care. First, based on race alone, there is a disproportionate prevalence of Black children in the child welfare system (23 percent are in foster care, versus the 14.6 percent Black population in the US). Second, in examining intersectional identities, one study indicated that approximately 57 percent of all LGBTQ children in out-of-home care also identify as youth of color (Dettlaff & Washburn, 2018). Given that communities of color approximate about 37.4 percent of the US population, but they represent 57 percent of the LGBTQ children in foster care, these numbers suggest LGBTQ people of color are 1.5 times more likely to be in foster care than LGBTQ White people. Meanwhile, another study found 5.6 percent of foster youth were transgender or gender nonconforming (Wilson et al., 2014). If only 2.25 percent of the general youth population identifies as TGNC, these numbers suggest TGNC youth are twice as likely to be in the child welfare system than cisgender youth

Studies have demonstrated that one of the reasons for the overrepresentation of LGBTQ people in the child welfare system is because the parents and guardians of these LGBTQ youth were not accepting of their children's sexual orientations or gender identities, leading to these LGBTQ youth getting kicked out of their homes or running away (Rosario et al., 2012). These experiences of family rejection may also contribute to the notion that 40 percent of homeless youth are LGBTQ—a prevalence that is almost 6.5 times higher than for the heterosexual, cisgender youth population (Quintana et al., 2010).

When LGBTQ youth are placed in foster or group homes, they are likely to encounter bullying, discrimination, and isolation because of their sexual orientation or gender identity (Woronoff, Estrada, & Sommer, 2006). As LGBTQ youth have a higher average number of foster care placements and a higher likelihood of living in a group home setting (Jacobs & Freundlich, 2006), each move or displacement potentially increases their feelings of being isolated, unwanted, ostracized, or unloved, which then negatively impacts their self-esteem and mental health (White et al., 2009). LGBTQ youth have fewer opportunities for permanency (e.g., family reunification or adoption), increasing their likeliness to age out of the system—increasing risk for contact with the criminal justice system, poverty, homelessness, or being victimized in adulthood (Irvine & Canfield, 2016; Fowler, Marcal, Zhang, Day, & Landsverk, 2017). Multiple studies have revealed how LGBTQ youth feel there is institutional desire to silence their experiences (Woronoff & Estrada, 2006).

As of 2018, there are only 17 states (and Washington, DC) that have explicit laws or policies to protect LGBTQ foster youth from discrimination based on both sexual orientation and gender identity; there are an additional 6 states that explicitly protect sexual orientation, but not gender identity (Warbelow et al., 2018). There are also only 7 states that require foster parents to undergo LGBTQ training, to equip them in working with LGBTQ youth (Warbelow et al., 2018). Moreover, there have been some court cases that have resulted in favorable outcomes for LGBTQ youth; for example, in *Doe v. Bell* (2003), a New York City circuit court judge acknowledged discrimination experienced by transgender youth in the child welfare system, as brought forth by a transgender girl who was not allowed to wear feminine clothes in her group home. Regardless, LGBTQ youth in foster care continue to be underserved. Thus, many scholars have described the need for child welfare agencies to adopt and enforce written policies that strongly forbid the discrimination and marginalization against LGBTQ youth by foster parents, staff, case workers, and all others who work with LGBTQ youth (McCormick et al., 2017).

QUEERING FAMILY LAW

In order to queer family law, one must always question and challenge the ways in which certain laws and policies were conceived and enacted, and how they were written through heterosexist and cissexist lenses. For instance, original legal definitions of what it means to be a family or a parent or a married couple are all different now than they were when laws were written centuries ago. Therefore, it becomes important to acknowledge that family law is one of the branches of law that has changed so consistently over time, in order to keep up with the society it is meant to serve. If more and more people are becoming families in historically non-traditional ways, and if more and more young people are identifying their sexual orientations and gender identities in unique ways, it becomes very important for laws to reflect those changing dynamics.

One example of family law that may need to be revisited is the child welfare system. The case study introduced a scenario in which a foster child was taken away from a home in which the baby had been with loving parents for several months. Although both foster parents were well-resourced, educated, and committed to starting a family, the foster system's first priority is keeping children with family or kinship first—regardless if the kin is actually biologically related to the child or if the kin would provide as many resources or opportunities as the foster family. There was no judge to make this decision; the child was simply removed from the foster home because the policies are rigid. Moreover, having a child removed from someone's home (espeically when one loves and cares for that child as their own) can be quite psychologically traumatizing for foster parents who are interested in starting families. Yet the system does not appear to consider the impact of these rigid laws on them. As a result, some potential foster parents may choose not to seek the foster system as a route for starting a family and seek other alternatives. And because there is no conclusive research that foster children fare better in kinship homes than in non-kinship homes, foster children may miss out on being placed in loving homes because agencies try to keep them in kinship homes.

At the same time, the child welfare system is also failing its LGBTQ youth. Perhaps they need to provide incentives for LGBTQ adults to become foster parents to these youth. Perhaps there need to be special mentorship programs in place for LGBTQ youth who age out of the system, so they feel a sense of family and connection that can assist in their abilities to thrive. However, without anyone challenging these existing policies or testing out alternatives, LGBTQ youth remain underserved in the system and miss out on having the same opportunities as heterosexual and cisgender youth, who may have an easier time navigating the system.

Given these factors, queering the child welfare system would include challenging the status quo and advocating for systemic reform, through legislative action or court precedent. Perhaps foster parents should be able to advocate their cases to a judge, instead of simply waiting for a foster agency to determine the child's future. Perhaps a judge can set a precedent by placing a foster child in a home that considers the child's well-being, instead of relying on focusing solely on family reunification or kinship placement first. Or perhaps individuals can lobby for an elected official to champion a bill for foster care reform, on local, state, and federal levels.

On an individual level, people may first advocate for change by learning and educating others about the various types of families that exist and the many legal obstacles that some families will face. Perhaps people who are committed to social justice will make intentional efforts to change public perceptions about what a family looks like—that some families consist of same-sex parents, one parent, a legal guardian, opposite-sex parents, and more, and that some families are created through adoptions, surrogacy, natural conceptions, and many other means. If society is more accepting of the different types of families that exist, perhaps laws and policies may be amended to better reflect (and protect) everyone. Further, advocating for justice in family law means gaining and maintaining awareness of one's privilege—whether it be heterosexual couples who recognize the privilege of being able to conceive and bear children, or LGBTQ people who acknowledge the privilege of having financial means to start their families with fewer legal obstacles. People with such privilege might use their voices to advocate for groups who have historically suffered from systemic oppressions, lessening the burden on people who are constantly trying to fight against institutional inequities. In using their privilege and power in positive ways, these people demonstrate—through their actions—that they are true allies.

EIGHT

Over the Rainbow and Across the Border

LGBTQ People and Immigration

THE CASE OF ROXANA HERNANDEZ

Roxana Hernandez was a 33-year-old Honduran woman who migrated to the US in May 2018, in hopes of seeking political asylum. Traveling with a caravan of other Central American migrants (which included a dozen other transgender women), she was detained upon arrival and was immediately held by local Immigration and Customs Enforcement (ICE) officials in New Mexico. After two weeks in the detention center, Ms. Hernandez died. ICE released a statement that proclaimed the cause of her death was a heart attack which was aggravated by dehydration, pneumonia, and other HIV-related complications; they also confirmed that Ms. Hernández was the sixth immigrant to die in its custody since October of 2017 (Green, 2018). A later analysis by NBC News reported 22 immigrants died in ICE custody from January 2017 to January 2019 (Seville, Rappleye, & Lehren, 2019).

Upon her death, an independent medical examiner determined that Ms. Hernandez was physically abused while in detention, with signs of bruising and fractured ribs (Garcia, 2018), caused by a baton or similar object while she was restrained by handcuffs (Lawler, 2018). It was also discovered that ICE officials had denied her access to antiretroviral drugs while in custody. Moreover, she was housed in freezing temperatures, a common condition for most detention centers that other detainees often referred to as an "ice box" (Green, 2018). Other detainees reported Ms. Hernandez was severely dehydrated (Garcia, 2018) and that she was denied adequate food, water, and medical care—to the point that other detainees reported begging authorities to provide her with water and medical care (Lawler, 2018). In December 2018, Senators Kamala Harris, Tom Udall, and Martin Heinrich demanded that ICE officials release a full report on Ms. Hernandez's death and failing to do so violates congressional requirements; however, over a full year later, they had not.

Sadly, Ms. Hernandez's death is not unique. In 2019, journalists reported the death of Johana "Joa" Medina Leon—a 25-year-old transgender Salvadorian woman who migrated to the United States, in April 2019, in hopes of seeking political asylum. When she arrived, she was detained at the Otero County Processing Center, a private detention center in New Mexico, died seven weeks later (Vasquez, 2019). When the government treats trans women like Ms. Hernandez and Ms. Leon in such inhumane ways, we begin to recognize how the system was not made for them. We also realize that while the United States often claims to be the country where people can seek life, liberty, and the pursuit of happiness, not everyone is welcome.

INTRODUCTION

The purpose of this chapter is to review the literature on LGBTQ immigrants in the US and the law, focusing on heterosexist and transphobic immigration policy, as well as the ways that LGBTQ immigrants navigate legal systems. While immigration has continued to be a contentious topic of debate in the United States, there are an array of issues concerning lesbian, gay, bisexual, transgender, and queer (LGBTQ) people and immigration. In fact, throughout American history, there has been a disparaging relationship between LGBTQ immigrants and the law. While there have been numerous discriminatory laws and policies that have negatively affected LGBTQ people in general (see chapter 1 for a review), there have been many anti-LGBTQ immigration laws preventing LGBTQ migrants from entering the country. There are also many contemporary obstacles for asylum seekers and undocumented queer immigrants—including their treatment in detention centers (see chapter 4 for a review).

A BRIEF HISTORY OF THE UNITED STATES

In order to understand the history of LGBTQ migrants in the US, we must briefly review the history of American immigration in general. When Christopher Columbus arrived in what is now known as San Salvador in 1492, he is often credited as "discovering" what he deemed "the New World" (and what people would later refer to as the Americas). While this may be something that many schoolchildren learn in their history books, archaeologists assert that indigenous people had been living in South America for at least 15,000 years (Goebel, Waters, & O'Rourke, 2008). Further, archaeological and historical evidence supports that there were multiple groups of non-indigenous people who had arrived in North America before Christopher Columbus arrived in the Americas; these included the Norse Vikings who traveled to Greenland and Iceland between 1000 and 1350 A.D. and the Polynesian seafarers who had arrived in Chile between the 1300s and early 1400s (Loewen, 2008).

Similarly, when English migrants landed in 1606 in what is now known as Jamestown, Virginia, and in 1620 in what is now known as Plymouth, Massachusetts, they are credited with "discovering" what would later become the United States. However, there were already millions of indigenous people and hundreds of tribes who were living in North America for thousands of years (Thornton, 1987). Additionally, prior to the Pilgrims' arrivals in the early 1600s, Spanish voyagers had already arrived in what is now California—with the earliest group led by Juan Rodríguez Cabrillo in 1542 (Costo & Costo, 1987). Finally, with Spanish trade between Spain, Mexico, and the Philippines, historical documents support that indigenous Filipinos arrived on the central coast of California in 1587 (Borah, 1995).

Revisiting the notion of who was "first" to arrive in the United States is important in understanding contemporary immigration debates because it demonstrates who gets to control the American historical narrative. As the old African proverb goes: "Until the lioness learns to write, every story will glorify the hunter." If American history books were written through the lens of Native Americans, instead of Europeans, perhaps we would label these Europeans not as "explorers" or as "settlers," but more accurately as "colonizers." Moreover, perhaps we would more accurately acknowledge that while these "founding fathers" were escaping religious persecution from the British Empire, they would aggressively instill their own religious and cultural values in the local indigenous peoples whose land they stole (Thornton, 1987). Similarly, perhaps we would acknowledge that Spanish conquistadors also used violent and exploitative tactics to force religion, culture, and language onto the Native Americans in both North and South America (Costo & Costo, 1987).

In these ways, the colonization of the Americas has often been described as a genocide of Native American people. If three of the criteria of genocide involve: (a) killing members of the group; (b) causing serious bodily or mental harm to members of the group; or (c) deliberately inflicting on the group conditions of life calculated to bring about its physical destruction in whole or in part, then European colonization of North America fit the criteria. Directly, violent tactics were used to force imprisonment, assimilation, or to even exterminate the population, so that colonizers could use the stolen land however they pleased; indirectly, millions of Native Americans were killed as a result of exposure to European diseases like smallpox, influenza, and measles (Costo & Costo, 1987). For context, prior to colonization, there were approximately 75 million indigenous people in North America; by the beginning of 1900, there were merely 4.5 million indigenous North Americans, or about 6 percent of the pre-colonial population (Thornton, 1987). Today, there are 2.9 million monoracial Native Americans and Alaskan Natives in the United States, with an additional 2.3 million multiracial people with indigenous North American heritage. (Norris, Vines, & Hoeffel, 2012). Moreover, only 372,095 Native Americans speak a Native North American language (Siebens & Julian, 2011), suggesting indigenous languages are slowly being obliterated over time.

Around the same time English colonizers began to arrive in North America, African slave trade began to take place. While transatlantic slavery had already existed for over a century, with slaves populating much of the Western Hemisphere in countries now known as Haiti and the Dominican Republic (Gates, 2011), the first slaves in the US were a group of 20 people of African descent who disembarked in Jamestown in 1619. In fact, out of the 12.5 million African people who were forcibly shipped to the New World between 1501 and 1866, less than half a million were brought to the US; 1.5 million had died in Middle Passage; and the remaining 10.5 million were distributed in the Caribbean and South America (Gates, 2011). Even as fewer Africans arrived via slave ships in the US, the Black American population grew significantly. By 1707, there were 25,000 slaves in the US, and by 1790, there were close to 700,000 Black people in the US (Du Bois, 2014).

The mentioning of Native American genocide and African slavery is crucial in discussing American immigration, as it is a way to counter false arguments that the US is solely an "immigrant country" or a "country built by immigrants"—two tropes that are often misused in immigration debates. While it is true that many immigrants from all over the world have been able to find opportunities for success in the US, the country was indeed built on stolen lands, through the atrocities of genocide and forced labor, and under the guise of colonization and the American Dream. And even if many Americans, today, are proud of the country they reside in, were raised in, and possibly may have only ever known, it is necessary to acknowledge the nation's racist and oppressive history, in order to understand the context of how immigration policies came to be and how they are utilized today.

THE HISTORY OF AMERICAN IMMIGRATION

Now that we are aware of the multiple ways that non-indigenous people arrived in the US, let's examine how immigration policies came to be. In order to do so, we must first examine immigration patterns. Dinnerstein

(2009) describes four major waves of immigrants into the United States: (a) Pre-1820s, (b) 1830s to 1890s, (c) 1890s to 1920s, and (d) Post–World War II. Jaggers, Gabbard, and Jaggers (2014) described five eras, based on policy: (a) Open Door Era: 1776–1881; (b) Era of Regulation: 1882–1916; (c) Era of Restriction: 1917–1964; (d) Era of Liberalization; and (e) Era of Devolution: 2001–present. Finally, Ewing (2012) describes six time periods of immigration: (a) Unrestricted Immigration: 1492–1874; (b) The First "Exclusion" Laws and Centralized Control of Immigration: 1875–1920; (c) The National Origins Quota System and End of Anti-Asian Exclusion: 1921–1964; (d) The End of National Origins Quotas and Creation of Refugee Resettlement: 1965–1985; (e) The Rise of Immigration Control and Limiting of Immigrants' Rights: 1986–2000; and (f) The Linking of Immigration Control to National Security: 2001–Present. Combining all three models, I identify six waves/ eras of immigration: (a) The First Wave/ Open Door Era: 1600s–1820s; (b) The Second Wave/ Era of Opportunity: 1820s–1880s; (c) The Third Wave/ Era of Regulations: 1890s–1920s; (d) The Fourth Wave/ Era of Restrictions: 1930s–1964; (e) The Fifth Wave/ Era of Liberalization: 1965–2001; and (f) The Sixth Wave/ Era of Fear and White Nationalism: 2001–Present Day.

The First Wave/ Open Door Era: 1600s–1820s

The first wave of American immigration initially consisted of individuals who arrived in the 1600s and 1700s—mainly people from England and other parts of Europe, who were escaping religious persecution and people from Spain who aimed to expand the Spanish empire, to spread Christianity, or both. The earliest members of this group did not need to apply to enter the US, as there were no formal immigration policies or regulations. They simply showed up and decided they could live on the land that was not theirs. Although the U.S. Constitution, written in 1787, did not mention anything directly about immigration, Congress passed the Naturalization Act of 1790 which allowed "free White persons" "of good character" to gain citizenship after two years of residence (Kerber, 1997, p. 841). In 1800, the minimum requirement was increased to five years of residence. This notion of allowing only Whites to become citizens is made evident through Thomas Paine's (1776) *Common Sense,* a text that later would be considered a classic. In his vision, he states: "Europe, not England, is the parent country of America" (Paine, 1776, p. 13). In this way, the view of the US as a "land of immigrants" was essentially meant to be restricted to White immigrants and their descendants.

Because only free White persons could gain citizenship, many groups could not—including Native Americans, Black slaves, and free people of color. The latter group would have included multiracial people and Haitian refugees (Dinnerstein, 2009), as well as the large settlement of Filipinos in Louisiana in 1763 who arrived as a result of the aforementioned trade between the Philippines, Mexico, and Spain (Mercene, 2007). While these people of color were legally allowed to live in the US, by being denied citizenship, they were denied the right to vote or the right to own property, among other things.

The Naturalization Act of 1790 was the first time the law explicitly affirmed children of citizens were considered citizens, regardless of where they were born. Yet, it also proclaimed citizenship would not be granted to "persons whose father has never been a resident in the United States" (Kerber, 1997, p. 839)—suggesting a child who is born to an American mother but to a non-American father would not be considered a citizen. In 1855, the U.S. Congress passed legislation declaring that women gained American citizenship when they married an American man with citizenship; yet, there was no explicit language about US-born women's citizenship or if an immigrant man who married a US-born woman was considered a citizen (Cott, 1998). In 1907, Congress further delegitimized American women's citizenship through a law enforcing American women who married a foreigner to take their husband's nationality (Cott, 1998). Taken together, these laws suggest women were only considered citizens because they were married to a man who was a citizen. So, although the U.S. Constitution used gender-neutral language, it was never meant to include women (Kerber, 1997).

In fact, if women were indeed full citizens, they would have been granted the ability to own property, serve on juries, serve in the military, or vote. Yet, women were prohibited from owning property in their own name, until states passed Women's Property Acts—beginning in 1839 (Warren, 2009). Women were barred from jury duty in many states for decades, and women were never drafted or called directly for military service (Cott, 1989). White women did not gain the right to vote until 1920, when the 19th Amendment to the Constitution prohibited voting restrictions based on sex (Terborg-Penn, 1997; Warren, 2009) and women of color could not vote until even later. Specifically, because Native Americans and Asian Americans could not become citizens until 1924 and 1952 respectively, women of these groups also could not vote (Minnis & Moua, 2015; Tsosie, 2016). Relatedly, voter suppression efforts effectually prevented Black women across the US from voting until the passage of the Voting Rights Act of 1965 (Terborg-Penn, 1997). Thus, women, especially women of color, were never full citizens of the US until the twentieth century. So, although the U.S. Constitution begins with "We the People," it has racist and sexist origins that were not originally intended to include all people.

The Second Wave/ Era of Opportunity: 1820s–1880s

Dinnerstein (2009) highlights a second wave of immigrants that arrived in the early to mid-1800s, mostly from European countries who had not come before. People from Ireland fled from famine and mainly settled on the East Coast; meanwhile, people from Germany and Scandinavia sought economic and farming opportunities and settled mainly in the Midwest. In the mid-1800s, amidst news of the gold rush in California, people from China arrived in search of wealth; later, these laborers would be credited as building the transcontinental railroads in the US (Chang & Fishkin, 2019). I label this time period as the era of opportunity because it begins a time in which immigrants viewed the US as a place where they could gain wealth or prospective success—and not necessarily just as a place to escape religious persecution. While this period is technically still an "open door" era, in that there were no restrictive laws on who could come to the US, this era would end with two major events that began to put restrictions on immigration.

First, the Chinese Exclusion Act of 1882 was enacted, preventing the migration of Chinese laborers into the country (Lew-Williams, 2018), becoming the first federal legislation that restricted immigration of a certain racial or ethnic group. The act, which initially was limited to 10 years, was renewed in 1902 and made permanent in 1904 (Leong & Okazaki, 2009). The passing of the act was fueled by an anti-Asian sentiment that began to increase in the mid-1800s, because Whites believed that Chinese migrants were stealing American jobs. This anti-Chinese sentiment, which was often directed at many other Asian groups, was sometimes referred to as a "Yellow Peril" (Lew-Williams, 2018, p. 35). So, although, these Chinese laborers worked in very poor conditions, and that anywhere between 50 and 1,200 Chinese railroad workers died as a result of work-related accidents or weather-related illness, or from smallpox, these Chinese migrants faced blatant discrimination and even violence from local Whites who did not want them in the US (Chang & Fishkin, 2019). For instance, in 1877, a Chinese laborer named Hing Kee was found dead in his bed in Port Madison, Washington; he suffered from two headwounds that penetrated his skull and a slit throat that was inflicted by either an axe or a cleaver (Lew-Williams, 2018). Sadly, such violence would foreshadow the treatment of many other immigrants who later would come to the US.

The second major event during this time period was the opening of Ellis Island in New York in 1892. Ellis Island, which was formerly a depot for processing New York immigrants, would then become the primary federal immigration depot in the country. Ellis Island would eventually become a ubiquitous symbol of American immigration, as it would become the hub in which more than 12 million immigrants began their lives in the US (Foner, 2000). Moreover, the opening of Ellis Island also symbolized the notion that state governments would no longer be responsible for processing immigration and that the federal government would have more control and regulation of who could legally enter the country.

The Third Wave/ Era of Regulations: 1890s–1920s

The third wave of immigration is one in which new ethnic groups began to arrive in large numbers; it is also one in which other ethnic groups were prohibited from coming to the US altogether. Most notably, the 1890s was the time period in which Ellis Island welcomed hundreds of thousands of Italians and over a million Jews from Eastern Europe (Foner, 2000). While the Jews were fleeing from religious persecution and genocide at the hands of Hitler and the Nazi regime (similar to the English from centuries prior), the Italians were in search of economic opportunities (similar to the Irish, Germans, and Chinese from the decades prior). While many of these new immigrants came with skills and were happy to start their new lives in the US, they were met with hostility by previous immigrants, namely by the Irish and Germans, who often stereotyped, and discriminated against, them. Nonetheless, this time period marked an era in which immigrants began to almost outnumber the native-born. As an example, it was reported 41 percent of all New York City residents in 1910 were foreign-born and that there was no clear majority ethnic group in the city (Foner, 2000).

At the turn of the century, some Asian Americans also began to migrate in larger numbers, in search of financial and vocational opportunities. While Chinese laborers were barred from entering the country, Japanese and Filipino laborers began to arrive, primarily on the West Coast and in Hawai'i (Daniels, Taylor, & Kitano, 2013; Mabalon, 2013). Some Filipinos immigrated as *pensionados*, or sponsored students, who sought educational opportunities at elite American universities, after the U.S. colonization of the Philippines (Nadal, 2011). However, there were still several obstacles for these new Asian immigrants. For example, California's 1913 Alien Land Law prohibited Asian Americans from owning property, deeming that purchasing of agricultural lands could only be by individuals who were eligible for citizenship (Leong & Okazaki, 2009).

This time period also marks the beginning of regulations of who could enter the US. The Chinese Exclusion Act of 1882 opened the door for subsequent laws prohibiting people not just on race, but also on other characteristics. First in 1903, Congress passed the Immigration Act of 1903, also known as the Anarchist Exclusion Act, which prohibited anarchists and people with extreme political beliefs from entering the US (Ewing, 2012); it would become the first immigration law to exclude people on the basis of political ideologies or beliefs. Second, the Immigration Act of 1907 added more exclusionary criteria, including the prohibition of immigrants who were "imbeciles," "feeble-minded" persons, individuals afflicted by a physical or mental disability that might impede their ability to earn a living or those with tuberculosis, children not accompanied by their parents, and individuals who admitted to having committed a crime of "moral turpitude" (Ewing, 2012, p. 4). While moral turpitude was not explicitly defined, federal judges used their own discretion and sometimes ruled sodomy as one of these crimes (Minter, 1993).

With the outbreak of the First World War, immigration declined overall; but, toward the end of the war, Congress passed the Immigration and Nationality Act of 1917, which resulted in three more major restrictions. First, it required immigrants who were 16 years old and above to pass a literacy test, in which they had to demonstrate they could read several words in a language of their choice (Jaggers et al., 2014). Second, it changed previous language (e.g., "imbeciles," "feeble-minded") to people who were "mentally defective" or of a "constitutionally psychopathic inferiority" (Davis, 1999, p. 19). Third, it prohibited any immigration from an "Asiatic Barred Zone" which consisted only of countries in Asia and the Pacific Islands (Leong & Okazaki, 2009, p. 353). The bill was vetoed twice by President Woodrow Wilson but was overridden by Congress. These new regulations demonstrate that immigration policies did not only discriminate on race, but also on educational levels and social class—countering the narrative of the US being a land of opportunities for all.

Perhaps the most significant regulations during this time period were ones involving quotas. The Emergency Quota Act of 1921 was the first immigration law to enforce numerical limits on immigration by country—by limiting it to a total of 350,000 immigrants per year and setting a quota of 3 percent of each country's population in the U.S. based on the 1910 Census (Ewing, 2012). Later, the Immigration Act of 1924, also known as the Johnson-Reed Act or the Asian Exclusion Act of 1924, banned entry of migrants from all Asian countries and amended the quota system to restrict entry to 2 percent of each country's population number from the 1890 U.S. Census (Bashi, 2004). Notably, the quota system only applied to countries in the Eastern Hemisphere and did not apply to Canada or Latin America (Massey & Pren, 2012).

The formula, which allowed approximately 150,000 total immigrants per year, was set so that 85 percent of new immigrants came from countries in Western European, with the highest quotas coming from the United Kingdom, Germany, and Ireland. Moreover, by using population numbers from the 1890 Census, the quota system from 1924 would decrease the numbers for countries who had come in larger numbers in 1910. In spite of this push for more immigrants from Western Europe, some of those countries could not fulfill their quotas. For example, there were 42,670 immigrants from the UK in 1929, representing only 55 percent of the quota allocated for that year (Bashi, 2004). Nevertheless, the Immigration Act of 1924 promoted more Whites in the country and prevented or halted non-Whites from entering the country—promoting even more racial hierarchies and tensions between the various groups.

The Fourth Wave/ Era of Restrictions: 1930s–1964

While new Asian immigrants were restricted from entering the US, those who were already living in the US were not deported and experienced more violence and discrimination. In the 1930s, on the West Coast, anti-Asian sentiment continued, with many working-class White men, again, believing that Asian Americans were stealing their jobs; however, a new sentiment developed that some Asian men were now stealing their women. For instance, in the 1920s and 1930s in Watsonville, California, tensions had risen between Filipino American farmworkers and working-class White men—many who had lost their jobs during the Great Depression (Mabalon, 2013; Showalter, 1989). The conflicts were exacerbated by White men's stereotyping of Filipino men as the "brown menace" or "hypersexual"; "splendid"; and "exceptional" dancers who wooed White women at the local dancehalls (Burns, 2008, pp. 23–24). In 1930, the Watsonville Riots ensued, with White men terrorizing the Filipino American men—with reports of beatings, burglaries, and destruction of their homes. The violence reached a fatal pinnacle with the murder of a 22-year-old Filipino American named Fermin Tobera who was shot through the heart (De Witt, 1979).

When World War II began in the 1940s, immigration continued to be minimal—particularly as a result of the quota system that generally remained in place. However, some Asian countries were eventually removed from the aforementioned barred zone and were allotted a quota of migrants who could enter the US. For example, the Tydings-McDuffie Act of 1934, otherwise known as the Philippine Independence Act, changed the status of Filipinos living in the US from "nationals" to "aliens"—to recognize the American occupation and colonization of the Philippines. In doing so, Filipinos were no longer banned from entry and a quota of 50 Filipino immigrants per year was established (Mabalon, 2013). Almost a decade later, the Magnuson Act of 1943 allowed for Chinese migrants to enter the US, with an annual quota of 105 people, effectually putting an end to the Chinese Exclusion Act of 1882 and allowing Chinese Americans to become U.S. citizens (Ewing, 2012; Minnis & Moua, 2015). Finally, at the end of World War II, the Luce-Celler Act of 1946 allocated a new annual quota for both the Philippines and India to 100 immigrants per year; it also allowed for Filipino and Indian Americans residing in the US to become U.S. citizens (Gonzales, 1986; Mabalon, 2013).

While these laws may have benefitted some Asian American groups, it was during this time period the federal government would engage in what would be considered one of the greatest injustices toward Asian Americans—the Japanese internment. In 1942, after the bombing of Pearl Harbor, the U.S. government violently forced approximately 120,000 Japanese Americans out of their homes and imprisoned them in "relocation" camps for three years, because they were viewed as threats to national security (Daniels et al., 2013; Dinnerstein, 2009; Ewing, 2012). This forced relocation resulted in 4 to 6 billion dollars in losses for Japanese Americans (many who were born and raised in the United States), whose homes and businesses were destroyed (Daniels et al., 2013). Decades later, President Ronald Reagan signed the Civil Liberties Act of 1988, providing reparations to survivors of the camps; in 1988, President George H. W. Bush formally apologized to the survivors of these camps, recognizing how racial prejudice led to the decision to uproot these innocent people's lives (Daniels et al., 2013).

A final major event during this time period was the signing of the 1952 Immigration Act, also known as the Walter-McCarran Immigration and Naturalization Act, which repealed the Johnson-Reed Act/Asian Exclusion Act of 1924 and put an end to the ban on immigration from all of the countries listed in the Asiatic Barred Zone. Furthermore, the act allotted an annual quota for the remaining Asian and Pacific Islander countries to 100 migrants and eliminated any laws banning Asian immigrants from becoming American citizens (Minnis & Moua, 2015). Thus, even though Asian people were severely restricted from entering the US, 1952 marked the first year that all Asian Americans were legally allowed to become American citizens.

The Fifth Wave/ Era of Liberalization: 1965–2001

In 1965, President Lyndon B. Johnson signed the Immigration and Naturalization Act of 1965, also known as the Hart-Celler Act of 1965, which effectively ended the quota system that prohibited migrants from many countries from entering the United States. In doing so, immigration began to increase significantly, at a rate that surpassed all other time periods (Nadal, 2011). For many Asian American groups, immigration after 1965 consisted mainly of professionals (e.g., doctors, nurses, engineers) who were highly educated and sought opportunities they did not view as possible in their home countries. Some migrants came to the US because of American colonization or American presence in their home country. For example, as a result of the Philippine-American War, in which Spain sold the Philippines to the US and the Philippines became an American colony for nearly 50 years, many Filipinos migrated to the US to achieve the American dream they were taught about in school systems (Nadal, 2011).

While the Hart-Celler Act of 1965 removed quotas from Asian and European countries it actually imposed an annual cap of 120,000 on entries from the Western Hemisphere, when there were no previous quotas placed on Latin American countries (Massey & Pren, 2012). In spite of this, the number of immigrants from Latin America increased significantly with 459,000 Latina/o/x immigrants in 1950 to a peak of 4.2 million during the 1990s, or 44 percent of all new immigrants (Massey & Pren, 2012). For Mexican Americans specifically, the population rose from 442,000 in the 1960s to 2.8 million in the 1990s (Massey, 2015). While the Latina/o/x population began to increase noticeably in the 1960s and 1970s, so did the anti-Latino immigrant sentiment; media images and political figures consistently portrayed Latina/o/x in negative and stereotypical ways, resulting in what would be referred to as the "Latino threat" narrative or an "immigration crisis" (Chavez, 2008).

During this time period, undocumented immigration also increased significantly, particularly for Mexican Americans—with an estimate of 1.13 million total undocumented Mexican Americans in 1984 (Warren & Passel, 1987) to an increase of 4.6 million undocumented Mexican Americans in 2000 (Hoefer, Rytyna, & Baker, 2009). Massey and Pren (2012) assert this increase of undocumented Mexican immigrants was highly influenced by the abrupt ending of the Bracero Program—a short-term foreign workers program, in which 450,000 Mexican immigrants were granted work visas annually and could travel between Mexico and the US. The cutting of the program disrupted the migration flow; thus, Mexican immigrants who were used to U.S. work opportunities now crossed the border without proper documentation.

In 1986, Congress passed the Immigration Reform and Control Act of 1986 (IRCA), which aimed to control and limit the number of undocumented immigrants in the US. Through IRCA, it became unlawful to hire (or continue to employ) undocumented people; it also authorized the expansion of the Border Patrol (Massey & Pren, 2012). However, through IRCA, approximately 1.7 undocumented immigrants who were able to demonstrate continuous residence in the country prior to 1982 were granted amnesty and were able to become permanent legal residents by 1990 (Woodrow, 1992). Yet, negative stereotyping of Latinx immigrants continued.

A final trend during this period was the creation of policies and programs for refugees, which were developed in response to the large amount of Southeast Asian refugees from the Vietnam War. In a short period of time, Congress passed two bills: 1) the Indochina Migration and Refugee Assistance Act of 1975, which created a domestic resettlement program for Vietnamese and Cambodian refugees in 1975 and Laotians in 1976; and 2) the Refugee Act of 1980 opened opportunities for refugees from all ethnic groups (Ewing, 2012).

The Sixth Wave/ Era of Fear and White Nationalism: 2001–Present Day

Jaggers and colleagues (2014) argue the current state is, or should be, one of devolution, or "the transfer of power from the central government to the state or local government" (p. 9). Part of their argument relies on the notion that Arizona has passed a series of propositions involving immigration, including Proposition 100 (which disallows bail for undocumented people who commit certain crimes); Proposition 200 (which restricts undocumented people from receiving state benefits); and Proposition 300 (which prohibits undocumented people from receiving in-state tuition at public universities). Additionally, Jaggers and colleagues highlight how states had responded to the failure of the federal Development, Relief, and Education for Alien Minors (DREAM) Act, which aimed to assist undocumented people who had come to the US as children, without consent or choice, and the US is the only country they had ever called home (Barron, 2011). For example, California passed their own DREAM Act in 2011, which granted undocumented students access to financial aid and in-state tuition (Whaley, 2012). Similarly, the Maryland Dream Act was passed in 2011, allowing undocumented students to attend public universities after proving their parents pay taxes and they attended a public high school for at least three years (Keyes, 2012).

In many ways, Jaggers and colleagues (2014) are correct, in that states have created and enforced their own policies regarding immigration. For example, many states have taken stances on whether or not to be "sanctuary states" in order to protect undocumented immigrants against inhumane and insensible deportation. As of June 2019, ten states plus Washington, DC are considered sanctuary states, while ten states have passed legislation prohibiting sanctuary cities and enforcing federal law (Morse, Polkey, Deatherage, & Ibarra, 2019). Herein lies the problem labeling this era one of devolution. The federal government is so entrenched in immigration law, particularly since the presidential election of 2016, that state immigration laws are typically created in reaction to federal laws and executive orders on immigration.

Because of this, I argue that this era is not about states being able to regulate immigration laws, as they previously had been able to do prior to 1790. Rather, this era is focused on fear and White nationalism. After the tragedies on September 11, 2001, the relationship between fear and increasing immigration followed similar historical patterns from the "Yellow Peril" and "Latino threat" tropes of the previous eras and was exacerbated. In October 2001, Congress passed the USA PATRIOT Act, which granted authorities the power to deport, without hearings or any presentation of evidence, all noncitizens (i.e., legal or illegal, temporary or permanent) who one may have reason to believe might commit, further, or facilitate acts of terrorism (Massey & Pren, 2012). As such, the PATRIOT Act granted power to the president of the U.S., the U.S. attorney general, and others to use their discretion in deporting individuals, which in many ways is denying individuals the constitutional right to a fair trial.

Other laws and policies that emerged included the National Security Entry-Exit Registration System (NSEERS) which effectively racially profiled foreign-born Muslims, Arabs, and South Asians in the name of antiterrorism, as well as the Enhanced Border Security and Visa Entry Reform Act of 2002, which implemented new procedures for the review of visa applicants, particularly scrutinizing individuals from countries that were deemed sponsors of terrorism (Koulish, 2010). Post-9/11 deportations increased significantly; from 2000 to 2009, the U.S. detained and deported 2.5 million individuals—a number only slightly higher than the total number of deportations between 1892 and 1999, a 107-year span (Coleman, 2012). In addition, although deportations were meant to be in direct response to terrorism, Mexican Americans, who played no part in the 9/11 tragedies, comprised 72 percent of deportations in 2009 (Massey & Pren, 2012).

Instilling fear has also been used as a way to promote White nationalism under the guise of American patriotism. When Donald J. Trump first announced his presidential candidacy in 2015, he referred to Mexicans as criminals, rapists, and drug dealers (Chavez, Campos, Corona, Sanchez, & Ruiz, 2019); focused his campaign on the slogan "Make America Great Again" (Eddington, 2018, p. 1); and encouraged his supporters to chant "Build that wall" at his rallies (Morey, 2018, p. 460). In January 2017, he issued three executive orders. First, he commanded that protecting the southern border was paramount and it required the building of a wall was a matter of national security and keeping American communities safe; second, he condemned jurisdictions that deemed themselves as sanctuaries—threatening to withhold any federal funding from those cities or states for not complying with his orders (Greene, 2018). Perhaps the most controversial of his executive orders was Executive Order No. 13,769, which would colloquially be known as the "Muslim travel ban" or more accurately the "Muslim Ban." Through this order, he suspended the entry of foreign nationals from seven Muslim-majority countries—namely Iran, Iraq, Libya, Sudan, Somalia, Yemen, and Syria—for 90 days; suspended the US refugee admissions program for a period of 120 days; decreased the number of refugees who could be admitted by half (i.e., 110,000 to 55,000 admissions); and indefinitely suspended refugees from Syria (Wadhia, 2018). These immigration policies often refer to "a national security threat" or the need to protect the American people—without any actual evidence that states that there are actual threats to individuals' safety.

With anti-immigrant rhetoric (as well as anti-Black, anti-LGBTQ, ableist, and sexist rhetoric), American citizens who hold similar sentiments are emboldened to engage in violence that aligns with these beliefs (Morey, 2018). For instance, in February 2017, in Olathe, Kansas, an Indian man named Srinivas Kuchibhotla was fatally shot by a White man, unprovoked, who screamed: "Get out of my country!" (Morey, 2018, p.462). In August 2017, in Charlottesville, Virginia, far-right White nationalists engaged in a torch-bearing march at the University of Virginia to protest the removal of a statue of Confederate leader Robert E. Lee.

Counter-protestors, who included anti-fascists, community members, and civil rights leaders, came to speak out against the hate. A White Nazi sympathizer named Alex Fields, Jr. drove his Dodge Challenger through a crowd of counter-protesters—injuring 35 people and killing one woman, a 32-year-old White woman named Heather Heyer (David, 2018).

Hate incidents like these are not rare; the Federal Bureau of Investigation (2018) reported in 2017 that hate crimes increased by 17 percent, with 80 percent of the cases involving race, ethnicity, or religion. The Southern Poverty Law Center reported a rapid increase in the number of hate groups (e.g., White supremacists, anti-Muslim groups, and anti-immigrant groups) in the country, citing specifically the number of hate groups with a focus on anti-immigration rising from 14 to 22 percent (Beirich & Buchanan, 2018).

In this way, I am reminded of the several aspects of American history that appear to be repeating themselves. First, the bans on these Muslim-majority countries are reminiscent of the Asiatic Barred Zone, which prevented any entry from certain Asian and Pacific Islander countries (and later led to an annual quota of 100 entrants from that country). Next, the notion of blanket groups of people being viewed as security threats is resonant of the Japanese internment camps, in which hundreds of thousands of innocent people were forcibly removed from their homes because they were deemed security threats. Finally, the anti-immigrant narrative and the violent desire to make America "great" again is a resurgence of both the Yellow Peril and the Latino threat, in which immigrants have been painted as stealing jobs and ruining the country.

LGBTQ PEOPLE AND IMMIGRATION POLICIES

Now that we have an understanding of how immigration laws and policies have affected immigrants in general, let's explore how LGBTQ people specifically have been affected by these aforementioned laws and by others. In this section, I will describe (a) LGBTQ Immigration Bans, (b) HIV/AIDS Ban, and (c) Marriage Laws.

LGBTQ Immigration Bans

First, as aforementioned, the Immigration and Nationality Act of 1917 prohibited people who were "mentally defective" or had a "constitutionally psychopathic inferiority" from entering the country (Davis, 1999, p. 19). Similar language appeared in the McCarran-Walter Act of 1952, which barred "aliens afflicted with a psychopathic personality, epilepsy, or a mental defect," and the Hart-Celler Act of 1965 which banned aliens afflicted with a "psychopathic personality, a mental defect, or sexual deviation" (Wheatley, 1985, p. 262). While not explicitly stated, each of these clauses could have been used to prohibit LGBTQ immigrants at the time.

In order to understand these connections, it is necessary to revisit the history of LGBTQ identities and behaviors being viewed as a mental illness. While sodomy had been criminalized since the inception of the US, homosexuality was not medically or clinically viewed as a mental disorder until 1952, with the American Psychiatric Association's first publication of the *Diagnostic and Statistical Manual of Psychiatric Disorders* (DSM) which listed homosexuality as a paraphilia. In the second revision of the DSM (published in 1968), homosexuality was listed as a "sexual orientation disturbance"; and in the third revision in 1973, it was removed altogether (van den Berg, 2017, p. 849).

So, while the Immigration Act of 1917 listed "mentally defective" as a characteristic that would prohibit one from legally immigrating to the US, homosexuality was not listed as an official psychiatric disorder until 1952. Consequently, this "mental defect" clause would not be the mitigating factor that would deny LGBTQ immigrants entrance into the US. Instead, these migrants could be denied citizenship because of the moral turpitude clauses that were cited in the Immigration Act of 1907. If an individual was found to not be of good moral character, they could be denied citizenship or naturalization. As such, if someone was caught (or admitted to) engaging in sodomy (which was still considered a crime), their behavior could deem them to be immoral. Subsequently, as long as sodomy was still considered a crime, particularly on the federal level, moral turpitude could be used to prohibit LGBTQ immigration into the US.

On the other hand, the original DSM was published, perhaps coincidentally or not, the same year as the McCarran-Walter Act of 1952. Thus, between 1952 and 1973, patients who were diagnosed with either of these disorders (i.e., paraphilia or sexual orientation disturbance) could be considered to have a mental defect and thus legally barred from immigration. They could also be subject to psychiatric institutionalization, in which they could be exposed to an array of severe (and ineffective) forms of treatments, such as castration, lobotomies, and electroshock therapy (Nadal, 2013).

Further, LGBTQ people were also prohibited from immigrating to the US as a result of the "psychopathic personality" clause in the McCarran-Walter Act of 1952—a law that would eventually be affirmed by the Supreme Court. In *Boutilier v. INS* (1967), through a 6–3 majority ruling, SCOTUS ruled how the inclusion of "psychopathic personality" in immigration laws was indeed intended to include homosexuals. Thereby, the court's ruling held a decision to deport Clive Michael Boutilier, an openly gay Canadian permanent resident who contended that despite his sexual orientation and past sexual history he did not have a psychopathic personality (Dueñas, 2000; Minter, 1993). Boutilier first arrived in the U.S. in

1955 when he was 21 years old; he applied for American citizenship in 1959, and his application was flagged by the Immigration and Naturalization Service, for deportation when he admitted to engaging in sodomy.

The court argued how the intention of Congress when they passed the McCarran-Walter Act of 1952 was to bar homosexuals from immigrating—citing congressional hearings in 1950, in which both the House and the Senate introduced revisions to previous immigration laws to list "sex perverts and homosexuals" as part of the disqualifying groups for immigration (Dueñas, 2000, p. 38). However, per the recommendation of the U.S. Public Health Service at the time, both bills were changed to include the more general language of "psychopathic personality," which Congress members were told would include homosexuals and other sexual deviants. One explanation for this change was because sexual behaviors could be concealed or covered up, while a homosexual personality was one that could be diagnosed by a medical professional (Minter, 1993). Through the decision, Mr. Boutilier was deported to Canada and thereby separated from his mother, stepfather, brother, and partner of 8 years— all of whom were living in the US. While the Hart-Celler Act of 1965 was even more explicit in their bias against LGBTQ people, in their adding of the phrase "sexual deviation" (which was meant to include sex workers, sexual predators, and LGBTQ people; Minter, 1993), the precedent set by *Boutilier v. INS* (1967) would prohibit homosexual immigrants from being legally admitted into the US.

When the American Psychiatric Association removed homosexuality as a disorder from the DSM in 1973, and when the American Psychological Association in 1975 followed suit and passed a resolution which proclaimed homosexual and bisexual orientations were not pathological, they complicated immigration laws as they were currently written. If medical and mental health professionals no longer viewed homosexuality to be a psychiatric disorder or a mental illness, INS would have difficulties in listing it alongside mental disorders. In fact, if both organizations moved it was unethical for any psychiatrist or psychologist to engage in any efforts to change one's sexual orientation, the rationale for excluding LGBTQ immigrants would be less robust. Despite this, the language of "sexual deviation" remained in immigration policy for nearly two decades. It was not until 1990, after years of lobbying by U.S. Congressman Barney Frank and others, that Congress removed the exclusion (Minter, 1993), effectually eradicating previous immigration acts, as well as the precedent of *Boutilier v. INS* (1967).

Under the revised Immigration and Naturalization Act of 1990, LGBTQ people would no longer be barred from entering or immigrating to the United States—at least not explicitly because of their sexual orientations or gender identities. However, even with this revision, LGBTQ immigrants were still subject to the aforementioned moral turpitude clause, in which they had to prove they were of good moral character and did not engage in any moral crimes. Yet, because sodomy was still illegal on a federal level (and would be until 2003), there was always a strong possibility LGBTQ people would be deemed immoral, by virtue of identifying as LGBTQ or engaging in same-sex sex.

To demonstrate the embedded heterosexism of these laws, let's visit the case of Richard John Longstaff—a native and citizen of the United Kingdom before he entered the US as a permanent resident in 1965 (Anglin, 217). On his application there was a question which read: "Are you now or have you ever been afflicted with psychopathic personality, epilepsy, mental defect, fits, fainting spells, convulsions or a nervous breakdown?" Longstaff answered "no"—as he did not have any history of psychopathy, mental illness, or any other related physical health issues. When he was granted permanent residency, he moved to Texas and went on to fulfill his dream of opening a retail clothing store. Fifteen years later, he tried to apply to become a naturalized citizen, never considering that he had ever broken the law. However, the district court denied his request because they learned, through a long interrogation with immigration authorities, that Longstaff had violated the Texas Penal Code by engaging in homosexual activity. When questioned about his original application in 1965, Longstaff attested he did not lie because he did not have any mental illness; however, given that having same-sex attraction was considered pathological by the American Psychiatric Association and that sexual deviance was enough to be rejected by the Immigration and Naturalization Service in 1965, he did indeed fit the criteria for a psychopathic personality or mental defect.

Further, Longstaff was tasked with proving that he was of good and moral character. Although his friends, neighbors, and other community members were able to speak to his kindness and civic engagement, he also lived in the state of Texas, where sodomy was illegal and where he could be arrested for engaging in consensual same-sex sexual behaviors, even in the privacy of his own home. While his ability to prove moral character was accepted by the court, he was still denied naturalization. In *Matter of Longstaff* (1983) the court asserted that he was never lawfully admitted to the US because his application was incorrectly completed. Because he had engaged in homosexual activity prior to his immigration to the US, the court ruled that he did have a mental defect; was considered a sexual deviant; and should be deported. Fortunately, Longstaff moved to San Francisco where he was protected, due to a federal appeals court in California which contradicted the decision in his case by ruling in another case of gay immigrants' ability to reside in the US. Years later, Mr. Longstaff was never granted US citizenship, though he was able to retrieve his green card and maintain status as a permanent resident (Anglin, 2017).

HIV/AIDS Immigration Ban

Another immigration policy which limited the immigration of LGBTQ people involved HIV/AIDS. As mentioned in chapter 1, the National Institutes of Health (NIH) Revitalization Act of 1993 added an amendment in which HIV was listed as a communicable disease. For almost two decades, people with HIV/AIDS diagnoses were excluded from legal migration, except under rare circumstances (Winston & Beckwith, 2011). So, while the U.S. Immigration Act of 1990 permitted entry for the first time to LGBTQ immigrants, the NIH Revitalization Act rescinded entry for LGBTQ people who were living with HIV. Though it is clear that not all people with HIV/AIDS are LGBTQ-identified or that all LGBTQ-identified people are living with HIV/AIDS, many LGBTQ people around the world who were indeed living with HIV/AIDS, may have wanted to seek refuge in the US, but would have been denied. These include people who would have benefitted from advanced access to HIV-related health care; people who wanted to live in a country where they encountered less anti-LGBTQ or anti-HIV stigma; and people who have wanted to seek asylum in the US due to their sexual identity, HIV status, or both.

While NIH's HIV travel ban prohibited immigrants from entering the country, two earlier asylum cases involved people already living in the US who were granted asylum due to their serostatus. First, José Patricio Boer-Sedano was a gay Mexican man living with HIV/AIDS who sought asylum in 1990 after he was sexually assaulted by a police officer and received numerous death threats (Bromer, 2006). One of the deciding factors in his victory was testimony from his American doctor who indicated that he was receiving HIV-related treatment that he could not obtain in Mexico, and that he would be unable to find a job due to his serostatus. Thus, deporting him would be bad for potential persecution, as well as for his health and well-being. Similarly, another case involved a woman living with HIV who was granted amnesty in 2000 because she was able to establish that because she was a married woman she would be imprisoned or physically harmed if she returned to India (Neilson, 2004). While both cases set a precedent for HIV status as an identity group for asylum cases, the HIV travel ban prevented so many others living with HIV from entering the country, potentially hindering them from surviving and thriving.

Marriage Laws and Immigration

While SCOTUS ruled state marriage bans were unconstitutional, which thereby legalized same-sex marriage in 2015, we recognize how marriage equality was also a major immigration issue. As discussed in chapter 1, the earliest same-sex marriage involved a Colorado gay couple—Tony Sullivan and Richard Adams—who were married in 1975;

when Sullivan applied for citizenship and listed Adams, a naturalized citizen, as his spouse, INS denied his application. Because same-sex marriage was not legal, especially on the federal level, their marriage could not be used as a way to streamline Sullivan's naturalized citizenship—a process that was possible for many opposite-sex couples since 1855.

In order to understand the impact of marriage laws on same-sex binational couples, we must examine the history of immigration laws for opposite-sex binational couples. As aforementioned, a woman could become naturalized when she married an American man with citizenship since 1855, though it is presumed the law only applied to White women who married White men (Cott, 1998). However, a man who married an American woman could not become naturalized until the Cable Act of 1922 removed gender-specific language from the previous legislation (Cott, 1998). Little else is written explicitly about marriage as a path to citizenship until World War II and the subsequent War Brides Act of 1945. The act allowed American military personnel to sponsor their foreign-born wives and children, waiving some of the previous visa requirements and time restrictions. In 1968, Congress amended the Hart-Celler Act of 1965 to add a family reunification clause, which allowed citizens to sponsor foreign-born family members—including spouses and children. Since then, annual immigration of foreign-born spouses increased from 26,345 in 1945 to 105,917 in 1985 (Thornton, 1992).

While the process in which an immigrant can use their binational marriage as a path to citizenship is one that is heavily regulated every step of the way (Abrams, 2007), it is an option that was impossible for LGBTQ immigrants before 2015. If Tony Sullivan, in 1975, submitted his application for citizenship and listed a wife as a sponsor, he may have been successful. And even if his marriage was recognized by the state of Colorado, it was not federally recognized, which then meant that INS, a federal agency, would not recognize it either.

A more recent situation involving this dilemma was one that first became popularized in 2009 through *People* magazine—the story of Shirley Tan and Jay Mercado, a same-sex female couple in California who met in 1986, gave birth to twin boys in 1997, and were registered as domestic partners in 2004 (Young, 2009). Tan, who was born in the Philippines and overstayed her visa, was at risk of deportation in 2009 after her asylum request was denied. While they were domestic partners in the state of California, and she was co-parenting two American citizens, their union was not recognized by the federal government. Their story is one that would be common for many LGBTQ binational couples and why LGBTQ people fought specifically for federal recognition of marriage. When *U.S. v. Windsor* (2013) overturned a provision in the Defense of Marriage Act which prohibited federal recognition of same-sex marriage, it allowed for state same-sex marriages to be recognized by the federal government, including Shirley Tan and Jay Mercado, who wed in 2014 (Araulla, 2013).

A final topic related to immigration and marriage is the notion of marriages of convenience—contracted agreements to wed for reasons other than love or romance (e.g., LGBTQ people who marry a U.S. citizen to stay in the country). Although heterosexual people may enter these types of agreements, prior to 2015, LGBTQ people may have had more difficulty in convincing immigration officials their marriages were bona fide, due to their sexual orientation, gender identity, or gender presentation. For example, one undocumented queer person avowed:

> I feel like there was definitely some hesitancy in coming out at one point in my life because I didn't want to cancel out my opportunities to getting a green card through marriage, which is fucked up, but that's a real thing, you know? You know, if you are openly out there and then you have a friend that comes along and wants to help you out, it's like, well what are you going to do now? Immigration is going to look up your background and see that you are queer. And yeah, they'll go on Facebook and see all my jota pictures. So that was a real thing because I was like, I want a green card. So that was a very real thing. (Cisneros & Bracho, 2019, p. 722)

Regardless, it must be noted that Immigration and Customs Enforcement (2016) views marriages of convenience as "marriage fraud" and are felony offenses which can result in a prison sentence of up to 5 years and a fine of up to $250,000 for both the immigrant and the U.S. citizen.

LGBTQ IMMIGRANTS AND ASYLUM

One of the greatest concerns between LGBTQ immigrants and the law is asylum. Because homosexuality and transgenderism (both identity and behaviors) are presently criminalized in more than 76 countries and are punishable by death in ten of those countries, many LGBTQ immigrants seek asylum as their only hope for survival and living as their truest and most authentic selves. Asylum seekers, also referred to as asylees, come to the US because they have suffered past persecution in their home country, have substantiated fears of future persecution in their home country, or both. In 1994, then U.S. Attorney General Janet Reno released Order 1895–1894, which reversed previous laws prohibiting gay and transgender people from seeking asylum. The precedent was set by the case of Fidel Armando Toboso-Alfonso—a gay Cuban man who suffered extensive physical and psychological abuse by the Cuban government and arrived in the US via a boatlift in 1990 (Shuman & Hesford, 2014). LGBTQ people were now considered for asylum because they had "membership in a particular social group that led to persecution" (Randazzo, 2005, p. 32).

While it is unclear how many LGBTQ asylum seekers there are in the US currently (as there is no public data on cases based on sexual orientation), earlier reports found in the first 9 years of eligibility, from 1994 to 2003, six hundred LGBTQ people were successfully granted asylum based on their sexual orientation (Randazzo, 2005). Current reports from attorneys and activists estimate the number of LGBTQ people seeking asylum each year is at least in the hundreds (Del Real, 2018). Though not specific to LGBTQ cases, the U.S. Department of Homeland Security (2019) reported, in 2017, there were 16,045 asylum applicants who were granted amnesty out of a total of 26,568 (a rate of about 60.4 percent); in 2016, the success rate was 11,582 out of 20,340 (or 56.9 percent); and in 2015, the success rate was 17,818 out of 26,011 (or 68.5 percent). The Organization for Refugee, Asylum, and Migration (ORAM, 2012) used data from the United Kingdom and Belgium to estimate that between 4 and 6 percent of all asylee cases involved LGBTQ identity. Using this formula, ORAM estimates that out of the 26,568 cases in the US in 2017, anywhere between 1,062 and 1,594 cases could be LGBTQ-related.

LGBTQ asylum claims are often difficult to win because individuals have to prove that (1) they are in fact queer or trans, and (2) they are being violently persecuted or are subject to being violently persecuted because of their sexual orientation or gender identity (Bromer, 2006). With such rigid tasks, asylum claims are often unsuccessful if the person is deemed to not appear to be gay, due to preconceived or stereotyped notions of what is meant by being LGBTQ; for instance, some masculine-presenting gay asylum seekers were denied because judges did not believe they were actually gay (Hanna, 2005). In fact, asylum seekers describe how their judicial process is one of interrogation and criminalization, instead of one of assistance and compassion. An asylee from Kenya described:

> I naively faced the process of seeking asylum, believing I would present my case and that I would be questioned in a non-adversarial manner. However, when the Immigration Officer interviewed me, I was surprised and offended by the battery of queries, particularly those designed to determine whether or not I was truly a gay man as I had asserted. From the start the interview felt like an inquisition. (Randazzo, 2005, p. 46)

Other flaws to the process include that proving one's sexuality and gender identity means doing so by using American definitions, which may contradict cultural definitions from the individual's home country; further, an unspoken requirement for an LGBTQ person to have been public about their sexuality or gender identity contradicts their need to be private in order to protect themselves (Shuman & Hesford, 2014). In other words, LGBTQ asylees must prove they were out as queer or trans in their home country (which may have led to severe violence) in order to be granted asylum from the severe violence they are trying to escape. In this way, the asylum process almost favors those who have experienced violence, without protecting people who have been fortunate enough to avoid violence altogether.

Previous research has found LGBTQ asylum seekers, especially transgender asylum seekers, face an array of obstacles in the process, which negatively affects their mental health (Nakamura & Morales, 2016). Some asylum seekers do not even make it to the US or to their trials due to violence they encounter along the way; others may not secure attorneys, which lessens their chance of winning their cases by 20 percent (Randazzo, 2005). Transgender asylum seekers experience psychological distress from being placed in facilities that do not match their gender identities or not receiving the proper health care or gender-affirming treatment, while increasing their risk for sexual assault (Del Real, 2018; Nakamura & Morales, 2016). Trans asylum seekers are often placed in solitary confinement, not because they deserve such treatment, but because detention centers do not know where to place them—a common binary-informed practice in incarceration (see chapter 5). As a result of these experiences, LGBTQ asylum seekers may undergo severe trauma and retraumatization, resulting in an array of PTSD symptoms (Nakamura & Morales, 2016).

Finally, perhaps one way to better understand what it means to be an LGBTQ person seeking asylum is to examine LGBTQ asylees' experiences through the lens of Queer Theory. Judith Butler (2012) argues the queer and trans migrant experience of diaspora is one that is based in loss and grief; one in which violence and persecution is a norm; and one in which an individual may never fully be at home. She describes how queers across the diaspora bond on the notion of being unwanted and exiled, stating that "we are all, in this sense, the unchosen but we are nevertheless unchosen together" (p. 25). Jose Esteban Muñoz (1999) describes how queers of color across the diaspora navigate race, ethnicity, gender, and sexuality in a way not previously identified in Queer Theory; he labels this process a disidentification, in that queers of color perform, survive, and fight in a world they do not fully fit in. Later, Munoz (2009) describes queerness as a utopia that has not been and may never be fully reached, urging people to move beyond a "here and now" vision and toward a futurist "then and there" vision.

UNDOCUMENTED LGBTQ IMMIGRANTS

Another LGBTQ subgroup who may have a spectrum of experiences with law and government are undocumented LGBTQ immigrants, or individuals who live and thrive at the intersection of their undocumented immigration statuses, their sexual orientations, and their genders and gender identities. Gates (2013b) estimates that there are approximately 904,000 LGBTQ immigrants in the US, with about 637,000 who are documented and 267,000 individuals who are undocumented. Out of the undocumented group, Gates estimates that 71 percent of undocumented LGBT adults are Latinx and 15 percent of undocumented LGBTQ adults are Asian or Pacific Islander, matching statistics for the overall undocumented population.

In recent years, undocumented LGBTQ people have self-identified as "undocuqueer"—a hybridized, political positionality of their multiple oppressed identities (Cisneros, 2013). Undocumented, gay, Filipino American activist Jose Antonio Vargas described: "Even though I came out as gay at age 18, I was in the closet about being undocumented until I was 30. The closet is a depressing, dangerous, isolating place to be. Now that I'm 'out' about both identities, I'm in the process of claiming myself fully" (Galluci, 2019).

For undocuqueer people, life requires navigating how or whether to come out of both the shadows and the closet—with shadows representing the ways they may learn to keep their undocumented statuses silent and in the dark, and closets representing where they are taught to hide or store their authentic sexual orientations and gender identities (Cisneros & Bracho, 2019).

Undocuqueer people circumnavigate how they conceal or disclose their sexual orientations, gender identities, undocumented immigration statuses—considering systems of oppression and the consequences in coming out. Some undocuqueers may have lived in the US for most of their lives; some are new arrivals. Some may seek asylum, while some may not. Regardless, there are a number of concerns they face as a result of these multiple and intersectional identities.

First, for undocumented LGBTQ people, finding employment and navigating work issues are common concerns. Because of a lack of papers, they may have difficulty securing a job. As an example, one undocuqueer person shared:

> I couldn't get a job. I kept looking for jobs and it was really hard to get jobs. You know people didn't want to give me jobs because I didn't have papers. So, you know, I just felt like, well, I think this is not. . . . I don't know, it just felt like I can't, I just can't do this. And I was really afraid. (Cisneros & Bracho, 2019, p. 723)

Even when undocuqueer people are able to obtain employment, they may take jobs they are not interested in, that do not promote their careers, or that do not utilize their fullest potentials. Further, because of the transience of their citizenship status, undocuqueers often undergo exploitation, abuse, and discrimination at work due to the fear of being outed, not being able to secure other employment, or being reported to immigration

(Burns, Garcia, & Wolgin, 2013). To demonstrate this phenomenon, an undocumented trans Latina immigrant described:

> Apart from being part of the LGBT community, we are Latinas, we are people that do not speak English. When we find work, they don't pay us well, and they don't give us work for not having papers, and sometimes even for being transgender within the LGBT community. They just don't. So, we are the ones that suffer the most, no? We know these are issues that affect the undocumented community, but if you identify as LGBT, it is going to affect you twice as much. (Cisneros & Bracho, 2019, p. 726)

As supported by her experience, the intersections of multiple oppressed identities harms undocuqueers', and perhaps more specifically undocuqueer trans Latinas', ability to prosper.

Second, undocuqueer people are more likely to encounter economic hardships, due to limited employment opportunities. While there is no known data that examines median income for undocuqueer people, previous scholars estimate undocumented people, in general, have a median income that is $14,000 a year less than the average median income; meanwhile LGBTQ people (especially trans people and LGBTQ people of color) tend to earn less money than their heterosexual cisgender counterparts (Burns et al., 2013). Therefore, by virtue of their intersectional identities, undocuqueer people may undergo economic issues that supersede those of LGBTQ people in general, immigrants in general, and undocumented people in general.

Third, the psychological stressors of navigating their intersectional identities is a common and conscious stressor for undocuqueer people. One undocuqueer person described:

> I was coming to terms with my identity within a relationship, but also having to hide that component of my life was another shadow . . . because I was hiding it . . . from my family, and I was hiding away with my family from society as being undocumented. So, it was living in both the closet and the shadow. (Cisneros & Bracho, 2019, p. 721)

Finally, undocuqueers describe the multiple forms of oppression they face, including heterosexism and heteronormativity within their families, racism and xenophobia within general LGBTQ communities, and the stigma of being undocumented and queer in general society (Cisneros, 2018). Some undocuqueers also identify some of the microaggressions they experience—even from well-intentioned allies. For example, while the DREAM Act was proposed to provide a pathway to citizenship for children who did not make the choice to come to the US, the usage of the term "DREAMers" by others has been used to create divisive narratives of "good" versus "bad" immigrants, instead of recognizing undocumented immigrants who did not come as children are good and moral immigrants too (Cisneros, 2018).

QUEERING IMMIGRATION

In queering immigration, we must reform the entire system—recognizing it was founded on racism, xenophobia, sexism, and heterosexism. We must also queer immigration by recognizing our country was built on stolen lands and that certain people have been allowed in, that others have been forced in against their will, and that others have been kept out altogether. We can address these in myriad ways—from teaching K–12 students about the real history of genocide and slavery, instead of perpetuating the false notion of a peaceful or humane colonization. For instance, instead of celebrating Thanksgiving and Columbus Day, the federal government can celebrate other holidays like LGBTQ Pride or the anniversary of Stonewall. Instead of school children learning about the alleged first Thanksgiving between the Pilgrims and Native Americans, perhaps they can learn about Native American history and heroes. When children learn about American history, they must also learn about the atrocities of slavery and the fight for Civil Rights. Teachers should not only teach about African Americans during Black History Month in February; rather, they should integrate conversations about systemic racism and oppression into all of their school subjects. As an example, when teaching about the Founding Fathers of the US, conversations about slavery, genocide, and sexism should be addressed too.

Queering immigration means learning about the faults of the current immigration system. It can mean reading works by Jose Antonio Vargas or understanding immigration legislation being championed by Alexandria Ocasio-Cortes. It can mean being familiar with organizations like the American Civil Liberties Union who advocate for immigrant rights, or the Sylvia Rivera Law Project who fight for trans rights (and trans immigrant rights). After learning more about the current state of affairs, it is necessary for people to have constant and persistent conversations about who is in power, who controls the best interests of the country, and who is viewed as invaluable or disposable. These conversations may occur among coworkers, at the dinner table, or even during story time with one's children. While it may feel awkward or anxiety-provoking to initiate these conversations, we must look at our country's history and acknowledge that speaking out against the status quo is the only way that disrupts normalized oppression. Finally, by teaching children about the true history of the United States, the fight for equity and justice will be the new normalized values for future generations.

NINE

The Queer Criminal Mind

LGBTQ People and Forensic Psychology

THE CASE OF ANDREW CUNANAN

On July 15, 1997, fashion designer Gianni Versace was shot twice in the back of the head and killed, in front of his beachfront home in Miami, Florida. At the time, Versace was considered one of the most high-profile fashion designers in the world, so his death came as a shock across the world. Hours after his murder, authorities identified their main subject — Andrew Cunanan, 27, a multiracial, self-identified gay man, who had been placed on the Federal Bureau of Investigation's Ten Most Wanted Fugitives a month prior (FBI, 2014). After eight days of global media attention and a national manhunt, FBI investigators discovered where Cunanan had been hiding — a houseboat that was just two miles away from Versace's home. Authorities found Cunanan's body with a self-inflicted gunshot wound into his mouth (FBI, 2014; Orth, 2008; 2017).

Prior to murdering Versace, Mr. Cunanan had killed four other men — two in Minnesota, one in Chicago, and one in New Jersey. The first two of Cunanan's victims were men whom he had known. Jeffrey Trail, 28, was a U.S. naval officer, who became friends with Cunanan while stationed in San Diego. Cunanan referred to Trail as his best friend, although the feeling was not mutual; Trail told people he felt sorry for Cunanan (Orth, 2008). Trail moved to Minnesota and befriended David Madson, 33, who was Cunanan's ex-lover and subsequently his second murder victim. On Sunday, April 27, 1997, while Cunanan was in Minneapolis visiting Madson, Cunanan asked Madson to invite Trail over to his apartment. After Trail arrived, an argument ensued. Forensic specialists determined Cunanan struck Trail with a hammer to the head, twenty-seven times, killing him. Authorities later found Trail's body wrapped in a rug. It is unknown if Madson and his dog were present at the time of the murder (Orth, 2017).

The next morning, a neighbor saw Madson and Cunanan in the elevator, along with Prince, Madson's dog. The next day, the same neighbor saw two men at a distance walking a dog. She presumed it was Madson and Prince, but they were too far away to identify. When Madson did not show up at work on Monday or Tuesday, his coworkers became concerned and called the police. Police discovered the body and initially presumed it was Madson's, but only later discovered it was Trail's. Madson was an immediate suspect, as the body was found in his loft apartment. However, a week later, Madson's body was found on a Minnesota lakeshore over 50 miles away, with multiple gunshot wounds in his back and head. With Madson no longer considered a murder suspect (and now a mere victim), police began their search for Cunanan.

A week later, on May 4, 1997, Cunanan killed his third victim—a business tycoon and philanthropist named Lee Miglin—in the garage of Miglin's Chicago home. When police arrived at the scene, they discovered that Miglin's head and body was bound completely with duct tape, with only a small breathing area under his nostrils. Miglin's ribs were broken, his throat was slashed by a saw, his face had contusions, and his body had been stabbed over 20 times with a screwdriver. Though Miglin's family denied it, police initially suspected that Cunanan and Miglin had a prior relationship and that Miglin may have been a closeted gay or bisexual. Because Miglin's face was brutalized, in similar ways that Trail's and Madson's were, it was presumed that Miglin's murder was personal and one that elicited anger in Cunanan (Orth, 2017).

Five days later, Cunanan killed his fourth victim—a cemetery caretaker named William Reese in New Jersey. Police labeled this murder as a "functional kill"—with Cunanan needing to steal Reese's red Chevrolet pickup truck, as he had been driving with Miglin's car—which he learned police were then searching for (Orth, 2008; 2017).

Cunanan drove Reese's car to Miami, where he lived for two months. Police later reported he did not lay low; he went out in public in the afternoons and evenings, and even pawned some of Miglin's jewelry and used his real name. When his body was found, there was no suicide note, leaving Cunanan's motive for killing Versace unclear. Some say the two had met 7 years prior in San Francisco, when Versace was designing costumes for the San Francisco Opera. Versace's family said the two never met at all. Some presume that Cunanan was delusional and had only imagined having ever known Versace. Others say that Cunanan targeted Versace because he was obsessed with his fame and fortune.

While the case of Andrew Cunanan was a hot topic in the summer of 1997, his infamy faded into obscurity, where it remained for almost twenty years. In January 2018, producer Ryan Murphy released the television series *The Assassination of Gianni Versace: American Crime Story*—featuring the murder spree of Andrew Cunanan, as well as some of the events that led up to that period of time. Based on Maureen Orth's novel, *Vulgar Favors: Andrew Cunanan, Gianni Versace, and the Largest Failed Manhunt in U.S. History*, the series starred Darren Criss in the role of Cunanan and went on to receive many accolades including an Emmy, a Golden Globe, and a Screen Actors Guild award for Criss. The series took many liberties in portraying the events that were not fully known (e.g., Cunanan's childhood, how Cunanan met Miglin, etc.). Nonetheless, the series illustrated possibilities of how Cunanan became a serial murderer.

Before the Murders

There are many factors to consider when trying to conceptualize Andrew Cunanan and his criminal mind and behaviors. First, what was erased in most mainstream media accounts before and after Cunanan's death, was the notion that Cunanan was biracial or multiracial. His father, Modesto (or "Pete"), a Filipino immigrant, became a U.S. Navy officer who was serving in the Vietnam War right when Andrew was born. Andrew's mother, Mary Ann Schillaci, an Italian American homemaker, took care of their four children: Christopher, Elena, Gina, and Andrew. Orth (2017) reports the two older children (Christopher and Elena) allegedly had a different life than their two younger siblings; they grew up in a time when the family had very few financial resources. When their mother inherited money, the family moved into a new house; when their father became a stockbroker in 1979, they were able to live more comfortably. As a result, Gina and Andrew had more opportunities than they did, and Andrew was especially favored from the start. In their new house, Modesto gave Andrew the master bedroom and later paid for his tuition at The Bishop's School—an elite college preparatory school in La Jolla, California—an opportunity not offered to the other children.

As a child, Andrew was deemed to be smart—a message that would be engrained in him from an early age. In some ways, such reinforcement was positive, in encouraging Andrew to read (he read and memorized encyclopedia pages and Bible passages). By junior high school, he was enrolled in a mentally gifted program, and he continued to excel academically. Meanwhile, he also began to tell elaborate lies that painted him as elite and wealthy—which contrasted with the reality of his middle-class immigrant roots. He became obsessed with the upper class—likely influenced by his father's teachings about being more superior than all others. Because these messages were so excessive (to the point that his classmates deemed him a pathological liar), the confidence that Modesto gave Andrew the boy would eventually transform into a narcissism and self-importance that Andrew would develop as a man. It was during this time his parents' marriage started to dwindle. His mother later avowed Modesto was physically abusive toward her by hitting her and pulling her hair. Nonetheless, Andrew's older siblings claim his childhood was unremarkable—stating that "he didn't have a violent bone in body" and "something horrible must have happened to him in his adult life" (Yanez, 1997).

One major event that occurred in Andrew's early adult life was when his father fled the country after being accused of embezzling more than $100,000. In doing so, Modesto left his wife and children with nothing—requiring them to sell their house and move to a humbler home. While Andrew's family was never wealthy, their house in an upper-middle-class neighborhood was enough to disguise the life that he had tried to hide from people. Andrew was a student at the University of California–San Diego at the time his father left; shortly after graduating, he left and moved to San Francisco. Purportedly, he would not speak to his siblings again.

Another major event during Andrew's young adulthood was when he began to live his life as a gay man. Orth (2017) reported he was teased by his peers as a child for being flamboyant; his first sexual experience was allegedly when he was 13 years old; and he began to come out to his friends sometime after. After his death, his siblings claimed he never disclosed his sexuality to them. In a Larry King interview, his father would deny his sexuality altogether, while his mother would say, "I was surprised because Andrew never admitted it openly . . . I wanted him to know that I loved him regardless of if he was an 'it' or 'she' or 'he' or what. I gave birth to him" (Kutchins & Sommers, 2017). Both of these sentiments from his parents demonstrate homophobic bias, but in different ways. While his father's denial would be considered overt homophobia, his mother's word choice but benevolent sentiment would be considered a microaggression that illustrates subtler bias (see Nadal, 2013).

Andrew's parents were both Catholic and, as aforementioned, one of the first books he learned to read was the Bible. Accordingly, it is likely that Andrew did not feel supported by his family regarding his sexual orientation and that he felt ashamed or unable to disclose his identity to them. In fact, research finds that coming out is very difficult in Filipino American families due to shame, stigma, and guilt derived from both Filipino and Catholic influences (Nadal & Corpus, 2013). Thus, it is possible that he believed that his parents would not love him if they knew about his sexuality—a common feeling for LGBTQ people and especially Filipino Americans (Nadal & Corpus, 2013). In this way, it seemed like Andrew was constantly seeking love and attention, perhaps as a way to validate his existence, or even to compensate for the love and acceptance he wished he could get from his parents.

One of Andrew's past sexual partners said that Andrew seemed "withdrawn" during sex and had a "prudish streak" that he wouldn't allow himself to explore sexually (Orth, 2017, p. 72). Sometime later, Andrew would indeed begin to explore his sexuality in a number of ways. For instance, reports indicated that he "had fallen in with the underground gay culture of San Francisco and was involved with drugs and well known as a popular sex slave. He appeared in many pornographic movies, got pleasure from sadomasochism, and truly enjoyed his status in the underground" (Douglas, Burgess, Burgess, & Ressler, 2013, p. 480). While some may view this behavior as "acting out" sexually, it could have been his way to gain sexual pleasure (especially when he did not feel pleasure in other parts of his life) or just an overall way to escape from reality and enjoy his sexuality.

Regarding race, there is not a lot mentioned about how Andrew felt about being multiracial or Filipino during his childhood, besides recollections of him never befriending other Filipino kids; one classmate stated: "Andrew always wanted to be part of a richer crowd" (Orth, 2007, p. 27). However, Andrew's older brother, Christopher, did refer to Andrew as the "White sheep" (p. 21), relaying how much their father favored Andrew; however, it is also possible that there is some racial meaning to this term. While Andrew may have appeared to be racially ambiguous to some, he was light-skinned and generally passed as White—a quality that is revered in Filipino culture, due to the history of Spanish and American colonization in the Philippines (David, 2013). In fact, Andrew's godfather asserted that Modesto invested so much time in Andrew because of his good looks (Orth, 2017). Thus, there is a possibility Andrew was favored by his father because he was White-presenting, light-skinned, or attractive—qualities that Modesto may have felt insecure about and projected onto Andrew.

As an adult, Andrew appeared to dismiss his Filipino heritage and associate only with White people. A friend at Berkeley said: "Filipino was the hot race on campus that year, [but] Andrew wanted to be blond and blue-eyed" (Orth, 2017, p. 71). His ex-boyfriend David Madson was White; his "best friend" Jeffrey Trail was White. When they rejected him, he was angered—perhaps not just for personal reasons but because of what they represented. Andrew had spent his entire life trying to be accepted by White people (especially White people who impressed him); so, to be rejected by these two men were not just emotional or narcissistic injuries; they potentially were also symbolic of his racial trauma (see Nadal, 2018). Even in death, Andrew's multiracial identity was in question. When his corpse was found, one attorney said: "I don't know that I'd recognize him. He looked very Filipino. I expected White preppy," while a detective shared: "I wouldn't describe him as Oriental, but even dead he was interesting-looking. He had interesting eyes. Even dead I could see a certain magnetism to him" (Orth, p. 494).

Personal Reflections on Cunanan

In July 1997, when I first heard news media reports about Andrew Cunanan, I was a college student at the University of California–Irvine. When I first saw Cunanan's name, I immediately thought he might be Filipino, as one of my friends from college had the same last name. When I saw his photo, I was certain he was Filipino American—potentially a multiracial Filipino (or a "mixed" Filipino as I probably would've said back then). He resembled many of my friends and cousins. His age aside, he was someone who would have easily blended in at our *Kababayan* (UCI's Filipino American student organization and also the Tagalog term for "fellow countrymen/countrywomen") meetings. Because my Filipino American friends and I did not see any Filipino Americans (positive or negative) in the media, we were intrigued and followed the case. We did not necessarily feel connected or empathetic toward him, but we wanted to learn more; after all, he was a *kababayan*. Additionally, as a closeted gay man at the time and as a psychology major, I was especially interested to watch how it would all unfold.

A short time after Cunanan's body was found, the news dwindled, and most people likely forgot about him. However, for many Filipino Americans, Cunanan would be a name that people would remember. As one of the few Filipinos on television for a number of years, he was, sadly, our claim to fame. Moreover, every once in a while, for a brief moment of time, when I would meet other gay men who would learn I was Filipino, some commented about whether I knew "the guy who killed Versace." Because Gianni Versace was such an icon in the mainstream gay community, many gay men of all races were intrigued about the case of Andrew Cunanan too.

My Filipino American friends and I had conversations about why we thought he might have done it all. We wondered if he had a strong Filipino American identity, whether he had Filipino American friends, if he felt supported or rejected by other Filipino Americans, and if his multiracial identity influenced any of his cognitions or behaviors. In fact, as I was enrolled in an Asian American Psychology summer course at the time, I learned about a number of cultural factors that influenced mental health issues, and I wondered about how Cunanan's cultural background may have influenced his psychopathy too.

It was not until after the release of Murphy's series in 2018, coupled with the timing of writing this book, that my interest in the Cunanan case reemerged. In wanting to learn more about his family, separate from what was portrayed in *American Crime Story*, I searched for academic articles on Mr. Cunanan. The first that emerged was from Christine Bacareza Balance (2008), a fellow Filipino American, who wrote about the internal conflict that Filipino Americans faced when they first heard news of Cunanan. Balance describes how she and her Filipino American friends and family similarly knew he was Filipino from the start, and how they joked with each other about people looking like him. She writes how Tom Brokaw and other journalists referred to Cunanan as the "homicidal homosexual" which, coupled with the bombarding of his mugshots over national news, "reiterated the brown and queer as deviant and the White, heterosexual male subject as a powerful norm" (p. 88). Further, Balance describes how the labeling of Cunanan as White and the erasure of his Filipinoness represented a greater problem of society's lack of understanding of Filipino Americans regarding race and historical context, as well as Filipino Americans' ability to adapt and blend into multiple spaces. Finally, she introduces many artistic pieces inspired by Cunanan, created by notable Filipino American writers and artists like Regie Cabico, Jessica Hagedorn, and Gina Apostol. In reading about all of these works, it is validating to learn that I was not alone in my complicated reaction to Cunanan.

INTRODUCTION

There is very little academic literature that has focused on the intersection of sexual orientation, gender identity, and criminal behavior. Forensic psychologists, criminologists, and other scholars have certainly written about individual criminals, who were either openly or likely lesbian, gay, bisexual, transgender, or queer (LGBTQ)—with notable names like Jeffrey Dahmer, Aileen Wuournos, and John Wayne Gacy. However, what is less common is that the scholars who write about LGBTQ people and communities are either openly queer or trans themselves, utilize a critical lens or social justice orientation, or are well-versed in Queer Theory, Critical Race Theory, Womanism, Feminism, or Intersectionality Theory. As academia is still predominantly controlled by White, cisgender, heterosexual, male narratives, I take a different approach in how to conceptualize or queer criminal behavior.

This chapter will focus on LGBTQ criminal offenders—or individuals who have engaged in violent or heinous crimes, particularly maliciously or knowingly, and who identify or have been identified by others as lesbian, gay, bisexual, transgender, or queer. While previous chapters have described the ways that many LGBTQ people have been unfairly criminalized (e.g., CeCe McDonald who was arrested for murder when she was protecting herself from a transphobic hate crime, or Michael Johnson who was criminalized for engaging in consensual condomless sex), this chapter will focus on LGBTQ people who have willfully hurt or brutalized people. A variety of criminal offenses will be covered—ranging from murder to child sexual abuse to intimate partner violence. I will begin the chapter by highlighting some of the previous literature on

LGBTQ criminal offenders and end with some of the mitigating factors which may contribute to their thought and behaviors.

Throughout the chapter, I will refer to cases, including Cunanan's, utilizing a critical and social justice approach to conceptualize some of the other variables that may have influenced his life. I acknowledge the caveat that in Cunanan's case, or any of the cases that I mention, that I do not condone any of their behaviors; rather, I present mere hypotheses, which I hope might assist in readers' understanding of each of the situations.

Television producer Ryan Murphy once shared: "No one is born a monster. Monsters are created" (De'Alessandro, 2018)—a sentiment that I share. I do not think that people who commit crimes were born to engage in such behavior; however, I strongly believe that trauma, systemic oppression, and other environmental variables may influence one's experiences to commit crimes. So, if we hope to minimize the amount of criminal behavior in our world, we have to address the factors that may influence them.

A REVIEW OF QUEER CRIMINAL BEHAVIOR

Scholars have asserted how the academic literature on LGBTQ people and criminal behavior is scant overall (Buist & Lenning, 2015; Dennis, 2014; Panfil, 2014; Woods, 2014, 2017), or how literature describes how crime-related research that focuses on sexual orientation and gender identity mainly LGBTQ people as victims or survivors of hate violence, bullying, or other forms of discrimination (Woods, 2014). Perhaps one of the difficulties in writing about LGBTQ criminals is that prior to just two decades ago, being LGBTQ in itself meant that a person could be classified as a criminal in the US. As noted in previous chapters of this text, sodomy laws were still active across many states until 2003, when SCOTUS ruled in *Lawrence v. Texas* (2003) that such laws were unconstitutional. Similarly, as described in chapter 8, LGBTQ immigrants were not even legally allowed to enter the US, as they were classified alongside sexual deviants, sex workers, pedophiles, and perverts. Dennis (2014) described this plight in the very first sentence of his work, citing: "It is problematic to write a chapter on the LGBT person as criminal offender, since for over 100 years, LGBT people were framed as the villains of every story and the culprits of every crime" (p. 86). Woods (2014) argues that after the 1970s, academic writings on LGBTQ offenders in criminology decreased so significantly, rendering them to be near invisible. In this section, I will describe the historical ways that academia has criminalized queer people, as well as movements toward "queering" criminology and forensic psychology.

Criminalizing Queer People

Prior to the Stonewall Uprising and the birth of the modern LGBTQ Civil Rights Movement in the late 1960s, there were multiple ways that LGBTQ people were criminalized as a result of their sexual orientations and gender identities. For example, in the 1930s, states began to enforce sexual psychopath laws, which resulted in gay men being arrested and institutionalized even without committing any actual criminal act; in the 1950s, with the Lavender Scare, LGBTQ people were fired from their jobs if they were outed or deemed to be "homosexual" (see chapter 1 for a review). While this societal anti-LGBTQ stigma may have been propagated by government leaders and the media, academic researchers in the middle of the twentieth century—across fields like psychology, criminology, sociology, and medicine—contributed to this criminalization. In fact, academic literature in the 1940s and early 1950s which depicted LGBTQ people as criminal, pathological, or both, was cited in the congressional reports that led to the firing of all LGBTQ people employed by the federal government.

In order to understand the sentiment about homosexuality at the time, let's review some of the influential scholars and publications at the time. First, physician Havelock Ellis (1944) defined homosexuality as "the most clearly defined of all sexual deviations, for it presents an impulse which is completely and fundamentally transferred from the normal object to an object which is normally outside the sphere of sexual desires, and yet possesses all the attributes which in other respects appeal to human affection" (p. 188). Regarding attempts at treatment, forensic psychiatrist Charles E. Smith (1953) stated:

> The treatment of homosexuality is unsatisfactory. Actually, no adequate method of modifying this condition has been demonstrated. The problem of treatment is further complicated by the fact that most homosexuals express no particular dissatisfaction with their state, so that, as a group, they seem to have very little motivation toward having their condition modified. (p. 591)

While transgender issues were not discussed explicitly, gender nonconformity was described by some scholars, including psychiatrist Bernard C. Glueck, Jr. (1956) who wrote:

> There is the problem of the very effeminate male homosexual, and the very masculine female homosexual. In addition to the attempts to copy the speech, mannerisms and dress of the opposite sex, which have a distinct social nuisance value, such individuals probably constitute a continuing source of social threat because of the marked degrees of emotional disturbance, including overt mental illness, found in this group." (p. 206)

Notably, there were some scholars who advocated against the criminalization of LGBTQ people, including psychiatrists Karl Bowman and Bernice Engle (1955) who wrote, "No state specifies homosexuality as a crime by that name. Every state, however, prohibits a number of homosexual acts, usually under the name of sodomy or crimes against nature" (p. 273).

During this time, a book was published by Donald Webster Cory, a self-identified gay man, as a way of providing personal insights and experiences of the very group of people who scholars had deemed as pathological criminals. *The Homosexual in America: A Subjective Approach* (1951) utilized the language and lenses of gay people at the time (referring to homosexuals as "gay" and heterosexual people as "straight"). It was written under a pseudonym as a way of protecting the author's career and family; two decades later, in 1974, the author was revealed to be Dr. Edward Sagarin, a professor of sociology at the City University of New York (Sears, 2013). Contrasting the work at the time which pathologized and criminalized queer people, Cory/Sagarin advocated that gay and lesbian people should be considered to be a minority group, writing: "It is my belief that another phase of the minority problem is demanding the attention of America. We who are homosexual constitute a minority that cannot accept the outlook, customs, and laws of the dominant group. We constitute a minority, and a unique one" (Cory, 1951, p. 4). While the book received praise from many including Albert Ellis and Alfred Kinsey, one psychologist reviewer critiqued it with: "The psychologist has little to gain from *The Homosexual in America*. . . . The discussion lacks scientific rigor. At best, the psychologist may find the book useful as a source of fresh hypotheses and 'background knowledge' which are often a pre-requisite of systematic scientific studies" (Bindra, 1953). Such a critique would mirror a commentary which would continue throughout academia for decades: that quantitative or empirical science needs to support the existence of an experience and that qualitative data or personal narratives would not suffice.

Post-Stonewall, in the 1970s, anti-LGBTQ organizations and openly homophobic scholars began to use research inappropriately or inappropriate research to miseducate people on the link between LGBTQ people and crime. For example, some people cite work from Paul Cameron, a psychologist who has claimed a link between homosexuality and violence since his publication *Sexual Gradualism: A Solution to the Sexual Dilemma of Teenagers and Young Adults* in 1978. His work has relied mostly on correlational analyses of data, and some of the work that is cited by the organization he founded—Family Research Institute (FRI)—was never published by a peer-reviewed academic journal. For example, FRI cites a paper presented at the 1983 Midwestern Psychological Association Conference in Chicago to claim a link between homosexuality and mass murders that was never published.

Moreover, as an example of the misuse or misinterpretation of data, the FRI cites the work of Swigert, Farrell, & Yoels (1976) who utilized records of a diagnostic and evaluation clinic. With a sample of 444 homicide cases between 1955 and 1973, the researchers identified a total of 5 cases that qualified as sexual homicides. Out of those 5 cases, there were 2 instances of consensual sex between defendant and victim (1 gay and 1 heterosexual), 2 cases of sexual sadism (1 gay and 1 heterosexual), and 1 pedophilia case of a man abusing a boy. Based on this study's results, the FRI suggests that because 3 out of 5 cases (or 60 percent) are gay, and because only 3 percent of the population identifies as gay, homosexuality must be a cause of sexual homicide. Using this correlational logic to make broad generalizations is problematic; not only is a sample of 5 cases too small or using data that is from 46–64 years ago too old to make a generalization, but they also don't include the rest of the findings of the study. While all five of the cases involve White male perpetrators from lower socioeconomic classes, with less than high school educations and unskilled jobs, the FRI doesn't make an argument about race, social class, education, or job type leading to sexual homicide.

In the 1980s and 1990s, with the HIV/AIDS epidemic, researchers began to investigate the causes of HIV and HIV transmission. While some studies examined intravenous drug users and origins in Africa, the majority of studies concluded homosexuality as the problem, with such perspectives implicitly and others more explicitly. For an example, in one of the first studies on HIV transmission that utilized blood samples, Darrow and colleagues (1987) wrote: "We conclude that HIV is transmitted during sexual activities between homosexual men. No sexual activities involving exposure to the semen, blood, or excretions of infected persons have been shown to be safe" (p. 482). In spite of these views, some academic researchers remained vigilant about not assigning blame and contributing to stigma. Some psychology scholars wrote: "Public and biomedical researchers who restrict attention to sexual behavior or ways in which gay persons differ from others draw on cultural stereotypes and strike gay persons at a most vulnerable place. These stereotypes cloud research into this poorly understood disease at a time when we need illumination" (Coates, Temoshok, & Mendel, 1984, p. 1313). In this way, while it was easy to criminalize LGBTQ people in a new way via HIV/AIDS, scholars can also assist in decreasing stigma and the perpetuation of hate, bias, or stereotypes.

Queering Crime

In order to understand criminal behavior, it is necessary to deconstruct how laws and policies in general have assumed heteronormativity and cisgender norms too. For instance, consider the definitions of sexual assault can include rape (sexual intercourse against one's will), forcible sodomy (anal or oral sex against a person's will), and forcible vaginal or anal object penetration, among others. The interpretation of which category certain crimes fit will depend on the law enforcement officer who first makes and files an arrest, the district attorney who files a charge, or the judge or jury who determine verdicts and sentences. For example, does "sexual intercourse" involve only vaginal sex, or does it include anal sex too? If a cisgender man is sexually assaulted by a man or trans woman via anal penetration, would the instance classify as a rape, sodomy, or both? Furthermore, is being assaulted by an object any less traumatic than being assaulted by intercourse? If rapes have harsher punishments than sodomy charges, and rapes of gay men or trans women get classified as sodomy, do perpetrators of sexual violence toward LGBTQ people get less lenient sentences?

Complicating the matters are that federal charges regarding sexual assault are defined differently than how states define sexually based crimes. The FBI classifies any type of forced or nonconsensual penetration as a rape, while some states define rape only as vaginal penetration. As a result of this discrepancy, two trends may emerge. First, men may not be counted as rape victims, resulting in the harsh undercounting of male rape survivors. Second, the same crime can be charged disparately in two different states—resulting in varying degrees of punishments. A well-known example of this discrepancy is the case of Brock Turner—a White male college student in California who penetrated an unconscious woman behind a dumpster with his fingers. While originally charged with two counts of rape, those charges were dropped because California state laws did not consider digital penetration to be rape. The trial resulted in Turner being convicted of three felony charges: (a) assault with intent to rape an intoxicated person, (b) sexually penetrating an intoxicated person with a foreign object, and (c) sexually penetrating an unconscious person with a foreign object. The sentences for the three charges traditionally would have resulted in up to 14 years. However, the judge sentenced him to 6 months, and he was released after 3 months (Rennison & Dodge, 2016). Thus, not only might people who commit rape (using federal definitions) get away with lesser charges, but they may also serve significantly less time, due to factors like judicial bias.

A third consideration regarding sexual crimes is whether or not it is appropriate to label certain acts as "homosexual," "bisexual," or "heterosexual." By definition, these three terms are sexual orientation, and describe the ways that people identify based on their sexual and romantic attractions, their sexual and romantic behaviors, and the people who share similar experiences. In this way, it is inappropriate to name something as a homosexual crime, if it is not clear how the person identifies. Further, crimes involving sex, particularly rape and child sexual abuse, are not just about sex; they are also about dominance and power (Murnen, Wright, & Kaluzny, 2002). In fact, many people who commit child sexual assaults may not identify with the sexual orientation people may presume (e.g., a male offender who molests both boys and girls may not identify as bisexual, while a male offender who molests boys only may identify as heterosexual). Earlier studies found the majority of offenders who sexually abused children identified as being heterosexual regardless of the gender of the children they abused (Groth & Birnbaum, 1978). In fact, many sex offenders are in heterosexual relationships with women, who are often surprised when their husband, boyfriend, or sexual partner is found to engage in pedophilia.

Additionally, crimes are rarely labeled as "heterosexual" crimes—perhaps because it is presumed that a crime that occurs between a man and a woman is normative, while a crime that occurs between two men is considered deviant and requires a unique label. Similarly, when crimes involve a female offender toward a male offender, it is also listed as a female crime (e.g., female serial killers, female sexual predators), as a way of differentiating the uniqueness of the case. Other times, gender changes whether the crime is even labeled as a crime, both legally and by the public. As an example, when middle school or high school teachers have sex with their adolescent students, male teachers are deemed as rapists or perverts, while sex with female teachers is deemed as consensual. Because of these factors, we must not label these crimes as "homosexual" crimes (nor as "bisexual" or "heterosexual" crimes). In order to be more accurate, crimes should be labeled in terms of their behavior (e.g., "crimes with male perpetrators and male victims"). If identifying people and their sexual orientations, it is appropriate to use labels like heterosexual, gay, and queer; however, people should still be mindful if people's sexual orientation identities are not disclosed. Finally, there are times when I may change language from "homosexual" to "gay or queer" as a way of using more contemporary and acceptable terms.

Queer Critical Criminology

In recent years, there has been a rapid growth of the concept of Queer Criminology or Queer Critical Criminology—a push for criminologists to recognize the homophobic and transphobic origins of criminology and to advocate for more LGBTQ-affirming and queer-centered scholarship. Buist and Lenning (2015) describe two goals of Queer Criminology are (a) to move LGBTQ people from the margins to the center of criminological inquiry, and (b) to investigate and challenge the ways that the criminal legal system has been used as a tool of oppression against Queer people" (p. 1). Later, they avow that "a true queer criminology moves beyond the traditional framework and shifts the spotlight from the rule breakers to the rule makers" (p. 4).

Woods (2015) offers a "homosexual deviancy thesis," in which criminologists are challenged to reconceptualize sexual orientation and gender identity and to consider LGBTQ people as both victims and offenders. Panfil (2014) describes how the fields of criminology and criminal justice have not addressed issues related to violence, gang membership, and crime commission among LGBTQ people—with reasons for omission including criminologists' unintentional presumption of criminal behavior being linked to heterosexuality or criminologists' general societal apathy toward queer experiences. Woods (2017) describes how even though it has been well-documented that LGBTQ people are involved with many factors that correlate with criminal justice systems (e.g., homelessness, poverty, exposure to foster care, etc.), there is a dearth of available data that examines LGBTQ people who come into contact with the criminal justice system, particularly criminal offenders.

Queer Forensic Psychology

While all of the work of all of these Queer Criminology scholars is very helpful in understanding the ways that criminologists can queer their work, I wondered about the ways that forensic psychology has been describing LGBTQ people and more specifically LGBTQ offenders. To explore this, I began with an online search in August 2019 of the academic database PsycInfo (the largest database in the field of psychology). I first searched for articles published in the journal *Law and Human Behavior (LHB)*—the official journal of the American Psychology-Law Society (AP-LS), the 41st division of the American Psychological Association (APA). AP-LS is known as the national organization that prominent forensic psychologists are members. In its 43 volumes (which consisted of 1,636 articles since 1977), there were a total of 4 articles published in LHB that mentioned the words "lesbian," "gay," "bisexual," "transgender," "queer," "homosexual." In examining each of the articles, I found all 4 articles did indeed focus on LGBTQ content—ranging from jury perceptions of gay offenders to workplace harassment. With this, it appears that 0.20 percent of articles published in the leading forensic psychology journal focus on LGBTQ issues.

Next, to assess how much Queer Psychology scholars were publishing on forensic issues, I used PsycInfo again to search for articles published in *Psychology of Sexual Orientation and Gender Diversity (PSOGD)*—the official journal of the Society for the Psychology of Sexual Orientation and Gender Diversity, otherwise known as APA's Division 44. Division 44 is known as the primary national professional organization for psychologists who study, teach, or advocate for LGBTQ issues. In its 6 volumes (which consisted of 342 articles since 2014), I found there were 11 articles that contained the word "forensic" or "criminal." After removing articles that were not primarily about forensic issues, 9 remained: 6 about hate crimes or the Pulse shooting; 2 about intimate partner violence; and 1 about jury bias. Thus, only 2.63 percent of articles published in the leading Queer Psychology journal focuses on anything about LGBTQ issues in forensic psychology.

Finally, I searched the entire PsycInfo database using the search terms "LGBTQ or lesbian or gay or homosexual or bisexual or transgender or homosexual or queer or sexual minority rights" and "forensic psychology." There were 133 hits—ranging in issues related to prison and incarceration to LGBTQ families custody and LGBTQ-related legislation and policy. For comparison, the term "forensic psychology" by itself had 22,556 hits, and the search "LGBTQ or lesbian or gay or homosexual or bisexual or transgender or homosexual or queer or sexual minority rights" had 41,581 hits. In this way, it is clear that forensic psychology has not taken the same steps as criminology to be more inclusive of LGBTQ concerns. It is also clear that Queer Psychology has not yet found ways to integrate issues related to Forensic Psychology.

Within my department and college, my colleagues and I have had several conversations about expanding the definition of forensic psychology, particularly in our doctoral program in Clinical Psychology, which has a Forensic Specialization and our MA degree programs in Forensic Mental Health Counseling and Forensic Psychology. Some of us have advocated for utilizing more broader conceptualizations of forensic psychology—above and beyond what it already or traditionally includes. For example, while traditional forensic psychology has focused on understanding perpetrators and offenders, a more critical or queer forensic psychology can also investigate experiences of survivors, families, and systems. Similarly, while traditional forensic psychology focuses on criminal behavior, eyewitness testimonies, and psychopathy, a more critical or queer forensic psychology can examine sociocultural influences of criminal behavior; immigration; or racial, gender, or sexual orientation disparities in the justice system. In this way, this chapter follows the lead of criminology scholars who have challenged their colleagues to "queer" their field and calls for a move toward a Critical and Queer Forensic Psychology.

TYPES OF OFFENDERS

Let's first begin by reviewing what we already know about offenders. As reviewed in chapter 5, Congress passed the Prison Rape Elimination Act in 2003, which allowed the DOJ's Bureau of Justice Statistics to collect data on sexual victimization of inmates; however, one of the unintentional consequences was creating a large database with crucial information on LGBTQ inmates (Wolff et al., 2006). One of those datasets was the National Inmate Survey of 2011–2012, which comprised 33,130 inmates; one major finding was that incarcerated LGBQ men and women were more likely than were heterosexual men and women to be incarcerated for violent sexual and nonsexual crimes, rather than crimes related to property, drugs, or parole violations (Meyer et al., 2017).

In this section, I will highlight a sampling of the types of offenders that exist in the criminal justice system, focusing particularly on (a) perpetrators of sexual violence, (b) serial murderers, (c) mass murderers, (d) perpetrators of intimate partner violence, and (e) juvenile offenders. If available, I will review the research or scholarship involving LGBTQ people in those groups (e.g., LGBTQ serial killers, LGBTQ mass murderers, etc.). I will report if there is data or literature on specific subgroups (e.g., gender differences, sexual orientation differences, etc.). Finally, I will discuss any other pertinent trends that may emerge within each category.

Perpetuators of Sexual Violence

Sexual assaults comprise a variety criminal acts which incorporate both sex and violence. Examples include rape (sexual intercourse against one's will), forcible sodomy (anal or oral sex against a person's will), forcible vaginal or anal object penetration, marital rape (nonconsensual or forced sex by a spouse), statutory rape (sex with a person not legally able to give consent), child sexual abuse, forcible touching, and many other sexual acts. As aforementioned, different jurisdictions may vary in their definitions of rape or sexual assault, often resulting in potentially unclear data, in addition to a variability of sentences, punishments, and charges for similar acts. Thus, because the FBI (2013) defines rape as "penetration, no matter how slight, of the vagina or anus with any body part or object, or oral penetration by a sex organ of another person, without the consent of the victim" (p. 1), one may presume the data they collect through their National Incident-Based Reporting System (NIBRS) would follow those same standards. However, because the NIBRS consists of law enforcement agencies who still use previous definitions, it is not completely clear they are using the same standards in reporting all of their data. Further, because not all state law enforcement agencies report their crime incidents to the NIBRS, it is not comprehensive of all crimes in the US.

With all of this in mind, NIBRS data provides some insights about the prevalence of sexual assault. Utilizing the "Victims of Violence" datasets by Puzzanchera, Smith, and Kang, (2018), there were a total of 33,950 reported rapes in 2016, in which 33,124 incidents were rapes toward women (or 97.57 percent of total rapes). Of those, 190 were committed by women perpetrators (or 0.57 percent of rapes toward women). Additionally, there were 826 rapes toward men (or 2.43 percent of total rapes). Of those, 71 were by male perpetrators (or 8.60 percent of rapes toward men). These findings align well with previous FBI reports which indicated 95 percent of the 3,888 recorded sexual homicides between 1976 and 2005 involved male offenders and 82 percent involved female victims.

The same dataset (Puzzanchera et al., 2018) can provide insight regarding child sexual assault; in total, there were 15,027 sexual assault cases consisting of an adult offender (18 years and older, or age unknown) and a minor victim (17 years and younger), consisting of 10,494 rapes, 3,176 sodomy cases, and 1,357 sexual assaults using an object. In cases that consisted of a male offender and a male minor victim there were 1,431 total sexual assaults (or 9.52 percent of total child sexual assaults); these included 44 rapes, 1,248 sodomy cases, and 139 sexual assaults using an object. In cases involving a female offender and a female minor victim, there were 270 total sexual assaults (or 1.80 percent of total child sexual assaults), including 73 rapes, 101 sodomy cases, and 96 sexual assaults involving an object. For comparison, between male offenders and female minor victims, there were 11,482 sexual assaults (9,120 rapes, 1,409 sodomy cases, and 953 sexual assaults with objects). Meanwhile, between female offenders and male minor victims, there were 387 total sexual assaults (244 rapes, 113 sodomy cases, and 30 sexual assaults involving objects). Given this, it is clear that men commit the most child sexual assaults and they tend to target girls; it is also clear that girls are more likely to be sexually assaulted by men and that boys are more likely to be assaulted by women, supporting previous literature affirming children are not at risk of being sexually abused by lesbian and gay adults (Jenny, Roesler, & Poyer, 1994).

In general, there is very little research on male offenders who commit rape toward other men, nor about female offenders who commit rape in general (Ryan, 2004); in fact, in spite of a historic public fear of gay men as rapists or sexual psychopaths, most of the literature that mentions "homosexual rape" or "gay rape" concentrates mostly on prison rape (Graham, 2006). Yet, there has been some previous research that has focused on male sexual offenders who have sexually abused boys. Scholars have described some of the possible etiological factors that contribute to pedophilia and subsequent child abuse, specifically for adult male pedophiles who sexually abuse boys. Seto (2018) argues how a history of childhood sexual abuse by a male perpetrator is a common factor for adult men who sexually abuse boys. Some studies find men who sexually abuse girls target ages 8 to 10 and men who sexually abuse boys tend to target ages 10 to 13 (Murray, 2000). Further, some studies find men who sexually abused boys had the highest rates of recidivism—suggesting treatment was less effective with this group than with other subgroups of sex offenders. (Maltezky & Steinhauser, 2002).

Serial Murderers

Serial murderers (often known colloquially as "serial killers") are defined as individuals "who either alone or with an accomplice, kill at least three people over a period of time, with cooling-off periods between the murders, indicating premeditation of each killing" (Miller, 2014, p. 4). Serial murderers are almost always White men between their 20s and 40s, though there are increasing cases of men of color, older men, women, and juveniles. Serial murders may involve various crimes, which result in different charges or different labels; for example, serial sexual homicide includes an offender murdering three or more victims while perpetrating some sort of sexual act pre- or post-mortem. Some murders may only involve two victims or are unrelated in their motive or pattern, which would more correctly be labeled as an offender who has committed multiple murders and not serial per se. As aforementioned, it is inaccurate to define anything as a "homosexual murder"; however, it is appropriate to examine patterns of behavior that may involve people of certain gender or sexual orientations.

Male Serial Murderers

There are three main theories that have investigated the various types of male serial killers who target adult men. Primarily referred to in the literature as "homosexual serial killers," scholars identify motives, victims, patterns, methods, locations, and other factors involved. Geberth (1996) has offered a six-fold typology of serial homicides involving male offenders and male targets: (a) Interpersonal violence-oriented disputes; (b) Forced sodomy; (c) Lust murder; d) Power murder; (e) Robbery-homicide; and (f) Homophobic murder. Interpersonal violence-oriented disputes are lover's quarrels that result in violence; in order to qualify as serial, there must be more than one homicide repeating the pattern. Forced sodomy involves dominant sex using blunt force or asphyxiation which leads to accidental suicide (that must be repeated to be considered serial). Lust murders are premeditated and sadistic; victims are stalked before being held captive, slowly tortured, or mutilated. Power murders are similar to lust murders, except they involve anger toward vulnerable populations like children, teens, homeless men, drug users, or sex workers. Robbery-homicides involve the seduction of vulnerable people to rob before murdering them; homophobic murders include gay-bashings that escalate to murder.

Beauregard and Proulx (2007) theorize a three-part typology of serial homicides involving male offenders and male victims: (a) avengers, (b) sexual predators, and (c) nonsexual predators. Avengers are sex workers who target their clients, often older men; the offender is triggered during sexual contact by something which reminds him of past traumas or abuses and results in an intense rage or heinous murder. Examples include strangulation or the blunt use of a weapon of opportunity (e.g., scissors, screwdriver, belt, cord, etc.). Sexual predators are similar to aforementioned lust murders or power murders; they are premeditated and sadistic—often involving stalking, abduction, torture, and mutilation. Finally, nonsexual predators are primarily motivated by robberies or theft; the offender may meet the victim at a gay bar or cruising area, may or may not involve sex, and often involves alcohol or drug use.

Miller (2014) reviewed the previous typologies and offers four conceptual commonalities among the various typologies:

a. Profit: homicides in which robbery or theft is the main motive.
b. Sadistic sexual gratification: homicides in which the offender experiences intense pleasure from torturing, mutilating, or abusing their victim
c. Power: homicides in which the primary motivations are domination and overpowering their victims and sexual contact is ancillary
d. Homophobia: homicides that derive from offenders' internalized homophobia, shame, or anger toward queer men who are more comfortable or open in their sexualities.

Across all these typologies, it appears that the majority of these serial homicides involve sex; however, there are some serial homicides that do not involve sex—at least not as the primary motive. These typologies align with a previous analysis by Morton, Tillman, and Gained (2015), which utilized the FBI database of NCAVC by federal, state, or local law enforcement agencies and examined 480 cases of serial murder involving 92 offenders from 1960 to 2006. In each of these cases, the researchers identified variables like motivation, victim selection and approach, method, and other related issues. Out of these 92 offenders, there were 7 offenders (or 7.6 percent of the sample) who only murdered male victims. Out of these 7 offenders, there were a total of 68 victims, and 57 (or 83.8 percent of these cases) involved sexual homicide, suggesting 11 (or 16.2 percent of the cases) did not include sex-related homicides.

Likely the most famous of serial sexual murderers was Jeffrey Dahmer, a gay White man who killed 17 men, mostly Black and Latino, over a period of 13 years. He commonly met these men in public and lured them to his home, with promises of sex, money, or both. Photos of his victims were found, at various stages of his torture and murder process; he often kept his victims' skulls or genitalia as souvenirs of his work. Schmidt (1994) asserted how Dahmer's infamous brutalities were horrific for gay men in Milwaukee, as they propagated homophobia among the community, instilled fear among gay people, and demonstrated how disposable queer people's lives were—particularly gay men of color—given that some of these men were missing for years but no one had been looking for them. Relatedly, Barnard (2000) discussed how there were few discussions about how Dahmer's victims were mostly Black and other people of color—describing how many of the Black men who were killed were known to distrust or dislike White men, and yet, their attractions to Dahmer eventually would lead to their deaths. Finally, Dahmer would likely fit the serial murderer condition of sadistic sexual gratification, in that he clearly derived some pleasure from torturing and mutilating his victims slowly and sexually abusing them at various points of the slow deaths.

Meanwhile, returning to the case of Andrew Cunanan, it may fit a few of the typologies or conditions presented previously. The murder of William Reese appeared to be solely for his pickup truck—the lone profit murder of his spree. The murder of Lee Miglin may have had elements of sadistic gratification (e.g., broken ribs, slitting of the throat, facial contusion, covered in tape); however, it is unclear if he gained any sexual gratification from it. The murder of his friend Jeffrey Trail may have been an interpersonal violence-oriented dispute gone awry, or it could have been one regarding power; and the murder of his ex-lover David Madson could have been an interpersonal violence-related dispute or a lust murder. Finally, his murder of Gianni Versace, who most claim he did not know at all, could have been one of power. Because Mr. Versace had so much success that Mr. Cunanan did not know, he felt the need to dominate him. And the one way he could do that was to take his life away. Yet, some authors may argue that Cunanan was not a serial killer and instead was a spree killer. Douglas and colleagues (2013) assert: "Serial killers tend to go about their lives and murdering on the side, while spree killers act in passion and without the emotional cooling-off period. In this sense, Cunanan seemed to be more of a spree killer" (p. 481).

Female Serial Murderers

Research concentrating on sexual homicides involving a female perpetrator and female victim is virtually nonexistent, particularly regarding female offenders who committed their crimes independently and not with male accomplices (Miller, 2014). Yet, Holmes and Holmes (1994) have elaborated a typology of female serial killers, which could include queer women:

a. Visionary serial killers: women who murder in response to psychotic symptoms like delusions of grandeur or hallucinations
b. Comfort-oriented serial killers: women who murder for financial or material gain
c. Power-seeking serial killers: women who kill for the thrill of power and dominance
d. Hedonistic serial killers: women who kill for sexual gratification.
e. Disciple serial killers: women who kill under the command of a charismatic leader (e.g., a cult leader).

Gurian (2011) describes women serial murderers who are solo or purpose-oriented offenders. These women generally commit their crimes alone—some with specific motives and others with psychosis. For example, "angels of death" murderers are nurses or doctors, primarily women, who target their medical patients. Other examples include "black widows" who kill their husbands or family members for money or women who commit infanticides (or murder their own or others' babies or young children) for various reasons. However, one critique is that these models do not concentrate on queer women explicitly.

Perhaps the most famous queer woman who has been labeled as a serial killer was Aileen Wuornos—a woman who was believed to identify as a lesbian, who worked as a prostitute and was convicted of killing six men. Despite claiming vehemently that she killed men who were her clients (also known as johns) out of self-defense, she was deemed a serial killer; was sentenced to death; and died by lethal injection in 2002. Chesler (1993) asserted that she did not believe Wuornos fit the description of a serial killer, citing the ways that Wuornos' trauma was a major contributor to her behavior. Pearson (2007) discussed how Wuornos' sexual deviance as a prostitute and a lesbian was used to criminalize her—a sentiment that is often used against lesbians or masculine-presenting women who defy female stereotypes, who fight back against men, or who threaten men's masculinities. Both authors allude to how male scholars, law enforcement, and journalists contributed to the pathologizing of Wuornos, instead of attempting to empathize with her, particularly given her extensive history of trauma. While we may never uncover the absolute truth, we do know that men, especially White heterosexual men, have historically been the gatekeepers about whether women, people of color, or LGBTQ people are telling the truth about their lived experiences. Therefore, it is worth postulating how Wuornos may have been both an offender and a victim.

Mass Murderers

In recent years, there has been an increased awareness in American society about mass murderers, or individuals "who kill multiple victims in a single incident, and whose fantasies tend to involve revenge against actual or imagined persecutors" (Miller, 2014, p. 4). A database created by *Mother Jones* found from August 1982 to August 2019, there were 116 cases of mass shootings in the US; of these, there were 934 people who were killed and 1,406 people who were injured (Follman, Aronsen, & Pan, 2019).

Researchers assert that most mass murderers in recent history have been men, with only 8 documented cases of women (Stone, 2015). Of these men, there have not been any known mass shooters or mass murderers who had openly disclosed having a queer, bisexual, or gay identity. However, there are some possible exceptions. First, it had been suspected that Omar Mateen, the Orlando Pulse nightclub shooter who killed 49 people and himself in June 2016, was potentially queer, gay, or bisexual, and that he had agonized with internalized homophobia (see chapter 2 for a review), though this was never fully supported. Second, prior to the Pulse massacres, the deadliest killing of LGBTQ people in a single incident was in 1973 through a fire at a gay bar in New Orleans called the Up Stairs Lounge. Thirty-two patrons died and no one was arrested. The main suspect was Roger Nunez—a gay male hustler who had been kicked out of the bar earlier that day. Nunez later confessed he had started the fire to at least three people; yet, a haphazard police investigation never led to his arrest. Nunez died by suicide in 1974 (Fieseler, 2018). In this way, Nunez fits the description of a mass murderer who sought revenge.

However, one commonality between a few of the mass murderers involved the threat of being perceived as gay or queer. In reviewing three major cases of mass murderers who died by suicide (i.e., the tragedies at Columbine High School, Virginia Tech, and Northern Illinois University), Kalish and Kimmel (2010) described how mass murderers were commonly teased for being gay or different, thereby threatening their masculinity and their entire personhood. Other cases have similar components too. For example, in Palm Bay, Florida in 1987, a man named William Cruse, 59, a retired librarian, killed two college students on his way to a supermarket, where he opened fire with one rifle, one revolver, and one shotgun. Killing 6 people and injuring 14, his motive was that he was paranoid that his neighbors were gossiping about him being gay (Follman et al., 2019). In Hamilton, Ohio in 1975, James Rupert killed eleven of his family members (which included his mother, his brother, his sister-in-law, and their 8 children). It later was revealed Rupert hated his mother who infantilized him and "made him feel gay" (Stone, 2015, p. 56). In West Paducah, Kentucky, Michael Carneal, a 14-year-old freshman, opened fire at his high school, killing 3 of his classmates; he later revealed they taunted him, falsely, for being gay (Stone, 2015). Either way, if these perpetrators were gay, bisexual, or queer, it is possible the teasing exacerbated their internalized homophobia, which led to violence; if they were indeed heterosexual, it is possible that toxic masculinity and fear of being perceived as gay was enough to incite violence.

Perpetuators of Intimate Partner Violence

Utilizing data from the FBI NIBRS by Puzzanchera and colleagues (2018), but now searching the "Victims of Domestic Violence" file (which consisted of family, household, or romantic relationship crimes), it was found in 2016, there were 420,973 cases involving simple assaults and 78,866 cases involving aggravated assaults. Of these, there were 6,771 simple assaults and 1,348 aggravated assaults that were listed as a "homosexual relationship." Thus, it appears that about 1.6 percent of simple assaults and 1.7 percent of aggravated assaults within households were by same-sex couples. Examining gender differences, there were 2,993 total assaults between male perpetrator and male victim; 2,429 were simple assaults and 564 were aggravated assaults. There were 5,124 total assaults between female perpetrator and female victim; 4,341 were simple assaults and 783 were aggravated assaults. For married same-sex female couples, there were 35 simple assaults and 3 aggravated assaults; for married same-sex male couples, there were 49 simple assaults and 3 aggravated assaults. Thus, while it appears that non-married same-sex female couples had a higher quantity of assaults than non-married same-sex male couples, the number of assaults was somewhat similar for the married couples.

Regarding previous research studies, it has been found within some male same-sex couples that each partner can often engage in both perpetrator and target behaviors (Craft & Serovich, 2005), complicating how characteristics of IPV perpetrators are measured. Yet, there have been some studies that have found traits of IPV perpetrators in male same-sex couples include a history of psychological and emotional abuse, particularly from one's family of origin (Toro-Alfonso & Rodríguez-Madera, 2004; Craft & Serovich, 2005). Examining both female and male same-sex couples, some studies have found common traits for perpetrators include being less educated, having lower self-esteem, and having more masculine traits (McKenry, Serovich, Mason, & Mosack, 2006). In this way, IPV may possibly be related more to male or masculine dominance, in both heterosexual and queer relationships. Additional studies indicate bisexual women report higher rates of IPV than lesbian women; gay and bisexual men report greater IPV than the general population; and gay men report more IPV than bisexual men (Goldberg & Meyer, 2013).

Finally, in comparing the brutality of IPV-related homicides between heterosexual, same-sex male, and same-sex female couples, Mize and Shackelford (2008) found there were significantly more brutal killings in queer couples (both same-sex male and female) than there were in heterosexual couples. Results from their sample also indicated that IPV-related homicides in queer male same-sex couples were higher than in both heterosexual and queer female same-sex couples. Looking at NIBRS data (i.e., Puzzanchera et al., 2018), there were 10 IPV-related homicides for same-sex male couples (non-married); 5 IPV-related homicides for same-sex female couples (non-married); and 0 murders for married same-sex couples of any gender. Comparatively, there were 159 IPV-related homicides for married heterosexual couples with male offenders; 48 IPV-related homicides for married heterosexual couples with female offenders; 196 IPV-related homicides for unmarried male offenders; and 54 IPV-related homicides for unmarried heterosexual couples with female offenders.

Juvenile Offenders

There are approximately 300,000 incarcerated LGBTQ juvenile offenders across the US (Hunt & Moodie-Mills, 2012). In general, young LGBTQ offenders tend to share many similar characteristics, including a history of running away or being homeless, engaging in sex work, unsupportive or oppressive school systems, or having lived in a foster home as a result of abuse (Irvine, Wilbur, & Canfield, 2017). Furthermore, Conover-Williams (2014) found LGBTQ juvenile offenders are more likely than heterosexual cisgender youth offenders to commit crimes that are both violent (e.g., fighting or physically hurting someone) and non-violent (e.g., vandalism, theft, or graffiti), and that protective factors like school and family attachment assisted in decreasing criminal offenses for LGBTQ youth. Belknap, Holsinger, and Little (2012) described how queer youth, particularly girls, reported a need for more counseling for sexual abuse and physical abuse treatment. Finally, discipline in schools is a contributing factor to LGBTQ youth incarceration; Himmelstein and Brückner (2011) found LGBTQ youth, especially gender variant or gender nonconforming girls, are more likely to experience harsh disciplinary treatment by school administrators than their heterosexual or cisgender counterparts.

FACTORS INFLUENCING VIOLENCE FOR LGBTQ OFFENDERS

While the chapter so far has examined a diverse spectrum of LGBTQ criminal offenders among the already diverse LGBTQ community, there are a few commonalities that can be explored in further research. In this next section, I will highlight four psychological factors that I hypothesize are risk factors of criminal behavior for LGBTQ people; these include: (a) History of Childhood Physical, Psychological, or Sexual Abuse; (b) Internalized Oppression; (c) Toxic Masculinity and Gender Role Socialization; and (d) Poor Emotional Regulation. With each of these variables, I will review previous literature, while also relating material to previously mentioned case studies, including Andrew Cunanan, Aileen Wuornos, and Jeffrey Dahmer.

History of Abuse

Numerous studies have found a connection between childhood sexual abuse (CSA) and criminal behavior, particularly for LGBTQ offenders. First, Meyer and colleagues (2017) used the National Inmate Survey for 2011–2012, which included approximately 80,000 participants and revealed sexual minority inmates were significantly more likely than heterosexual inmates to have been sexually abused as children. Sexual abuse was prevalent among both men and women in the sample, with

33.4 percent of gay and bisexual men reporting CSA and 53.7 percent of lesbian and bisexual women reporting CSA. These findings align with previous studies that link childhood sexual abuse and incarceration; for example, Belknap and colleagues (2012) found lesbian, gay, and bisexual girls in Ohio reported more experiences with abuse than heterosexual girls, while Irvine and colleagues (2017) reported many LGBTQ offenders had experienced abuse by their families of origin or in the foster system.

Previous research has found LGBTQ people, in general, are more susceptible to childhood sexual abuse than their heterosexual counterparts. For instance, Friedman and colleagues (2011) conducted a meta-analysis and found LGBQ adolescents were 2.9 times more likely than heterosexual youth to report a history of childhood sexual abuse. For gay, bisexual, or queer boys, the number was significantly higher; they were 4.9 times more likely to experience childhood sexual abuse, compared with heterosexual boys. Given this, it is especially important to not just prevent children from experiencing CSA, but to ensure they seek the proper treatment when they do experience the abuse.

In general, when children are abused, they become more likely to engage in violence than they would if they were not abused (Widom, 2017). Being sexually abused as children is a common trait in serial murderers like Jeffrey Dahmer and John Wayne Gacy; in fact, Mitchell and Aamodt reported in a review of 50 serial murderers who were convicted before 2000 that 36 percent were physically abused; 26 percent were sexually abused; and 50 percent were psychologically abused. One case of persistent childhood abuse was Aileen Wuornos, who was sexually abused by her grandfather, her older brother, and her grandfather's friend (who impregnated her at age 14). By the time Wuornos became a sex worker as an adult, she had already suffered from so much complex trauma that any violence (perceived or actual) may have triggered violence (Chesler, 1993; Pearson, 2007). If Wuornos went from being a survivor of violence to a perpetrator of violence, perhaps the perpetrators of her violence should be held accountable too.

Internalized Oppression

Another common factor that is prevalent in many LGBTQ offenders is the notion of internalized oppression, or the notion that individuals turn upon themselves and their communities the distress patterns and hatred that result from the systems of dominance of historically majority groups (David, 2014). Internalized oppression can take multiple forms, including internalized racism for people of color, internalized sexism for women, internalized homophobia for queer people, internalized transphobia for trans people, and colonial mentality for any group that has been colonized by another group. Internalized oppression can affect numerous factors including mental health issues, self-esteem, behaviors, relationships, and even health problems (David, 2014). It can also be overt (e.g., self-hating comments people make about themselves or their group) or subtle (e.g., covert behaviors that individuals may or may not be conscious of engaging in). When discussing internalized oppression, it is very important to acknowledge how the systems of oppressions are the source of the oppression, while the individual is merely the agent through which they manifest. Such a nuance is important, as it lessens or eliminates the blame on the individual and holds the system responsible.

Numerous scholars have described the ways that Jeffrey Dahmer struggled with internalized homophobia and how he took it out on other gay men (or men he perceived as gay). For instance, Schmidt (1994) stated: "Dahmer symbolized the result of internalized homophobia in its most extreme, alienating, and isolating form. [For] the lesbians and gay men in Milwaukee, it was difficult to incite pride, instill activism, and strengthen community bonds, when Dahmer could only represent 'the worst nightmare possible'" (p. 84–85). Barnard (2000) added that "Dahmer had internalized societal homophobia to such an extent that he felt guilt, shame, discomfort, and hatred about his own homosexuality, and that a logical result of these feelings could have been the urge to destroy those with whom he attempted to satisfy his proscribed sexual desires" (p. 70). Barnard also continues describes the ways that Dahmer targeted mostly Black men and other men of color, demonstrating the deadly combination of his racial bias and his sexual desire for men of color. In this way, Dahmer may have battled internalized homophobia (hatred toward himself) and racism (hatred toward people of color) simultaneously.

It can be hypothesized that Andrew Cunanan suffered from two forms of internalized oppression: internalized racism and internalized homophobia. As described previously, he often denied his Filipino heritage and tried to blend in as White. This internalized racism may have been a reason why he overcompensated so much, which eventually resulted in his delusions of grandeur or his need to lie about his history. He also may have suffered from internalized homophobia—in that he was never fully comfortable with his gay identity and displaced his discomfort and anger onto gay men who were comfortable with their identities (and whose families were accepting too). For example, some of his friends described how Cunanan would lie about his father being gay and having a boyfriend around his age (Orth, 2017). The specificity of such a lie is very telling—potentially indicative of his need or desire for his father's acceptance.

With all of these examples, it must be made exceptionally clear that internalized oppression does not directly result in criminal behavior, nor that people who suffer from internalized oppression should be permitted to commit crimes, especially crimes that harm other people. Rather, it should be understood that internalized oppression is something that should be acknowledged and addressed. If people like Jeffrey Dahmer or Andrew Cunanan learned to love and accept themselves, instead of feeling the shame they did, perhaps the trajectories of their lives (and their victims') would be different.

Toxic Masculinity and Gender Role Socialization

Another commonality among many LGBTQ offenders is the concept of toxic masculinity—or the constellation of socially regressive male traits that serve to foster domination, the devaluation of women, homophobia, and wanton violence (Kupers, 2005). While toxic masculinity is a common trait for offenders of different orientations and who commit various crimes, it may manifest differently for different people. For instance, for serial murderers, toxic masculinity is a typical primary factor for dominating their victims who they view as weak or vulnerable. For mass murderers, toxic masculinity may emerge as one of the reasons why they are seeking revenge. Relatedly, an area of further exploration would be how masculinities may affect women or gender nonconforming people who develop or uphold negative and traditional traits of masculinity— including a need for dominance, jealousy, rage, and more.

Poor Emotion Regulation

Previous research has cited that deviant and criminal behavior often stems from individuals' inabilities to manage their emotions; this process is often referred to as emotion regulation or "an individual's awareness, understanding, and acceptance of emotional experience, as well as ability to modulate behavioral and emotional responses to meet goals and situational demands" (Edwards & Wupperman, 2017, p. 1160). For LGBTQ offenders, poor regulation is often related to trauma, particularly childhood traumas. Charak, Villarreal, Schmitz, Hirai, and Ford (2019) reported how LGBQ people who were survivors of child abuse or adult victimization have a more difficult time in regulating their emotions. Seto (2018) revealed people who are more emotionally dysregulated may often become more disinhibited in their behaviors, when they use alcohol or drugs as a way of coping with distress. Bryant-Davis (2019) reminds us that "chronic invalidation and discrimination can result in emotional and behavioral dysregulation, so although skills training may be helpful, it must be rooted in an acknowledgment of oppression" (p. 402). Thus, when people of historically marginalized groups exhibit symptoms of dysregulation, it is necessary to attempt to be empathetic and understanding, instead of pathologizing or blaming them for their experiences.

Furthermore, when individuals who are emotionally dysregulated have more characteristics of alexithymia (e.g., lack of connection to emotional experiences, difficulty communicating feelings, or focus on facts versus feelings), they are more likely to engage in deviant behaviors like impulsive aggression (Edwards & Wupperman, 2017). In other words, when people who have difficulty in managing their emotions also have difficulty in identifying or communicating their emotions, they might be more susceptible to engaging in deviant behaviors like violent aggression. For example, Andrew Cunanan's first act of violence may have been a demonstration of his inability to manage his emotions. An argument with a friend resulted in him repeatedly striking that friend in the head with a hammer; a rejection from an ex-lover resulted in him shooting him point-blank. In this way, perhaps Cunanan should be classified more as a spree killer—most motivated by emotion and each exacerbating the other. In this way, perhaps his motive for killing Gianni Versace was because he viewed it as the only way that he could ever gain the fame and status that he had always wanted.

QUEERING FORENSIC PSYCHOLOGY

In this chapter, we queered previous literature, by attempting to understand the societal and systemic factors that may influence criminal behavior, without focusing solely on further pathologizing and criminalizing of offenders. Perhaps one way to queer forensic psychology is to consider ways to apply more humanistic approaches in working with LGBTQ offenders, while considering systemic approaches to prevent future LGBTQ offenders. For instance, clinical psychology training programs have traditionally incorporated medical models of psychotherapy, which is defined as any therapeutic approach that focuses on modalities and techniques, using a medical schema and language to describe what is taking place (Elkins, 2016). In this way, consumers are often referred to as patients, and their presenting problems in therapy are often referred to using diagnostic criteria and evidenced-based treatment methods, instead of considering other factors that assist in the therapeutic process. Moreover, training programs must acknowledge how the field of forensic psychology is not just about criminal profiling or forensic assessments, but about "the application of the scientific, technical, or specialized knowledge of psychology to the law and the use of that knowledge to assist in resolving legal, contractual, and administrative disputes" (American Psychological Association, 2013, p. 19). In this way, training programs need to ensure they cover all aspects of psychology and the law—examining topics related to victims, family law, immigration, and working with historically marginalized groups, including LGBTQ communities.

Forensic mental health practitioners (psychiatrists, psychologists, nurses, etc.) tend to utilize the medical model too (Bartlett, 2010), often pathologizing and criminalizing their constituents concurrently. In the past few decades, practitioners and scholars have advocated for integrating humanistic approaches into forensic mental health (Barnao, Ward, & Robertson, 2016), concentrating on clients' strengths. Some scholars have advocated for avoiding labels in working with people who have committed crimes, as it can be stigmatizing and debilitating (Willis, 2018). Further, in using a wellness model, practitioners focus on all of the parts of an individual, while understanding how systems and external factors have influenced one's personal struggles or mental health issues (Myers & Sweeney, 2004). In this way, even criminal offenders who have committed the most heinous of crimes are still viewed as humans, who often developed faulty, maladaptive, or harmful cognitions and behavior. Perhaps another way to queer forensic psychology is by utilizing restorative justice—or "an approach to discipline that engages all parties in a balanced practice that brings together all people impacted by an issue or behavior" (Gonzalez, 2012, p. 281). When offenders hear the impact of their actions from survivors or families of victims, perhaps they can gain some insight and feel accountable; when survivors (who choose to) are able to confront their offenders, they may gain some healing.

Another way to queer forensic psychology is to concentrate on prevention and policy change, particularly for historically marginalized groups. Because systemic oppression serves as a contributing factor to criminal behavior, policymakers, practitioners, educators, and others must create programs and identify solutions to prevent systemic oppression. For instance, for youth of color, some have described a school-to-prison pipeline, describing the ways educational systems have enforced disciplinary actions that result in incarceration (Gonzalez, 2012). Such systemic issues affect LGBTQ people, too; as an example, when transgender people (especially trans people of color) face obstacles in accessing health care, correcting their gender markers, or securing employment, they may have little choice than to engage in survival behaviors (e.g., sex work, drug use or dealing) that result in their entrance into the system. Thus, systems must be disrupted, so that people from historically marginalized groups are no longer deemed the problem; rather, systems which perpetuate these problems must be held accountable instead.

Conclusion

Through the previous ten chapters, we have examined a number of issues related to LGBTQ communities and the law. As stated in the introduction, there would be four recurring themes throughout this text, including: (a) LGBTQ people are both victimized and criminalized; (b) intersectional identities matter; (c) gender binaries are harmful and dangerous; and (d) advocacy creates change. In this final chapter, I will review how each of these themes apply to the various topics that have been reviewed. I will also provide real, practical recommendations for how to improve, dismantle, and queer various parts of the justice system.

LGBTQ PEOPLE ARE BOTH VICTIMIZED AND CRIMINALIZED

Throughout this text, there been many examples of (a) how LGBTQ are victimized, (b) how LGBTQ are criminalized, (c) how LGBTQ victimization leads to criminalization, and (d) how LGBTQ criminalization leads to victimization. The ways that LGBTQ people are victimized are innumerable. First, we have learned how LGBTQ people have been historically targeted by hate violence—with the Orlando Pulse massacre as a most recent example. We also have learned how systemic homophobia has persistently perpetuated through government, media, and other systems leading to discrimination, violence, or erasure. In contemporary times, we know LGBTQ people are victimized by hate crimes and bullying, which both can be considered life-threatening epidemics: 1) Hate crime homicides are disproportionately prevalent for transgender women of color, and 2) bullying is a strong predictor of suicide for LGBTQ youth. We have also learned many ways that LGBTQ people have been criminalized throughout history. Through many examples, we reviewed how LGBTQ people are victimized by heterosexist and transphobic laws, which have often resulted in their persecution. Specifically, through the Stonewall Uprising and the events at Cooper's Doughnuts and Compton's Cafeteria, we learned how LGBTQ people were harassed and arrested, simply for gathering in a space with each other, or for dressing and engaging in behaviors that were considered deviant.

Throughout the text, we learned how LGBTQ victimization led to criminalization—with the case of CeCe McDonald exemplifying situations in which LGBTQ people defend themselves after being targeted by violence and being arrested themselves. We also covered scenarios in which LGBTQ people have been victimized by systemic oppression, which have led to survivor behaviors like sex work, selling drugs, or theft. Finally, we learned how criminalization leads to victimization, with the most salient examples involving LGBTQ people who are incarcerated being physically and sexually assaulted in correctional facilities.

With this, it is necessary for LGBTQ community leaders, community members, and their advocates to continue to understand the links between criminalization and victimization. Because one informs the other (and vice versa), advocates must pay attention in not merely addressing one without the other. In other words, when LGBTQ advocates address the high number of hate crimes toward LGBTQ people, but then turn their backs on (or remain ignorant about) experiences of sex workers who are being violently arrested by police officers, they fail to recognize how both problems stem from a greater system of heterosexism and transphobia. LGBTQ people from privileged groups, specifically, need to reflect on the ways they may perpetuate bias and violence toward other LGBTQ people. By stigmatizing other LGBTQ people (e.g., sex workers, drug users, homeless youth, etc.), privileged LGBTQ people contribute to the ways that LGBTQ people are criminalized and targeted by violence.

Intersectional Identities Matter

In analyzing each of the case studies that were presented, we uncovered the importance of unpacking the many ways that intersectional identities may have affected how we conceptualized various cases or scenarios. For instance, the tragedy at Pulse in 2016 was even more complicated because most of the victims were Latinx (and specifically Puerto Rican), while the assailant was a US-born Muslim Afghan American. Michael Johnson's case involving HIV transmission was significantly impacted by his identity as a masculine-presenting Black man, who the media painted as a violent and dangerous sex offender. Similarly, Andrew Cunanan's identity as a multiracial person of Filipino heritage, alongside his family's lack of acceptance of his gay identity, may have contributed to his murder spree. Race and gender identity negatively impacted how trans women of color leaders like Sylvia Rivera and Marsha P. Johnson were accepted (or not accepted) into the mainstream gay or lesbian movement.

Intersectional identities must always be considered when discussing issues related to LGBTQ communities. While there are still many systemic issues affecting LGBTQ people in general, those issues are compounded by LGBTQ people's other identities, including race, gender identity, age, socioeconomic status, religion, size, ability status, and many other demographic variables. When LGBTQ data is disaggregated, there are always unique findings regarding different subgroups. Admittedly, throughout this text, there were few explicit references to experiences of LGBTQ people with disabilities and the law, with the exception of some mentions of LGBTQ people with mental illness or LGBTQ people living with HIV/AIDS. Because several scholars have described the dearth of literature involving the intersections of sexual orientation, gender identity, and ability status in general (Duke, 2011), it is especially important for researchers to disaggregate data on ability status, in order to highlight the experiences of LGBTQ people with disabilities and to ensure they are being properly served and advocated for in the system.

Gender Binaries Are Harmful and Dangerous

Another common theme throughout the text involved the danger of maintaining gender binaries among all aspects of law and the justice system. Rigid binaries result in transgender and gender nonconforming people being housed in facilities that do not match their gender identities—resulting in the increased likeliness of their sexual victimization and lack of safety. Gender binaries also affect various other aspects of government and the law—from trans and genderqueer people's inability to get identification cards that match their gender identities or their ability to access proper gender-affirming health care. When transgender and gender nonconforming people are denied these basic rights and needs, they are placed in situations in which they are more likely to come in contact with law enforcement.

There have been movements in certain jurisdictions to allow flexibility in gender identification. For example, in New York City, beginning in 2015, transgender people have been allowed to change their gender markers on their birth certificates, regardless of having any gender-affirming surgeries or medical procedures (Lee, Gurr, & Van Wye, 2017). In 2019, gender nonconforming people in New York City were given the option of changing their birth certificates to an "X" (Simko-Bednarski, 2019). Indeed, more cities and states must begin to think beyond the binary, as a way to normalize the deconstruction of gender binaries.

Advocacy Creates Change

A final theme that was pervasive throughout the various chapters was the notion that advocacy leads to change. Positive changes for LGBTQ people came because LGBTQ community leaders and their allies advocated for it. The decrease of overt police harassment of queer spaces began from the revolutionary actions of Stonewall veterans. The end of sodomy laws and the movement for marriage equality came from individuals who fought to have their cases heard by the Supreme Court of the US. The decrease in sexual violence of incarcerated prisoners came from political lobbying of congressional leaders to pass the Prison Rape Elimination Act. Although systemic change is difficult to achieve, previous advocacy efforts have demonstrated it is possible. Further, we can learn from the mistakes of previous advocacy efforts to ensure that change can come efficiently and inclusively.

As an example, the fight for marriage equality was one that was powerful and problematic. It was powerful in showing how LGBTQ people across the country could organize and create systemic change via congressional votes, state propositions, or court decisions. Yet, it was also problematic in centering the perspectives of White, cisgender, upper-class couples and ignored the plights of many trans people of color living in poverty and other subgroups of LGBTQ people who would be unaffected by whether same-sex marriages were legal or not. In fact, many Queer Studies scholars described how marriage equality symbolized the fight between assimilationism and radicalism—how some people were pro-marriage as a way of being heteronormative, while others were anti-marriage as a way of fighting heteronormativity (Weber, 2015). So, when national organizations deemed marriage equality as their main cause, other radical causes were ignored or put on hold.

However, other LGBTQ concerns did not become a priority for many of these organizations, and some groups even dismantled shortly after the SCOTUS decision. One national organization included Freedom to Marry, whose main mission was focused on marriage equality, disbanded just weeks after SCOTUS (Heller, 2015). Another New York–based organization, Empire State Pride Agenda, declared their top priorities had been accomplished and they completed their mission of serving LGBTQ communities (Cohen & Carpenter, 2015). O'Brien (2019) cites that a major reason for organizations disbanding was because they lost financial support of major donors who were interested primarily in marriage equality.

A similar dynamic occurred in the fight for federal employment non-discrimination laws. When the Employment Non-Discrimination Act (ENDA) was re-introduced to Congress in 2007, gender identity was removed as a protected class (focusing only on sexual orientation). Such betrayals must be prevented in the future; when only privileged groups are included in advocacy efforts, while other marginalized groups are excluded, organizers are using similar oppressive tactics by the mainstream. Thus, in advocating for systemic change, activists must acknowledge whether funding and privilege dictate what is fought for, while being intentional in ensuring that movements center individuals who are marginalized, have less access to resources, or have fewer opportunities to have their voices heard.

Relatedly, when privileged LGBTQ people subscribe to narratives in which some LGBTQ people are viewed as "good" while others are viewed as "bad," they engage in similar biases that have historically targeted LGBTQ communities. For instance, some LGBTQ people in monogamous marriages or relationships are critical of those who are in open or polygamous relationships—a similar judgment that heterosexual people have had of queer people and relationships. These dynamics are often referred to as "respectability politics"—or the idea in which some LGBTQ people attempt to put LGBTQ relationships, behaviors, and norms into mainstream, heteronormative conceptualizations rather than attempt to garner societal acceptance for difference and deviation (Matsick & Conley, 2015).

Therefore, to "queer" means to always question what is considered socially acceptable and to recognize there are always others who hold identities or engage in behaviors that are stigmatized. Queering norms can occur within LGBTQ communities as well; for instance, as covered in the introduction, there have been an array of new, diverse sexual orientation and gender identifiers that have emerged in recent years. Thus, in similar ways that queer and trans people have been rejected by mainstream societies, many groups (e.g., transgender, bisexual, people of color, people with disabilities, and other subgroups) have been marginalized within mainstream LGBTQ communities. Accordingly, LGBTQ people must not reject people with identities that are new or different or enact biases or microaggressions toward them, as they would be perpetrating similar types of oppression that heterosexual and cisgender people (and other privileged groups) enact toward LGBTQ people and other marginalized groups (Nadal, 2019).

RECOMMENDATIONS

At the conclusion of each chapter, I brainstormed possibilities of how to queer each system (e.g., queering incarceration, queering law enforcement, etc.). Building on those specific suggestions, I provide further practical recommendations across various sectors of government and the justice system.

Education, Training, and Organizational Accountability

It is clear that across each sector, there is a need for individuals to become more knowledgeable about LGBTQ issues; to become more aware of their implicit and explicit biases about LGBTQ people (and people of historically marginalized groups in general); and to be held accountable when they actively incite discrimination or violence toward any of their constituents. Though there have been some efforts for mandatory LGBTQ-affirming training in law enforcement (see chapter 3) and the child welfare system (see chapter 7), there are still many states that do not require such programs. Moreover, there are few efforts to mandate any sort of cultural competence training in correctional facilities, courtrooms, or juries. Thus, while LGBTQ trainings are ethical requirements for medical professionals (Joint Commission, 2014) and psychologists (Singh, 2016), governing organizations across other fields must mandate such trainings for employees of all ranks in various government and legal agencies.

Trainings must be frequent, and they must move beyond a one-day model, as previous research has found one-day trainings are less effective at reducing heterosexist or transphobic biases. Further, related to transgender-affirming training, research finds it is more effective to introduce personal narratives and dialogues, rather than relying solely on didactic or informational lectures (Walch et al., 2012). Mandated frequent training is one way to ensure that an organization can communicate to its staff members how committed they are to LGBTQ issues. For example, in New York City's Administration for Children Services, it is required for all foster parents to complete annual LGBTQ training and for all staff members to complete LGBTQ training every two years (Perry & Green, 2014). Given the research on LGBTQ communities is consistently growing and that laws and policies are always changing, such trainings are also necessary so that staff members and foster parents are constantly aware of the most appropriate terminology, trends, and concerns for LGBTQ youth in the system.

Furthermore, it is necessary for employers to create organizational accountability through both written policy and action; employees must be held accountable for their discriminatory actions with mandated training, demotion, or termination. Disciplinary actions must be as transparent as possible, in order to communicate that discrimination will not be tolerated. When organizations fail to address issues of discrimination or violence effectively, they engage in what scholars have referred to as "institutional betrayals" or "institutional action and inaction that exacerbate the impact of traumatic experiences" (Smith & Freyd, 2014, p. 577). If organizations are truly committed to advocating for justice, they will address institutional betrayals expeditiously and effectively, while integrating social justice into all aspects of their work.

Community-Based Participation and Policy Reform

While policy reform is necessary on all levels, one way to ensure systems and organizations can hold themselves accountable is to create opportunities involving community-based participation. For example, Brown, Canfield, and Irvine (2014) describe how creating an LGBTQ task force committed to juvenile justice could be helpful in building community relations, while also implementing community-informed policies. Community advisory boards can be helpful with police departments, district attorney offices, and other sectors too. For example, in Washington, DC, the Mayor's Office of LGBTQ Affairs appoints a group of community members who meet to address LGBTQ communities and to innovate ways of addressing those concerns. By engaging community members, government leaders demonstrate their commitment to LGBTQ citizens, while genuinely providing opportunities to improve the quality of life of their LGBTQ constituents.

Cities can also hold town halls or public meetings as a way for community members to voice their concerns to their elected officials. As an example, the Seattle LGBTQ Commission meets monthly in their city hall as a way for the community to share their perspectives on a number of issues ranging from hate crime laws to LGBTQ homelessness to LGBTQ veterans' issues. In doing so, elected officials provide access to community members and hear firsthand concerns from their constituents. Additionally, LGBTQ community members, who historically may have felt voiceless or marginal, gain insight about the political process and perhaps may get involved or engaged as a result.

Lobbying for Justice

One more important way to advocate for change is through lobbying—or persuading or influencing lawmakers and policymakers to consider perspectives they had not. Specific to LGBTQ issues and the law, lobbying can include talking with state legislators about the need to decriminalize HIV/AIDS or sex work. Lobbying can involve writing letters to governors or congresspeople about combatting gender binaries in correctional or detention facilities. Lobbying can consist of setting up meetings with local city council members to discuss LGBTQ concerns. Because lobbying might seem like a difficult strategy for some, Markarian (2017) shares simple but helpful tips for lobbying effectively, including:

a. Identifying yourself and stating a clear objective: introducing yourself by name; sharing your relationship to the individual; and asserting the purpose of your meeting (e.g., "Hello, I'm Kevin Nadal, I'm a resident in your district, and I wanted to speak with you today about integrating LGBTQ education into K–12 curriculum.").
b. Explain why the issue is personally important to you (e.g., "As a queer person, I am advocating for mandatory LGBTQ-inclusive curriculum in primary and secondary education because I know first-hand how LGBTQ history can combat negative internalized feelings about being LGBTQ.").
c. Share as much supporting information as possible, without lying or misleading (e.g., "In California, state senators passed laws to mandate LGBTQ Studies and Ethnic Studies into their curriculum. Research studies described the positive impact of Ethnic Studies on students of color, with some studies demonstrating increased self-

esteem, GPAs, and mental health. Thus, I hypothesize this would occur for LGBTQ students too.").

Furthermore, effective lobbying involves working with legislative staff, if the elected official is not available. Finally, it is always important to thank the individual for meeting with you and to be polite yet persistent if you do not hear back from them in a timely manner.

Research for Justice

A final recommendation is to conduct empirical research that can be utilized in advocating for justice. Nadal (2017) describes the historical ways that psychologist-activists have been influential in systemic change—from the Clark doll experiments that influenced the *Brown v. Board of Education* decision to the LGBTQ researchers who have been cited in court cases involving marriage equality. In these ways, research in LGBTQ issues must increase in both quality and quantity—particularly in areas that continue to be understudied. For instance, as aforementioned, there is still limited research on the intersections of ability status, sexual orientation, gender identity, and law. Similarly, more research is needed involving other LGBTQ subgroups including, but not limited to, genderqueer or gender nonconforming people, bisexual men and women, LGBTQ Asian Americans and Pacific Islanders, LGBTQ Muslim Americans, transgender men, LGBTQ people living with mental health disorders, LGBTQ people living with personality disorders, LGBTQ sex offenders, LGBTQ trauma survivors, and so forth. Because such research can be used to support programming and services for these populations, researchers must use their voices to advocate for justice and better the human condition.

A CALL TO ACTION

I conclude this book with a call to action. I reiterate the directive once proclaimed by Black gay Civil Rights activist Bayard Rustin: "We need, in every community, a group of angelic troublemakers" (Houtman, Naegle, & Long, 2019, p. vii). We have identified the problems that exist and recognize that systemic change must occur in order for justice to prevail. We must collectively work together to address the wrongdoings of our country's past, while advocating for changes for the future. People must organize and advocate for justice, using strategies in which they are both compassionate and relentless. It is indeed a daunting task to challenge the status quo; however, from history, we have learned that it takes the masses to speak out against injustice in order for major change to occur, and that the revolution often begins with one person. I hope you recognize that the revolution toward justice begins with you.

References

Abrams, K. (2007). Immigration law and the regulation of marriage. *Minnesota Law Review, 91*, 1625–1709.
Alarid, L. F. (2000). Sexual orientation perspectives of incarcerated bisexual and gay men: The county jail protective custody experience. *The Prison Journal, 80*, 80–95.
Albelda, R., Badgett, M. L., Schneebaum, A., & Gates, G. (2009). Poverty in the lesbian, gay, and bisexual community. Los Angeles: The Williams Institute at UCLA. Retrieved from http://papers.ccpr.ucla.edu/index.php/pwp/article/download/855/238 .
Alexander, M. (2012). *The New Jim Crow: Mass incarceration in the age of colorblindness.* New York: New Press.
Allegretto, S. A., & Arthur, M. M. (2001). An empirical analysis of homosexual/heterosexual male earnings differentials: unmarried and unequal? *Industrial and Labor Relations Review, 54*, 631–646.
American Bar Association (2011). *Model Code of Judicial Conduct.* Washington, DC: ABA Book Publishing.
American Psychiatric Association (1952). *Mental disorders: Diagnostic and statistical manual.* Washington, DC: Author.
American Psychological Association. (2013). Specialty guidelines for forensic psychology. *The American Psychologist, 68*, 7–19.
Amnesty International USA. (2005). *Stonewalled: Police abuse and misconduct against lesbian, gay, bisexual and transgender people in the U.S.* New York, NY: Author.
Anglin, M. (2017, December). Richard Longstaff. *The Dallas Way.* Retrieved from: http://www.thedallasway.org/stories/written/2017/12/8/richard-longstaff.
Antecol, H., Jong, A., & Steinberger, M. (2008). The sexual orientation wage gap: The role of occupational sorting and human capital. *Industrial and Labor Relations Review, 61*, 518–543.
Arkles, G. (2009). Safety and solidarity across gender lines: Rethinking segregation of transgender people in detention. *Temple Political & Civil Rights Law Review, 18*, 515–560.
Arnup, K. (1999). Out in this world: The social and legal context of gay and lesbian families. *Journal of Gay & Lesbian Social Services, 10*, 1–25.
Averett, P., Nalavany, B., & Ryan, S. (2009). An evaluation of gay/lesbian and heterosexual adoption. *Adoption Quarterly, 12*, 129–151.
Badgett, M. V. L., Lau, H., Sears, B., & Ho, D. (2007). *Bias in the workplace: Consistent evidence of sexual orientation and gender identity discrimination.* Los Angeles, CA: UCLA School of Law and The Williams Institute.
Badgett, M. V. L., Durso, L. E., & Schneebaum A. (2013). *New patterns of poverty in the lesbian, gay, and bisexual Community.* Los Angeles: The Williams Institute and UCLA School of Law.
Balance, C. B. (2008). Notorious kin: Filipino America re-imagines Andrew Cunanan. *Journal of Asian American Studies, 11*, 87–106.
Baldwin, J. (1981). Black English: A Dishonest Argument. In G. Smitherman (Ed.), *Black English and the Education of Black Children and Youth: Proceedings of the National Invitational Symposium on the King Decision* (pp. 53–60). Detroit, MI: Center for Black Studies, Wayne State University.
Barnao, M., Ward, T., & Robertson, P. (2016). The good lives model: a new paradigm for forensic mental health. *Psychiatry, Psychology and Law, 23*, 288–301.

Barnard, I. (2000). The racialization of sexuality: The queer case of Jeffrey Dahmer. *Thamyris Overcoming Boundaries: Ethnicity, Gender and Sexuality 7*, 67–97.
Barron, E. (2011). Development, Relief, and Education for Alien Minors (DREAM) Act. *The Harvard Journal on Legislation, 48*, 623–655.
Bartlett, A. (2010). Medical models of mental disorders. In A. Bartlett & G. McGaulery (Eds.), *Forensic mental health: Concepts, systems, and practice* (pp. 5–19). Oxford, UK: Oxford University Press.
Bashi, V. (2004). Globalized anti-blackness: Transnationalizing Western immigration law, policy, and practice. *Ethnic and Racial Studies, 27*, 584–606.
Bass, S., Shields, M. K., & Behrman, R. E. (2004). Children, families, and foster care: Analysis and recommendations. *The Future of Children, 14*, 5–29.
Bausum, A. (2015) *Stonewall: Breaking out in the fight for gay rights*. New York, NY: Speak.
Beauregard, E., & Proulx, J. (2007). A classification of sexual homicide against men. *International Journal of Offender Therapy and Comparative Criminology, 51*, 420–432.
Beck, A. J. (2014). *Sexual Victimization in Prisons and Jails Reported by Inmates, 2011–12, Supplemental Tables: Prevalence of Sexual Victimization Among Transgender Adult Inmates*. Washington, DC: U.S. Department of Justice, Bureau of Justice Statistics.
Beck, A. J. (2015a). *Prison Rape Elimination Act of 2003 Data Collection Activities, 2015*. Washington, DC: U.S. Department of Justice, Bureau of Justice Statistics.
Beck, A. J. (2015b). *Use of Restrictive Housing in U.S. Prisons and Jails, 2011–12*. Washington, DC: U.S. Department of Justice, Bureau of Justice Statistics.
Beck, A. J., Berzofsky, M., Caspar, R., & Krebs, C. (2013). *Sexual Victimization in Prisons and Jails Reported by Inmates, 2011–2012*. Washington, DC: U.S. Department of Justice, Bureau of Justice Statistics.
Beirich, H., & Buchanan, S. (2018, February 19). *2017: The Year in Hate and Extremism*. Montgomery, AL: Southern Poverty Law Center.
Belknap, J., Holsinger, K., & Little, J. (2012). Sexual minority status, abuse, and self-harming behaviors among incarcerated girls. *Journal of Child & Adolescent Trauma, 5*, 173–185.
Bell, T., & Romano, E. (2017). Permanency and safety among children in foster family and kinship care: A scoping review. *Trauma, Violence, & Abuse, 18*, 268–286.
Ben-Ezra, M., Hamama-Raz, Y., Mahat-Shamir, M., Pitcho-Prelorentzos, S., & Kaniasty, K. (2017). Shattering core beliefs: Psychological reactions to mass shooting in Orlando. *Journal of Psychiatric Research, 85*, 56–58.
Benner, L. A. (2011). Eliminating Excessive Public Defender Workloads. *Criminal Justice, 26*, 24–33.
Berke, D. S., Maples-Keller, J. L., & Richards, P. (2016). LGBTQ perceptions of psychotherapy: A consensual qualitative analysis. *Professional Psychology: Research and Practice, 47*, 373–382.
Berrill, K. T. (1990). Anti-gay violence and victimization in the United States: An overview. *Journal of Interpersonal Violence, 5*, 274–294.
Bérubé, A. (2003). The history of gay bathhouses. *Journal of Homosexuality, 44*, 33–53.
Bethard, R. (2004). New York's Harvey Milk School: A Viable Alternative. *Journal of Law Education, 33*, 417–424.
Biber, K., & Dalton, D. (2009). Making art from evidence: Secret sex and police surveillance in the Tearoom. *Crime, Media, Culture, 5*, 243–267.
Biller, R., & Rice, S. (1990). Experiencing multiple loss of persons with AIDS: Grief and bereavement issues. *Health & Social Work, 15*, 283–290.
Bindewald, B. J., Rosenblith, S., & Green, B. (2017). The Aftermath of Hobby Lobby and Obergefell: A Reconceptualization of Religious Freedom in the U.S. and Its Potential Implications for Public Schools and Pluralist Democracies. *Educational Studies, 53*, 1–20.
Bindra, D. (1953). Review of The Homosexual in America: A Subjective Approach. *Canadian Journal of Psychology, 7*, 92–93.

Black, D., Makar, H., Sanders, S., & Taylor, L., (2003). The earnings effects of sexual orientation. *Industrial and Labor Relations Review, 56*, 449–469.
Blandford, J., (2003). The nexus of sexual orientation and gender in the determination of earnings. *Industrial and Labor Relations Review, 56*, 622–642.
Borah, E. G. (1995) Filipinos in Unamuno's California Expedition of 1587. *Amerasia Journal, 21*, 175–184.
Borchert, J. (2017). A New Iron Closet: Failing to Extend the Spirit of Lawrence v. Texas to Prisons and Prisoners. In D. Halperin & T. Hoppe (Eds.). *The War on Sex* (pp. 191–210). Durham, NC: Duke University Press.
Bostwick, W. B., Meyer, I., Aranda, F., Russell, S., Hughes, T., Birkett, M., & Mustanski, B. (2014). Mental health and suicidality among racially/ethnically diverse sexual minority youths. *American Journal of Public Health, 104*, 1129–1136.
Bowman, K. M., & Engle, B. (1956). A psychiatric evaluation of laws of homosexuality. *American Journal of Psychiatry, 112*, 577–583.
Boykin, F. F. (1991). The AIDS crisis and gay male survivor guilt. *Smith College Studies in Social Work, 61*, 247–259.
Blount, J. M. (2006). *Fit to teach: Same-sex desire, gender, and school work in the twentieth century*. Albany, NY: SUNY Press.
Bowman, K, & Engle, B. (1955). A psychiatric evaluation of the laws of homosexuality. *Temple Law Quarterly, 29*, 273–326.
Bowman, K. M., & Engle, B. (1956). A psychiatric evaluation of laws of homosexuality. *American Journal of Psychiatry, 112*, 577–583.
Brewer, R. A., Magnus, M., Kuo, I., Wang, L, Liu, T., & Mayer, K. H. (2014). The High Prevalence of Incarceration History Among Black Men Who Have Sex with Men in the United States: Associations and Implications. *American Journal of Public Health, 104*, 448–454.
Brewer, R. A., Magnus, M., Kuo, I., Wang, L., Liu, T., & Mayer, K. H. (2014). Exploring the relationship between incarceration and HIV among Black men who have sex with men in the United States. *Journal of Acquired Immune Deficiency Syndrome, 65*, 218–225.
Brooklyn Daily Eagle (1913, September). Trondle girl in dresses. Retrieved from https://www.newspapers.com/clip/7789167/elizabeth_trondle_a/.
Bromer, Z. (2006). Boer-Sedano v. Gonzales: The increasing influence of HIV/AIDS status on asylum claims based on homosexual identity. *Law & Sexuality: Review of Lesbian, Gay, Bisexual, and Transgender Legal Issues, 15*, 163–174.
Bronski, M. (2011). *A queer history of the United States*. Boston, MA: Beacon Press.
Brower, T. (2001). Of courts and closets: a doctrinal and empirical analysis of lesbian and gay identity in the courts. *San Diego Law Review, 38*, 565–627.
Burns, C., Garcia, A., & Wolgin, P. (2013). *Living in Dual Shadows*. Washington, DC: Center for American Progress.
Burns, L. M. S. P. (2008). "Splendid Dancing": Filipino "exceptionalism" in taxi dancehalls. *Dance Research Journal, 40*, 23–40.
Butler, J. (2012), *Parting ways: Jewishness and the critique of Zionism*. New York, NY: Columbia University Press.
Brower, T. (2007). Multistable figures: sexual orientation visibility and its effects on the experiences of sexual minorities in the courts. *Pace Law Review, 27*, 141–198.
Brown, B. E., Canfield, A., & Irvine, A. (2014). *Practice Guide: Creating a Juvenile Justice LGBTQ Task Force*. Washington, DC: National Council on Crime and Delinquency.
Brown, J. G. (2000). Sweeping Reform from Small Rules: Anti-Bias Canons as a Substitute for Heightened Scrutiny. *Minnesota Law Review, 85*, 363–449.
Brown, R. (2008, November). Murder of Transgender Woman Revives Scrutiny. *New York Times*. Retrieved from https://www.nytimes.com/2008/11/18/us/18memphis.html.
Brown, R. S. (1958). *Loyalty and Security: Employment Tests in the United States*. New Haven, CT: Yale University Press.

Brundage, W., & Cunningham, E. (2017). Unemployment holds steady for much of 2016 but edges down in the fourth quarter. *Monthly Labor Review.* Washington, DC: U.S. Department of Justice, Bureau of Justice Statistics.
Bryant-Davis, T. (2019). The cultural context of trauma recovery: Considering the posttraumatic stress disorder practice guideline and intersectionality. *Psychotherapy, 56,* 400–408.
Brydum, S. (2015). Fateful Typo Discovered in Ky Peterson's Sentencing. *The Advocate.* Retrieved from https://www.advocate.com/politics/transgender/2015/04/17/fateful-typo-discovered-ky-petersons-sentencing.
Brydum, S., & Kellaway, M. (2015). This Black Trans Man Is in Prison for Killing His Rapist. *The Advocate.* Retrieved from https://www.advocate.com/politics/transgender/2015/04/08/black-trans-man-prison-killing-his-rapist.
Brydum, S. (2016, July). Puerto Rico's First LGBT Monument Honors Orlando Victims. *The Advocate.* Retrieved from https://www.advocate.com/pride/2016/7/03/puerto-ricos-first-lgbt-monument-honors-orlando-victims .
Buist, C. L., & Stone, C. (2014). Transgender victims and offenders: Failures of the United States criminal justice system and the necessity of queer criminology. *Critical Criminology, 22,* 35–47.
Bullock, D. (2004). Lesbian cruising: An examination of the concept and methods. *Journal of Homosexuality, 47,* 1–31.
Burch, T. (2015). Skin color and the criminal justice system: Beyond black-white disparities in sentencing. *Journal of Empirical Legal Studies, 12,* 395–420.
Burks, D. J. (2011). Lesbian, gay, and bisexual victimization in the military: An unintended consequence of "Don't Ask, Don't Tell." *American Psychologist, 66,* 604–613.
Burns, C. (2007). *The corporate leavers survey: The cost of employee turnover due solely to unfairness in the workplace.* Oakland CA: Level Playing Institute.
Byne, W. (2018). Resilience and action in a challenging time for LGBT rights. *LGBT Health, 5,* 1–5.
Cabeldue, M. K., Cramer, R. J., Kehn, A., Crosby, J. W., & Anastasi, J. S. (2018). Measuring attitudes about hate: Development of the hate crime beliefs scale. *Journal of Interpersonal Violence, 33,* 3656–3685.
California Supreme Court (2018). *California Code of Judicial Ethics.* San Francisco, CA: Author.
Callanan, V. J., & Rosenberger, J. S. (2011). Media and public perceptions of the police: Examining the impact of race and personal experience. *Policing and Society, 21,* 167–189.
Calton J. M., Cattaneo, L. B., & Gebhard, K. T. (2016). Barriers to help seeking for lesbian, gay, bisexual, transgender, and queer survivors of intimate partner violence. *Trauma, Violence & Abuse, 17,* 585–600.
Campero, S. C., & Nanclares, S. (2019, July). These Transgender Latinas Want New York State to Decriminalize Sex Work. *The Daily Beast.* Retrieved from https://www.thedailybeast.com/these-transgender-latinas-want-new-york-state-to-decriminalize-sex-work.
Carpenter, C. S. (2007). Revisiting the income penalty for behaviorally gay men: Evidence for NHANES III. *Labour Economics, 14,* 25–34.
Carson, E. A. (2015). Prisoners in 2014. Washington, DC: U.S. Department of Justice, Bureau of Justice Statistics.
Carter, D. (2004). *Stonewall: The riots that sparked the gay revolution.* New York, NY: Macmillan.
Cathcart, K., & Gabel-Brett, L. (Eds.). (2016). *Love unites us: Winning the freedom to marry in America.* New York, NY: New Press.
Center for Constitutional Rights. (2012). *Stop and frisk: The human impact; the stories behind the numbers, the effects on our communities.* New York, NY: Author.
Centers for Disease Control and Prevention. (2016). *Sexual Identity, Sex of Sexual Contacts, and Health-Risk Behaviors Among Students in Grades 9–12: Youth Risk Behavior Surveillance.* Atlanta, GA: U.S. Department of Health and Human Services.

Centers for Disease Control and Prevention (2018). *HIV Surveillance Report, 2017.* Atlanta, GA: Author. Retrieved from http://www.cdc.gov/hiv/library/reports/hiv-surveillance.html.
Centers for Disease Control and Prevention (2019). *HIV and STD Criminal Laws.* Atlanta, GA: Author. Retrieved from https://www.cdc.gov/hiv/policies/law/states/exposure.html.
Chambers, D. L., & Polikoff, N. D. (1999). Family law and gay and lesbian family issues in the twentieth century. *Family Law Quarterly, 33,* 523–542.
Chammah, M. (2014, January). The Mystery of the San Antonio Four. *Texas Observer.* Retrieved from https://www.texasobserver.org/mystery-san-antonio-four/.
Chandra, A., Mosher, W. D., Copen, C., & Sionean, C. (2011). *Sexual behavior, sexual attraction, and sexual identity in the United States: Data from the 2006–2008 National Survey of Family Growth* (National Health Statistics Reports No. 36). Hyattsville, MD: National Center for Health Statistics.
Chang, G. H., & Fishkin, S. F. (Eds.). (2019). *The Chinese and the iron road: Building the transcontinental railroad.* Stanford, CA: Stanford University Press.
Chang, S., & Skolnik, A. (2017). Transgender day of remembrance. In K. Nadal (Ed.), *The Sage encyclopedia of psychology and gender* (pp. 1698–1699). Thousand Oaks, CA: Sage.
Charak, R., Villarreal, L., Schmitz, R. M., Hirai, M., & Ford, J. D. (2019). Patterns of childhood maltreatment and intimate partner violence, emotion dysregulation, and mental health symptoms among lesbian, gay, and bisexual emerging adults: a three-step latent class approach. *Child Abuse & Neglect, 89,* 99–110.
Chauncey, G. (1995), *Gay New York: Gender, Urban Culture, and the Making of the Gay Male World, 1890–1940.* New York: Basic Books.
Chávez, K. (2013). *Queer migration politics: Activist rhetoric and coalitional possibilities.* Urbana, IL: University of Illinois Press.
Chavez, L. R. (2008). *The Latino threat: Constructing immigrants, citizens, and the nation.* Stanford, CA: Stanford University Press.
Chavez, L. R., Campos, B., Corona, K., Sanchez, D., & Ruiz, C. B. (2019). Words hurt: Political rhetoric, emotions/affect, and psychological well-being among Mexican-origin youth. *Social Science & Medicine, 228,* 240–251.
Chernin, J. N., & Johnson, M. R. (2003). *Affirmative psychotherapy and counseling for lesbians and gay men.* Thousand Oaks, CA: Sage.
Chesler, P. (1993). A woman's right to self-defense: The case of Aileen Carol Wuornos. *St. John's Law Review, 66,* 933–978.
Chesney-Lind, M., & Eliason, M. (2006). From invisible to incorrigible: The demonization of marginalized women and girls. *Crime, Media, Culture, 2,* 29–47.
Children's Bureau (2018). The AFCARS Report. Washington, DC: U.S. Department of Health and Human Services, Administration for Children and Families, Administration on Children, Youth and Families, Children's Bureau. Retrieved from https://www.acf.hhs.gov/sites/default/files/cb/afcarsreport25.pdf.
Chin, J. J., Leung, M., Sheth, L., & Rodriguez, T. R. (2007). Let's not ignore a growing HIV problem for Asians and Pacific Islanders in the US. *Journal of Urban Health, 84,* 642–647.
Cisneros, J. (2018). Working with the complexity and refusing to simplify: Undocuqueer meaning making at the intersection of LGBTQ and immigrant rights discourses. *Journal of Homosexuality, 65,* 1415–1434.
Cisneros, J., & Bracho, C. (2019) Coming out of the shadows and the closet: Visibility schemas among undocuqueer immigrants. *Journal of Homosexuality, 66,* 715–734.
Clemens, A. M. (2005). Executing homosexuality: Removing anti-gay bias from capital trials. *Georgetown Journal of Gender & Law, 6,* 71–103.
Clements-Nolle, K., Marx, R., Guzman, R., & Katz, M. (2001). HIV prevalence, risk behaviors, health care use, and mental health status of transgender persons: Implications for public health intervention. *American Journal of Public Health, 91,* 915–921.

Civic Science (2017). *Counting Counts: Quantifying LGBTQ Experiences & Sentiment*. Pittsburgh, PA: Author.

Cleves, R. H. (2015). "What, Another Female Husband?": The Prehistory of Same-Sex Marriage in America. *The Journal of American History, 101*, 1055–1081.

Cisneros, J. (2018). Working with the complexity and refusing to simplify: Undocuqueer meaning making at the intersection of LGBTQ and immigrant rights discourses. *Journal of Homosexuality, 65*, 1415–1434.

Coates, T. J., Temoshok, L., & Mandel, J. (1984). Psychosocial research is essential to understanding and treating AIDS. *American Psychologist, 39*, 1309–1314.

Cochran, B. N., Stewart, A. J., Ginzler, J. A., & Cauce, A. M. (2002). Challenges faced by homeless sexual minorities: Comparison of gay, lesbian, bisexual, and transgender homeless adolescents with their heterosexual counterparts. *American Journal of Public Health, 92*, 773–777.

Cohen, C. (2017). Losing Your Children: The Failure to Extend Civil Rights Protections to Transgender Parents. *George Washington Law Review, 85*, 536–565.

Cohen, D. S., & Carpenter, L. (2015, December). In the movement for LGBTQ equality, the mission isn't even close to accomplished. *Slate*. Retrieved from https://slate.com/human-interest/2015/12/empire-state-pride-agenda-closing-claims-mission-accomplished.html.

Coleman, M. (2012). The "local" migration state: The site-specific devolution of immigration enforcement in the US South. *Law & Policy, 34*, 159–190.

Colvin, R. A. (2009). Shared perceptions among lesbian and gay police officers: Barriers and opportunities in the law enforcement work environment. *Police Quarterly, 12*, 86–101.

Colvin, R. (2014). Policing the lesbian and gay community: The perceptions of lesbian and gay police officers. In. D. Peterson & V. R. Panfil (Eds.), *Handbook of LGBT communities, crime, and justice* (pp. 183–205). New York, NY: Springer.

Comstock, G. D. (1991). The police as perpetrators of anti-gay/lesbian violence. In G. D. Comstock (Ed.), *Violence against lesbians and gay men* (pp. 152–162). New York: Columbia University Press.

Conclara, R. (2014, August). Pinay lesbian couple marries despite deportation fear. *ABS-CBN*. Retrieved from https://news.abs-cbn.com/global-filipino/08/20/14/pinay-lesbian-couple-marries-despite-deportation-fear.

Connell, R. W., & Messerschmidt, J. W. (2005). Hegemonic masculinity: Rethinking the concept. *Gender and Society, 19*, 829–859.

Conover-Williams, M. (2014). The Queer Delinquent: Impacts of Risk and Protective Factors on Sexual Minority. In D. Peterson & V. R. Panfil (Eds.), *Handbook of LGBT communities, crime, and justice* (pp. 449–472). New York, NY: Springer.

Cortopassi, A. C., Driver, R., Eaton, L. A., & Kalichman, S. C. (2019). A New era of HIV risk: It's not what you know, it's who you know (and how infectious). *Annual Review of Psychology, 70*, 673–701.

Costo, R., & Costo, J. H. (1987). *The missions of California: A legacy of genocide*. San Francisco, CA: Indian Historian Press.

Cott, N. F. (1998). Marriage and women's citizenship in the United States, 1830–1934. *The American Historical Review, 103*, 1440–1474.

Craft, S. M., & Serovich, J. M. (2005). Family-of-origin factors and partner violence in the intimate relationships of gay men who are HIV positive. *Journal of Interpersonal violence, 20*, 777–791.

Cramer, M. (2013, February). Boston, transgender woman settle lawsuit. *Boston Globe*. Retrieved from https://www.bostonglobe.com/metro/2013/02/05/transgender-woman-settles-lawsuit-with-boston-over-treatment-during-arrest-sues-city-after-police-arrested-humiliated-bathroom-for-using-woman/.

Cramer, R. J., Laxton, K. L., Chandler, J. F., Kehn, A., Bate, B. P., & Clark, J. W., III (2017). Political Identity, Type of Victim, and Hate Crime-Related Beliefs as Predictors of Views Concerning Hate Crime Penalty Enhancement Laws. *Analyses of Social Issues and Public Policy, 17*, 262–285.

Crenshaw, K. (1989). Demarginalizing the intersection of race and sex: A Black feminist critique of antidiscrimination doctrine, feminist theory, and antiracist politics. University of Chicago Legal Forum.

Croff, J. M., Hubach, R. D., Currin, J. M., & Frederick, A. F. (2017). Hidden rainbows: Gay bars as safe havens in a socially conservative area since the Pulse nightclub massacre. *Sexuality Research and Social Policy, 14*, 233–240.

Crompton, L. (1976). Homosexuals and the Death Penalty in Colonial America. *Journal of Homosexuality, 3*, 277–293.

Curley, C. (2018). Sexual orientation, sexual history, and inequality in the United States. *Feminist Economics, 24*, 88–113.

Currah, P. (2008). Expecting bodies: The pregnant man and transgender exclusion from the employment non-discrimination act. *Women's Studies Quarterly, 36*, 330–336.

D'Emilio, J. (2012). *Sexual politics, sexual communities*. Chicago, IL: University of Chicago Press.

Dale, M. C. (2001, November). Town in Schuylkill County sued over teenager's suicide. *The Philadelphia Inquirer*.

Daneshvary, N. C., Waddoups, J., & Wimmer, B. S. (2009). Previous marriage and the lesbian wage premium. *Industrial Relations: A Journal of Economy and Society, 48*, 432–453.

Daniels, R., Taylor, S. C., & Kitano, H. H. (Eds.). (2013). *Japanese Americans: From relocation to redress*. Seattle, WA: University of Washington Press.

Dank, M., Yu, L., Yahner, J., Pelletier, E., Mora, M., & Conner, B. (2015). *Locked in: Interactions with the criminal justice and child welfare systems for LGBTQ youth, YMSM, and YWSW who engage in survival sex*. Washington, DC: Urban Institute.

Darrow, W. W., Echenberg, D. F., Jaffe, H. W., O'Malley, P. M., Byers, R. H., Getchell, J. P., & Curran, J. W. (1987). Risk factors for human immunodeficiency virus (HIV) infections in homosexual men. *American Journal of Public Health, 77*, 479–483.

Daum, C. W. (2015). The war on solicitation and intersectional subjection: Quality-of-life policing as a tool to control transgender populations. *New Political Science, 37*, 562–581.

Dart, T. (2019, June). Texas clings to unconstitutional, homophobic laws—and it's not alone. *The Guardian*. Retrieved from https://www.theguardian.com/world/2019/jun/01/texas-homophobic-laws-lgbt-unconstitutional.

David, E. J. R. (2013). *Brown Skin, White Minds: Filipino/American Postcolonial Psychology*. Charlotte, NC: Information Age.

David, E. J. R. (Ed.). (2014). *Internalized oppression: The psychology of marginalized groups*. New York, NY: Springer Publishing Company.

David, M. D. (2018). Confronting Charlottesville: Using interdisciplinary research as critical engagement praxis. *Politics, Groups, and Identities, 6*, 303–308.

Davis, L. (2017a). Passing. In K. Nadal (Ed.), *The Sage encyclopedia of psychology and gender* (pp. 1279–1280). Thousand Oaks, CA: Sage.

Davis, L. (2017b). Queer. In K. L. Nadal (Ed.), *The Sage encyclopedia of psychology and gender* (pp. 1383–1385). Thousand Oaks, CA: Sage.

Davis, T. J. (1999). Opening the doors of immigration: Sexual orientation and asylum in the United States. *Human Rights Brief, 6*, 19–20.

Day, N. E., & Schoenrade, P. (1997). Staying in the closet versus coming out: Relationships between communication about sexual orientation and work attitudes. *Personnel Psychology, 50*, 147–163.

De'Alessandro, A. (2018, August). How 'The Assassination of Gianni Versace' Still Resonates Today. *Vanity Fair*. Retrieved from https://deadline.com/2018/08/ryan-murphy-ricky-martin-look-back-on-the-assassination-of-gianni-versace-emmy-nominee-1202446351/.

de Blasio, B., & Malalis, C. (2019). NYC Commission on Human Rights legal enforcement guidance on discrimination on the basis of gender identity or expression: Local Law No. 3 (2002); N.Y.C. Admin. Code § 8-102. New York, NY: New York

City Commission on Human Rights. Retrieved from https://www1.nyc.gov/assets/cchr/downloads/pdf/publications/2019.2.15%20Gender%20Guidance-February%202019%20FINAL.pdf.
De Witt, H. A. (1979). The Watsonville anti-Filipino riot of 1930: a case study of the Great Depression and ethnic conflict in California. *Southern California Quarterly, 61,* 291–302.
de Vogue, A. (2019). Supreme Court won't take up case of death row inmate who claims juror discrimination against him for being gay. *CNN.* Retrieved from https://www.cnn.com/2019/04/15/politics/supreme-court-charles-rhines/index.html.
Del Real, J. A. (2018, July). "They Were Abusing Us the Whole Way": A Tough Path for Gay and Trans Migrants. *New York Times.* Retrieved from: https://www.nytimes.com/2018/07/11/us/lgbt-migrants-abuse.html.
DeMilia, S. (1978, February). Homosexuals as Police Officers? No . . . *New York Times,* p. 28. Retrieved from https://www.nytimes.com/1978/02/10/archives/homosexuals-as-police-officers-no-yes.html.
Dennis, J. P. (2014). LGBT Offenders. In D. Peterson & V. R. Panfil (Eds.), *Handbook of LGBT communities, crime, and justice* (pp. 87–102). New York, NY: Springer.
DeSouza, E. R., Wesselmann, E. D., & Ispas, D. (2017). Workplace Discrimination against Sexual Minorities: Subtle and not-so-subtle. *Canadian Journal of Administrative Sciences, 34,* 121–132.
Dettlaff, A. J., & Washburn, M. (2018). Lesbian, gay, and bisexual (LGB) youth within in welfare: prevalence, risk and outcomes. *Child Abuse & Neglect, 80,* 183–193.
Deutsch, T. (2017). Asexuality. In K. L. Nadal (Ed.), *The Sage encyclopedia of psychology and gender* (pp. 95–97). Thousand Oaks, CA: Sage.
Diaz, E. M., & Kosciw, J. G. (2009). *Shared Differences: The Experiences of Lesbian, Gay, Bisexual, and Transgender Students of Color in Our Nation's Schools.* New York, NY: GLSEN.
Dinnerstein, L. (2009). *Ethnic Americans: A History of Immigration.* New York, NY: Columbia University Press.
Dispenza, F., Kumar, A., Standish, J., Norris, S., & Procter, J. (2018). Disability and sexual orientation disclosure on employment interview ratings: An analogue study. *Rehabilitation Counseling Bulletin, 61,* 244–255.
Dixon, E., Ray, A., & Tillery, B. (2019). *Pride and Pain: A Special NCAVP Report on Anti-LGBTQ Violence During Pride Season 2019.* New York, NY: The National Coalition of Anti-Violence Programs.
Donahue, D. M. (2014). Learning from Harvey Milk: The limits and opportunities of one hero to teach about LGBTQ people and issues. *The Social Studies, 105,* 36–44.
Donahue, J. (2011). Making it happen, mama: A conversation with Miss Major. In E. A. Stanley & N. Smith (Eds.), *Captive genders: Trans embodiment and the prison industrial complex* (pp. 267–280). Chico, CA: AK Press.
Douglas, J. E., Burgess, A. W., Burgess, A. G., & Ressler, R. K. (2013). *Crime classification manual: A standard system for investigating and classifying violent crime.* New York: John Wiley & Sons.
Drescher, J. (2015). Can sexual orientation be changed? *Journal of Gay & Lesbian Mental Health, 19,* 84–93.
Du Bois, W. E. B. (2014). *The suppression of the African slave-trade to the United States of America.* Oxford, United Kingdom: Oxford University Press.
Duberman, M. (2019). *Stonewall: The Definitive story of the LGBTQ rights uprising that changed America.* New York: Plume.
Dueñas, C. A. (2000). Coming to America: The immigration obstacle facing binational same-sex couples. *Immigration & Nationality Law Review, 21,* 29–59.
Duke, T. S. (2011). Lesbian, gay, bisexual, and transgender youth with disabilities: A meta-synthesis. *Journal of LGBT Youth, 8,* 1–52.
Dunn, T. R. (2010). Remembering Matthew Shepard: Violence, identity, and queer counterpublic memories. *Rhetoric & Public Affairs, 13,* 611–652.

Durkin, J. (1998). Queer studies I: An examination of the first eleven studies of sexual orientation bias by the legal profession. *UCLA Women's Law Journal, 8,* 343–378.

Durso, L.E., & Gates, G. J. (2012). *Serving our youth: Findings from a national survey of service providers working with lesbian, gay, bisexual, and transgender youth who are homeless or at risk of becoming homeless.* Los Angeles: The Williams Institute.

Dwyer, A. E. (2011). "It's not like we're going to jump them": How transgressing heteronormativity shapes police interactions with LGBT young people. *Youth Justice, 11,* 203–220.

Eddington, S. M. (2018). The communicative constitution of hate organizations online: A semantic network analysis of "Make America Great Again." *Social Media and Society, 4,* 1–12.

Edwards, E. R., & Wupperman, P. (2017). Emotion regulation mediates effects of alexithymia and emotion differentiation on impulsive aggressive behavior. *Deviant Behavior, 38,* 1160–1171.

Eigenberg, H. (1992). Homosexuality in male prisons: Demonstrating the need for a social constructionist approach. *Criminal Justice Review, 17,* 219–234.

Eliason, M. (2010). Introduction to special issue on suicide, mental health, and youth development. *Journal of Homosexuality, 58,* 4–9.

Elliott, R., Utyasheva, L., & Zack, E. (2009). HIV, disability and discrimination: Making the links in international and domestic human rights law. *Journal of the International AIDS Society, 12,* 29–44.

Ellis, H. (1944). *Psychology of Sex: A Manual for Students.* New York, NY: Emerson.

Elkins, D. N. (2016). *The human elements of psychotherapy: A nonmedical model of emotional healing.* Washington, DC: American Psychological Association.

Eskridge, W. N. (2009). *Gaylaw: Challenging the apartheid of the closet.* Cambridge, MA: Harvard University Press.

Ewing, W. A. (2012). *Opportunity and exclusion: A brief history of US immigration policy.* Washington, DC: Immigration Policy Center of the American Immigration Council.

Eyerman, R. (2012). Harvey Milk and the trauma of assassination. *Cultural Sociology, 6,* 399–421.

Faderman, L., & Timmons, S. (2009). *Gay LA: A history of sexual outlaws, power politics, and lipstick lesbians.* Berkeley, CA: University of California Press.

Fairyington, B. (2013, December). Two decades after Brandon Teena's murder, a look back at Falls City. *The Atlantic.* Retrieved from https://www.theatlantic.com/national/archive/2013/12/two-decades-after-brandon-teenas-murder-a-look-back-at-falls-city/282738/.

Federal Bureau of Investigation (2013). Rape. *Crime in the United States.* Washington, DC: Author. Retrieved from: https://ucr.fbi.gov/crime-in-the-u.s/2013/crime-in-the-u.s.-2013/violent-crime/rape/rapemain_final.pdf.

Federal Bureau of Investigation (2014). Serial Killers, Part 6: Andrew Cunanan murders a fashion icon. Washington, DC: Author. Retrieved from https://www.fbi.gov/news/stories/serial-killers-part-6-andrew-cunanan.

Federal Bureau of Investigation (2018). Hate Crimes Statistics, 2017. Washington, DC: Author. Retrieved from https://ucr.fbi.gov/hate-crime/2017.

Federal Bureau of Investigation (2019a). Definitions of terrorism in the U.S. Code. Retrieved July 8, 2019 from https://www.fbi.gov/investigate/terrorism.

Federal Bureau of Investigation (2019b). *Hate crimes.* Retrieved July 8, 2019 from https://www.fbi.gov/investigate/civil-rights/hate-crimes.

Feinberg, L. (2006). Street Transvestite Action Revolutionaries. *Workers World.* Retrieved from https://www.workers.org/books2016/Lavender_and_Red.pdf.

Ferguson, K. M., Bender, K., Thompson, S., Xie, B., & Pollio, D. (2011). Correlates of street-survival behaviors in homeless young adults in four US cities. *American Journal of Orthopsychiatry, 81,* 401–409.

Fiani, C. N., Nadal, K. L., Han, H., Mejia, D., Deutsch, T., & Murillo, M. (2017). A System of Transphobic Injustice: Microaggressions toward Transgender and Gender Nonconforming People in the Criminal Justice System. *New York State Psychologist, 29,* 5–15.

Fidas, D. & Cooper, L. (2019). *A Workplace Divided: Understanding the Climate for LGBTQ Workers Nationwide.* Washington, DC: Human Rights Campaign. Retrieved from https://www.hrc.org/resources/a-workplace-divided-understanding-the-climate-for-lgbtq-workers-nationwide.

Fieseler, R. W. (2018). *Tinderbox: The untold story of the Up Stairs Lounge fire and the rise of gay liberation.* Liveright Publishing.

Fillichio, C. A. (2006). The new beat. *The Public Manager, 35,* 56–59.

Fischer, M. (2016). #Free_CeCe: the material convergence of social media activism, *Feminist Media Studies, 16,* 755–771.

Fitzsimmons, T. (2018, December). Judge clears records of wrongfully convicted "San Antonio 4." *NBC News.* Retrieved from https://www.nbcnews.com/feature/nbc-out/judge-clears-records-wrongfully-convicted-san-antonio-four-n943751.

Flaks, D. K. (1994). Gay and lesbian families: Judicial assumptions, scientific realities. *William & Mary Bill of Rights Journal, 3,* 345–372.

Follman, M., Aronsen, G., & Pan, D. (2019). US Mass Shootings, 1982–2019: Data from Mother Jones' Investigation. *Mother Jones.* Retrieved August 28, 2019 from https://www.motherjones.com/politics/2012/12/mass-shootings-mother-jones-full-data/.

Foner, N. (2000). *From Ellis Island to JFK: New York's two great waves of immigration.* New Haven, CT: Yale University Press.

Forbes, A. (2014). LGBTQ experiences with the courts: The role of gender nonconformity and assertiveness (Unpublished doctoral dissertation). City University of New York, New York, NY.

Fowler, P. J., Marcal, K. E., Zhang, J., Day, O., & Landsverk, J. (2017). Homelessness and aging out of foster care: A national comparison of child welfare-involved adolescents. *Children and Youth Services Review, 77,* 27–33.

Fradella, H. F., Owen, S. S., & Burke, T. W. (2009). Integrating gay, lesbian, bisexual, and transgender issues into the undergraduate criminal justice curriculum. *Journal of Criminal Justice Education, 20,* 127–156.

Frankel, A. (2016). *"Do you see how much I'm suffering here?": Abuse against transgender women in U.S. immigration detention.* New York, NY: Human Rights Watch.

Friedman, M. S., Marshal, M. P., Guadamuz, T. E., Wei, C., Wong, C. F., Saewyc, E. M., & Stall, R. (2011). A meta-analysis of disparities in childhood sexual abuse, parental physical abuse, and peer victimization among sexual minority and sexual nonminority individuals. *American Journal of Public Health, 101,* 1481–1494.

Gal, N., Shifman, L., & Kampf, Z. (2016). "It Gets Better": Internet memes and the construction of collective identity. *New Media & Society, 18,* 1698–1714.

Galletly, C. L., & Lazzarini, Z. (2013). Charges for criminal exposure to HIV and aggravated prostitution filed in the Nashville, Tennessee prosecutorial region 2000–2010. *AIDS and Behavior, 17,* 2624–2636.

Gallucci, N. (2019, June). Jose Antonio Vargas on the LGBTQ movement, immigration, and the importance of storytelling. *Mashable.* Retrieved from https://mashable.com/article/jose-antonio-vargas-storytelling-immigration/.

García, A. M., & Slesaransky-Poe, G. (2010). The heteronormative classroom: Questioning and liberating practices. *The Teacher Educator, 45,* 244–256.

Garcia, S. E. (2018, November). Independent Autopsy of Transgender Asylum Seeker Who Died in ICE Custody Shows Signs of Abuse. *New York Times.* Retrieved from https://www.nytimes.com/2018/11/27/us/trans-woman-roxsana-hernandez-ice-autopsy.html.

Gardiner, S., & Firger, J. (2011, September). Rare Charge Is Unmasked. *Wall Street Journal.* Retrieved from https://www.wsj.com/articles/SB10001424053111190419460 4576581171443151568.

Gares J. (Director), & Cox, L. (Producer). (2016). *Free CeCe!* [Motion Picture]. USA: Jac Gares Media, Inc.

Garnette, L., Irvine, A., Reyes, C., & Wilber, S. (2011). Lesbian, gay, bisexual, and transgender (LGBT) youth and the juvenile justice system. In F. Sherman & F. Jacobs (Eds.), *Juvenile justice: Advancing research, policy, and practice* (156–173). New York, NY: Wiley.

Garsd, J. (2019, March). Should sex work be decriminalized? Some activists say it's time. *NPR*. Retrieved from https://www.npr.org/2019/03/22/705354179/should-sex-work-be-decriminalized-some-activists-say-its-time.

Gartrell, N. K., Bos, H. M. W., Peyser, H., Deck, A., & Rodas, C. (2011). Family characteristics, custody arrangements, and adolescent psychological well-being after lesbian mothers break up. *Family Relations, 60*, 572–585.

Gates, G. J. (2013a). *LGBT parenting in the United States*. Los Angeles, CA: The Williams Institute, UCLA School of Law. Retrieved from http://williamsinstitute.law.ucla.edu/wp-content/uploads/LGBT-Parenting.pdf.

Gates, G. J. (2013b). *LGBT Adult Immigrants in the United States*. Los Angeles: Williams Institute at UCLA School of Law. Retrieved from http://williamsinstitute.law.ucla.edu/research/census-lgbt-demographics-studies/us-lgbt-immigrants-mar-2013/.

Gates, H. L. (2011). *Life upon these shores: Looking at African American history, 1513–2008*. New York, NY: Alfred A. Knopf, Inc.

George, M. (2016). Agency nullification: Defying bans on gay and lesbian foster and adoptive parents. *Harvard Civil Rights-Civil Liberties Law Review, 51*, 363–422.

Geberth, V. J. (1996). *Practical homicide investigation: Tactics, procedures, and forensic techniques* (3rd ed.). Boca Raton, FL: CRC Press.

Ghaziani, A., & Brim, M. (Eds.). (2019). *Imagining Queer Methods*. New York: NYU Press.

Gillespie, W. (2008) Thirty-five years after Stonewall: An exploratory study of satisfaction with police among gay, lesbian, and bisexual persons at the 34th annual Atlanta pride festival. *Journal of Homosexuality, 55*, 619–647.

Gius, M. (2015). The impact of state and federal assault weapons bans on public mass shootings. *Applied Economics Letters, 22*, 281–284.

Glueck, B. C. (1956). An Evaluation of the Homosexual Offender. *Minnesota Law Review, 41*, 187–210.

Goebel, T., Waters, M. R., & O'Rourke, D. H. (2008). The late Pleistocene dispersal of modern humans in the Americas. *Science, 319*, 1497–1502.

Gold, J. (2019). 3 Trans Women Have Been Killed in Dallas This Past Year. *The Cut*. Retrieved from https://www.thecut.com/2019/06/trans-woman-chynal-lindsey-murdered-in-dallas.html.

Goldberg, N. G., & Meyer, I. H. (2013). Sexual orientation disparities in history of intimate partner violence: Results from the California Health Interview Survey. *Journal of Interpersonal Violence, 28*, 1109–1118.

Goldberg, S. K. & Conron, K. J. (2018). How many same-sex couples in the U.S. are raising children? Los Angeles, CA: The Williams Institute and UCLA School of Law. Retrieved from https://williamsinstitute.law.ucla.edu/research/parenting/how-many-same-sex-parents-in-us/.

Goldstein, A. B. (1988). History, homosexuality, and political values: Searching for the hidden determinants of Bowers v. Hardwick. *Yale Law Journal, 97*, 1073–1104.

Goltz, D. B. (2013). It gets better: Queer futures, critical frustrations, and radical potentials. *Critical Studies in Media Communication, 30*, 135–151.

Gonzales, J. L. (1986). Asian Indian immigration patterns: The origins of the Sikh community in California. *International Migration Review, 20*, 40–54.

Gonzalez, T. (2012). Keeping kids in schools: Restorative justice, punitive discipline, and the school to prison pipeline. *Journal of Law Education, 41*, 281–336.

Goodrich, K. M., Harper, A. J., Luke, M., & Singh, A. A. (2013). Best practices for professional school counselors working with LGBTQ youth. *Journal of LGBT Issues in Counseling, 7*, 307–322.

Goodrich, K. M., Luke, M., & Kassirer, S. (2017). Heteronormativity. In K. L. Nadal (Ed.), *The Sage Encyclopedia of Psychology and Gender*.

Graham, R. (2006). Male rape and the careful construction of the male victim. *Social & Legal Studies, 15*, 187–208.

Grant, J. M., Mottet, L. A., Tanis, J., Harrison J., Herman, J. L., & Keisling, M. (2011). *Injustice at every turn: A report of the national transgender discrimination study.* Washington, DC: National Center for Transgender Equality and National LGBTQ Task Force.

Graves, K. (2009). *And they were wonderful teachers: Florida's purge of gay and lesbian teachers.* Champaign, IL: University of Illinois Press.

Green, C. (2018, May). Transgender Honduran woman's death in US 'ice box' detention prompts outcry. *The Guardian.* Retrieved from: https://www.theguardian.com/us-news/2018/may/31/roxana-hernandez-transgender-honduran-woman-dies-us-ice-box.

Greene, J. (2018). Confronting Immigration Enforcement under Trump: A Reign of Terror for Immigrant Communities. *Social Justice, 45*, 83–132.

Griffin, J. L. (1993, August). Primary label for gay police officers is cop. *Chicago Tribune.* Retrieved from https://www.chicagotribune.com/news/ct-xpm-1993-08-25-9308250142-story.html.

Groth, A. N., & Birnbaum, H. J. (1978). Adult sexual orientation and attraction to underage persons. *Archives of Sexual Behavior, 7*, 175–181.

Gruber-Miller, S. (2019, July). Jury decides Terry Branstad discriminated against gay employee as governor, awards employee $1.5 million. *Des Moines Register.* Retrieved from https://www.desmoinesregister.com/story/news/politics/2019/07/15/terry-branstad-gay-official-discrimination-chris-godfrey-workers-compensation-commissioner-verdict/1714302001/.

Gurian, E. A. (2011). Female serial murderers: Directions for future research on a hidden population. *International Journal of Offender Therapy and Comparative Criminology, 55*, 27–42.

Gutt, P. S. (1987, January). Homosexual parents winning some custody cases. *New York Times.* Retrieved from https://www.nytimes.com/1987/01/21/garden/homosexual-parents-winning-some-custody-cases.html.

Haider, S. (2016). The shooting in Orlando, terrorism or toxic masculinity (or both?). *Men and Masculinities, 19*, 555–565.

Haldeman, D. (2017). Marriage equality. In K. Nadal (Ed.), *The Sage encyclopedia of psychology and gender* (pp. 1106–1108). Thousand Oaks, CA: Sage.

Hale, C. J. (1998). Consuming the Living, Dis(re)membering the Dead in the Butch/FTM Borderlands. *GLQ: A Journal of Lesbian and Gay Studies, 4*, 311–348.

Hancock, K. A., & Haldeman, D. C. (2017). Between the lines: Media coverage of Orlando and beyond. *Psychology of Sexual Orientation and Gender Diversity, 4*, 152–159.

Haney, C. (2018). The psychological effects of solitary confinement: A systematic critique. *Crime and Justice, 47*, 365–416.

Hanna, F. (2005). Punishing masculinity in gay asylum claims. *Yale Law Journal, 114*, 913–921.

Harris, K., Udall, T., & Heinrich, M. (2018). 12.05.18 Roxana Hernandez letter [Letter written December 5, 2018 to R. Vitiello]. Retrieved September 11, 2019 from https://www.harris.senate.gov/imo/media/doc/12.05.18%20Roxana%20Hernandez%20letter[1].pdf.

Hasenbush, A., Flores., A., Kastanis, A., Sears, B., & Gates, G. J. (2014). *The LGBT Divide: A Data Portrait of LGBT People in the Midwestern, Mountain & Southern States.* Los Angeles: The Williams Institute and UCLA School of Law.

Heller, K. (2015, July). Freedom to Marry is going out of business. And everybody's thrilled. *Washington Post.* Retrieved from https://www.washingtonpost.com/lifestyle/style/freedom-to-marry-is-going-out-of-business-and-everybodys-thrilled/2015/07/30/5ca89b5c-322b-11e5-8f36-18d1d501920d_story.html.

Herek, G. M. (1993). Sexual orientation and military service: A social science perspective. *American Psychologist, 48*, 538–549.

Herek, G. M. (2007). Confronting sexual stigma and prejudice: Theory and practice. *Journal of Social Issues, 63*, 905–925.
Herek, G. M. (2010). Sexual orientation differences as deficits: Science and stigma in the history of American psychology. *Perspectives on Psychological Science, 5*, 693–699.
Herek, G. M. (2017). Documenting hate crimes in the United States: Some considerations on data sources. *Psychology of Sexual Orientation and Gender Diversity, 4*, 143–151.
Higdon, M. J. (2009). Queer teens and legislative bullies: The cruel and insidious discrimination behind heterosexist statutory rape laws. *Davis Law Review, 42*, 195–253.
Hill, E. (2011, January). Ricky Martin on Fatherhood, Coming Out, and His Big Return. *Parade*. Retrieved from https://parade.com/93035/erinhill/31-ricky-martin/.
Hill, M. L. (2012, May). Why Aren't We Fighting for CeCe McDonald? *Ebony*. Retrieved from https://www.ebony.com/news/why-arent-we-fighting-for-cece-mcdonald/.
Hill, N., & McCaughan, A. (2017). Intersex. In K. L. Nadal (Ed.), *The Sage encyclopedia of psychology and gender* (pp. 972–975). Thousand Oaks, CA: Sage.
Himmelstein, K. E. W., & Bruckner, H. (2011). Criminal justice and school sanctions against nonheterosexual youth: A national longitudinal study. *Pediatrics, 127*, 49–58.
Hoefer, M., Rytina, N., & Baker, B. C. (2009). *Estimates of the Unauthorized Immigrant Population Residing in the United States: January 2008*. Washington, DC: Office of Immigration Statistics, U.S. Department of Homeland Security.
Holder, A., Jackson, M. A., & Ponterotto, J. G. (2015). Racial microaggression experiences and coping strategies of Black women in corporate leadership. *Qualitative Psychology, 2*, 164–180.
Holloway v. Arthur Andersen and Company (1977) 566 F.2d 659 (9th Cir. 1977).
Holsinger, K., & Hodge, J. P. (2016). The experiences of lesbian, gay, bisexual, and transgender girls in juvenile justice systems. *Feminist Criminology, 11*, 23–47.
Houtman, J., Naegle, W., & Long, M. G. (2019). *Troublemaker for Justice: The Story of Bayard Rustin, the Man Behind the March on Washington*. San Francisco, CA: City Lights Books.
Human Rights Campaign (2019a). *Corporate Equality Index 2019: Rating workplaces on lesbian, gay, bisexual, transgender, and queer equality*. Washington, DC: Author. Retrieved from https://assets2.hrc.org/files/assets/resources/CEI-2019-FullReport.pdf.
Human Rights Campaign (2019b). Violence Against the Transgender Community in 2018. Retrieved from https://www.hrc.org/resources/violence-against-the-transgender-community-in-2018.
Hunt, J., & Moodie-Mills, A. (2012). *The unfair criminalization of gay and transgender youth: An overview of the experiences of LGBT youth in the juvenile justice system*. Washington, DC: Center for American Progress.
Hunt, J. S. (2015). Race, ethnicity, and culture in jury decision making. *Annual Review of Law and Social Science, 11*, 269–288.
Immigration and Customs Enforcement (2016). Marriage fraud is a federal crime. Washington, DC: Author. Retrieved from https://www.ice.gov/identity-benefit-fraud#tab2.
Inch, M. S. (2018). *Change notice: Transgender offender manual*. Federal Bureau of Prisons. Washington, DC: U.S. Department of Justice. Retrieved from https://www.bop.gov/policy/progstat/5200-04-cn-1.pdf.
Irvine, A. (2010). We've had three of them: Addressing the invisibility of lesbian, gay, bisexual, and gender nonconforming youths in the juvenile justice system. *Columbia Journal of Gender and Law, 19*, 675–701.
Irvine, A., & Canfield, A. (2016). The overrepresentation of lesbian, gay, bisexual, questioning, gender nonconforming and transgender youth within the child welfare to juvenile justice crossover population. *American University Journal of Gender, Social Policy and the Law, 24*, 243–262.

Irvine, A., Wilber, S., & Canfield, A. (2017). *Lesbian, Gay, Bisexual, Questioning, and/or Gender Nonconforming and Transgender Girls and Boys in the California Juvenile Justice System: A Practice Guide.* Oakland, CA: Impact Justice and the National Center for Lesbian Rights.

Israel, T., Harkness, A., Avellar, T. R., Delucio, K., Bettergarcia, J. N., & Goodman, J. A. (2016). LGBTQ-affirming policing: Tactics generated by law enforcement personnel. *Journal of Police and Criminal Psychology, 31,* 173–181.

Israel, T., Harkness, A., Delucio, K., Ledbetter, J. N., & Avellar, T. R. (2014). Evaluation of police training on LGBTQ issues: Knowledge, interpersonal apprehension, and self-efficacy. *Journal of Police and Criminal Psychology, 29,* 57–67.

Jackson, R. (2016). If they gunned me down and criming while White: An examination of Twitter campaigns through the lens of citizens' media. *Cultural Studies? Critical Methodologies, 16,* 313–319.

Jackson, S. D. (2017). "Connection is the antidote": Psychological distress, emotional processing, and virtual community building among LGBTQ students after the Orlando shooting. *Psychology of Sexual Orientation and Gender Diversity, 4,* 160–168.

Jacobs, J. & Freundlich, M. (2006) Achieving Permanency for LGBTQ Youth. *Child Welfare, 85,* 299–316.

Jaggers, J., Gabbard, W. J., & Jaggers, S. J. (2014) The Devolution of U.S. Immigration Policy: An examination of the history and future of immigration policy. *Journal of Policy Practice, 13,* 3–15.

James, S. E., Herman, J. L., Rankin, S., Keisling, M., Mottet, L., & Ana, M. (2016). *The Report of the 2015 U.S. Transgender Survey.* Washington, DC: National Center for Transgender Equality. Retrieved from https://transequality.org/sites/default/files/docs/usts/USTS-Full-Report-Dec17.pdf.

Jenness, V., Maxson, C. L., Matsuda, K. N., & Sumner, J. M. (2007). Violence in California correctional facilities: An empirical examination of sexual assault. *Bulletin, 2,* 1–4.

Jennings, K. (2015, October). Leelah Alcorn and the continued struggle for equity for LGBT students. *The Educational Forum, 79,* 4, 343–346.

Jenny, C., Roesler, T. A., & Poyer, K. L. (1994). Are children at risk for sexual abuse by homosexuals? *Pediatrics, 94,* 41–44.

Jepsen, L. K. (2007). Comparing the earnings of cohabiting lesbians, cohabiting heterosexual women, and married women: Evidence from the 2000 census. *Industrial Relations: A Journal of Economy and Society, 46,* 699–727.

Johnson, D. K. (2009). *The Lavender Scare: The Cold War persecution of gays and lesbians in the federal government.* Chicago: University of Chicago Press.

Johnson, H. (2017, June). Being gay in prison is ten times harder: Inmates tell of abuse, use of solitary. *The Progressive.* Retrieved from: http://progressive.org/dispatches/'being-gay-in-prison-is-ten-times-harder'-inmates-tell-of-ab/.

Joint Commission. (2014). *Advancing effective communication, cultural competence, and patient- and family-centered care for the lesbian, gay, bisexual, and transgender (LGBT) community: A field guide.* Oak Brook, IL: The Joint Commission.

Jones, R. (2019, August). Richard meets . . . Margaret Cho. *Queer Forty.* Retrieved from https://queerforty.com/richard-meets-margaret-cho.

Jost, J. T., Rudman, L. A., Blair, I. V., Carney, D. R., Dasgupta, N., Glaser, J., & Hardin, C. D. (2009). The existence of implicit bias is beyond reasonable doubt: A refutation of ideological and methodological objections and executive summary of ten studies that no manager should ignore. *Research in Organizational Behavior, 29,* 39–69.

Kaeble, D. (2018). Time Served in State Prison, 2016. *Bureau of Justice Statistics.* Washington, DC: U.S. Department of Justice. Retrieved from https://www.bjs.gov/content/pub/pdf/tssp16.pdf.

Kaeble, D., & Cowhig, M. (2018). *Correctional populations in the United States.* Washington, DC: US Department of Justice, Bureau of Justice Statistics.

Kalish, R., & Kimmel, M. (2010). Suicide by mass murder: Masculinity, aggrieved entitlement, and rampage school shootings. *Health Sociology Review, 19,* 451–464.

Kane, M. D. (2007). Timing matters: Shifts in the causal determinants of sodomy law decriminalization, 1961–1998. *Social Problems, 54,* 211–239.
Kaufman, M., Fondakowski, L., Pierotti, G., & Paris, A. (2014). *The Laramie Project and the Laramie Project: Ten Years Later.* New York, NY: Vintage.
Kellaway, M. (2015, March). Trans Teen Activist, Former Homecoming King, Dies in Charlotte, NC. *The Advocate.* Retrieved from https://www.advocate.com/obituaries/ 2015/03/24/trans-teen-activist-homecoming-king-dies.
Keyes, E. (2012). Examining Maryland's views on immigrants and immigration. *University of Baltimore Law Forum, 43,* 1–34.
Killough, A. (2019, May). House passes Equality Act to increase protections for sexual orientation and gender identity. *CNN.* Retrieved from: https://edition.cnn.com/ 2019/05/17/politics/houses-passes-equality-act/index.html.
King, E. B., Dunleavy, D. G., Dunleavy, E. M., Jaffer, S., Morgan, W. B., Elder, K., & Graebner, R. (2011). Discrimination in the 21st century: Are science and the law aligned? *Psychology, Public Policy, and Law, 17,* 54–75.
Kingshott, B. F. (2013). Revisiting gender issues: Continuing police reform. *Criminal Justice Studies, 26,* 366–392.
Kinsey, A. C., Pomeroy, W. B., Martin, C. E., & Gebhard, P. H. (1953). *Sexual behavior in the human female.* Philadelphia, PA: W. B. Saunders Company.
Knauer, N. J. (2012). Legal consciousness and LGBT research: The role of the law in the everyday lives of LGBT individuals. *Journal of Homosexuality, 59,* 748–756.
Koppelman, A. (1997). Romer v. Evans and invidious intent. *William & Mary Bill of Rights Journal, 6,* 89–146.
Koulish, R. (2010). *Immigration and American democracy: Subverting the rule of law.* New York: Routledge.
Krebs C. P., & Simmons, M. (2002). Intraprison HIV transmission: An assessment of whether it occurs, how it occurs, and who is at risk. *AIDS Education and Prevention, 14,* 53–64.
Krutzsch, B. (2019). *Dying to Be Normal: Gay Martyrs and the Transformation of American Sexual Politics.* Oxford, UK: Oxford University Press.
Kupers, T. A. (2005). Toxic masculinity as a barrier to mental health treatment in prison. *Journal of Clinical Psychology, 61,* 713–724.
Kutchins, P. (Series Producer), & Sommers, C. (Producer) (2017). The Gianni Versace Murder. [Television Series Episode] in *How it really happened with Hill Harper.* Atlanta, GA: HLN.
La Fountain-Stokes, L. (2018). Recent developments in Queer Puerto Rican history, politics, and culture. *Centro Journal, 30,* 502–540.
Lam, K. (2019, February). LGBT police officers say they've faced horrible discrimination, and now they're suing. *USA Today.* Retrieved from https:// www.usatoday.com/story/news/2019/02/08/lgbt-law-enforcement-officers-sue-over-workplace-discrimination/2404755002/.
Lambda Legal (2007). *2005 Workplace Fairness Survey.* New York, NY: Author.
Lambda Legal (2015). *Protected and served?* New York, NY: Author. Retrieved from https://www.lambdalegal.org/sites/default/files/publications/downloads/ ps_executive-summary.pdf.
Lambda Legal (2016). *Transgender Rights Toolkit: A legal guide for trans people and their advocates.* New York: Author.
Lave, T. R. (2008). Only yesterday: The rise and fall of twentieth century sexual psychopath laws. *Louisiana Law Review, 69,* 549–591.
Laver, M., & Khoury, A. (2008). *Opening doors for LGBTQ youth in foster care: A guide for lawyers and judges.* Washington, DC: American Bar Association.
Lawler, O. G. (2018, December), What happened to Roxana Hernández, the trans woman who died in ICE custody? *The Cut.* Retrieved from https:// www.thecut.com/2018/12/roxana-hernndez-a-transgender-woman-died-in-ice-custody.html.

Lawless, J. F. (2017). The deceptive fermata of HIV-criminalization law: Rereading the case of Tiger Mandingo through the juridico-affective. *Columbia Journal of Gender and Law, 35,* 117–160.

Lee, C., & Kwan, P. (2014). The trans panic defense: Masculinity, heteronormativity, and the murder of transgender women. *Hastings Law Journal, 66,* 77–132.

Lee, E. J., Gurr, D., & Van Wye, G. (2017). An evaluation of New York City's 2015 birth certificate gender marker regulation. *LGBT Health, 4,* 320–327.

Leitsinger, M. (2014, November). Judge strikes down Montana ban on same-sex marriage. *NBC News.* Retrieved from https://www.nbcnews.com/news/us-news/judge-strikes-down-montanas-gay-marriage-ban-n252016.

Leong, F. T., & Okazaki, S. (2009). History of Asian American psychology. *Cultural Diversity and Ethnic Minority Psychology, 15,* 352–362.

Leppel, K. (2009). Labour force status and sexual orientation. *Economica, 76,* 197–207.

Levy, A. (2013, September). The Perfect Wife. *The New Yorker.* Retrieved from https://www.newyorker.com/magazine/2013/09/30/the-perfect-wife.

Lew-Williams, B. (2018). *The Chinese must go: Violence, exclusion, and the making of the alien in America.* Cambridge, MA: Harvard University Press.

Lim, J. R., Sullivan, P. S., Salazar, L., Spaulding, A. C., & DiNenno, E. A. (2011). History of arrest and associated factors among men who have sex with men. *Journal of Urban Health, 88,* 677–689.

Lloren, A., & Parini, L. (2017). How LGBT-supportive workplace policies shape the experience of lesbian, gay men, and bisexual employees. *Sexuality Research and Social Policy, 14,* 289–299.

Loewen, J. W. (2008). *Lies my teacher told me: Everything your American history textbook got wrong.* The New Press.

Lorde, A. (2007). *Sister outsider: Essays and speeches.* Berkeley, CA: Crossing Press.

Lydon, J., Carrington, K., Low, H., Miller, R., & Yazdy, M. (2015). *Coming Out of Concrete Closets: A Report on Black & Pink's National LGBTQ Prisoner Survey.* Dorchester, MA: Black & Pink.

Mabalon, D. B. (2013). *Little Manila is in the heart: The making of the Filipina/o American community in Stockton, California.* Raleigh, NC: Duke University Press.

Mackenzie, S., Rubin, E., & Gómez, C. (2016). "Prison is one place you don't want your sexuality": Sexuality, desire and survival among incarcerated behaviorally bisexual Black men in the United States. *Penal Field, 13,* 1–27.

Majd, K., Marksamer, J., & Reyes, C. (2009). *Hidden injustice: Lesbian, gay, bisexual and transgender youth in juvenile courts.* San Francisco: Legal Services for Children, National Juvenile Defender Center, and National Center for Lesbian Rights.

Major, R. H. (1950). New moral menace to our youth. *Coronet, 28,* 101–08.

Make the Road New York (2012). *Transgressive policing: Police abuse of LGBTQ communities of color in Jackson Heights.* New York: Author.

Mallory, C., Hasenbush, A., & Sears, B. (2013). *Discrimination against Law Enforcement Officers on the Basis of Sexual Orientation and Gender Identity: 2000 to 2013.* Los Angeles: The Williams Institute.

Mangan, D. (2012, October). Judge rejects birth mother & gives custody to partner. *New York Post.* Retrieved from https://nypost.com/2012/10/01/judge-rejects-birth-mother-gives-custody-to-partner/.

Maramba, D. C., & Nadal, K. L. (2013). Exploring the Filipino American Faculty Pipeline: Implications for Higher Education and Filipino American Students. In R. Bonus & D. C. Maramba (Eds.), *The "Other" Students: Filipino Americans, Education and Power* (pp. 297–307). Charlotte, NC: Information Age.

Markarian, M. (2017, September). 11 Habits of highly effective lobbyists. *Huffington Post.* Retrieved from: https://www.huffpost.com/entry/11-habits-of-highly-effec_b_254041.

Marksamer, J. (2008). "And by the way, do you know he thinks he's a girl?" The failures of law, policy and legal representation for transgender youth in juvenile delinquency courts. *Sexuality Research & Social Policy, 5,* 72–92.

Mariner, J. (2001). *No Escape: Male rape in U.S. prisons.* New York: Human Rights Watch.
Marshal, M. P., Friedman, M. S., Stall, R., King, K. M., Miles, J., Gold, M. A., . . . & Morse, J. Q. (2008). Sexual orientation and adolescent substance use: a meta-analysis and methodological review. *Addiction, 103,* 546–556.
Maschi, T., Rees, J., & Klein, E. (2016). "Coming Out" of Prison: An Exploratory Study of LGBT Elders in the Criminal Justice System. *Journal of Homosexuality, 63,* 1277–1295.
Massey, D. (2015). Uninformed Policies and Reactionary Politics: A Cautionary Tale from the United States. In C. Dustmann (Ed.), *Migration: Economic Change, Social Challenge* (pp. 118–137). Oxford, UK: Oxford University Press.
Massey, D. S., & Pren, K. A. (2012). Unintended consequences of US immigration policy: Explaining the post-1965 surge from Latin America. *Population and Development Review, 38,* 1–29.
Masters, T. (2007, November). 10 years later, firestorm over gay-only ENDA vote still informs movement. *Los Angeles Blade.* Retrieved from https://www.losangelesblade.com/2017/11/06/10-years-later-firestorm-gay-enda-vote-still-informs-movement/.
Matsick, J. L., & Conley, T. D. (2015). Maybe "I Do," Maybe I Don't: Respectability Politics in the Same-Sex Marriage Ruling. *Analyses of Social Issues and Public Policy, 15,* 409–413.
Maxwell, M. E., & Kelsey, G. (2014). Second parent adoption: Same-sex and the best interest of the child. *Journal of Health and Human Services Administration,* 260–299.
McCabe, S. E., Bostwick, W. B., Hughes, T. L., West, B. T., & Boyd, C. J. (2010). The relationship between discrimination and substance use disorders among lesbian, gay, and bisexual adults in the United States. *American Journal of Public Health, 100,* 1946–1952.
McCormick, A., Schmidt, K., & Terrazas, S. (2017). LGBTQ youth in the child welfare system: An overview of research, practice, and policy. *Journal of Public Child Welfare, 11,* 27–39.
McKenry, P. C., Serovich, J. M., Mason, T. L., & Mosack, K. (2006). Perpetration of gay and lesbian partner violence: A disempowerment perspective. *Journal of Family Violence, 21,* 233–243.
McKinley, J. (2019, June). Bills to Decriminalize Prostitution Are Introduced. Is New York Ready? *New York Times.* Retrieved from: https://www.nytimes.com/2019/06/11/nyregion/prostitution-legal-ny.html.
McLemore, M. (2012). *Sex workers at risk: Condoms as evidence of prostitution in four US cities.* New York: Human Rights Watch.
Meiners, E. R. (2011). Ending the school-to-prison pipeline/building abolition futures. *The Urban Review, 43,* 547–565.
Mercene, F. L. (2007). *Manila men in the new world: Filipino migration to Mexico and the Americas from the sixteenth century.* Quezon City, Philippines: University of Philippines.
Mertus, J. B. (2011). Barriers, hurdles, and discrimination: The current status of LGBT intercountry adoption and why changes must be made to effectuate the best interests of the child. *Capital University Law Review, 39,* 271–312.
Meyer, D. (2019). Omar Mateen as US citizen, not foreign threat: Homonationalism and LGBTQ online representations of the Pulse nightclub shooting. *Sexualities,* 1–20. Advanced online publication.
Meyer, I. H., Flores, A. R., Stemple, L., Romero, A. P., Wilson, B. D., & Herman, J. L. (2017). Incarceration rates and traits of sexual minorities in the United States: National Inmate Survey, 2011–2012. *American Journal of Public Health, 107,* 267–273.
Miller, L. (2014). Serial killers: I. Subtypes, patterns, and motives. *Aggression and Violent Behavior 19,* 1–11.
Miller, N. (2002). *Sex-crime panic: A journey to the paranoid heart of the 1950s.* New York, NY: Alyson Books.

Miller, S. L., Forest, K. B., & Jurik, N. C. (2003). Diversity in blue: Lesbian and gay police officers in a masculine occupation. *Men and Masculinities, 5*, 355–385.

Minnis, T. A., & Moua, M. (2015). *Fifty Years of the Voting Rights Act: The Asian American Perspective*. Washington, DC: Asian Americans Advancing Justice. Retrieved from https://www.advancingjustice-aajc.org/sites/default/files/2016-09/50-years-of-VRA.pdf.

Minter, S. (1993). Sodomy and public morality offenses under US immigration law: Penalizing lesbian and gay identity. *Cornell International Law Journal, 26*, 771–818.

Mitchell, H., & Aamodt, M. G. (2005). The incidence of child abuse in serial killers. *Journal of Police and Criminal Psychology, 20*, 40–47.

Mitchell, K. (2018, May). Transgender inmate raped, beaten in Cañon City prison hours after judge denied motion to keep her in safer quarters. *Denver Post*. Retrieved from https://www.denverpost.com/2018/05/03/transgender-inmate-raped-beaten-canon-city/.

Mize, K. D., & Shackelford, T. K. (2008). Intimate partner homicide methods in heterosexual, gay, and lesbian relationships. *Violence and Victims, 23*, 98–114.

Mock, J. (2014). *Redefining realness: My path to womanhood, identity, love & so much more*. New York: Simon and Schuster.

Mohatt, N. V., Thompson, A. B., Thai, N. D., & Tebes, J. K. (2014). Historical trauma as public narrative: A conceptual review of how history impacts present-day health. *Social Science & Medicine, 106*, 128–136.

Mondel, J. A. (2016). Mentally awake, morally straight, and unfit to sit: Judicial ethics, the First Amendment, and the Boy Scouts of America. *Stanford Law Review, 68*, 865–894.

Moore, M. H. (1992). Problem-solving and community policing. In M. Tonry & N. Morris (Eds.), *Modem Policing* (pp. 99–158). Chicago: University of Chicago Press.

Moreau, J. (2018, May). Bureau of Prisons rolls back Obama-era transgender inmate protections. *NBC News*. Retrieved from https://www.nbcnews.com/feature/nbc-out/bureau-prisons-rolls-back-obama-era-transgender-inmate-protections-n873966.

Morey, B. N. (2018). Mechanisms by which anti-immigrant stigma exacerbates racial/ethnic health disparities. *American Journal of Public Health, 108*(4), 460–463.

Morse, A., Polkey, C., Deatherage, L., and Ibarra, V. (2019). *Sanctuary Policy FAQ*. Washington, DC: National Conference of State Legislatures.

Mountz, S. E. (2016). That's the sound of the police: State-sanctioned violence and resistance among LGBT young people previously incarcerated in girls' juvenile justice facilities. *Affilia, 31*, 287–302.

Movement Advancement Project (2019a). Equality Maps: State Non-Discrimination Laws. Boulder, CO: Author. Retrieved August 15, 2019 from: http://www.lgbtmap.org/equality-maps/non_discrimination_laws.

Movement Advancement Project (2019b). Local Nondiscrimination Ordinances. Boulder, CO: Author. Retrieved from: https://www.lgbtmap.org/equality-maps/non_discrimination_ordinances.

Muñoz, J. E. (1999). *Disidentifications: Queers of color and the performance of politics*. Minneapolis, MN: University of Minnesota Press.

Muñoz, J. E. (2009). *Cruising utopia: The then and there of queer futurity*. New York, NY: New York University Press.

Murnen, S. K., Wright, C., & Kaluzny, G. (2002). If "boys will be boys," then girls will be victims? A meta-analytic review of the research that relates masculine ideology to sexual aggression. *Sex Roles, 46*, 359–375.

Murray, J. B. (2000). Psychological profile of pedophiles and child molesters. *The Journal of Psychology, 134*, 211–224.

Myers, J. E., & Sweeney, T. J. (2004). The indivisible self: An evidence-based model of wellness. *Journal of Individual Psychology, 60*(3), 234–245.

Mykhalovskiy, E. (2015). The public health implications of HIV criminalization: past, current, and future research directions. *Critical Public Health 25*, 373–385.

Myrick, A., Nelson, R. L., & Nielson, L. B. (2012). Race and representation: Racial disparities in legal representation for employment civil rights plaintiffs. *Journal of Legislation and Public Policy, 15,* 705–757.

Nadal, K. L. (2011). *Filipino American psychology: A handbook of theory, research, and clinical practice.* New York: Wiley.

Nadal, K. L. (2013). *That's So Gay! Microaggressions and the Lesbian, Gay, Bisexual, and Transgender Community.* Washington, DC: American Psychological Association.

Nadal, K. L. (2017). "Let's Get in Formation": On Becoming a Psychologist-Activist in the 21st Century. *American Psychologist, 72,* 935–946.

Nadal, K. L. (2018). *Microaggressions and traumatic stress: Theory, research, and practice.* Washington, DC: American Psychological Association.

Nadal, K. L. (2019). A Decade of Microaggression Research and LGBTQ Communities: An Introduction to the Special Issue. *Journal of Homosexuality, 66,* 1309–1316.

Nadal, K. L., & Corpus, M. J. H. (2013). "Tomboys" and "baklas": Experiences of lesbian and gay Filipino Americans. *Asian American Journal of Psychology, 4,* 166–175.

Nadal, K. L., Davidoff, K. C., Allicock, N., Serpe, C., & Erazo, T. (2017). Perceptions of police, racial profiling, and psychological consequences: A mixed methodological study. *Journal of Social Issues, 73,* 808–830.

Nadal, K. L., Davidoff, K. C., & Fujii-Doe, W. (2014). Transgender women and the sex work industry: Roots in systemic, institutional, and interpersonal discrimination. *Journal of Trauma and Dissociation, 15,* 169–183.

Nadal, K. L., Erazo, T., Fiani, C.N., Murillo Parilla, M.C., & Han, H. (2018). Navigating microaggressions, overt discrimination, and institutional oppression: Transgender and gender nonconforming people and the criminal justice system. In C. L. Cho, J. K. Corkett, & A. Steele (Eds.), *Exploring the Toxicity of Lateral Violence and Microaggression in Multiple Contexts and Disciplines: Poison in the Watercooler* (pp. 51–74). New York, NY: Palgrave Macmillan.

Nadal, K. L., Issa, M. A., Leon, J., Meterko, V., Wideman, M., & Wong, Y. (2011). Sexual orientation microaggressions: "Death by a thousand cuts" for lesbian, gay, and bisexual youth. *Journal of LGBT Youth, 8,* 234–259.

Nadal, K. L., Quintanilla, A., Goswick, A., & Sriken, J. (2015). Lesbian, gay, bisexual, and queer people's perceptions of the criminal justice system: Implications for social services. *Journal of Gay & Lesbian Social Services, 27,* 457–481.

Nadal, K. L., Skolnik, A., & Wong, Y. (2012). Interpersonal and systemic microaggressions: Psychological impacts on transgender individuals and communities. *Journal of LGBT Issues in Counseling, 6,* 55–82.

Nadal, K. L., Vargas, V., Meterko, V., Hamit, S., & Mclean, K. (2012). Transgender female sex workers: Personal perspectives, gender identity development, and psychological processes. In M. A. Paludi (Ed.), *Managing Diversity in Today's Workplace: Strategies for Employees and Employers, Volume 1: Gender, Race, Sexual Orientation, Ethnicity, and Power* (pp. 123–153). Santa Barbara, CA: Praeger.

Nakamura, N., & Morales, A. (2016). The criminalization of transgender immigrants. In R. Furman, A. Ackerman, & G. Lamphear (Eds.), *The immigrant other: Lived experiences in a transnational world* (pp. 48–61). New York, NY: Columbia University Press.

Nash, M. A., & Silverman, J. A. (2015). "An Indelible mark": Gay purges in higher education in the 1940s. *History of Education Quarterly, 55,* 441–459.

National Center for Transgender Equality (2018). LGBTQ criminal justice reform: Real steps LGBTQ advocates can take to reduce incarceration. Washington, DC: Author. Retrieved from: https://transequality.org/reduceincarceration.

National Review (1985). AIDS, nature, and the nature of AIDS. Author, *37,* 18.

Nawyn, S. J., Richman, J. A., Rospenda, K. M., & Hughes, T. L. (2000). Sexual identity and alcohol-related outcomes: Contributions of workplace harassment. *Journal of Substance Abuse, 11,* 289–304.

Neumark, D. (2018). Experimental research on labor market discrimination. *Journal of Economic Literature, 56,* 799–866.

Neilson, V. (2004). On the Positive Side: Using a Foreign National's HIV-Positive Status in Support of an Application to Remain in the United States. *AIDS and Public Policy Journal, 19*, 45–53.

Noelle, M. (2002). The ripple effect on the Matthew Shepard murder: Impact on the assumptive worlds of members of the targeted group. *American Behavioral Scientist, 46*, 27–50.

Nolan, T. (2009). Behind the blue wall of silence: Essay. *Men and Masculinities, 12*, 250–257.

Norris, T., Vines, P. L., & Hoeffel, E. M. (2012). The American Indian and Alaska Native Population: 2010. *2010 Census Briefs*. Washington, DC: U.S. Census Bureau. Retrieved from https://www.census.gov/history/pdf/c2010br-10.pdf.

O'Brien, M. E. (2019) The influence of donors on cross class social movements: Same sex marriage and trans rights campaigns in New York State. *Social Movement Studies, 18*, 586–601.

Ok, R. J. (2018). Sex Is Messy (and Always Has Been): A Textualist Argument for Application of Title VII to Sexual Orientation Discrimination. *Lewis & Clark Law Review, 22*, 1361–1392.

Onwuachi-Willig, A. (2016). The trauma of the routine: Lessons on cultural trauma from the Emmett Till verdict. *Sociological Theory, 34*, 335–357.

Organization for Refugee, Asylum, and Migration (2012). Rainbow Bridges: A Community Guide to Rebuilding the Lives of LGBTI Refugees and Asylees. San Francisco, CA: Author.

Orth, M. (2008). The Killer's Trail. *Vanity Fair*. Retrieved from https://www.vanityfair.com/magazine/1997/09/cunanan199709.

Orth, M. (2017). *Vulgar favors: Andrew Cunanan, Gianni Versace, and the largest failed manhunt in US history*. New York: Bantam.

Overland, S. (2009). Strategies for Combating Anti-Gay Sentiment in the Courtroom. *The Jury Expert, 21*, 1–5.

Owen, S. S., Burke, T. W., Few-Demo, A. L., & Natwick, J. (2018). Perceptions of the Police by LGBT Communities. *American Journal of Criminal Justice, 43*, 668–693.

Paine, T. (1776). *Common Sense*. Philadelphia, PA: Author.

Panfil, V. R. (2014). Better left unsaid? The role of agency in queer criminological research. *Critical Criminology, 22*, 99–111.

Park, N. K., Kazyak, E., & Slauson-Blevins, K. (2016). How law shapes experiences of parenthood for same-sex couples. *Journal of GLBT Family Studies, 12*, 115–137.

Pasulka, N. (2012, May). The Case of CeCe McDonald: Murder—Or Self-Defense against a Hate Crime? *Mother Jones*. Retrieved from https://www.motherjones.com/politics/2012/05/cece-mcdonald-transgender-hate-crime-murder/.

Pattavina, A., Hirschel, D., Buzawa, E., Faggiani, D., & Bentley, H. (2007). A comparison of the police response to heterosexual versus same-sex intimate partner violence. *Violence Against Women, 13*, 374–394.

Patterson, C. J. (2009). Children of lesbian and gay parents: Psychology, law, and policy. *American Psychologist, 64*, 727–736.

Patterson, C., & Riskind, R. G. (2010). To be a parent: Issues in family formation among gay and lesbian adults. *Journal of GLBT Family Studies, 6*, 326–340.

Patti, C. (2017). *Hively v. Ivy Tech Community College*: Losing the battle but winning the war for Title VII sexual orientation discrimination protection. *Tulane Journal of Law and Sexuality: Review of Sexual Orientation and Gender Identity in the Law, 26*, 133–146.

Pearson, K. (2007). The trouble with Aileen Wuornos, feminism's "first serial killer." *Communication and Critical/Cultural Studies, 4*, 256–275.

Peek, C. (2003). Breaking out of the prison hierarchy: Transgender prisoners, rape, and the Eighth Amendment. *Santa Clara Law. Review, 44*, 1211–1248.

Perry, J. R., & Green, E. R. (2014). *Safe & respected: Policy, best practices, & guidance for serving transgender & gender non-conforming children and youth involved in the child welfare, detention, and juvenile justice systems*. New York, NY: New York City Administration for Children's Services.

Pew Research Center (2013). *A Survey of LGBT Americans: Attitudes, Experiences and Values in Changing Times.* Washington, DC: Author. Retrieved from http://www.pewsocialtrends.org/2013/06/13/a-survey-of-lgbt-americans.
Pinello, D. R. (2003). *Gay Rights and American Law.* Cambridge: Cambridge University Press.
Platt, L. F., & Lenzen, A. L. (2013) Sexual orientation microaggressions and the experience of sexual minorities. *Journal of Homosexuality, 60,* 7, 1011–1034.
Ploscowe, M. (1962). *Sex and the Law.* New York, NY: Ace Books.
Pope, M. (2017). Two-spirited people. In K. Nadal (Ed.), *The Sage encyclopedia of psychology and gender* (pp. 1743–1748). Thousand Oaks, CA: Sage.
Popova, M. (2018). Inactionable/Unspeakable: Bisexuality in the Workplace. *Journal of Bisexuality,* 18:1, 54–66.
Printz, H. (2018). Some MSM blood donors move from a lifetime deferral to a one-year ban: Finally, or not good enough. *Journal of Health Care Law & Policy, 21,* 71–85.
Puzzanchera, C., Smith, J., & Kang, W. (2018). Easy access to NIBRS victims, 2016: Victims of domestic violence. Available at https://www.ojjdp.gov/ojstatbb/ezanibrsdv/.
Quindlen, A. (1981, December). About New York: A tough month in the new life of a policeman. *New York Times,* p. 29. Retrieved from https://www.nytimes.com/1981/12/05/nyregion/about-new-york-a-tough-month-in-the-new-life-of-a-policeman.html.
Quintana, N. S., Rosenthal, J., & Krehely, J. (2010). *On the Streets: The Federal Response to Gay and Transgender Homeless Youth.* Washington, DC: Center for American Progress.
Ragins, B. R., Cornwell, J. M., & Miller, J. S. (2003). Heterosexism in the workplace: Do race and gender matter? *Group & Organization Management, 28,* 45–74.
Ramirez, J. L., Gonzalez, K. A., & Galupo, M. P. (2018). "Invisible during my own crisis": Responses of LGBT people of color to the Orlando shooting. *Journal of Homosexuality, 65,* 579–599.
Randazzo, T. J. (2005). Social and legal barriers: Sexual orientation and asylum in the United States. In E. Luibhéid & L. Cantú Jr. (Eds.), *Queer migrations: Sexuality, U.S. citizenship, and border crossings* (pp. 30–60). Minneapolis: University of Minnesota Press.
Reisner, S. L., Bailey, Z., & Sevelius, J. (2014). Racial/ethnic disparities in history of incarceration, experiences of victimization, and associated health indicators among transgender women in the US. *Women & Health, 54,* 750–767.
Rennison, C. M., & Dodge, M. (2016). *Introduction to criminal justice: Systems, diversity, and change.* Thousand Oaks, CA: Sage.
Resnick, C. A., & Galupo, M. P. (2019). Assessing experiences with LGBT microaggressions in the workplace: Development and validation of the microaggression experiences at work scale. *Journal of Homosexuality, 66,* 1380–1403.
Reynolds, D. (2017). Drag Race's Peppermint Comes Out as Transgender. *The Advocate.* Retrieved from https://www.advocate.com/television/2017/4/28/drag-races-peppermint-comes-out-transgender.
Ricketts, W., & Achtenberg, R. (1989). Adoption and foster parenting for lesbians and gay men: Creating new traditions in family. *Marriage & Family Review, 14,* 83–118.
Riley, J. (2017, August). New York City found liable in man's beating by police at gay house party *Metro Weekly.* Retrieved from https://www.metroweekly.com/2017/08/new-york-city-found-liable-mans-beating-police-gay-house-party/.
Riskind, R., Patterson, C., & Nosek, B. (2013). Childless lesbian and gay adults' self-efficacy about achieving parenthood. *Couple and Family Psychology, 2,* 222–235.
Ritenhouse, D. (2011). What's orientation got to do with it? The best interest of the child standard and legal bias against gay and lesbian parents. *Journal of Poverty, 15,* 309–329.

Rivera, R. R. (1991). Sexual Orientation and the Law. In J. C. Gonsiorek & J. D. Weinrich (Eds.), *Homosexuality: Research implications for public policy* (pp. 81–100). Thousand Oaks, CA: Sage Publications.

Rosario M., Schrimshaw, E.W., & Hunter, J. (2012). Risk factors for homelessness among lesbian, gay, and bisexual youths: A developmental milestone approach. *Children and Youth Services Review, 34*, 186–193.

Routh, D., Abess, G., Makin, D., Stohr, M. K., Hemmens, C., & Yoo, J. (2017). Transgender inmates in prisons: A review of applicable statutes and policies. *International Journal of Offender Therapy and Comparative Criminology, 61*, 645–666.

Rubenstein, W. B. (1998). Queer Studies II: Some Reflections on the Study of Sexual Orientation Bias in the Legal Profession. *UCLA Women's Law Journal, 8*, 379–406.

Ryan, H. (2019). *When Brooklyn was queer: A history*. New York, NY: St. Martin's Press.

Salerno, J. M., Najdowski, C. J., Bottoms, B. L., Harrington, E., Kemner, G., & Dave, R. (2015). Excusing murder? Conservative jurors' acceptance of the gay-panic defense. *Psychology, Public Policy and Law, 21*, 24–34.

Santos, R. (2018). *Beyond gender binaries: The history of trans, intersex, and third-gender individuals*. New York, NY: Rosen.

Sarwar, O. (2016, June) American Muslims must address religiously sanctioned homophobia. *The Advocate*. Retrieved July 5, 2019 from http://www.advocate.com/commentary/2016/6/16/american-muslims-must-address-religiously-sanctioned-homophobia.

Satuluri, S., & Nadal, K. L. (2018). LGBTQ perceptions of the police: Implications for mental health and public policy. *LGBTQ Policy Journal, 8*, 43–55.

Saunders, J. (2018, June). Florida Supreme Court targets juror's anti-gay bias in 2005 death penalty case. *Orlando Weekly*. Retrieved from https://www.orlandoweekly.com/Blogs/archives/2018/06/15/florida-supreme-court-targets-jurors-anti-gay-bias-in-2005-death-penalty-case.

Sawyer, K., Thoroughgood, C., & Webster, J. (2016). Queering the gender binary: Understanding transgender workplace experiences. In T. Köllen (Ed.), *Sexual Orientation and Transgender Issues in Organizations: Global Perspectives on LGBT Workforce Diversity* (pp. 21–42). Wiesbaden, Germany: Springer.

Scharron-del Río, M. (2017). Latina/o Americans and transgender identity. In K. Nadal (Ed.), *The Sage encyclopedia of psychology and gender* (pp. 1034–1038). Thousand Oaks, CA: Sage.

Schmich, M. (1992, June). One cop's courage risks a way of life. *Chicago Tribune*. Retrieved from https://www.chicagotribune.com/news/ct-xpm-1992-06-26-9202260352-story.html.

Schmidt, M. A. (1994). Dahmer discourse and gay identity: The paradox of queer politics. *Critical Sociology, 20*, 81–105.

Schontzler, G. (2016, August). Gay couple's dream of adopting ends in bias charge against Montana. *Bozeman Daily Chronicle*. Retrieved from https://www.bozemandailychronicle.com/news/gay-couple-s-dream-of-adopting-ends-in-bias-charge/article_9dde90ec-45d7-5734-82cb-81f0c0f18e17.html.

Schultz, K., Cattaneo, L. B., Sabina, C., Brunner, L., Jackson, S., & Serrata, J. V. (2016). Key roles of community connectedness in healing from trauma. *Psychology of Violence, 6*, 42–48.

Scott, A., Klein, F. K., & Onovakpuri, U. (2017). *Tech leavers study*. Oakland, CA: Kapor Center for Social Impact.

Sears, B., Hunter, N. D., & Mallory, C. (2009). *Documenting discrimination on the basis of sexual orientation and gender identity in state employment*. Los Angeles, CA: The Williams Institute and UCLA. Retrieved from https://williamsinstitute.law.ucla.edu/wp-content/uploads/ExecutiveSummary1.pdf.

Sears, B., & Mallory, C. (2014). Employment discrimination against LGBT people: Existence and impact. In C. M. Duffy (Ed.), *Gender Identity and Sexual Orientation Discrimination in the Workplace: A Practical Guide* (pp. 1–19). Arlington, VA: Bloomberg.

Sears, J. T. (2013). *Behind the mask of the Mattachine: The Hal Call chronicles and the early movement for homosexual emancipation*. New York, NY: Routledge.

Segers, G. (2019, January). New York legislature passes historic bill against transgender discrimination. *CBS News*. Retrieved from https://www.cbsnews.com/news/new-york-legislature-passes-historic-anti-transgender-discrimination-bill/.

Serpe, C. R., & Nadal, K. L. (2017). Perceptions of Police: Experiences in the Trans* Community. *Journal of Gay and Lesbian Social Services, 29*, 280–299.

Serrano, R. A. (1990, September). Gay Police Leave the Shadows. *Los Angeles Times*. Retrieved from https://www.latimes.com/archives/la-xpm-1990-09-03-mn-1514-story.html.

Seto, M. C. (2018). *Pedophilia and sexual offending against children: Theory, assessment, and intervention*. Washington, DC: American Psychological Association.

Seville, L. R., Rappleye, H., & Lehren, A. W. (2019, January). 22 immigrants died in ICE detention centers during the past 2 years. *NBC News*. Retrieved from https://www.nbcnews.com/politics/immigration/22-immigrants-died-ice-detention-centers-during-past-2-years-n954781.

Sexton, L., Jenness, V., & Sumner, J. M. (2010). Where the margins meet: A demographic assessment of transgender inmates in men's prisons. *Justice Quarterly, 27*, 835–866.

Shapiro, J. (2013). The law governing LGBT-parent families. In A. E. Goldberg & K. R. Allen (Eds.), *LGBT-parent families: Innovations in research and implications for practice* (pp. 291–304). New York: Springer.

Shepard, J. (2009). *The Meaning of Matthew: My Son's Murder in Laramie, and a World Transformed*. New York, NY: Penguin.

Shipherd, J. C., Maguen, S., Skidmore, W. C., & Abramovitz, S. M. (2011). Potentially traumatic events in a transgender sample: Frequency and associated symptoms. *Traumatology, 17*, 56–67.

Shortnacy, M. B. (2001). Guilty and gay: A recipe for execution in American courtrooms: Sexual orientation as a tool for prosecutorial misconduct in death penalty cases. *American University Law Review, 51*, 309–365.

Showalter, M. P. (1989). The Watsonville Anti-Filipino Riot of 1930: A Reconsideration of Fermin Tobera's Murder. *Southern California Quarterly, 71*, 341–348.

Shuman, A., & Hesford, W. S. (2014). Getting out: Political asylum, sexual minorities, and privileged visibility. *Sexualities, 17*, 1016–1034.

Siebens, J. & Julian, T. (2011). Native North American Languages Spoken at Home in the United States and Puerto Rico: 2006–2010. *American Community Survey Briefs*. Washington, DC: U.S. Census Bureau. Retrieved from https://www2.census.gov/library/publications/2011/acs/acsbr10-10.pdf.

Simko-Bednarski, E. (2019, January). New York City birth certificates get gender-neutral option. *CNN*. Retrieved from https://www.cnn.com/2019/01/03/health/new-york-city-gender-neutral-birth-certificate-trnd/index.html.

Simon, D. (2017, April). Lesbian plaintiff in work discrimination suit sticking to fight. *CNN*. Retrieved from https://www.cnn.com/2017/04/05/us/lgbt-employees-appeals-court-plaintiff/index.html.

Singh, A. A., & Dickey, l. (2016). Implementing the APA guidelines on psychological practice with transgender and gender nonconforming people: A call to action to the field of psychology. *Psychology of Sexual Orientation and Gender Diversity, 3*, 195–200.

Smith, A. (2009, June). The NYPD's Anti-Gay Violence. *Socialist Worker*. Retrieved from https://socialistworker.org/2009/06/09/nypd-antigay-violence.

Smith, C. E. (1953). The homosexual federal offender: A study of 100 cases. *Journal of Criminal Laws, Criminology, & Police Science, 44*, 582–591.

Smith, C. P., & Freyd, J. J. (2014). Institutional betrayal. *American Psychologist, 69*, 575–587.

Smith, R. J. (2015). Reducing racially disparate policing outcomes: Is implicit bias training the answer? *University of Hawai'i Law Review, 37*, 295–312.

Smith, R. (2017). Hegemonic masculinity. In K. Nadal (Ed.), *The Sage encyclopedia of psychology and gender* (pp. 830–831). Thousand Oaks, CA: Sage.

Spade, D. (2015). *Normal Life: Administrative Violence, Critical Trans Politics, and the Limits of Law*. Durham, NC: Duke University Press.

Spitznagel, E. (2014, May). Laverne Cox: Blending in was never an option. *New York Times Magazine*. Retrieved from https://www.nytimes.com/2014/06/01/magazine/laverne-cox-blending-in-was-never-an-option.html.

St. John, P. (2015, August). In a first, California agrees to pay for transgender inmate's sex reassignment. *The Los Angeles Times*. Retrieved from https://www.latimes.com/local/california/la-me-inmate-transgender-20150810-story.html.

Stafford, Z. (2019, January). NYPD Sued After Arresting Trans Woman with Pink Handcuffs. *The Advocate*. Retrieved from https://www.advocate.com/transgender/2019/1/22/nypd-sued-after-arresting-trans-woman-pink-handcuffs.

Stapel, S. (2008). Falling to Pieces: New York State civil legal remedies available to lesbian, gay, bisexual, and transgender survivors of domestic violence. *New York Law School Law Review, 52*, 248–277.

Steinberg, V. (2005). A heat of passion offense: Emotions and bias in "Trans Panic" mitigation claims. *Boston College Third World Law Journal, 25*, 499–512.

Stern, M., Oehme, K., & Stern, N. (2016). Test to identify and remedy anti-gay bias in child custody decisions after Obergefell. *UCLA Women's Law Journal, 23*, 79–100.

Stone, M. H. (2015). Mass murder, mental illness, and men. *Violence and Gender, 2*, 51–86.

Stotzer, R. L. (2009). Violence against transgender people: A review of United States data. *Aggression and Violent Behavior, 14*, 170–179.

Stoudt, B. G., Fine, M., & Fox, M. (2011). Growing up policed in the age of aggressive policing policies. *New York Law School Law Review, 56*, 1331–1370.

Strader, J. K., & Hay, L. (2019). Lewd stings: Extending Lawrence v. Texas to discriminatory enforcement. *American Criminal Law Review, 56*, 465–509.

Streib, V. (1995). Death penalty for lesbians. *National Journal of Sexual Orientation Law, 1*, 105–127.

Struckman-Johnson, C., Struckman-Johnson, D., Rucker, L., Bumby, K., & Donaldson, S. (1996). Sexual coercion reported by men and women in prison. *Journal of Sex Research, 33*, 67–76.

Stryker, S. (2008). *Transgender history*. Berkeley, CA: Seal Press.

Sutherland, E. H. (1949). The sexual psychopath laws. *Journal of Criminal Law & Criminology, 40*, 543–554.

Swanson, K. (2017, August). A 1995 TV show surprised him with his gay secret admirer. *Washington Post*. Retrieved from https://www.washingtonpost.com/news/morning-mix/wp/2017/08/23/a-1995-tv-show-surprised-him-with-his-gay-secret-admirer-this-week-he-leaves-prison/.

Swigert, V. L., Farrell, R. A., & Yoels, W. C. (1976). Sexual homicide: Social, psychological, and legal aspects. *Archives of Sexual Behavior, 5*, 391–401.

Sylvia Rivera Law Project. (2007). "It's war in here": A report on the treatment of transgender and intersex people in New York State men's prisons. New York, NY: Author.

Syrett, N. L. (2007). The boys of Beaver Meadow: A homosexual community at 1920s Dartmouth College. *American Studies, 48*, 9–18.

Terborg-Penn, R. (1997). African American Women and the Vote: An Overview. In A. D. Gordon (Ed.), *African American Women and the Vote, 1837–1965* (pp. 10–23). Amherst, MA: University of Massachusetts Press.

Thornton, M. C. (1992). The quiet immigration: Foreign spouses of US citizens, 1945–1985. In M. P. P. Root (Ed.), *Racially mixed people in America* (pp. 64–76). Thousand Oaks, CA: Sage.

Thornton, R. (1987). *American Indian holocaust and survival: A population history since 1492*. Norman, OK: University of Oklahoma Press.

Thrasher, S. (2014, July). How College Wrestling Star "Tiger Mandingo" Became An HIV Scapegoat. Buzzfeed. Retrieved from https://www.buzzfeed.com/steven-thrasher/how-college-wrestling-star-tiger-mandingo-became-an-hiv-scap.

Thrasher, S. (2019, July). "Tiger Mandingo," who got 30 years for not telling sex partners he had HIV, is free 25 years early. *Buzzfeed News*. Retrieved from https://www.buzzfeednews.com/article/steventhrasher/tiger-mandingo-who-got-30-years-for-not-telling-sex.

Tillery, B., Ray, A., Cruz, E., & Waters, E. (2018). *Lesbian, Gay, Bisexual, Transgender, Queer and HIV-Affected Hate and Intimate Partner Violence in 2017*. New York, NY: National Coalition of Anti-Violence Programs (NCAVP).

Tobias, C. (2018). Appointing Lesbian, Gay, Bisexual, Transgender and Queer Judges in the Trump Administration. *Washington University Law Review Online, 96*, 11–22.

Tomei, J., & Cramer, R. J. (2016). Legal policies in conflict: The gay panic defense and hate crime legislation. *Journal of Forensic Psychology Practice, 16*, 217–235.

Toro-Alfonso, J., & Rodríguez-Madera, S. (2004). Domestic violence in Puerto Rican gay male couples: Perceived prevalence, intergenerational violence, addictive behaviors, and conflict resolution skills. *Journal of Interpersonal Violence, 19*, 639–654.

Townsend, C. (2012). Interrogating gender politics and Black Power in Newark NJ: An interview with Charles Bennett Brack, producer of "Dreams Deferred: The Sakia Gunn Film Project." *Transforming Anthropology, 20*, 169–171.

Tsosie, R. (2016). The Politics of Inclusion: Indigenous Peoples and US Citizenship. *UCLA Law Review, 63*, 1692–1751.

Tyler, T. R. (2007). Procedural Justice and the Courts. *Court Review: The Journal of the American Judges Association , 44*, 26–31.

Tyler, T. R. (2008). Legitimacy and cooperation: Why do people help the police fight crime in their communities? *Ohio State Journal of Criminal Law, 6*, 231–275.

United Nations (1951). *Convention on the prevention and punishment of the crime of genocide*. New York, NY: Author.

United Nations (2016). *Standard Minimum Rules for the Treatment of Prisoners (the Nelson Mandela Rules)*. New York: Author.

U.S. Census Bureau (2019). Race and Hispanic Origin. *QuickFacts*. Washington, DC: Author. Retrieved from https://www.census.gov/quickfacts/fact/table/US/IPE120217.

U.S. Department of Homeland Security and U.S. Department of Justice (2019). Table 16. Individuals Granted Asylum Affirmatively or Defensively: Fiscal Years 1990 to 2017. Washington, DC: Author. Retrieved from https://www.dhs.gov/immigration-statistics/yearbook/2017/table16.

U.S. Department of Labor (2019). Unemployment rate unchanged at 3.6 percent in May 2019. Bureau of Labor Statistics. Washington, DC: Author. Retrieved from https://www.bls.gov/opub/ted/2019/unemployment-rate-unchanged-at-3-point-6-percent-in-may-2019.htm.

U.S. Department of Justice (2014). *Community policing defined*. Washington, DC: Office of Community Oriented Policing Services, U.S. Department of Justice.

U.S. Senate, Committee on Expenditures in the Executive Departments by its Committee on Investigations (1950). *Employment of Homosexuals and Other Sex Perverts in Government*, S. Doc. 241, 81st Congress, 2nd Session.

Valentine, S. (2010). When your attorney is your enemy: Preliminary thoughts on ensuring effective representation for queer youth. *Columbia Journal of Gender and Law, 19*, 773–804.

van den Berg, J. (2017). Heterosexist bias in the DSM. In K. L. Nadal (Ed.), *The Sage encyclopedia of psychology and gender* (pp. 849–852). Thousand Oaks, CA: Sage.

Van Gilder, B. J. (2017). Coping with sexual identity stigma in the US military: An examination of identity management practices prior to and after the repeal of "Don't Ask, Don't Tell." *Identity, 17*, 156–175.

Vasquez, T. (2019, June). The Details of Johana Medina Leon's detainment and death matter. *Rewire News*. Retrieved from https://rewire.news/article/2019/06/06/the-details-of-johana-medinas-detainment-and-death-matter/.

Villaseñor, M. (2019). The Law and Economics of Religious Exemptions for Adoption Agencies in Cases of Same-Sex Fostering and Adoption. *California Legal Studies Journal*, 43–60.

Vitiello, M., & Nadal, K. L. (2019). Microaggressions towards People Living with HIV/AIDS. In J. Pierce (Ed.), *Living with HIV/AIDS: Challenges, Perspectives and Quality of Life* (pp. 57–82). Hauppauge, NY: Nova Publishers.

Vitulli, E. (2010). A defining moment in civil rights history? The Employment Non-Discrimination Act, trans-inclusion, and homonormativity. *Sexuality Research and Social Policy*, 7, 155–167.

Wadhia, S. (2018). National security, immigration and the Muslim bans. *Washington and Lee Law Review*, 75, 1475–1506.

Walch, S. E., Sinkkanen, K. A., Swain, E. M., Francisco, J., Breaux, C. A., & Sjoberg, M. D. (2012). Using intergroup contact theory to reduce stigma against transgender individuals: Impact of a transgender speaker panel presentation. *Journal of Applied Social Psychology*, 42, 2583–2605.

Wallace, M. (1992). Gays in Law Enforcement [Television series episode]. In Hewitt, D. (Executive Producer), *60 Minutes*. New York: CBS.

Walls, N.E., & Bell, S. (2011). Correlates of engaging in survival sex among homeless youth and young adults. *Journal of Sex Research*, 48, 423–36.

Walker, A. (2004). *In search of our mothers' gardens: Womanist prose*. Boston, MA: Houghton Mifflin Harcourt.

Warbelow, S., Oakley, C., & Kutney, C. (2018). *2018 State Equality Index*. Washington, DC: Human Rights Campaign Foundation.

Ward, J. (2008). White normativity: The cultural dimensions of whiteness in a racially diverse LGBT organization. *Sociological Perspectives*, 51, 563–586.

Warren, J. W. (2009). *Women, money, and the law: Nineteenth-century fiction, gender, and the courts*. Iowa City, IA: University of Iowa Press.

Warren, R., & Passel, J. S. (1987). A count of the uncountable: Estimates of undocumented aliens counted in the 1980 Census. *Demography* 24: 375–393.

Waters, E. (2017). *Lesbian, gay, bisexual, transgender, queer, and HIV-affected hate violence in 2016*. New York, NY: National Coalition of Anti-Violence Programs (NCAVP).

Weber, S. (2015). Daring to marry: Marriage equality activism after proposition 8 as challenge to the assimilationist/radical binary in queer studies. *Journal of Homosexuality*, 62, 1147–1173.

Weinstein, B. S. (2004). A Right with No Remedy: Forced Disclosure of Sexual Orientation and Public Outing under 42 USC 1983. *Cornell Law Review*, 90, 811–838.

Weisheit, R. A., Falcone, D. N., & Wells, L. E. (1999). *Crime and policing in rural and small-town America* (2nd ed.). Prospect Heights, IL: Waveland Press.

West, E., & Meterko, V. (2015). Innocence project: DNA exonerations, 1989–2014: Review of data and findings from the first 25 years. *Albany Law Review*, 79, 717–794.

Whaley, W. (2012). California Dream Act: A Dream (not DREAM) Come True. *McGeorge Law Review*, 43, 625–643.

Wheatley, M. (1985). In Re Longstaff: Lesbian and Gay Aliens Denied Naturalization. *Loyola of Los Angeles International & Comparative Law Journal*, 8, 161–182.

Wheeler, L. (1983, January). A Pair of Standouts on D.C. Police. *Washington Post*. Retrieved from https://www.washingtonpost.com/archive/local/1983/01/24/a-pair-of-standouts-on-dc-police/c725e6c1-5253-4d3f-8c29-342aa8dc132e/.

White, C. R., O'Brien, K., Pecora, P. J., English, D., Williams, J. R., & Phillips, C. M. (2009). Depression among alumni of foster care: Decreasing rates through improvement of experiences in care. *Journal of Emotional and Behavioral Disorders*, 17, 38–48.

Whitman, C. N., & Nadal, K. L. (2015). Sexual minority identities: Outness and well-being among lesbian, gay, and bisexual adults. *Journal of Gay & Lesbian Mental Health*, 19, 370–396.

Widom, C. S. (2017). Long-term impact of childhood abuse and neglect on crime and violence. *Clinical Psychology: Science and Practice, 24*, 186–202.
Williams Institute (2019, January). *LGBT demographic data interactive*. Los Angeles, CA: The Williams Institute, UCLA School of Law. Retrieved from https://williamsinstitute.law.ucla.edu/visualization/lgbt-stats/?topic=LGBT.
Willis, G. M. (2018). Why call someone by what we don't want them to be? The ethics of labeling in forensic/correctional psychology. *Psychology, Crime & Law, 24*, 727–743.
Wilson, B. D. M., Cooper, K., Kastansis, A., & Nezhad, S. (2014). *Sexual and Gender Minority Youth in Foster Care: Assessing Disproportionality and Disparities in Los Angeles*. The Williams Institute, UCLA School of Law. Available at http://williamsinstitute.law.ucla.edu/wp-content/uploads/LAFYS_report_final-aug-2014.pdf.
Wilson, B. D., Jordan, S. P., Meyer, I. H., Flores, A. R., Stemple, L., & Herman, J. L. (2017). Disproportionality and disparities among sexual minority youth in custody. *Journal of Youth and Adolescence, 46*, 1547–1561.
Winston, S. E., & Beckwith, C. G. (2011). The impact of removing the immigration ban on HIV-infected persons. *AIDS Patient Care and STDs, 25*, 709–711.
Wolff, K. B., & Cokely, C. L. (2007). "To protect and to serve?": An exploration of police conduct in relation to the gay, lesbian, bisexual, and transgender community. *Sexuality and Culture, 11*, 1–23.
Wolff, N., Blitz, C. L., Shi, J., Bachman, R., & Siegel, J. A. (2006). Sexual violence inside prisons: Rates of victimization. *Journal of Urban Health, 83*, 835–848.
Woodrow, K. A. (1992). A consideration of the effect of immigration reform on the number of undocumented residents in the United States. *Population Research & Policy Review, 11*, 117–144.
Woods, J. B. (2009). Don't tap, don't stare, and keep your hands to yourself! Critiquing the legality of gay sting operations. *Journal of Gender, Race, & Justice, 12*, 545–578.
Woods, J. B. (2014). "Queering criminology": Overview of the state of the field. In D. Peterson & V. R. Panfil (Eds.), *Handbook of LGBT communities, crime, and justice* (pp. 15–41). New York, NY: Springer.
Woods, J. B. (2017). LGBT Identity and Crime. *California Law Review, 105*, 667–733.
Woronoff, R., & Estrada, R. (2006). Regional Listening Forums: An examination of the methodologies used by the Child Welfare League of America and Lambda Legal to highlight the experiences of LGBTQ youth in care. *Child Welfare, 85*, 341–360.
Wright, W. (2005). *Harvard's secret court: The savage 1920 purge of campus homosexuals.* New York: Macmillan.
Wurth, M. H., Schleifer, R., McLemore, M., Todrys, K. W., & Amon, J. J. (2013). Condoms as evidence of prostitution in the United States and the criminalization of sex work. *Journal of the International AIDS Society, 16*, 1–3.
Xavier, J. M., Bobbin, M., Singer, B., & Budd, E. (2005) A needs assessment of transgendered people of color living in Washington, DC. *International Journal of Transgenderism, 8*, 31–47.
Yanez, Y. (1997, August). Cunanan siblings speak out. *Sun Sentinel.* Retrieved from https://www.sun-sentinel.com/news/fl-xpm-1997-08-07-9708070133-story.html.
Young, S. (2009). A Gay Mom Faces Deportation. *People.* Retrieved from https://people.com/archive/a-gay-mom-faces-deportation-vol-71-no-15/.
Zemsky, B., & Sanlo, R. L. (2005). Do policies matter? In R. Sanlo (Ed.), *New directions for student services: Gender identity and sexual orientation, research, policy, and personal perspectives* (pp. 7–15). Hoboken, NJ: Wiley.

Index

activism, 6, 8, 51, 70, 119, 209, 214
Adams, Richard, 34, 169–170
Administration for Children's Services, 212
adoption, LGBTQ People and, 35, 137, 139, 143, 144, 145
advocacy. *See* activism
African Americans. *See* Black Americans
Alcorn, Leelah, 48
Alexander, Michelle, 2, 4, 73
Almstead, Bobby, 66
American Bar Association, 77
American Disabilities Act, 30
American Psychiatric Association, 25, 166, 167, 168
American Psychological Association, 167, 190, 204
Amnesty International, 2, 59, 60, 64
androgynous, 12
Anti-Violence Project, 32, 35
aromantic, 10
asexual, 10
Asian Americans and Pacific Islanders: HIV/AIDS and, ix; immigration and, 160; incarceration and, 100
Asian Exclusion Act of 1924, 159, 161
asylum seekers, 30, 95, 101, 103, 169, 171, 172, 173
attorney bias, 80–84

Babet v. Johsnon, 142
Baldwin, James, 21
bathhouses, 22, 54
Batts, Deborah, 79
biological sex. *See* sex assigned at birth
bisexuality, 10
bisexual people: intimate partner violence and, 199; invisibility and, 95, 124; prison experiences of, 95

Black and Pink, 96, 109, 111
Black Americans : criminalization of, 73, 84; historical trauma and, 44; incarceration of, 4, 100; police killings of, 4; prison overrepresentation of, 4; racial profiling of, 4; slavery and, 154
Black Lives Matter, 70
Black transwomen : hate violence and, 4, 47; identity and, 13; incarceration of, 4, 97; police violence toward, 62
blood donations, ban on. *See* Food and Drug Administration (FDA)
Boer-Sedano, José Patricio, 169
Bogan, Ron, 66
Booker, Muhlaysia, 47
Bottoms, Kay, 140
Boutilier v. INS (1967), 166, 167
Bowers v. Hardwick (1986), 30
Boy Scout Exception, 79
Boy Scouts of America, Inc. and Monmouth Council, et al., Petitioners v. James Dale (2000), 30
Boyle, Mary, 66
Brockington, Blake, 48
Brown, Rusty, 24
Brown v. Board of Education , 214
buggery, 22
bullying, ix, 47, 48, 49
Bush, George W, 95
butch women, 12, 59
Butler, Judith, 173

Campbell, Jabbar, 62
Carson, Mark, 47
Chase, Raymond, 47
Cho, Margaret, 133
child abuse, 179, 193
child custody, 78, 79, 82, 139, 140, 141, 142, 143, 144, 145

243

child sexual abuse, 78, 193, 200, 201
Child Welfare System, 138, 139, 146, 147, 148
Chinese Americans, 157, 160
Chinese Exclusion Act of 1882, 157, 158, 160
clinical psychology, 204
Clementi, Tyler, 47
Clinton, Bill, 79
Cochrane, Charles, 66
collective trauma, 46, 48, 49
colonization, 153, 154, 158, 160, 161, 176, 181
Columbus, Christopher, 152, 176
Compton's Cafeteria Uprising, 19, 207
community policing, 68
condoms as evidence, 20, 36, 59, 60
Cooper's Doughnuts Uprising, 19, 207
Cory, Donald Webster, 186
correctional officers, abuse by, 95, 106, 107, 111
Council, et al., Petitioners v. James Dale (2000), 31
Cox, Laverne, 1, 114
Crenshaw, Kimberlé, 8
crime reporting, 56, 57, 106, 133
crimes against nature, 22, 32, 85, 186
criminal justice reform, 69, 113
cross-dressing, 12, 23
Criss, Darren, 178
cruising, 22, 194
Cubilette-Polanco, Layleen, 102–103, 114
Cunanan, Andrew, 7, 177, 178, 179, 182

Dahmer, Jeffrey, 183, 195, 200, 201, 202
Davenport, Bonnie, 66
deadnaming, 12, 49
death penalty, 86
Defense of Marriage Act, 34, 170
dehumanization, 64, 65, 86, 88, 111
demisexual, 10
detention centers: immigration, 95, 101, 103, 106, 110, 151, 152, 173; juvenile, 78, 84, 99, 111, 114
DeLarverie, Stormé, 18
DeSerrano, Joseph and Luis, 135, 136, 137, 143

Development, Relief, and Education for Alien Minors (DREAM) Act, 162, 175
devolution, 154, 162
Diagnostic Statistical Manual of Psychiatric Disorders, 25, 51, 166, 167
discrimination: court cases, 30, 31, 74, 116, 125; definitions of, 14; laws, 20, 28, 38, 65, 117, 118, 119, 120, 121, 122, 143, 146, 147; police and, 56, 67; systemic, 14, 123, 132; trauma and, 50; within group, 70; workplace, 116, 117, 118, 123, 124, 125, 126, 127, 129, 130
Doe v. Bell (2003), 147
domestic terrorism, 40
domestic violence. *See* intimate partner violence
Don't Ask Don't Tell (DADT) policies, 20, 33
drag, 12, 13, 17
DREAMers. *See* Development, Relief, and Education for Alien Minors (DREAM) Act.
Dukakis, Michael, 142

Eisenhower, Dwight, 27
Ellis Island, 157, 158
Emergency Quota Act of 1921, 159
emotional dysregulation, 200, 203
Empire State Agenda, 210
Employment Law, 117, 132, 133
Employment Nondiscrimination Act (ENDA), 117, 118, 119
Equality Act, 118, 119
Evans v. Georgia Regional Hospital Department of Behavioral Health and Developmental Disabilities (2017), 121
excessive force, 55, 61, 62
explicit bias, 5, 211

family law, 139, 140, 141, 142, 143, 144, 145, 147, 148
Family Research Institute, 186
Federal Bureau of Investigation, 2, 32, 39, 40, 102, 165, 177, 188, 192, 195, 198
Federal Bureau of Prisons, 102

federal laws, 20, 28, 34, 35, 84, 116, 117, 118, 119, 137, 163
female serial murderers, 196, 197
feminism, 8, 183
femme, 12, 13, 105
Filipino Americans : academia and, x; colonization of, 181; immigration of, 158, 160; Labor Movement and, 69; sexual orientation and, 180; stereotyping of, 160
fluidity, 10
Food and Drug Administration (FDA), 29
forensic mental health, 204–205
forensic psychology, 8, 183, 190, 191, 204, 205
foster children, 138, 148
Frank, Barney, 118, 167
Free CeCe Movement, 1, 35
Freedom to Marry, 210

Garza, Alicia, 70
gay bars, 40, 194, 197
gay men, 9, 12, 17, 22; arrests of, 25, 185; discrimination toward, 26, 36, 68; entrapment and, 22, 58, 64; HIV/AIDS and, 49; incarceration and, 95, 193; intimate partner violence and, 57, 199; LGBTQ community and, 119; microaggressions and, 63, 87; poverty and, 131; sex work and, 60; sexualization of, 65; unemployment and, 116; wage earnings, 127
Gay Officers Action League, 66
gay panic defense, 82, 85
Gay Related Immune Deficiency, 28, 49
Gay Student Services v. Texas A&M University (1984), 89
gender affirming medical treatments, 11, 102, 103, 107, 120, 123, 133, 173, 209
gender, definitions of, 11, 12, 13
gender binaries, 3, 5, 6, 10, 11, 101, 102, 103, 110, 112, 113, 207, 209, 213
gender confirmation surgeries. *See* gender affirming medical treatments
gender dysphoria, 51, 103
gender identity, 11, 12, 20

gender identity disorder, 51, 103
gender presentation, 13, 59, 76, 97
gender pronouns, 12, 49, 76, 87, 112, 128
gender roles, 12, 119
gender role socialization, 43, 203
Gentili, Cecilia, 35
Gacy, John Wayne, 183, 201
Godfrey, Chris, 126
Grey, Jeannette, 62
Gunn, Sakia, 47

Harris, Kamala, 151
Hart Celler Immigration Act of 1965, 161, 166, 167, 170
hate crimes, 3, 20, 32, 39, 44, 45, 46, 47, 56, 84
hate violence. *See* hate crimes
hegemonic masculinity, 43, 67, 68
help-seeking behaviors, 35, 48, 56, 57
Hernandez, Roxana, 151, 152
heteronormativity, 20, 40, 89, 124, 128, 139, 175, 187, 210
heterosexism, 8, 14, 15, 21, 41, 67, 76, 86, 87, 123, 124, 128, 137
heterosexuality, 9, 67, 89, 95, 124, 128
hiring practices, 66, 126
historical trauma, 44, 47, 49, 50, 51
HIV/AIDS: criminalization of, 30, 72, 90; diagnoses, ix, 28, 30, 72, 187; discrimination, 30, 49, 61; epidemic, 29, 30, 49, 187; immigration ban, 30, 169; legislation, 29, 72; stigma, 28, 29, 30, 49
Hively, Kimberly, 115, 116
Hively v. Ivy Tech Community College (2017), 116
Hollingsworth v. Brown , 34
Holloway v. Arthur Andersen and Company (1977), 120
homelessness, ix, 116, 131; homeless shelters, 63, 131; incarceration and, 96, 98; LGBTQ youth and, 18, 99, 100, 130, 132, 146, 200; survival behaviors and, 132
homophobia, 2, 42, 43, 57, 75, 118, 137, 195, 201, 202, 203
homophobic language, 1, 4, 13, 47, 62, 64, 68, 75, 76, 77, 87, 111, 128, 129

homosexual deviancy thesis, 189
homosexual serial killers, 194
hormone treatment, 11, 12, 102, 103, 107
Human Rights Campaign, 118
Hurley v. Irish-American Gay, Lesbian, and Bisexual Group of Boston (1995), 31

immigration, waves of, 154–165
Immigration Act of 1903, 158
Immigration Act of 1907, 158, 166
Immigration and Nationality Act of 1917, 166
Immigration Act of 1942. *See* Asian Exclusion Act of 1924
Immigration Act of 1952. *See* Walter-McCarran Immigration and Naturalization Act of 1952
Immigration Act of 1990, 169
Immigration and Customs Enforcement, 101, 151, 171
Immigration Reform and Control Act of 1986, 162
implicit bias, 4, 14, 69, 84, 90
incarcerated LGBTQ people, 2, 5, 95, 96–101, 191, 200
indigenous people: genocide of, 22, 44, 153; history of, 152, 153, 156; incarceration experiences of, 94, 97, 100; sexuality and gender fluidity among, 13, 22
Indochina Migration and Refugee Assistance Act of 1975, 162
Internal Revenue Service (IRS), 34
Islamophobia, 42, 43
institutional betrayals, 212
institutional oppression. *See* systemic oppression
internalized homophobia. *See* internalized oppression
internalized oppression, 43, 195, 197, 198, 200, 201, 202
International Transgender Day of Remembrance (ITDOR), 32
intersectional identities, ix, 3, 4, 5, 8, 41, 42, 49, 56, 57, 69, 129, 146, 174, 175, 208
Intersectionality Theory, 8, 183

intersex, 11, 101, 102
intersex people and incarceration, 102, 103
intimate partner violence, 20, 57, 61, 183, 190, 192, 198, 199

Japanese Americans : immigration of, 158; internment of, 160, 165
"Jenny Jones Murder," 82
Jimenez, Tiffany, 62
Johnson, Duanna, 62
Johnson, Marsha P, 8, 18, 70, 208
Johnson, Michael L, 71, 72, 73, 74
judicial bias, 75, 77, 78, 79, 139, 188
jury bias, 80, 84, 85, 86, 190
juvenile justice, 76, 98, 99, 100, 212

Khan-Cullors, Patrisse, 70
Knudson, Dorothy, 66

Lambda Legal, 61, 116, 127
Latino threat, 161, 163, 165
Latinx Americans, 37; hate crimes and, 39; homophobia and, 42; immigration and, 162, 163, 165, 173; incarceration and, 62, 98, 100; Pulse massacre and, 41; racial profiling and, 58; unemployment and, 131
Lavender Scare, 26, 28, 33, 36
Lawrence v. Texas (2003), 20, 74, 184
Lesbians: arrests of, 17, 24, 57; discrimination toward, 26, 31, 33, 35, 36, 89, 123; gender presentation among, 12; identity of, 9; incarceration of, 81, 99, 104, 108; intimate partner violence and, 199; parenting and, 145; police brutality toward, 62; stereotyping of, 23, 80, 81, 86, 140, 141, 197; wages and, 127
Leon, Johana Joa Medina, 152
LGBTQ Movement, 8, 19
LGBTQ immigration bans, 165, 166, 167, 168
LGBTQ federal judges, 79
LGBTQ parenting, 139, 140, 141, 142
LGBTQ people of color. *See* queer and trans people of color
LGBTQ police officers, 65, 66, 67
LGBTQ Pride Month, 41

LGBTQ youth of color, ix, 98, 131
Limon, Matthew, 86
Lindsey, Chynal, 47
lobbying, 6, 114, 167, 209, 213, 214
Longstaff, Richard John, 168
Lorde, Audre, 15
Lucas, Billy, 47, 48, 49

Madson, David, 177, 178
Major, Miss, 113
"Make America Great Again," 164, 165
Marquez-McCool, Brenda Lee, 37
marriage equality, 20, 34, 74, 169, 209, 210, 214
Martin, Ricky, 138
masquerade laws, 23, 24
mass murderers, 192, 197, 198, 203
Matthew Shepard and James Byrd, Jr. Hate Crimes Prevention Act, 20
McCarthyism, 26
McDonald, CeCe, 1, 3, 4, 5, 6, 91
medical models of psychotherapy, 204
Mercado, Jay, 170
Mercado, Jorge Stephen Lopez, 47
mental health, 55, 98, 103, 112, 113, 130, 146, 201, 204
Mexican Americans: immigration and, 161, 162, 163; labor movement and, 69
Michigan v. Schmitz. See "Jenny Jones Murder".
microaggressions, 14, 26, 30, 42, 63–65, 87–90, 110–112, 124, 128–130, 133, 175
microaggressive trauma, 50, 51
Miglin, Lee, 178, 196
military: gays and lesbians in, 20, 26, 33, 74; legislation and, 27, 33, 170; transgender people in, 20, 33; women and, 156
Milk, Harvey, 45, 46
Miller, Terry, 48
misgendering, 12, 64, 76, 112
mistrust toward police, 55, 57
Mock, Janet, 35, 45
monogamous relationships, 10, 29, 142, 210
Moscone, George, 45
Mother Emmanuel shootings, 40

Movement Advancement Project, 121, 122
Muñoz, Jose Esteban, 35, 173
Murphy, Ryan, 178, 184
Murray, Akya, 37
Muslim Americans, 37, 42, 214
Muslim travel bans, 164, 165

National Coalition of Anti-Violence Programs, 32, 118
National Gay and Lesbian Task Force, 30, 61
National Inmate Survey of 2011–2012, 97, 191, 200
National Security Entry Exit Registration System (NSEERS), 163, 164
National Transgender Discrimination Survey, 5, 62, 97, 104, 116, 126, 130, 131
Native Americans. *See* indigenous people
Native Hawaiians, 13
Naturalization Act of 1790, 155, 156
Nelson Mandela Rules, 110
Nettles, Islan, 47
New York Police Department, 54, 58, 59, 62, 65
Nineteenth Amendment, 156
Nonviolent Homosexual Advance Defense. *See* Gay Panic Defense

Obama, Barack, 20, 30, 33, 46, 48, 79, 102
Obergefell v. Hodges (2015), 20, 34, 139
Ocasio-Cortes, Alexandria, 176
offenders, types of, 191–200
offenders, factors explaining behaviors of, 200–203
Orlando Pulse massacre, 37–44, 197, 207
outness, 124–126

pansexual, 10
parental custody, 79
Parkland, Florida, shootings in, 40
passing, 12
Pearlman, Joanie
Pelosi, Nancy, 118

Penn, Sean, 45
Peppermint, 12
per se rule, 77
Perceptions of Police Scale, 56
Peterson, Ky, 83, 87
Pilgrims, 22, 153, 176
police bias, 4, 56
police brutality. *See* police violence.
police culture, 64, 67, 68, 69
police killings of Black civilians, 4
police misconduct, 61
police, mistrust toward. *See* mistrust toward police.
police profiling, x, 35
police raids, 18, 19
police training, 69
police violence, 19, 55, 62, 69
polyamory, 10
polygamous relationships, 210
poverty, 116, 130, 131, 132, 144, 146, 189, 210
Pride Month, 41
prison abolition, 113
prison culture, 105
prison industrial complex, 2, 113
prison rape, 103, 104, 105, 106, 193
Prison Rape Elimination Act of 2003, 94, 95, 106, 191, 209
procedural justice, 55, 56, 76, 77
promotions and wages, biases in, 126, 127
prostitution. *See* sex work.
Puerto Ricans, 37, 41, 42, 208

queer advocacy, 35, 50, 51, 69, 90, 113, 132, 133, 147, 148, 176, 204
queer identity, 10, 13
queer criminology. *See* queer critical criminology
queer critical criminology, 189
queer forensic psychology, 190, 191, 204
queer psychology, 190, 191
queer sanctuaries, 40, 41, 42
Queer Studies, 46
Queer Theory, 8, 183
queer and trans people of color, 5, 13, 30, 49, 83, 94, 113, 125, 130, 205, 210

racial profiling, 4, 55
racial trauma, 50, 181
rape. *See* sexual assault
Reagan, Ronald, 29, 30, 160
recidivism, 193
Reese, William, 178, 196
reflexivity, 7
refugees, 30, 155, 162, 164, 172
Refugee Act of 1980, 162
religious freedom laws, 20, 143
religious persecution, 22, 153, 155, 156, 158
Reno, Janet, 171
restorative justice, 204
retraumatization, 49, 55, 173
Rhines, Charles, 86
Rivera, Sylvia, 8, 18, 19, 70, 208
Romeo and Juliet Laws, 86
Romer v. Evans (1996), 31
runaways, LGBTQ, 99, 100, 132, 146, 200
Rustin, Bayard, 214

same-sex marriage. *See* marriage equality
San Antonio Four, 81–82, 91
sanctuary states and cities, 163
Savage, Dan, 48
Saunders-Velez, Lindsay, 93–94
school-to-prison pipeline, 205
secondary trauma, 44
sentencing, Anti-LGBTQ biases in, 80, 83, 84, 85
September 11th Attacks, 163
serial murderers, 193–197
sex assigned at birth, 11
sex work: arrests, 59, 60, 99; decriminalizing, 35, 113, 114, 213; incarceration and, 100, 102; laws, 90; survival sex and, 132, 200, 205, 207
sex worker. *See* sex work
sexual assault, 61, 103, 104, 105, 106, 173, 187, 188, 192, 193
sexual attraction, 10, 95, 120, 168
sexual deviation, 165, 167
sexual misconduct laws, 104, 108, 109
sexual orientation, 9–10
sexual psychopath laws, 25–26

sexual victimization in incarceration, 94, 100, 103–106
Shepard, Judy, 46
Shepard, Matthew, 32, 45, 46
Shine, Aubrey Mariko
slavery. *See* Black Americans
sodomy, definitions of sodomy, 17
sodomy laws, 17, 18, 21, 22, 23
solitary confinement, 1, 5, 6, 71, 78, 100, 102, 103, 106, 108, 110
Southern Poverty Law Center, 165
spree murders, 178, 196, 203
Spyer, Thea, 34
stealth mode, 12
stereotype, definition of, 14
Stonewall Uprising, 13, 17–19, 207
Stop, Question, and Frisk, 58
substance use and abuse, 114, 130
suicide, death by, ix, 47, 48, 49, 197
Sullivan, Tony, 34, 169, 170
Supreme Court of the United States (SCOTUS), 20, 30, 31, 38, 54, 74, 79, 121, 166, 209
survival behaviors, 99, 132, 205
survivors of trauma, 44, 160
survivors of violence, 61, 80, 84, 184, 203
Swank, Hillary, 54
Sylvia Rivera Law Project, 35, 176

Tan, Shirley, 170
Teena, Brandon, 53–54
Tennant, Woody, 66
terrorism, 37, 38, 39, 40, 163
Thrasher, Stephen, 71, 90
three-article rule, 17, 24
Tintiangco-Cubales, Allyson, 15
Title VII of the Civil Rights Act of 1964, 28, 116, 119, 120
Tobera, Fermin, 160
toxic masculinity. *See* hegemonic masculinity
Trail, Jeffrey, 177, 181, 196
transgender and gender nonconforming people: child welfare system and, 146; court systems and, 76, 77, 87; hate crimes toward, 32; identity of, 6, 12, 14; incarceration and, 76; police and, 56, 57, 62, 63; poverty, 131; unemployment and, 116; workplace discrimination and, 116, 126, 127, 128
transphobia, 14, 15, 21, 41, 42, 57, 67, 88, 119, 137, 201, 208
transphobic language, 76, 87, 111, 128
trans asylum seekers, 173
trans panic defense, 82, 85, 90
trauma: definitions of, 44, 50, 51; symptoms of, 50, 51
Trump, Donald J, 164
two-spirited people, 13, 22
Tydings-McDuffie Act of 1934, 160

Ulane v. Eastern Airlines (1984), 120, 121
undercover police officers, 17, 18, 58, 59
undocumented immigrants, 101, 114, 162, 163, 173, 174
undocuqueers, 171, 174–175
unemployment, 96, 116, 117, 130, 131
United Nations, 110
U.S. Department of Homeland Security, 172
U.S. Department of Justice, 2
U.S. Government Accountability Office, 106
U.S. Transgender Survey, 24, 98, 104, 116
US v. Windsor, 34, 170

Vargas, Jose Antonio, 174, 176
Versace, Gianni, 177, 178, 182, 196, 203
vicarious trauma, 44
victims. *See* survivors of violence
Violence Against Women Reauthorization Act of 2013, 20
Voting Right Act of 1965, 156

Walker, Alice, 8
Walker-Hoover, Carl Joseph, 48
Walsh, Seth, 47
Walter-McCarran Immigration and Naturalization Act of 1952, 161
Wayman, Marcus, 60
Wernikoff, Brenda, 63
White, Brittany, 47
Williams Institute, The, 67, 116, 138

Windsor, Edie, 34
witch hunts, 26, 27, 28, 91
Womanism, 8
Women's Property Acts, 156
workplace culture, 124, 125

workplace discrimination. *See* discrimination, workplace
Wournos, Aileen, 183, 197, 200, 201

Yellow Peril, 157, 163, 165

About the Author

Kevin Leo Yabut Nadal, PhD, is a professor of psychology at John Jay College of Criminal Justice and The Graduate Center at the City University of New York (CUNY). His numerous leadership positions include former Executive Director of the CLAGS: The Center for LGBTQ at the Graduate Center; former President of the Asian American Psychological Association; the founder of the LGBTQ Scholars of Color Network; and National Trustee of the Filipino American National Historical Society. He has published over 100 works on multicultural issues, including 10 books such as *Filipino American Psychology: A Handbook of Theory, Research, and Clinical Practice* (Wiley, 2011) and *Microaggressions and Traumatic Stress* (APA, 2018). He has contributed to the *Huffington Post* and *Buzzfeed*, and he has been featured on NBC, CBS, ABC, FoxNews, The Weather Channel, and HGTV. He has received numerous awards, including the 2017 American Psychological Association Distinguished Contributions to the Public Interest and the 2019 Robert Wood Johnson Foundation New Connections Thought Leadership Award. In 2016, he was invited to speak at President Obama's White House and at the U.S. Capitol.

CPSIA information can be obtained
at www.ICGtesting.com
Printed in the USA
LVHW022008261221
707061LV00003B/107